Central Banking in a Post-Pandemic World

This book addresses the urgent need to examine central bank policies in response to the global supply and demand shock brought on by the COVID-19 pandemic, asking whether central banks are doing enough to address inequalities and concerns around climate change and emerging technologies. Adopting an interdisciplinary, critical perspective, the contributors to this volume provide novel theoretical, methodological, and empirical insights on central banks around the world, including in advanced, emerging, and developing economies. The chapters in this book explore the evolution of central bank mandates, the policy tools central banks are utilizing, why and how monetary policy takes different shapes (including unconventional monetary policy), the key dynamics influencing central bank policies, how central banks are adapting to the new realities and addressing emerging challenges, and how monetary policy is perceived in the wider economic policy framework. With novel theoretical approaches and diverse empirical evidence from a variety of countries, this book will appeal to readers interested in central banking, monetary policy, the economics of the pandemic, and political economy.

Mustafa Yağcı is Assistant Professor of International Political Economy at İstinye University, İstanbul, Turkey. His research interests lie at the intersection of comparative and international political economy, political economy of development, central banking, and public policy. He has published various articles and book chapters on political economy of central banking, public policy, and international political economy. He is the editor of the book *The Political Economy of Central Banking in Emerging Economies* published by Routledge. He is the co-editor of the book *The China Puzzle: The Economic Rise of China, Transformation in International Relations, and Turkey* published in Turkish.

Routledge Critical Studies in Finance and Stability

Edited by **Jan Toporowski**, *School of Oriental and African Studies, University of London, UK*

The 2007–8 Banking Crash has induced a major and wide-ranging discussion on the subject of financial (in)stability and a need to revaluate theory and policy. The response of policy-makers to the crisis has been to refocus fiscal and monetary policy on financial stabilisation and reconstruction. However, this has been done with only vague ideas of bank recapitalisation and 'Keynesian' reflation aroused by the exigencies of the crisis, rather than the application of any systematic theory or theories of financial instability.

Routledge Critical Studies in Finance and Stability covers a range of issues in the area of finance including instability, systemic failure, financial macroeconomics in the vein of Hyman P. Minsky, Ben Bernanke and Mark Gertler, central bank operations, financial regulation, developing countries and financial crises, new portfolio theory and New International Monetary and Financial Architecture.

Emerging Economies and the Global Financial System
Post-Keynesian Analysis
Edited by Bruno Bonizzi, Annina Kaltenbrunner and Raquel A. Ramos

Financialisation in Emerging Economies
Changes in Central Banking
Juan Pablo Painceira

Financialization and Macroeconomics
The Impact on Social Welfare in Advanced Economies
Giovanni Scarano

Central Banking in a Post-Pandemic World
Challenges, Opportunities, and Dilemmas
Edited by Mustafa Yağcı

For more information about this series, please visit: www.routledge.com/series/RCSFS

Central Banking in a Post-Pandemic World

Challenges, Opportunities, and Dilemmas

Edited by Mustafa Yağcı

Routledge
Taylor & Francis Group
LONDON AND NEW YORK

First published 2024
by Routledge
4 Park Square, Milton Park, Abingdon, Oxon OX14 4RN

and by Routledge
605 Third Avenue, New York, NY 10158

Routledge is an imprint of the Taylor & Francis Group, an informa business

British Library Cataloguing-in-Publication Data
A catalogue record for this book is available from the British Library

ISBN: 978-1-032-34670-0 (hbk)
ISBN: 978-1-032-34671-7 (pbk)
ISBN: 978-1-003-32328-0 (ebk)

DOI: 10.4324/9781003323280

Typeset in Times New Roman
by KnowledgeWorks Global Ltd.

To my wife, son, and daughter.

Contents

List of Contributors ix
Preface xiii

Introduction 1
MUSTAFA YAĞCI

1 **Rethinking Monetary Policy for the New Challenges: Inequality and Climate Change** 3
JUAN-FRANCISCO ALBERT AND CARLOS OCHANDO

2 **Capitalist Central Banks, War Finance, and Covid** 18
JOCELYN F. PIXLEY

3 **Central Bank Digital Currencies in the Post-pandemic Era** 34
DOMINIQUE TORRE AND QING XU

4 **The Federal Reserve, COVID-19, and the Governance of the International Monetary System** 53
AYCA ZAYIM

5 **Public Banking for a Public-Financed Post-pandemic Transition: A Proposal for a New Public Bank System in Spain** 72
JORGE GARCIA-ARIAS, NURIA ALONSO, EDUARDO FERNÁNDEZ-HUERGA AND DAVID TRILLO

6 **The Political Economy of Asset versus Consumer Inflation** 91
CHRISTOPH SCHERRER AND NORA HORN

7 **The Effects of Institutional Independence on Initial Central Bank Responses to the COVID-19 Crisis** 109
IOANNIS GLINAVOS

8 Open Banking on Different Sides of the Atlantic: A Comparative Study between Brazil and the United Kingdom 127
VINÍCIUS KLEIN AND RODOLFO RODRIGUES DA COSTA FARIAS

9 Central Banking in Russia, Ukraine, and Belarus in the Face of Pandemic, War, and Sanctions 145
CORNELIA SAHLING

10 Climate Change on the Policy Agenda of Central Banks in Central and Southeast Europe 167
TATJANA JOVANIĆ

11 Crises of Authoritarian Financialization: Monetary Policy in Hungary and Türkiye in the Polycrisis 186
DAVID KARAS AND PINAR E. DÖNMEZ

12 Diversity of Monetary Regimes and Reactions to the COVID-19 Pandemic Crisis in the Balkan Countries 221
NIKOLAY NENOVSKY AND TSVETELINA MARINOVA

13 The PBOC in the Post-Covid World: Multitasking, Perseverance and Self-Discipline 240
ORHAN YAZAR

14 Central Banking and the Impact of the COVID-19 Pandemic: Some Insights from Ghana 257
PATRICK K. TUTU, FRANKLIN NAKPODIA AND GEOFRY ARENEKE

Index *273*

Contributors

Juan-Francisco Albert holds a Ph.D. in Economics and Teaching Assistant at the University of Valencia (Spain). He holds a M.Sc. in Economics from the University of Alicante (Spain) and a M.Sc. in Philosophy from the UNED (Spain). His research interest covers Monetary Policy and Theory, Economics of Inequality, Welfare Economics, and Applied Macroeconomics. He has published several scientific articles in international peer-reviewed journals such as *Structural Change and Economic Dynamics*, *Papers in Regional Science*, *Journal of Economic Policy Reform*, and *Health Education Journal*. Juan Francisco Albert has been Visiting Researcher at the London School of Economics (UK) and De Nederlandsche Bank (Netherlands). He has been awarded as a young researcher to carry out different projects related to his doctoral thesis (the effects of monetary policy on income and wealth inequality) by the Ministry of Science in Spain, Fundación Alternativas, and Fundación Banco Sabadell.

Nuria Alonso is an Associate Professor at the Department of Economics, Rey Juan Carlos University, Spain, and Research Associate at the Complutense Institute for International Studies, Complutense University, Spain. She has been Head of Analysis of the Official Credit Institute. Her main research lines are connected to public economics, public debt, and public banking. Her research has been published in academic journals such as *Journal of World Economy*, *Water International*, *Papeles de Europa*, *Procedia-Social*, and *Behavioral Sciences*, among others.

Geofry Areneke is a Senior Lecturer at Manchester Metropolitan University in the UK. He has developed a world-class research profile in corporate governance and firm financing in emerging economies. His research has been published in globally reputable journals, including Journal of World Business, Journal of Business Research, Research in International Business and Finance, Managerial Auditing Journal, and Finance Research Letters. His research has also been presented and published in internationally referred conference proceedings, including Academy of Management (AOM) and African Accounting and Finance Association (AAFA) Conferences.

Pinar E. Dönmez is a Senior Lecturer in International Relations in the Faculty of Arts, Design& Humanities at De Montfort University. Her research considers (de-/re-)politicisation of governance and social relations, politics of crisis & restructuring from a critical political economy perspective.

Eduardo Fernández-Huerga is an Associate Professor at the Department of Economics and Statistics, University of Leon, Spain. His main lines of research have been linked to heterodox economics (mainly post-keynesian and institutional economics) and International Political Economy. His research has been published in many academic journals.

Jorge Garcia-Arias is a Full Professor at the Department of Economics and Statistics, University of Leon, Spain, and Research Associate at the Department of Development Studies, School of Oriental and African Studies (SOAS), University of London (UK). His main research lines are related to International Political Economy and Critical Development Studies. His research has been published in academic journals such as *Environmental Politics, Globalizations, Environment & Planning, Global Policy, Water International, Journal of Post Keynesian Economics, Latin American Perspectives*, or the *European Journal of Development Research*, among many others.

Ioannis Glinavos, Senior Lecturer in Law, University of Westminster, London, UK.

Nora Horn is a student in the MA Global Political Economy and Development, University of Kassel.

Tatjana Jovanić is a Professor of Economic Law and Market Regulation at the University of Belgrade, Faculty of Law. Since 2012, she has been an advisor to the Governor of the National Bank of Serbia. She served as a member of Serbian Government's Negotiating Team for Accession Negotiations of Serbia to the European Union.

David Karas earned his PhD in 2015 from the European University Institute. He is currently a postdoctoral research fellow at CEU Democracy Institute where his research focuses on the political economy of development, statecraft, and finance.

Vinícius Klein, PhD in Law from the Rio de Janeiro State University, PhD in Economic Development from Paraná Federal University, Visiting Scholar at Columbia University in 2012, Professor of Law, and Economics at Paraná Federal University. Director at the Brazilian Institute for Competition and Innovation – IBCI (www.ibcibr.com.br).

Tsvetelina Marinova, PhD, is an Associate Professor at the Department of economics at the New Bulgarian University, Sofia, Bulgaria and Associate Researcher at the LEFMI, University of Picardie Jules Verne, Amiens, France. Her publications are focused on social and solidarity economy in the Balkans, history of economic thought and economic history as well as European economic and monetary integration of Eastern European countries.

Franklin Nakpodia, Accounting Department, Durham University, Durham, UK.

Nikolay Nenovsky, DSc, is a Professor at the University of Picardie Jules Verne, LEFMI, Amiens, France and Professor and Associate Researcher at the SU HSE as well at the RUDN in Moscow. He has published mainly in the areas of currency boards and central banking, especially of post-communist countries as well as in the fields of history of economic thought and economic history of the Balkan countries and Russia. He has a long, practical experience as a researcher and as a member of the Governing Council of the Bulgarian National Bank.

Carlos Ochando holds a PhD in Economics and Professor of Economic Policy in the Department of Applied Economics at the University of Valencia (Spain). He has held visiting professorships at the University of South Bank University of London, the University of Chile, and as an external researcher at the European University Institute in Florence. He has published several articles and books on issues related to income policy, income distribution, the organization and results of the welfare state, and the institutional reforms carried out in the social security systems of various countries. Since 2020 he has been director of the Master's degree in Economic Policy and Public Economics at the University of Valencia.

Jocelyn F. Pixley is an honorary professor in sociology at Macquarie University Sydney, Australia. Among many publications her most relevant are Central Banks, Democratic States, and Financial Power, Cambridge University Press, 2018 and co-authored 'Central bank independence: A social economic and democratic critique' by J. F. Pixley. *The Economic and Labour Relations Review* 2013, Vol. 24 (1): 32–50, and co-edited Financial crises and the nature of capitalist money: Mutual developments from the challenge of Geoffrey Ingham (eds.) J. F. Pixley and G. C. Harcourt, 2013, She has a chapter in The Future of Central Banking edited by Sylvio Kappes, Louis-Philippe Rochon and Guillaume Vallet, Edward Elgar, out in August 2022.

Rodolfo Rodrigues da Costa Farias is a MSc Candidate in Economics at Paraná Federal University, Specialization in Strategic Business Management from Fundação Getúlio Vargas. Bachelor of Laws from Unicuritiba. Research Assistant at the Center for Human Rights and International Justice at Stanford University, supporting the Responsible Digital Leadership in the Financial Sector project.

Cornelia Sahling is an independent researcher (in Germany) and is currently working on central banking in Russia, Belarus, and Ukraine. Her main interests are related to the historical development of central banking in transition economies, the economic history of resources and rents in Russia, and financial stability and regulation. She received her M.A. from Technische Universität Dresden in 2014 and completed her doctoral studies (PhD in economics) in 2017 at RUDN University in Moscow where she was working as a lecturer in 2018-2019. Her recent publications and presentations are related to central banking in transition economies and Southeastern Europe.

Christoph Scherrer is a Full Professor of globalization and politics, Executive Director of the International Center for Development and Decent Work (ICDD) at the University of Kassel. He holds PhDs in political science from the FU Berlin (Dr. habil.) and the U of Frankfurt (Dr. phil.) and a M.A. in economics (U of Frankfurt). Recent publications include: Biden's Foreign Economic Policy: Crossbreed of Obama and Trump? (accepted 2022), America second? Die USA, China und der Weltmarkt, Berlin (2021); The Phantom of Upgrading in Agricultural Supply Chains: A Cross-Country, Cross-Crop Comparison of Smallholders, Baden-Baden, co-edited (2021), The 'Nested' Power of TNCs: Smallholders' Biggest Challenge, (2021). Public Banks in the Age of Financialization: A Comparative Perspective, Cheltenham, edited (2017).

Dominique Torre is an Emeritus Professor of Economics at Université Côte d'Azur (UCA) and member of GREDEG research team (UCA – CNRS). His research interests are digital economics, microeconomics, monetary theory, tourism economics, and history of monetary analysis. He wrote more than 60 research articles, book chapters and books in those different areas. He visited or presented seminar in more than 20 Universities in France and other countries, supervised/ses 20 PhD and 3 HDR. He works as scientific expert of many assessment bodies, scientific reviews, and associations.

David Trillo is an Associate Professor at the Department of Economics, Rey Juan Carlos University, Spain, and Director of the "European economic structures and dynamics" research group at Complutense Institute for International Studies. His main research lines are related to public finance and gender studies. He has several published books on public economics and finance, and articles in many academic journals.

Patrick K. Tutu, PhD Student, University of South Africa, South Africa.

Qing Xu is an Associate Professor of Finance at Université Catholique de Lille (Faculté de Gestion, Économie & Sciences) and an associate member of GREDEG research team (CNRS). She received a PhD in economics from Université Côte d'Azur in 2014. Her primary research interest is in m-payment in Asia & Africa, exporting the m-payment models to other countries, but also fintech development, digital currency, and innovation in finance.

Orhan H. Yazar is an Associate Professor of International Business at the Dongbei University of Finance and Economics and The University of Surrey's international business program in China. Dr. Yazar received his PhD from the University of Sydney's Department of Government and International Relations and master's degree from London School of Economics in the field of international political economy. His research interests are financial regulation, central banking, state-market relations, business negotiations, and organizational justice.

Ayca Zayim is an Assistant Professor of Sociology at Mount Holyoke College. She received her Ph.D. from the University of Wisconsin-Madison in 2018. Her research focuses on power, finance, and central banks in emerging economies. Her work has appeared in Socio-Economic Review, Contexts, and The Political Economy of Central Banking in Emerging Economies.

Preface

After COVID-19, we are living in a different world. Not because COVID-19 changed everything in our lives but because it symbolized a significant "critical juncture" about how we view ourselves, our lifestyles, the economy, society, and politics. In a way, it forced us to rethink our assumptions about life. Many people interpreted COVID-19 as a sign that we could not ignore, we had to change.

COVID-19 pandemic struck the world after we had submitted our final chapters to Routledge for our book "The Political Economy of Central Banking in Emerging Economies." In our book, we underlined that the global and domestic political economy context within which central banks operate should be incorporated in our analysis. That's why we could not expect central banks in emerging and developing countries to operate in the same way that they are operating in advanced economies. Furthermore, many emerging and developing country central banks operate under distinct conditions because of political, social, economic, and historical reasons. Thus, we need to recognize and identify these dynamics to have a better understanding of central banking.

Our current book aims to advance our understanding of central banking in a post-pandemic world because many historical forces that were building up before the pandemic have come to light. Geopolitical conflicts, fierce rivalry between the United States and China, reshaping of global production networks, digitalization, climate change, rising inequality, and inflation are all changing our world, and central banks need to adapt to these changes. In their adaptation, however, they face numerous challenges, opportunities, and dilemmas. We examine these dynamics in an interdisciplinary manner with no geographical distinction.

We hope that with both empirical and normative orientation, our book will enrich the debates on central banking and will open new horizons to explore for the future.

Mustafa Yağcı
İstanbul, Türkiye

Introduction

Mustafa Yağcı

The world is changing and evolving, and central banks are no exception. The history of central banking shows us that central banks adapt to the changing times to be relevant. In the current period we are living in, central banks face new challenges, opportunities, and dilemmas. Starting with the COVID-19 pandemic, central banks are operating under peculiar conditions. Geopolitical conflicts, the rivalry between China and the United States, reshaping of global production networks, climate change, digitalization, evolution of cryptocurrencies, rising inequality, and inflation are intensifying the debates on the role of central banks in an economy, their mandates, and contributions to overall social welfare. The chapters in our volume address these transformations and how central banks in different regions are coping with the new global and domestic political economy context.

Juan-Francisco Albert and Carlos Ochando focus on climate change and rising inequality in addressing the shifts in central bank policies. Jocelyn Pixley distinguishes between capitalist and non-capitalist central banks and examines central banks with respect to the post-pandemic dynamics and war finance. Dominique Torre and Qing Xu investigate monetary policy debates on central bank digital currencies and provide examples from around the world. Ayca Zayim examines Federal Reserve's lender of last resort role in the aftermath of the COVID-19 pandemic and reflects on the governance of international monetary system.

Jorge Garcia-Arias, Nuria Alonso, Eduardo Fernández-Huerga, and David Trillo examine the case of Spain with respect to public banking and how it is related to central bank operations. Christoph Scherrer and Nora Horn differentiate between asset and consumer inflation with respect to financialization and compares Federal Reserve and European Central Bank's role in addressing it. Ioannis Glinavos analyzes how institutional independence affected central bank responses to COVID-19 and highlights the importance of coordination between fiscal and monetary policy.

Vinícius Klein and Rodolfo Rodrigues da Costa Farias focus on how central bank authorities in Brazil and the United Kingdom approach open banking practices with divergent regulatory policies. Cornelia Sahling scrutinizes central bank practices in Russia, Ukraine, and Belarus within the context of pandemic, conflict, and sanctions. Tatjana Jovanić brings the climate change agenda of Central and

DOI: 10.4324/9781003323280-1

Southeast European countries to our attention and reviews the factors influential in this respect.

David Karas and Pınar Dönmez provide a comparative case study of monetary policy practices and political economy context in Türkiye and Hungary in the face of the pandemic. Similarly, Nikolay Nenovsky and Tsvetelina Marinova investigate the central bank policies of Balkan countries in the aftermath of the pandemic. Orhan Yazar examines the activities of Chinese central bank and provides an analysis of how the pandemic has changed the political economy dynamics within which Chinese central bank is operating. Finally, Patrick K. Tutu and Franklin Nakpodia present an analysis of central banking practices in Ghana following the COVID-19 the pandemic.

1 Rethinking Monetary Policy for the New Challenges: Inequality and Climate Change

Juan-Francisco Albert and Carlos Ochando

Introduction

In recent years, the world economies have suffered major unexpected shocks. The economic crisis triggered by the COVID-19 pandemic has had devastating effects on economies worldwide. In addition, there is the uncertainty generated and the still unpredictable effects of Russia's invasion of Ukraine. These effects overlap with the scars left by the Great Recession. The pre-pandemic crisis already left a more than worrying scenario: low inflation, nominal interest rates at their lower bound, low economic growth, financial crises, and low productivity growth. If this succession of crises in almost a decade of time has shown anything, it is that economies experience frequent shocks, both on the demand and supply side, generating significant fluctuations in activity and business cycles. Moreover, we now know that the financial sector is also at the root of these economic fluctuations.

In this context, monetary policy has had to engage in a profound exercise of innovation. Since 2008, monetary policy has undergone a profound overhaul, both in terms of its traditional objectives and its instruments (Howells and Biefang-Frisancho, 2011). The exhaustion of conventional monetary policy instruments in a scenario of liquidity traps or interest rates close to their effective lower bound has forced most central banks to apply new monetary policy measures known as "unconventional". The Great Recession and, more recently, the crisis stemming from the COVID-19 pandemic have led to major changes in monetary policy design and the role of central banks. The secular decline of interest led central banks to adopt a broad set of policies such as forward guidance, quantitative easing, long-term refinancing operations, or negative interest rates.

One of the most substantial institutional changes in monetary policy in recent years has been the Federal Reserve's decision in 2020 to adopt average inflation targeting as part of its long-run monetary strategy framework in 2020. This strategy allows inflation to rise and fall such that it averages 2% over time. Until then, most central banks followed inflation targeting in their actions. It is especially in the wake of the financial crisis of 2007–2008 that the need for central banks to follow new targets was put on the economic agenda. These include nominal GDP, economic growth, employment, or the establishment of a long-term growth path for prices (price-level targeting).

DOI: 10.4324/9781003323280-2

Another extension of central banks' objectives has come from the need to integrate monetary policy objectives with the regulation of the financial system. Two objectives have stood out in this respect: the need to monitor the evolution of financial asset prices and the assumption of greater responsibilities in macroprudential financial regulation to guarantee long-term financial stability. Substantial progress has been made in this respect: central banks have increasingly assumed greater responsibilities in the macroprudential and regulatory function of financial intermediaries.

On the other hand, the debate on the independence of central banks has been present since the origin of their constitution. The Great Recession led some authorities to exceed the legal limits of their competence and led central banks to reduce, in their praxis, their independence. According to Blinder (1999), "independence means two things: first, that the central bank is free to decide how it will pursue its objectives and, second, that its decisions are very difficult to reverse by any other political institution". Blinder adds that a central bank should be independent in its choice of instruments, but not in its choice of objectives. Arguments in favor of independence have always dominated the academic mainstream (see, for example, Alesina and Summers, 1993 or Tucker, 2020). According to these arguments, central bank independence would lend credibility and stability to monetary policy, distancing it from electoral cycles, lengthening the time horizon for target setting, and ultimately allowing inflation to be reduced with lower social costs (Haldone, 2020). However, some authors point out that there are problems related to time inconsistency and central bank independence itself that have been little studied (Arias, 2009; Baumann et al., 2021): (1) the risk that the obsession with the pursuit of central banks' reputation dominates everything, moving away from the goals of society; (2) that the two proposed solutions to time inconsistency (monetary rule and independence) will contradict each other; (3) that the credibility theory is fundamentally biased by the inflation fear factor; (4) the necessary coordination of monetary policy with other economic policies, especially fiscal policy; (5) the problems of democratic legitimacy of independent bodies; (6) the assumption of extensive new macroprudential regulatory tasks may compromise the independence of central banks; (7) the "problems of democratic legitimacy of independent bodies"; (8) "regulatory capture problems", i.e., the possibility that monetary policy may serve specific interests that favor the financial system. In any case, the current challenges open the debate on the possibility of central banks adopting multidimensional objectives.

Finally, we are currently in a context of high energy prices and bottlenecks that push inflation higher than desired and force central banks to maintain a difficult balance between consolidating economic recovery and maintaining stable inflation. In this regard, many central banks note that while the post-pandemic recovery, energy prices, and geopolitical factors may put pressure on inflation in the short term, deflationary forces have not disappeared, and they expect inflation rates to moderate again in the coming years (European Central Bank, 2022).

In addition to these current challenges, we must add two major challenges that threaten the role of economic policies and the very survival of the current economic and social system. These are growing inequalities and climate change. Faced with the rise of these phenomena, which will undoubtedly mark the fate of the coming years, many voices, even within central banks (Schnabel, 2020), are beginning to ask what role monetary policy can play in helping to mitigate these threats. It is in this context that this paper is framed.

The rest of the chapter is structured as follows. Section 2 discusses how climate change may affect monetary policy. Section 3 discusses the relationship between monetary policy and economic inequalities. Section 4 explains why the climate challenge and economic inequalities need to be addressed together. Section 5 discusses the role that monetary policy can play in addressing these two challenges. Finally, section 6 presents the conclusions.

Monetary Policy and Environmental Sustainability

In recent years, climate change has become one of the most important challenges facing humanity. The effects of climate change and global warming are currently evident. Globally, the number of heat waves and extreme heat events, precipitation, floods, droughts, coastal erosion, changes in marine ecosystems, and the melting of glaciers have increased. In Figure 1.1, we can see the evolution of these adverse climatic events at the planetary level during the last years. Moreover, these events are heterogeneous between countries. The countries most affected by climatic events in recent years are developing countries such as Haiti, Pakistan, Puerto Rico, Myanmar, the Dominican Republic, and the Philippines. However, the increasing evolution of these episodes occurs in all countries almost without exception.

In response to this situation, many public institutions around the world have developed plans to try to mitigate the harmful effects of climate change. For example, the European Commission adopted a set of proposals to adapt EU climate, energy, transport, and taxation policies to reduce net greenhouse gas emissions by at least 55% by 2030 compared to 1990 levels. The main objectives of the European Green Deal are no net greenhouse gas emissions in 2050, achieving zero pollution

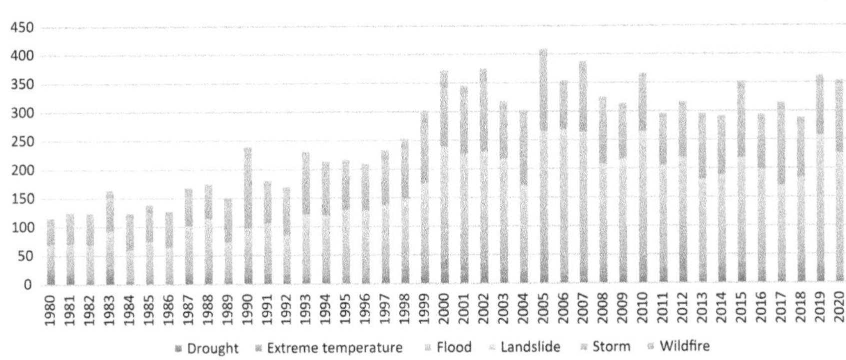

Figure 1.1 Frequency of natural disasters

Source: International Monetary Fund.

in a toxic-free environment, clean, affordable, and secure energy supply, preserving and restoring ecosystems and biodiversity, mobilizing industry for a clean and sustainable economy, achieving a fair, healthy, and environmentally friendly food system, efficient use of energy and resources in construction and renovation, and accelerating the transition to sustainable and smart mobility. In this context, more and more voices are arguing in favor of central banks taking an important role in the fight against climate change. Some authors argue that central banks should become more involved in the fight against climate change as a public and democratic institution in the face of the existential challenge we face (Bartholomew and Diggle, 2021). Other authors point out that environmental protection falls within the secondary objectives of many central banks, which would force them to act (Honohan, 2019). For example, according to Article 3 of the Treaty on the Functioning of the European Union, the ECB's secondary objectives include the duty to promote sustainable growth with particular regard to improving the quality of the environment. Similarly, by 2021 the Bank of England has incorporated the fight against climate change into its mandates with a number of explicit environmental objectives. However, without the need to change mandates or address secondary objectives, it is possible to argue that monetary authorities should pay more attention to climate change because it may have significant implications for what is usually the primary objective of most central banks: price stability.

In this regard, Schnabel (2020) points to three transmission channels through which climate change could affect price stability: (1) Direct effects on inflation dynamics – both the consequences of climate change and the measures to mitigate it could have a direct impact on the evolution of inflation. For example, adverse weather events such as droughts or floods could destroy harvests and lead to higher food prices. Alternatively, pollution mitigation measures could also lead to an increase in some commodity prices such as energy and subsequent spillovers to other prices in the economy. (2) Effects on the monetary policy transmission channel – the consequences of climate change could adversely affect financial institutions' balance sheets and financial stability and thus damage the monetary policy transmission channel (Brunnermeier and Landau, 2020). For example, financial institutions could be affected by losses in physical capital or depreciation in the value of various assets (Löyttyniemi, 2021). Central banks themselves are exposed to these potential losses as they hold on to their balance sheets many assets of financial and non-financial institutions purchased in their asset purchase programs and with depreciation risk or in the form of collateral provided by counterparties in regular monetary policy operations. (3) Effects on the equilibrium or natural rate of interest – the natural rate of interest theory predicts that this long-term interest rate is determined by the forces of saving and investment. Assuming the veracity of this theory, climate consequences could further reduce the natural rate of interest and thus the room for monetary authorities to implement expansionary monetary policy measures in two ways. First, uncertainty caused by adverse weather events could increase households' precautionary savings. On the other hand, extreme weather shocks could reduce labor productivity, force a reallocation of productive factors, and thus reduce investment incentives.

Given these channels, the traditional way of conceiving climate change from the central bankers' point of view within their primary objectives is as a series of negative supply shocks that are likely to cause a contraction in the productive capacity of the economy, thereby generating higher prices and lower growth rates. Moreover, as Economides and Xepapadeas (2018) point out, the more persistent these shocks are, the greater the likelihood that they will lead to a permanent reduction in potential output, affecting not only business cycles but also their long-term trends. However, some empirical studies suggest that some climate change mitigation measures such as carbon taxes would not be inflationary, but deflationary. In this regard, Konradt and di Mauro (2021) point out that carbon taxes could lead to higher energy prices in the first place, but the higher taxation could reduce consumers' real income by acting as a negative demand shock and leading to a fall in aggregate consumption and prices of other types of goods and services. Similarly, Dietrich et al. (2021) point out that negative news of the impact of climate change could affect consumer expectations and lead to a reduction in present consumption, inflation, and the real interest rate. Finally, Faccia and Stracca (2021) find empirically that the rise in temperatures in recent decades has inflationary effects in the short term, but deflationary effects in the medium and long term. According to these authors, short-term supply disruption in agriculture may lead to more lasting downward pressure on demand over time. Thus, the effects of climate change on the traditional objectives of central banks – price stability and full employment – are not fully understood and will need further and better assessment.

In any case, in recent years a growing number of studies have focused on how central banks could contribute to the environmental sustainability. Pérez-Moreno et al. (2021) summarize some of these proposals at the international level. On the one hand, Zerbib (2017) and Schoenmaker (2021) suggest that central banks could redirect their asset allocation and collateral used as collateral in regular monetary policy operations toward low-carbon sectors with the aim of reducing their cost of capital and channeling investments from more polluting sectors to lower-emission sectors. Similarly, Giuliani et al. (2017) propose that central banks can refocus and increase the purchase of "green" assets in their asset purchase programs. Finally, Hilmi et al. (2021) advocate coordinating monetary and environmental policies for the same purpose: to attract investment from companies that are committed to clean energy and low carbon emissions.

Monetary Policy and Economic Inequalities

The implementation of the new monetary policy measures has coincided with high and rising levels of inequality. This has raised concerns about the potential relationship between monetary policy and inequality. On the one hand, a growing number of studies have assessed the possible effects of a monetary shock on income and wealth inequality. Traditionally, monetary policy has been considered neutral in the long run and it was fiscal and/or labor policies that had to deal with distributional issues (Bernanke, 2015). However, with the implementation of extraordinarily loose unconventional monetary policy measures in many Western economies, along with rising levels of both income and wealth inequality in these developed economies, concerns about the potential distributional effects of monetary policy have resurfaced.

Figures 1.2 and 1.3 show for the United States and the Eurozone, respectively, the negative correlation between 10-year government bond interest rates and the income share of the top 1% of the population. It shows that since the 1980s there has been a fall in interest rates that has coincided with a continuous rise in income inequality. These two trends are one of the factors that has motivated the study of the relationship between monetary policy and inequality in order to discern whether there is a causal relationship.

In recent years, much theoretical and empirical work has attempted to quantify the transmission channels through which monetary policy might imply changes in both income and wealth inequality (see, for example, Coibion et al., 2017 or Colciago et al., 2019). These studies establish that monetary policy could affect income inequality through different channels: (1) the income heterogeneity channel: reductions in the interest rate that manage to increase the level of employment and wages benefit more households at the bottom of the distribution that are usually the most sensitive to the business cycle and most dependent on labor income (Carpenter and Rodgers, 2004; Heathcote et al., 2010); (2) redistributive savings channel: unexpected reductions in interest rates reduce debt payments and thus benefit the most indebted households – typically low-income households (Nakajima, 2015); (3) financial segmentation channel: households that are more connected to financial markets or more financially educated may be able to extract better returns from changes in monetary policy (Williamson, 2008).

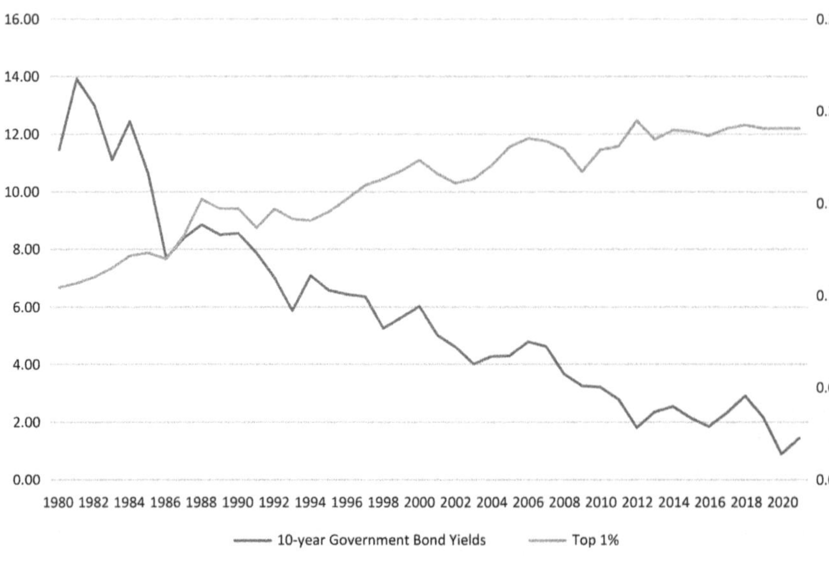

Figure 1.2 Evolution of interest rate and income inequality in the United States

Source: World inequality database and FRED.

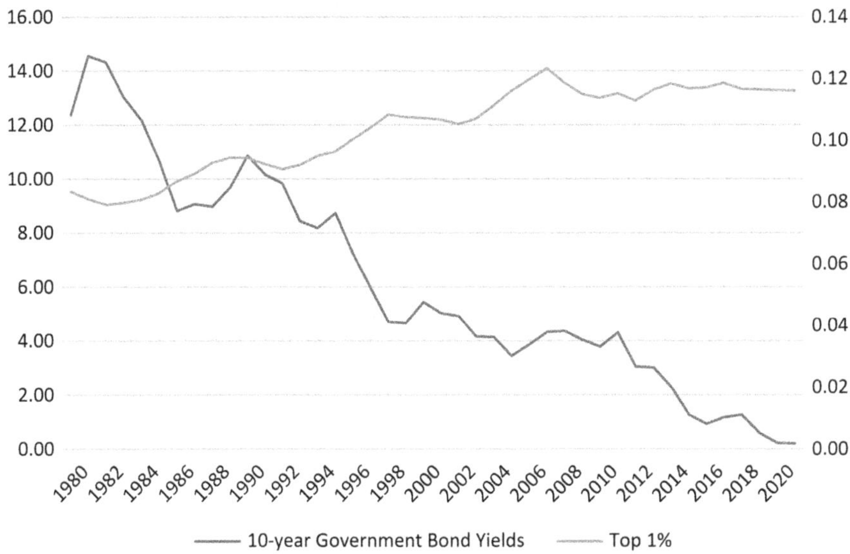

Figure 1.3 Evolution of interest rate and income inequality in the Eurozone

Source: World inequality database and FRED.

Despite the existence of competing channels, the consensus of empirical evidence suggests that expansionary monetary policy shocks could reduce income inequality in some contexts through job creation and subsequent wage increases (see Coibion et al., 2017 for the United States; Mumtaz and Theophilopoulou, 2017 for the United Kingdom, or Lenza and Slačálek, 2018 for the Eurozone).

There are other channels that link monetary policy to wealth inequality: (1) portfolio channel: reductions in the interest rate increase the price of financial assets and, therefore, benefit households with higher wealth who typically own the highest proportion of these financial assets (Albert et al., 2019); (2) housing channel: increases in house prices brought about by a reduction in the interest rate will benefit households with a higher proportion of housing in their wealth; (3) Fisher channel: increases in inflation induced by a more expansionary monetary policy will benefit households with higher debts and more inflation-protected assets (Auclert, 2019).

Empirical work on the effects of monetary policy on wealth distribution is inconclusive and finds mixed results. On the one hand, some papers find that an expansionary monetary policy shock significantly increases wealth inequality through an increase in the price of financial assets (Albert and Gómez-Fernández, 2022 for the United States; Mumtaz and Theophilopoulou, 2020 in the United Kingdom). However, other studies find more modest or no effects (Lenza and Slačálek, 2018 for the Eurozone). The empirical evidence from these papers suggests that while an expansionary monetary policy shock tends to reduce income inequality through job creation and higher wages, the effect on wealth inequality is more ambiguous.

Moreover, alongside the study of the effects of monetary policy on income and wealth inequality, there has been a growing interest in exploring the other causal direction. That is, to study whether high inequality has consequences for the effectiveness and performance of monetary policy. These studies suggest that high inequality may affect the effectiveness of monetary policy through two channels.

First, high inequality may partially explain the secular decline in the long-term equilibrium interest rate. Empirical studies have shown that the marginal propensity to consume (MPC) of higher relative income households is lower than the MPC of lower income households (Jappelli and Pistaferri, 2010). High inequality could therefore reduce total consumption, increase saving, and reduce the equilibrium natural rate of interest (Auclert and Rognlie, 2018; Mian et al., 2021).

Second, in the aftermath of the Great Recession, several studies have focused on the effects of inequality on macroeconomic variables and monetary policy transmission mechanisms. Thus, for example, Keynesian heterogeneous agent models (HANK) have become popular in recent years, highlighting the importance of heterogeneity in the MPC and wealth composition in explaining the transmission of monetary policy to consumption (Kaplan et al., 2018). In this vein, several theoretical papers incorporating heterogeneity have highlighted the importance of how different wealth composition and consumption heterogeneities influence the transmission of monetary policy (Iacoviello, 2005; Auclert, 2019).

Simultaneously, much empirical work has been developed thanks to the availability of data and improvements in microeconomic techniques. This research has shown the relevance of heterogeneity across households. The empirical literature has shown how, in the face of unexpected changes in interest rates, young households, with a higher mortgage burden, lower savings, and more prone to unemployment, adjust their consumption more than other households (Jappelli and Pistaferri, 2010; Di Maggio et al., 2017; Jappelli and Scognamiglio, 2018). All these theoretical and empirical papers emphasize the distributional effects and the importance of inequality in the transmission and effectiveness of monetary policy.

Climate Change and Economic Inequalities: Two Interdependent Challenges

Climate change and socioeconomic inequalities are often considered independently. However, it is not possible to address either of these challenges without addressing the other. It seems plausible that the consequences of climate change will have dramatic effects on inequality, poverty, and equality of opportunity. For example, the increased frequency of adverse weather events hits the most vulnerable workers, especially in agricultural areas, and increases the willingness to migrate in search of a better future. However, lower economic resources favor migration, but only of those with sufficient means to do so (Gray and Mueller, 2012). Thus, the most vulnerable groups in society have fewer resources to protect themselves from climate events and to recover from them when they occur. The climate crisis is therefore quite likely to significantly increase economic

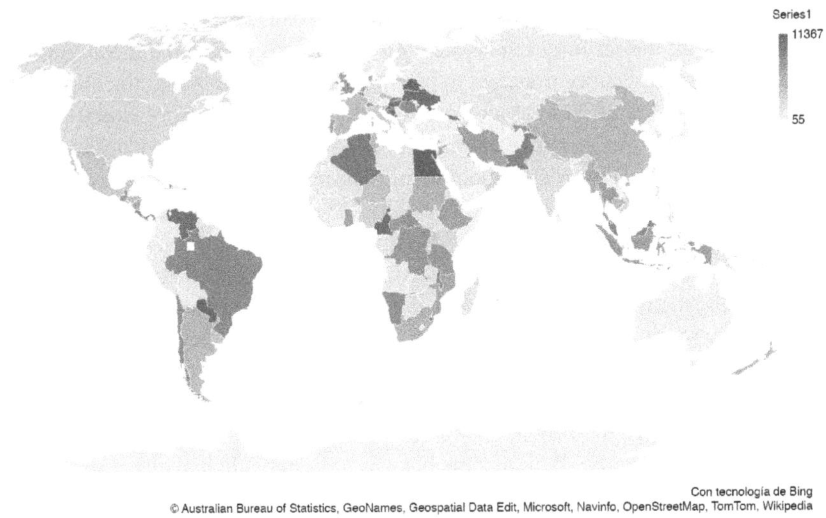

Figure 1.4 Global climate risk index

Source: Germanwatch. Climate risk index.

inequalities. Figure 1.4 shows the Global Climate Risk Index developed by Germanwatch. This index identifies the extent to which countries have been affected by extreme weather events such as tropical storms or tornados, hydrological events such as storm surges or flash floods, or climatological events such as wildfires or droughts. Although all countries are affected, the index seems to show that, historically, those most affected by climate change (represented with darker color) have been developing countries. Based on current data and forecasts, it seems plausible that the consequences of climate change may be a determining factor in the coming years of increased poverty and inequality.

At the same time, poverty and inequality may also aggravate the environmental crisis. Polarization and socioeconomic inequalities directly affect support for public policies. For the decarbonization of our economies to be politically acceptable, serious consideration must be given to who will bear the cost. Protests such as the "yellow vest" in France or the "war on coal" in the United States are direct consequences of the interaction between climate change and socioeconomic inequalities.

In this context, we are faced with a dilemma with a complex solution. On the one hand, a Pigouvian carbon tax seems to be an indispensable tool to address the environmental challenge (Stiglitz and Stern, 2017). However, such a corrective tax tends to be regressive and with little public acceptance (Dinan and Rogers, 2002). Klenert et al. (2018) point out that advances in political science and behavioral economics can help design carbon taxation to improve public acceptance. Factors related to public perception, salience of benefits, cultural worldviews, or general trust in politicians help explain why in some countries carbon taxes are better accepted by taxpayers. Among other considerations, the authors point out that citizens tend to ignore the positive effects of implementing a Pigouvian tax. However, they point out that earmarking the resources generated with the tax to benefit the most vulnerable population, compensatory transfers to households, or talking about the concept of a "social tax or dividend" help to increase the acceptability of the tax. Some countries have set up specific successful programs. For example, in 2008, Switzerland created a specific "CO2levy" with the objective of making fossil fuels more expensive. To increase the acceptability of the tax, two-thirds of the revenue raised is redistributed annually to the population, regardless of the amount of energy consumed. Similarly, in some Canadian provinces, citizens receive a tax benefit called the "Climate Action Incentive Payment" to compensate for the increase in the price of fossil fuels due to the tax increase. For example, a family of four members receives a tax incentive of 1,000 Canadian dollars in Saskatchewan, 720 dollars in Manitoba, 600 dollars in Ontario, and 981 dollars in Alberta. In addition, rural residents receive 10% more than urban residents, to account for the fact that they probably use more energy and do not have as many public transport options to reduce their fuel consumption. It is important to note that these types of tax transfers or subsidies are progressive in that all citizens receive a similar amount regardless of the energy consumed – higher income households tend to consume more of the energy burden.

What Can Monetary Policy Do in the Face of These Interdependent Challenges?

In the face of new challenges that require shared solutions, there is a need for coordination between different institutions and policies. More specifically, close coordination between monetary policy and fiscal and environmental policies is possible.

Central banks were certainly not designed to address these challenges and should not be the institution leading a response to the climate crisis and high inequalities. First, central banks are not set up to deliver the ecological transition and do not have the resources to adequately measure pollutant emissions. Moreover, in a context of high uncertainty, where we do not know the future technologies that will enable the creation and storage of clean energy, investment by central banks in certain projects may have a very high opportunity cost. In this sense, climate experts argue that there is no alternative to carbon dioxide taxation, and it is governments, not central banks, which have the tools to do so. Finally, there is also no justification today for central banks to act on the grounds that climate change affects the primary objective of price stability. As discussed above, recent studies on the effects of climate change on inflation have not been conclusive.

However, within unconventional monetary policy instruments, there may be some scope for central banks to help mitigate new global challenges. For example, monetary authorities could, as an additional policy instrument, finance part of the energy offset transfers to households in order to make carbon taxes more attractive and acceptable.

In this regard, many authors have developed various proposals for what is commonly referred to as a "monetary helicopter". In a context where inflation is persistently below target – without taking into account a possible temporary price increase caused by the consequences of the health crisis and high energy prices – interest rates are at their effective minimum and where additional expansionary monetary policy measures will be needed in the future, several papers have argued for the need to go beyond the traditional interest rate channel and provide the economy with direct stimulus through direct central bank financing via newly created money to individuals or fiscal authorities (Bartsch et al., 2019; Coppola, 2019). Thus, for example, Muellbauer (2014) proposed the unconditional distribution by the ECB of €500 to all European citizens of adult age as a stimulus measure to cope with the Great Recession. More recently, Jourdan (2020) advocated extending the amount of such a transfer to €1000 to address the uncertainty generated by the COVID-19 crisis. Alternatively, other authors have proposed specific formulas for monetary transfers that allow for an effective countercyclical response but based on rules to prevent the central bank from overstepping its functions and to minimize the potential risks of loss of independence and excessive inflation (Beckworth, 2020).

In this context, the creation of a program of cash transfers to citizens that is justified as a kind of "energy social dividend" and partly financed by the central bank as long as macroeconomic conditions permit – low inflation and the need for unconventional monetary policy measures – could serve to provide further stimulus to the economy, to reduce inequalities through progressive transfers and thus improve the effectiveness of monetary policy transmission, and to improve the acceptability of the carbon tax.

In this environment, where conventional monetary policy is exhausted and central banks are forced to be imaginative and use new instruments, why not design new instruments that are both effective with the primary objective of price stability and more diligent with the secondary objectives and the major challenges of our societies?

However, we have to bear in mind that after more than three decades in which inflation was trending downward in both advanced economies and emerging markets, inflation has soared in the last few years (2021/2022) in virtually all areas of the world. In this scenario, many of the major central banks have already started to tighten monetary policy and, therefore, the space to implement the measures described above is much more limited. There is therefore a high degree of uncertainty whether in the medium-long term the global economy will return to a regime characterized by low real interest rates that prevailed before the pandemic, and inflation will be on target, or whether we are facing a structural change with de-anchored inflation expectations and high volatility (Gopinath, 2022). In the latter case, central banks would face new challenges in dealing with supply shocks, forcing them to make difficult trade-offs between fighting inflation and supporting employment or growth. New expansionary monetary policy instruments that can help mitigate the effects of climate change and inequality would therefore be less feasible and harder to justify.

The war in Ukraine needs to be mentioned separately in relation to climate change. On the one hand, the consequences of the war in terms of rising energy and other commodity prices may force central banks to act decisively and adjust their monetary policy and, consequently, limit the room for the expansionary monetary policies explained above. However, it is also true that the ambition to eliminate the dependence on Russian gas that exists in many European countries can be a major impetus for the construction of renewable energy infrastructures that will ultimately favor environmental sustainability. The shift to greener technologies could reduce price pressures over the longer run, but it could also broaden the sources of energy shocks during the transition (Schnabel, 2022). In short, the world has changed substantially in recent years and while we cannot be sure that we will not return to a world of low inflation and interest rates, neither can we rule out the hypothesis of structural change.

Conclusions: Challenges, Dilemmas, and Opportunities

In an environment of high uncertainty, with economies hit simultaneously by two severe economic crises in just over a decade and subject to geopolitical tensions, central banks have been exposed to numerous problems and changes: new instruments, new goals, erosion of independence, etc. In this difficult context and in the face of two of the new challenges facing humanity such as climate change and economic inequalities, this chapter has analyzed how monetary policy interrelates with these global challenges and what role it can play to help mitigate them.

Throughout the chapter, the relationship between monetary policy and the new challenges has been set out. It is also argued that inequalities and the climate emergency cannot be treated in isolation but are closely linked.

Throughout this chapter, it has been argued that central banks have experienced a period of opportunity before the pandemic with economies characterized by low and stable inflation and low interest rates. In this context and in certain exceptional situations where central banks need to implement new expansionary policies to achieve their price stability objectives, it is argued that these policies could be designed in coordination with fiscal authorities in such a way as to provide greater incentives to economies, help reduce economic inequalities, and make a carbon tax that can help reverse the environmental crisis more bearable and acceptable to middle- and low-income households. Smart and innovative design and close policy coordination could be the most efficient and effective way to meet the great challenges of our time.

However, in a more current context of rising inflation not seen for many years, central banks face difficult dilemmas. As discussed in the last section, there is a high risk of a structural reversal of the pre-pandemic path with high and volatile inflation and de-anchored inflation expectations. If such a negative scenario were to occur, the space for central banks to be more proactive on climate change and inequalities would be reduced and the proposals for monetary and fiscal coordination outlined in the chapter would be less feasible. On the other hand, while it is true that emerging market central banks have made great strides in monetary policy credibility and stability over the past two decades, achieving a much greater degree of control over inflation, current shocks pose greater challenges than in advanced economies. The transmission of commodity price shocks and exchange rate changes to inflation tends to be much larger and more persistent than in advanced economies. The higher rise in inflation means that central banks in emerging countries would have to raise interest rates more aggressively to reduce inflationary pressures at the cost of lower growth. If this scenario materializes, central banks in emerging economies would have even less room to collaborate on social inclusion and ecological transition.

Finally, although it is true that we are in a period of high uncertainty and there is no certainty about what may happen in the coming years, we cannot rule out that the environment of low inflation and low interest rates will once again dominate the international sphere in the middle-long term. Factors such as high inequality, demographic aging, or low productivity are still present and could reduce equilibrium interest rates and inflation again once the current tensions subside. In this case, the space for central banks to be innovative is widened and measures such as those presented in this chapter could help to mitigate two of the great current challenges: economic inequalities and climate change.

References

Albert, J. F., Gómez-Fernández, N., & Ochando, C. 2019, "Effects of unconventional monetary policy on income and wealth distribution: Evidence from United States and eurozone", *Panoeconomicus*, 66(5), 535–58.

Albert, J. F., & Gómez-Fernández, N. 2022, "Monetary policy and the redistribution of net worth in the U.S." *Journal of Economic Policy Reform*, 25(4), 420–434.

Alesina, A., & Summers, L. 1993, "Central bank independence and macroeconomic performance: Some comparative evidence", *Journal of Money, Credit and Banking*, 20(1), 151–62.

Arias, X. C. 2009, *La Crisis De 2008 y La Naturaleza De La Política Económica*. Instituto Universitario de Análisis económico y Social. Universidad de Alcalá de Henares.

Auclert, A. 2019, "Monetary policy and the redistribution channel", *American Economic Review*, 109(6), 2333–67.

Auclert, A., & Rognlie, M. 2018, "Inequality and aggregate demand", *National Bureau of Economic Research* No. w24280.

Bartholomew, L., & Diggle, P. 2021, "Central Banks and Climate Change-The Case for Action". Available in SSRN 3895605.

Bartsch, E., Boivin, J., Fischer, S., Hildebrand, P., & Wang, S. 2019, "Dealing with the next downturn: From unconventional monetary policy to unprecedented policy coordination", *SUERF Policy Note*, 105, 1–16.

Baumann, P., Rossi, E., & Schomaker, M. 2021, "Central Bank Independence and Inflation: Weak Causality at Best". Available in Voxeu.org.

Beckworth, D. 2020, "COVID-19 Pandemic, Direct Cash Transfers, and the Federal Reserve". *Mercatus Center Research Paper Series*, Special Edition Policy Brief.

Bernanke, B. S. 2015, "Monetary Policy and Inequality", Brookings. Available in https://www.brookings.edu/blog/ben-bernanke/2015/06/01/monetary-policy-&inequality/, June 01.

Blinder, A. S. 1999. *El Banco Central. Teoría y Práctica*. Antoni Bosch Ed.

Brunnermeier, M., & Landau, J. P. (2020), "Central Banks and Climate Change". Available in VoxEU.org, January 15.

Carpenter, S. B., & Rodgers, W. M. 2004, "The disparate labor market impacts of monetary policy", *Journal of Policy Analysis and Management*, 23, 813–30.

Coibion, O., Gorodnichenko, Y., Kueng, L., & Silvia, J. 2017, "Innocent bystanders? Monetary policy and inequality", *Journal of Monetary Economics*, 88, 70–89.

Colciago, A., Anna, S., & de Haan, J. 2019, "Central bank policies and income and wealth inequality: A survey", *Journal of Economic Surveys*, 33(4), 1199–231.

Coppola, F. 2019, *The Case for People's Quantitative Easing*. Polity Press, London.

Di Maggio, M., Kermani, A., Keys, B. J., Piskorski, T., Ramcharan, R., Seru, A., & Yao, V. 2017, "Interest rate pass-through: Mortgage rates, household consumption, and voluntary deleveraging", *American Economic Review*, 107(11), 3550–88.

Dietrich, A., Gernot, J. M., & Schoenle, R. 2021, "The Expectations Channel of Climate Change: Implications for Monetary Policy", *CEPR Discussion Paper* 15866.

Dinan, T., & Rogers, D. 2002, "Distributional effects of carbon allowance trading: How government decisions determine winners and losers", *National Tax Journal*, 55(2), 199–221.

Economides, G., & Xepapadeas, A. 2018, "Monetary Policy Under Climate Change", *Cesifo Working Paper* 7021/2018.

European Central Bank. 2022, *Economic Bulletin*, Issue 2/2022. Frankfurt.

Faccia, D., & Stracca, P. M. L. 2021, "Feeling the Heat: Extreme Temperatures and Price Stability", *ECB Working Paper*, ECB Working Paper, No. 2626, ISBN 978-92-899-4913-2

Giuliani, D., Kidney, S., & Meng, A. 2017, "Recommendations for Central Banks on How to Support the Development of the Green Bond Market", Paper presented at the CEP-DNB Workshop on Central Banking and Green Finance, Amsterdam, November 28–29, 2017.

Gopinath, G. 2022, "How Will the Pandemic and War Shape Future Monetary Policy?" Speech at the Jackson Hole Symposium. August 26, 2022.

Gray, C. L., & Mueller, V. 2012, "Natural disasters and population mobility in Bangladesh", *Proceeding of the National Academy of Science*, 109(16), 6000–5.

Haldone, A. 2020, "What Has Central Bank Independence Ever Done For Us" UCL Economists´Society Economics Conference. Bank of England.

Heathcote, J., Perri, F., & Violante, G. L. 2010, "Unequal we stand: An empirical analysis of economic inequality in the United States 1967–2006", *Review of Economic Dynamics*, 13(1), 15–51.

Hilmi, N., Djoundourian, S., Shahin, W., & Safa, A. 2021, "Does the ECB policy of quantitative easing impact environmental policy objectives?". *Journal of Economic Policy Reform*, 25(3), 259–271.

Honohan, P. 2019, "19–18 Should Monetary Policy Take Inequality and Climate Change in Account?", *PIIE Working paper*.

Howells, P., & Biefang-Frisancho, I. 2011, "Desarrollos recientes en la política monetaria", *Información Comercial Española* No. 858, 7–22.

Iacoviello, M. 2005, "House prices, borrowing constraints, and monetary policy in the business cycle", *American Economic Review*, 95(3), 739–64.

Jappelli, T., & Pistaferri, L. 2010, "The consumption response to income changes", *Annual Review of Economics*, 2, 479–506.

Jappelli, T., & Scognamiglio, A. 2018, "Interest rate changes, mortgages, and consumption: Evidence from Italy", *Economic Policy*, 33(94), 183–224.

Jourdan, S. 2020, "Helicopter Money as a Response to the Covid-19 Recession", Positive Money Report.

Kaplan, G., Moll, B., & Violante, G. L. 2018, "Monetary policy according to HANK", *American Economic Review*, 108(3), 697–743.

Klenert, D. L., Mattauch, E., Combet, O., Edenhofer, C., Hepburn, R., & Stern, N. 2018, "Making carbon pricing work for citizens", *Nature Climate Change* 8(8), 669–677.

Konradt, M., & di Mauro, W. 2021, "Carbon Taxation and Inflation: Evidence from Canada and Europe", *CEPR Discussion Paper* 16396.

Lenza, M., & Slačálek, J. 2018, "How Does Monetary Policy Affect Income and Wealth Inequality? Evidence from Quantitative Easing in the Euro Area", *ECB Working Paper* 2190, ECB European Central Bank, Frankfurt am Main.

Löyttyniemi, T. 2021, "Integrating Climate Change into a Financial Stability Framework". Available in Disponible en VoxEU.org, July 8.

Nakajima, M. 2015, "The redistributive consequences of monetary policy", *Federal Reserve Bank of Philadelphia Business Review*, 2, 9–16.

Mian, A., Straub, L., & Sufi, A. 2021, "Indebted demand", *The Quarterly Journal of Economics*, 136(4), 2243–307.

Muellbauer, J. 2014 "Combatting Eurozone Deflation: QE for the People". Available in VoxEU.org, December 23/2014.

Mumtaz, H., & Theophilopoulou, A. 2017, "The impact of monetary policy on inequality in the UK. An empirical analysis", *European Economic Review*, 98, 410–23.

Mumtaz, H., & Theophilopoulou, A. 2020, "Monetary policy and wealth inequality over the great recession in the UK. An empirical analysis", *European Economic Review*, 130, 103598.

Pérez-Moreno, S., Martín-Fuentes, N., & Albert, J. F. 2022, Rethinking Monetary Policy in the Framework of Inclusive and Sustainable Growth. In *Economic Policies for Sustainability and Resilience* (pp. 319–64). Palgrave Macmillan, Cham.

Schnabel, I. 2020, "When Markets Fail – The Need For Collective Action Tackling Climate Change", Speech at the European Sustainable Finance Summit, Frankfurt am Main, September 2020.

Schnabel, I. 2022, "Monetary policy and the Great Volatility", Speech at the Jackson Hole Symposium. August 27, 2022.

Schoenmaker, D. 2021, "Greening monetary policy", *Climate Policy*, 21(4), 581–92.

Stiglitz, J., & Stern, N. 2017, "Report of the High-Level Commission on Carbon Prices", World Bank.

Tucker, P. 2020, "Sobre la independencia del banco central" *Finanzas y Desarrollo*, junio 2020, pp: 44–7.

Williamson, S. D. 2008, "Monetary policy and distribution", *Journal of Monetary Economics*, 55(6), 1038–53.

Zerbib, O. 2017, "The Green Bond Premium", CEP-DNB Workshop on Central Banking and Green Finance, Amsterdam, November 28–29, 2017.

2 Capitalist Central Banks, War Finance, and Covid

Jocelyn F. Pixley

The chapter starts with variations in capitalist central banks. These state-established banks are beholden to private financial sectors and to their capitalist states. Neither accepts an intrusive central bank, and this refusal by state and financial forces limits what central banks (CBs) can do. In comparison, East Asian CBs have more potential for control over private banks. China is obvious as communist but even capitalist Japan appreciates CB controls. East Asian CBs are also different from the *West* in their thorough acceptance of earlier Western central bank reforms like the US Federal Reserve of 1934. Such reforms were later abolished in capitalist countries although some central bankers maintain respect for the reforms partly sparked by President Franklin D. Roosevelt's global influence in introducing controls over private banks. FDR's and other reforms were introduced elsewhere before World War II, such as requiring banks to invest in productive ventures and not just in speculation. It is called "window" or "forward" guidance and America's role as the currency hegemon had the dominant yet then, beneficial influence (Polanyi 1944).

The chapter's main theme is that monetary policy is always *political*. Governments establish central banks and design their purposes and remits. Governments can change CBs, sack CB officials, and limit them, according to the political context and class make-up of a country, and changes in the economic fashions and trends of the day. Most capitalist CBs have little control over the banking sectors they serve. It is mostly unknown that banks create most of the money the West uses in comparison to state currency money. Changes to private banks depend on governments, treasuries, and the strength of political and class demands.

CBs must fund state wars they had no part in, and often troubled banks. During the 2007 Global Financial Crisis, the US Fed had little influence over President Obama's decisions in 2010 for example. He refused stimulus despite the Fed's pleading. Furthermore, most people do not understand what CBs do; they tend to be blamed often wrongly for disasters not caused by them. In the 2022 inflations, few mention the inflation from war funding. In World War II, that was a key concern now forgotten, despite more war funding required with which CBs must cope. My view is that CBs can do very little without permission to act. Governments or banks make the decisions.

Second, the chapter moves to the varied responses of central banks to the Covid disaster and the potential for constructive money creation to emerge, or not, which was often dominant. Much central bank money creation eventually fostered

DOI: 10.4324/9781003323280-3

socially useless, capitalist bank market speculation (after deregulation of financial controls, and privatisation of state assets), whereas there might previously have been investment in constructive state-owned (and not neoclassical private) health systems. Covid vaccines should also have been free to all the world. The key remedy was that central banks provide "forward guidance" over private banks (Werner 2016: 375; 2020: 8–9) to prevent central bank funds from being spent purely on speculation on Wall Street as they were, under the misleading Quantitative Easing (QE) tag. Banks could have been told to have a long-term, socially useful component of their investment which can be paid off but were not. In the Covid case, state-run vaccine research and development could stop intellectual property rights being used as a stick against low-income countries by releasing the same vaccines for free. In his *Post-Corona capitalism*, Andreas Nölke (2022) does not see capitalism changing since the Corona virus.

Japan, South Korea, and China still use forward guidance as was practiced by the US Fed and Australia since World War II and Sweden, differently. The 1980s saw those bank rules dismissed in most capitalist countries on the grounds of "financial repression". This alleged repression was an exaggeration given the existing wealth of bankers and *rentiers* (Pixley 2018). Privatisations grew also in health care to banking's advantage but not for the sick; there are other factors in the pandemic worth mentioning like trust. Neoclassical economics, which came to dominate policy in capitalist countries, saw no need for trust relations, even after the privatisations of health systems. In fact, *rentiers*, wealthy from unearned income, gained more. However, informal trust between people proved its worth during Covid, see below.

The third contrast is the current explosion of war finance spending and not only on the Ukraine invasion but US invasions. All wars are, by definition, destructive. The losses are uncountable and unrecoverable. While the tragedy of war is the public's concern, there are very few capitalist CBs that are permitted to worry about suffering, when their states are insistent on starting wars. Few mention that arms races are inflationary, and the main way to curb war profiteers (as FDR called them) is through war taxes. These limit financial market speculation on government bonds issued, meaning the state borrows to pay for war finance. Taxes help pay back these debts and reduce other inflations. However, democratic states are reluctant to tax on what the public will perceive as disastrous wars, as most are. The historical antecedents of unpopular war savagery, not only the expenses and inflation of financial warfare, are discussed briefly. The British pound hegemon was able to pass inflationary costs off onto other countries. The same occurred with the later US dollar hegemony. These hegemons have been predominant in pursuing brutal wars in the world.

Variations in Central Banks

The consequences of the US Fed's global dominance are that few notice outlying capitalist central banks (see Ugolini 2011 and Epstein 2006). The Bank of Canada (BoC) and the Reserve Bank of Australia (RBA) with relatively small populations of initially mainly white settlers are too boring for others to mention. Bank of England types wrongly assume their ex-*colonies'* central banks are modelled on it. During the 1930s–40s, BoE Governor Montagu Norman did try to force its model so that the British could further exploit the commonwealth and colonial countries through the intended financial subservience to the British empire. Canada, India, New Zealand, and Australia rejected these blatant schemes. As white English-speaking countries, it was easiest to be heard (Pixley 2018). Epstein (2006: 16–17) stresses that all CBs across the world have financed governments and used allocation methods to engage in sectoral policy. He asks what *kind* of developmental policy CBs should conduct. England and the US focused on promoting the financial sector, which makes countries "vulnerable to financial panics".

Yet during the 1940s, even the Fed helped promote many new CBs to encourage economic development and internal stability (Epstein 2006: 13–14). Another highly social model is the Swedish Rehn-Meidner model which makes the Riksbank nearly irrelevant, save for its Keynesian views (Erixon 2010). In contrast, France has not ceded many of its former French African colonies any monetary sovereignty to this day (Idrissa 2021). The Banque de France controls their money creation. A recent translation of *Africa's last colonial currency: the CFA franc story* (Pigeaud and Sylla 2021) shows that France's earlier colonial push was mercantile.

That was unlike Britain where King Charles II *defaulted* on London's merchant-lenders in the 1670s. These merchants overthrew James I by arranging for William of Orange to invade England in 1688. Loans were for William's European wars and, only by chartering the privately owned Bank of England in 1694, were lenders prepared to fund the Crown's wars. That gave England a huge military advantage over Europe and Ireland, from which William III benefited. The condition was that lenders would be assured of no defaults by hobbling the Crown in Parliament in London, by forcing the government to tax. Max Weber (1981: 264–5) saw it as a memorable alliance: states would make war and merchant classes would make money. A British Prime Minister two centuries later said King William had put the state in "a position of subserviency to induce monied men to be lenders" (cited Kynaston 1995: 19–20). This pattern of mutual deals for war finance, which central banks arranged, spread in warmongering capitalist countries.

It was early capitalist money. The *hypostatisation* of money, complained Cartelier (2007) of Classical liberalism, refuses to accept the difference from trading with shells, or exchange of cattle in local markets, and their various *social contexts* as he and the social economists have long said. Capitalist money is specific to one system, and it needs strong controls by trustworthy authorities.

Money, being a fragile social institution of multiple, mutual relations, is the least predictable, as Simmel and Durkheim explained more than a century ago (in Orléan 2014). Capitalist money is a three-way relation between lenders, debtors, and the suffering community. But orthodoxy tries to make capitalist money with shaky war finance into a thing (like shells). These attempts to hypostatise money (Cartelier 2007) always fail in various ways like depressions, bubbles, crashes, and bailouts.

Otherwise, in France, Britain, and Belgium, European earlier colonial pushes were about centuries-old trade in which local currencies and commodities (shells, e.g. Idrissa 2021) were originally valid in commercial zones. They were not using capitalist money. The Niger's *dala* was derived from Austria's *thaler*. It later as the *dollar* became the US sovereign currency. But the *dalar* circulated as a trade currency from Aden to Mexico without central banks. When the British East India Company (EIC) became the Crown's affair – nationalised due to EIC corruption (Dalrymple 2019), the British currency pound sterling had to be used in all colonial trade and territorial takeovers, with the Bank of England (BoE) supervising. Idrissa (2021) explains how the state currency of the franc emerged with Napoleon's establishing the Banque de France in 1800. It is debt-credit not savings, which creates money; but French African banks were forbidden from creating modern money for entrepreneurial Africans. This "staggering blow" left France's African possessions at the mercy of colonial capitalism managed by the Banque de France (Idrissa 2021).

After the gold standard collapsed in 1930, France imposed a system of *imperial preference* on its African colonies. It resembled the efforts of the Bank of England to keep Britain's colonies dependent on the pound. Some Commonwealth countries were white and politically independent, sufficient to reject such attempts to retain Empire. Meantime India and other non-white UK colonies or newly independent countries did join the BoC or RBA in resisting. Not so the French sub-Saharan and equatorial African countries, although Idrissa refuses to despair about France's domination since some African countries did quite well. This is not an excuse (Pigeaud and Sylla 2021).

The US Federal Reserve was not designed or enacted in 1913 to be like the BoE which had to undertake Lender of Last Resort after bank collapses. CB-Lenders can inspect the banks' books under last resort lending. The US Fed designers met under secrecy, to thwart mid-west American demands to democratise money that were vociferous in the late 1800s, with "Cross of Gold" slogans. The Fed was designed to destroy the City of London in favour of Wall Street. This occurred through British determination to increase its debts to Wall Street and "win" the gruesome slog of World War I. War debt meant the UK lost its currency hegemony to the USA through Wall Street deals which forced Britain, France, and Italy to repay their WW1 debts in US dollars (Pixley 2018: Chapters 1 and 2). Their taxes were far too slight to retain much control.

During the Depression, US President Roosevelt and Marriner Eccles, Fed Chair, achieved many bank controls, but they lost in the Senate when trying to nationalise the District Feds. The New York District Fed remains privately owned by Wall Street banks, and it has enormous influence on the national Federal Reserve in Washington DC. Most central banks are state-owned. The BoE was nationalised in the immediate postwar Labour government under PM Attlee. But the BoE has never been as forward thinking as the Bank of Japan (BoJ), BoC, RBA, and others in controlling the direction of private bank loans. The US Fed Board Chairs' records – after Eccles' and McChesney Martin's "lean against the wind" strategy against private banks, and via President Eisenhower's somewhat stronger achievement of peace (Wheatcroft 2021) – are patchy. Fed Chair Bernanke, a historian of the Great Depression, had no idea that his QE during the Global Financial Crisis was a gift to Wall Street through his ridiculous "loanable funds" idea (Pixley 2018: 367–8). Schumpeter delves back to Adam Smith on this about savings; in depressed times, savings will diminish economic activity, since what is saved is not spent. (Bibow 2015: 17 argues Keynes agreed, it was hoarding; Schumpeter 1954: 318–20.) CBs always help banks overnight, and thus QE is merely lots more. Bernanke's antecedent was Greenspan's "put", which also favoured Wall Street. These Fed Chairs vociferously supported deregulation which resulted in a loss of controls for central banks and treasuries over banks' unadmitted capacities to create money.

When the 2007 crash hit America, everyone knowledgeable could see it coming – just not *when* it would happen (interviews in Pixley 2004). Regardless, the US Fed and Treasury kept feeding the multiple bubbles, notably from derivatives, until the edifice collapsed. Britain had assiduously copied the USA and likewise the BoE Governor dithered even when Northern Rock was already bankrupt. Meanwhile Canada and Australia escaped the worst of the 2007 crash, somewhat differently. Both countries had a large element of financial deregulation in the 1980s but had different mechanisms to cope, and both prevented the biggest banks from mergers.

In Canada, the original 1871 Bank Act legislation retained some of its features. Notably, the Ottawa Parliament was required to review the Bank Act's provisions every ten years, and since 1992, every five. This is unheard of in other English-speaking countries because it requires banks to front up every five years and demonstrate that they are worthy of bank licences to create money. Parliament did waive through various deregulations, but MPs were mindful of their own constituencies possibly losing branches, if banks should become too big to fail (Kobrak and Martin 2018: 210–211). As a result, Canadian banks have usually been well-controlled, as Ryan-Collins says too (2015).

In Australia in the 20007 crash, much had been deregulated but the RBA was quick-witted and worked closely with a new Treasury. A Labor government had just inherited the mess of a far-right one. Treasury immediately introduced stimulus programmes, particularly a new building of their choice for every Australian school. The RBA has retained its full employment remit (FE) to this day (as has the US Fed), which helps prevent drastic rate rises. The Fed wilfully ignores its FE remit, often creating ruinous unemployment. Australia emerged from the 2007 financial crisis with the best reputation in the western world (Pixley 2018).

Covid and Central Banks

By 2020, Western central banks could do nothing new about the Covid pandemic but use the QE of the *great Atlantic financial crisis*, the Chinese name for the GFC. Capitalist CBs had lost all the controls they could have used after neoclassical economics had doomed economic activity. This was done to central banks by putting them under tight control of governments, through inflation targets. This now *orthodoxy* had wrongly blamed governments for alleged inflationary spending on people's needs and aiming for Full Employment (FE) with decent wages and conditions. The neoclassical *cure* rested on telling governments to hobble central banks and make tax cuts. They in fact did obey orthodoxy to the letter by accepting the opinions of this small group which was primarily anti-social and pro-banks. Reagan and Thatcher led the way, not in understanding the mysticisms of neoclassical types, of course, only in their anti-communism. The rise of *finance economics* was fraudulent, and André Orléan (2014), an economist at Sciences Po, has made fun of their alleged theories that capitalist financial markets were rational, or efficient or, barring any *psychotic* event, were always predictive. This has never been the case for 400 years.

Under silly hopes of finding *certainty*, many central banks became mute and social democracy died in capitalist countries, although not all. South America always endured rough treatment, and the faintest hint of a country's own money creation for social democracy led to US financial and real warfare. Governments should be minimal, sell off everything state-owned, and shut down the school, health, housing, and social security provisions. Central banks must be controlled tightly to abolish aims for FE and forward guidance over private banks. Inflation Targets were to *club the economic activity* that had flourished during the postwar time. Just as non-whites and women were getting toeholds on secure jobs, particularly in health services and education, these chances were abolished. The USA never had much that was state-owned, whereas Europe and other Anglo-American countries did. The US Fed barely noticed because "free enterprise" dominated (Pixley 2018).

Meantime, East Asian central banks retrieved regulations like forward guidance, dumped in Anglo-America decades ago. They flourished while Anglo-America did not, except for their financial sectors. The pandemic was ignored in many Western countries until some governments realised that health protection came above economic activity. When or if the pandemic eases, the blame is now cast on central banks, but treasuries have the power to reduce various inflations that hurt those who are already impoverished and distressed. Taxes are effective, and another tool like guidance is Asset-Backed Reserve Requirements, used in Europe, Japan, and earlier the RBA. CBs can raise or lower the requirements to dampen or renew banks' propensity for money creation (Epstein 2006: 12). A few central banks call for wage rises in vain, such as the RBA, while East Asian CBs aim for sharing wealth. This is anathema to Wall Street.

Nölke (2020: 169–70) notes that the pandemic occurred just when China-US relations became very tense. President Trump's efforts to blame China for "Covid" were in accord with the US Democrats' consistent hawk leanings for decades. Pressure on Australia, which is a huge trading partner with China, to accuse China of *creating* COVID-19, lost Australia much trading. The USA promptly took these trade avenues: so much for the US-Australia alliance. Fine wool graziers in Australia who trade with Shanghai are furious about this imbroglio. Australia has a world monopoly of fine wool; China has the best wool processors and now a huge market for a cold climate. Interviews confirm these farmers enjoy their friendships in Shanghai.

Plenty of pandemics had occurred before – it's a long list of dangerous infectious diseases, some still prevalent like polio and AIDS. Quarantine centres were built for recovery from cholera and back to the 1918 world "Spanish" influenza (now believed to have originated in the USA no less). There was an arc of countries from Japan to New Zealand which had not forgotten the recent SARS outbreak that had swept these countries. But Australia was by then a pure neoclassical government. Quarantines were torn down; hospitals and the Medicare state progressive health insurance system were heavily modified with largesse to the high wealth side. State-owned hospitals struggled and doctors, nurses, and specialists were hobbled by harsher Medicare rules and a low-tax regime.

In Australia, the leaders of the Australian Council of Trade Unions (ACTU) forced the government to provide Covid sick leave and higher income supplements. But the Commonwealth government refused to fund age-care centres properly although it has the responsibility to prevent elderly people from malnutrition and to improve the lack of Covid nurses and other experts (Refs in Australian press and journals). On 21 May 2022, this government lost office to a Labor government with Greens and independents in Parliament. There is a huge mess to fix, but some optimism.

In a slight economic examination of Covid in America, Paul Krugman, now opinion page economic writer for the *NYT*, discussed "Covid's Economic Mutations" (2022). He agrees that the USA did not cope well with Covid and indeed there were more Covid deaths after Biden was inaugurated. Krugman dismisses the line that "centralised social control" – countries like China – are better able to cope with crises like Covid than Western liberal orders. He suggests Western countries developed vaccines rapidly, whereas he claims China's vaccines "appear to be less effective" than the West's. He admits a centralised country like Denmark with high vaccine rates returned to lockdowns in 2021. So did many capitalist countries with more controls than the USA. His (questionable) conclusions are that autocratic countries "suffer from their lack of openness" in the long run. This is unproven although Krugman rightly skewers the economists for failing to consider global bottlenecks from Covid shutdowns, with clogged ports and crucial parts for factories lacking, hence price inflation. He dubiously praises the US Fed for forestalling a likely deep recession.

Krugman misses a further interesting qualification to Covid analyses. At Oxford, two researchers compared "interpersonal" levels of trust, not trust in government or institutions like CBs, but trust in each other, neighbours, strangers, friends, or co-workers (Hale 2022). The US and UK scored well in pandemic preparedness but two years later these OECD (allegedly open) countries were among those with the greater loss of life. In the study, countries with these characteristics cannot be classified as authoritarian or *Western*, as Krugman does, but a variety. People spent far less time in lockdowns and other restrictions because this kind of trust involves collective action "if everyone takes part" and trust that others won't break the rules.

In 2020 and 2021, the main countries with fewer Covid deaths were Thailand, South Korea, and Australia, a mixed bunch. The researchers admit these correlations may need more contextual factors to be fully explanatory, but they are worth pondering. Central banks, at a guess, have least connections to interpersonal trust. But if they have fruitful outcomes for most, that can help trust maintenance.

How they expanded to deal with Covid expenditure varies; Australia followed the QE route. Paul Krugman in a *NYT* regular article still uses the argument about a singular inflation not multiple inflations, while Wall Street cries "Inflation" constantly and wrongly (Auerback 2022).

The RBA has no control over how this Covid accommodation was used by banks and financial markets (the Fed could control margin loan requirements but does not). The RBA has kept its rate very low, however, on the grounds that wages are in *deflation* and households are heavily indebted. Like the USA, Australia has Covid inflations from bottleneck shortages, price rises, and from US sanctions against Russia, particularly gasoline or petrol. Australia also closed all entry to the country for at least a year! Citizens had the same lockouts. Raising RBA rates will have no effect on these different inflations, nor property inflation and other asset bubbles. South Korea in contrast does have a central bank with forward guidance on banks, whereas Thailand has nothing like the wealth of either South Korea or Australia. Australia's Treasury, however, completely misread the pandemic; its right-wing government was slow on preventative measures, so Australia's good record is mainly due to the population's ethics of caring for each other in bad times, like during recent flooding across Eastern Australia.

Financial Warfare

Central banks are simultaneously facing Covid problems, and the war finance demanded by governments, which requires CBs to accommodate states' heavy expenditure-debts on military arsenals. The US arms spending data is staggering and exceeds all other countries' *combined* military build-up; it can be said the US is only ahead of the rest of the world in its vast military stockpile of arsenals. The Fed can do nothing although it rarely calls on Treasury for tax increases. On most other calculations, Wall Street is also huge but is profitable purely for *rentiers (and capitalist military firms)*, not for productive, green, and social developments. Other countries foster that fruitful mix.

American beliefs that their country is the greatest are not slackening. This mostly includes the Fed. The US under President Biden has stepped up threats that are alleged to be coming from China, differently from President Trump's initial blaming China for Covid; this amplified in Biden's threats against Russia, as far as commentators can make out. The US plans to have nuclear missile bases in countries like South Korea and Australia (Brown 2022) on top of the world's largest number of US bases (the Australian peoples were not consulted, nor have we accepted any nuclear power). There is also the question of US financial sanctions on Iraq, Afghanistan, Venezuela, and now Russia. It is far more globally important than the other war-scarred countries under US sanctions, many of which barely function. The consequences of America's previous invasions have shattered these already disadvantaged countries; recently was the White House's "freeze" of the Afghani Central Bank's reserves (Conley 2022). The connections to the US Fed are secret.

The number of problems for central banks in funding war finance is multifarious – but the early capitalist central banks were *designed* to finance European warfare, with taxes to minimise inflation. However, in the variations discussed above, some central banks had remits primarily to serve national social welfare as well as being bankers to private banks. Problems of war inflation lie there when governments borrow from private banks to fund unpopular wars. The USA post-1945 has funded the bulk of wars in this way, many with NATO, nearly all ending in bitter failures (Jimmy Carter in Wilkins 2019) and unbearable levels of inflationary war debt. War expenditure is inflationary because it does not bring socially useful economic returns: nothing is said on this by CBs. Taxes help to reduce warfare's destructive waste, as was stressed for World War II (Keynes 1940; for Australia see Pixley 2018). Today's central banks cannot control war inflation to stabilise currencies.

The US financial warfare against Russia starting in March 2022 "breaks all rules of the game" (Hendrickson 2022). Whether the "great powers of the world" eventually regret this dangerous decision or end in triumph over Russia is unpredictable. The major prognoses come from their fast-moving moments in time. The dominant narrative is Western promoted and has been believed in a simple caricature: Vladimir Putin is an evil monster; Russia is bad; Ukraine is perfect, and the USA is self-righteously *exceptional*. This propaganda is very like the British empire's in their wars against Tsarist Russia and, globally linked, the British carving up of the Middle East and Afghanistan. These were all to protect Britain's largest colony India and further east, notably UK opium-peddling incursions into China.

The present US conflict has some similarities; the US leaves Ukraine to fight. Financial sanctions include confiscating the Russian central bank reserves. In *The American Conservative* (9 March 2022), Hendrickson argues the "freezing" in Biden's words, of Russian foreign exchange reserves, is like a financial H-Bomb. "This action means that all previous economic contracts between Russia and the West are invalid" and the US and allies are badly underestimating the fallout. "Remarkably, they did this against the backdrop of a worldwide crisis in supply chains (largely from Covid lockdowns). That is about to get a lot worse".

As he says whilst… "much debate [is] about what the West is willing to buy, little attention is on the terms on which Russians are willing to sell, if they are willing to sell at all. They are in a position to impose staggering costs on the West in retaliation".

In another paper (March 23), Hendrickson gives reliable evidence that financial sanctions on Russia were

> … cooked up in a couple of hours by US government staffers. In name the central bank actions are a *freeze*, but in actuality they constitute a debt repudiation, a default, on a far bigger scale than anything engineered by the Bolsheviks, who put the debts of the Tsar to the torch when they came to power.
>
> The situation is made all the more incredible by two facts. First, the contemporary default occurred at the center of the financial order, not at its periphery. That makes it staggering and unlike any other. Previous discussions of sanctions had treated Russia's removal from SWIFT as the Absolute Weapon [but with] … Full faith and credit", now repudiated, had been no mere phrase

[but signified countries' respect for funding, even if the countries are at war]. "This suffering is on the US government" he concludes.

Other criticisms focus on the Afghan humanitarian disaster caused by the USA. Biden's February 2022 seizure of the US$7 billion in assets held by the Afghan central bank is dooming many Afghans to die of starvation as we speak. Human rights groups are appalled and economists who understand money insist the country needs a functioning central bank with banks that citizens can use. Children are dying, report *Médecins sans Frontiers*, from malnutrition and common baby contagions. Few Afghanis can access bank-money to buy food (Hendrickson 9 March), whereas the Taliban have their own funding sources (Weisbrot 2022).

The difference in Afghanistan is that the alleged moral superiority (in Ukraine) of the USA vanishes. President Biden imposed central bank "freezes" that are heavily weighted not by the Afghan starvation now unmentionable and irrelevant to financial markets, but by the Russian freeze with its global economic impacts. The politics of sanctions have entailed huge pressure on reluctant countries to agree to United Nations condemnations of Russia's invasion of the Ukraine. The UN also condemned the US invasion of Iraq. Narratives vary widely. Biden did not rearm the Ukraine on his own; according to Caitlin Johnstone (2022), President Trump began this rearmament, not such a Kremlin puppet that the Democrats allege. Obama had "refused demands" from neoconservatives and liberal hawks to arm Ukraine, because he feared that rearming might provoke an attack by Russia. But Trump "spent his term pouring weapons into Ukraine, shredding treaties with Russia and ramping up cold war escalations against Moscow", she alleges. The Central Bank of Russia has so far responded competently (discussed below).

This dangerous situation was avoidable, not just by the USA, since the Kremlin had other options than brutal invasion. Its gas and wheat could have been refused to "unfriendly" countries. This to me is hard to imagine since the US decided to take over the EU's foreign and trade policies and stop Russia's gas lines (Auerback 2022). The ECB has been quiet. But the Kremlin could have urged the UN to play a peace-keeping role. The Russians took umbrage about NATO encroachments. However, Russia and Ukraine are holding peace talks, but the US is not interested. Why? The Fed narrative blames the Russians for invading, correctly. It then wrongly blames Russia on shortages when they are due to US sanctions.

In Australia, some of us sceptics are stressing the now former belligerent pro-US government is taking umbrage at China's relations with the tiny Solomon Islands. Exactly like the Kremlin, Canberra is livid and imagines Chinese nuclear bases will be bristling against Australia any day now. So far, the Chinese have only signed a draft mutual aid and protection idea. The Chinese also built a beautiful, fully equipped hospital in Fiji some years ago. This is part of the PBoC's forward guidance to Chinese banking, to encourage Keynesian-type investment which brings good returns for Chinese spending, albeit indirectly. Australia's former government patronised Pacific Island governments and fostered more carbon emissions, against all Islands' wishes. The RBA had lost all power to encourage private bank investment in the Pacific. Moreover, we are not even armed for defence. We rely on the USA for "defence", which according to some American "crackpot realists" involves putting more US nuclear missiles around China (Brown 2022). They will be in Japan, South Korea, and further south to Australia. The USA will avoid the nuclear replies, but we will not. The UK and Australia have long been vassal states to the USA; America is working on collecting more vassals. East Asian states are proving disobliging. Australia's new Labor government has a brilliant Foreign Minister who actively shows that Australia will renew ties to SE Asia and the Pacific Islands. This is far from White House policy, but early days for spending more via the RBA.

The US record in interfering with Russia emerging from the Soviet Union is poor. David Woodruff (1999) argues the IMF gurus and Yeltsin's neoclassical minister had no clue about money. No one *in charge* insisted a capitalist state must have a central monopoly over the creation and definition of money payments (debts), by its central bank. In its absence, due to neoclassical ignorance, in Russia by 1994 *regional* authorities accepted barter as a means of payment between sophisticated firms, to prevent destruction of industries, because intricate obligations had to be met. Soviet banks became commercial under Gorbachev, without central bank controls. During 1990–91 Yeltsin boasted everyone could have "choices" and pursued a "radical and rapid transition". Russia above all needed action on monetary consolidation with its central bank but instead endured a decade of misery (Woodruff 1999: 111–113; 713–4).

Today, the White House's use of the central bank of Russia's reserves is still unfolding. Biden promised the rouble was reduced to "rubble" which so far has not happened as its value has held so far. The Governor of Russia's central bank has world respect for her monetary policy. In 2014, Governor Elvira Nabiullina switched the currency to a free float, and in 2022, she raised interest rates after Biden's sanctions so that the rouble was not "rubble" (Maki, 2022). Other changes are that the EU is facing many worries but with France's elections in 2022, and criticisms inside Germany of the government's weaknesses in acceding to the USA, these concerns may not be tempered. The ECB is strangely silent, yet the EU seems hobbled by the USA and NATO. Italy is looking to northern Africa for alternative energy sources. It is well-known that the US does not like a competitor as capable (and white) as the EU, but it's also true that most hegemonic powers are reluctant to see their own empires decline gracefully. The British empire clung to its financial warfare long after it lost its pound hegemony during World War I debts to the USA. As mentioned in the first section, Britain remained brutal wherever it could get away with it (Pixley 2018). However, as Wall Street took over world financial domination, the City of London had fewer tricks which had been richly supported by the Bank of England and Treasury. PM Thatcher produced "Big Bang" a quaint term that meant the City was to open itself to all financial competitors. Eventually, this was mainly Wall Street banks. The BoE was thereby weakened.

In 2019, former President Jimmy Carter, aged 94, gave a speech on how he had told Trump that China's success was due to its peaceful foreign policies. He cites how China built thousands of kilometres of high-speed rail, while the USA has none, broken US bridges are not repaired, or new hospitals built. Then US Fed Chair Yellen called Obama for infrastructure spending, but US Treasury refused. The Fed has done less on making calls on war finance inflation. Carter had the figures: since 2001, $5.9 trillion has been spent on US military arms and warfare. The USA has kept at peace for 16 of its 242 years as a nation and is the "most warlike country" in the world, to Carter. Many nations view the US as a threat to world peace (Carter cited Wilkins 2019). The Fed has not remarked that other countries are trying to avoid using the US Dollar.

Although France's franc managed by the Banque de France never had the pound's global hegemony, its own abuse of France's former Sub-Sahara and Equatorial colonies remains (Pigeaud and Sylla 2021). This is somewhat like President Biden's "expropriation" of *all* of Russia's central bank reserves. Hardly known elsewhere, France expropriates fifty per cent of these African countries' CB reserves. France's former northern African colonies like Algeria refused to accept the CFA franc and preferred to have their own currencies and budgets with which to invest as necessary and to local Africans.

The Equatorial countries were not allowed this ordinary, essential sovereignty. From 1960, they were under a "reciprocal preferential" regime through the currency. Earlier, from 1954 the *lesser* currencies in use locally *only* were pegged to the franc, whereby one French franc was worth 50 CFA francs and after 1999 with the Euro. CFA francs went straight to Paris.

> The CFA franc, used by fourteen countries yet economically bound to France, is the last colonial currency on the African continent. French and international media had long taken its existence as something of a dirty secret, even though it is used by some 187 million people. … the CFA franc instead points to … the persistence of what has for decades served as a tool of French neocolonialism.
>
> (Sylla 2022)

Other currency blocs in Africa were dismantled with postwar independence (pound sterling, Spanish peseta, Belgian and Portuguese escudo currency areas). But the CFA franc stayed, with few sub-Saharan Africans believing French ministerial claims in April 2017 that "France is there as a friend" (Pigeaud and Sylla 2021: 34). The French tried severe repression for countries escaping control of the Banque de France (winning brutally against Guinea and Togo). There are many benefits for France, which amount to Sylla (2022) as a "recipe for underdevelopment" for central African countries unable to have their own central banks. The system is cumbersome and difficult to detect, but it has not stimulated trade among members, nor economic development. "It has deprived countries of chances to conduct an autonomous monetary policy" but this "mug's game" is excellent for French interests and the African ruling classes (Pigeaud and Sylla 2021: 27; 137). Chronic overvaluation makes exports very unattractive, whereas luxury imports for African elites are apparently wonderful (Sylla 2022).

Rather than stray into the messy, uncertain present, there are various reasons why many African countries are currently choosing to be neutral to Russia's Ukraine invasion (Ajala 2022). One is the lack of their own central banks, of course. In 2012, Namibia argued NATO's invasion and overthrow of Libya's Gaddafi should be condemned for destabilising North Africa. President Obama played a role. More recently, military alliances developed with Ethiopia, Mali, and Nigeria. Ajala notes the low emphasis on human rights makes Russia attractive say in Nigeria. Conflicting stories (save on CBs) swirl everywhere.

Although White House sanctions are hurting the EU since late March 2022 onwards, EU opinion is divided. Greece for example found in a poll (April 2022) that sixty per cent "understood" Russia's position. The Central Bank of Greece has defended its efforts to be free of EU influence. Pressure on Germany to rearm thoroughly, despite its post-World War II abhorrence of armaments, started to "waver" (12 April 2022, NYT). Much of the EU wants some "normality" returned, to keep its gas supply stream from Russia as it further builds alternative energy.

One of the questions unable to be asked at present is the number of "kleptocrats" in the world (Bernstein 2021) not only Russians. In late 2021, they still thrived since the USA came to provide loopholes and money laundering for American and global kleptocrats. New Jersey state was clipped of "shady" practices in the 1900s; the Fed appears to have played no role, but Delaware stepped in with tax-free gifts as long as a company did no business in Delaware. One of Ukraine's oligarchs did much damage to US firms' workers, but that is silenced at present. It is a mark of how little is controlled by the US Fed, and Treasury could act, but fails.

Conclusion

Capitalist central banks have an ambiguous position in a massive conflict over the conditions of control over money production. For capitalist banks and firms, the state must not participate directly in the economy. In Canada, however, we saw the Parliament still scrutinises banks about whether they are worthy of a licence to create money (Kobrak and Martin 2018). The strength of parliamentary scrutiny depends on the balance of political forces, but incredibly, banks are by law held to account in Canada's public sphere.

Equally, full employment (FE) is designed for central banks to maintain a *balance* between monetary stability and FE. This is a strength of the RBA, we discussed, with the Fed only drawing on it by Chair Yellen against President Obama's weakness with Treasury. Money can never be depoliticised so there is no chance of a *neutral* central bank (Keynes's hope). In Sweden, the CB played little part in Sweden's social policies (Erixon 2010). Australian social economists up to the 1990s saw that politics is the *essence* of monetary policy. This is the key conclusion of this chapter. The RBA and the BoC are noteworthy here. In the World War II era, these governments widely understood that inflation is not a singular claim, because the context must provide distinctions or else "inflation" merely defends sectional interests. War finance is inflationary in certain circumstances, so that too much money in war also chases few goods and services. Banks also create more money, if deregulated, merely for consumer lending or speculation, not useful activities with taxes ensured, which brings money inflation and asset inflation. Full employment is not necessarily accompanied by wage inflation. In 2022 Australia, wages were deflating long before the Corona pandemic and the huge amounts on war finance to support *American* exceptionalism. Austerity had long before entailed wage suppression, ironically a drive of neoclassical economics which wrongly blamed FE for all inflations (we saw, also Pixley 2018). Small businesses had few customers, and thus with business and household debt build-ups, the RBA was left during the pandemic keeping them from bankruptcy with a low CB rate.

Whereas China, Japan, and South Korea had forward guidance to insist that banks invest part of their profits on ventures that were profitable, even green, Australia and Canada had lost these controls (in Pixley 2018: 187–91). But these two capitalist CBs resisted harsh inflation targets. Targets were, we saw, designed to prevent economic activity. Now other CBs, like the US Fed and the BoE, are at a loss. The appalling deaths from Covid in both countries are also a mark of the thorough deregulation of the finance sector, the public health sector, and much more. The USA never had a welfare state, but Britain's is fast unravelling from its desire to escape the EU in Brexit. Labour shortages in its fabled NHS will not be overcome by a feeble BoE, which has rarely worked in tandem with UK Treasury. The US Fed appears to have no control or potential to cooperate with a belligerent White House. Its rate rises can only do more harm, except to Wall Street banks, while war finance and sanctions are inflationary. CBs lack control in most pure capitalist contexts.

References

Ajala, O. 2022. 'Five reasons why many African countries choose to be neutral' https://johnmenadue.com/olayinka-ajala-russias-war-with-ukraine-five-reasons-why-many-african-countries-choose-to-be-neutral/

Auerback, M. 2022. 'Inflation isn't a Putin problem: It's made in America' *The Scrum* May 4.

Bernstein, J. 2021. 'Loopholes for kleptocrats' *NYRB* 2 December: 23–25.

Bibow, J. 2015. *The Euro's Savior? Assessing the ECB's Crisis Management Performance*. Macroeconomic Policy Institute (IMK), Study, June, 42.

Brown, J. 2022. 'Washington's crackpot realism' *NYRB* 24 March: 12–14.

Cartelier, J. 2007. 'The hypostasis of money: an economic point of view', *Cambridge Journal of Economics* No. 31, 217–233.

Conley, J. 2022. 'The Afghan humanitarian disaster is caused by the US' reprinted from *CommonDreams* by *Menadue.com.au*. March 27, 2022.

Dalrymple, W. 2019. *The Anarchy: The Relentless Rise of the East India Company*. London: Bloomsbury.

Epstein, G. 2006. 'Central Banks as Agents of Economic Development', *United Nations University (UNU-Wider)*, Research Paper No. 2006/54, May: 1–20.

Erixon, L. 2010. "The Rehn-Meidner Model in Sweden" *Journal of Economic Issues*, Vol XLIV (3): 677–715.

Hendrickson, D. 2022. 'Why this economic war on Russia breaks all the rules of the game' Responsible Statecraft https://responsiblestatecraft.org/2022/03/23/why-this-economic-war-on-russia-breaks-all-rules-of-the-game/

Hendrickson, D. 2022. See also his https://www.theamericanconservative.com/articles/weapons-of-financial-destruction-and-the-new-world-disorder/

Idrissa, R. 2021. 'Countries without currency' *LRB* 2 December: 27–30.

Johnstone, C. 2022. 'Revisiting Russiagate in light of the Ukraine war.' https://caitlinjohnstone.com/2022/03/28/re-visiting-russiagate-in-light-of-the-ukraine-war/

Keynes, J. M. 1940. *How to Pay for the War: a Radical Plan for the Chancellor of the Exchequer*. London: Macmillan and Co.

Kobrak, C. and Martin, J. 2018 *From Wall Street to Bay Street: History of American and Canadian Finance*. University of Toronto Press.

Krugman, P. 2022. 'Covid's economic mutations' *NYRB* 10 March: 19–20.

Kynaston, D. 1995. 'The Bank of England and the Government' in R. Roberts & D. Kynaston eds. *The Bank of England*. Oxford: Oxford University Press: 19–55.

Hale, T. 2022. 'We've found one factor that predicts which countries best survive Covid' The Guardian: https://www.theguardian.com/commentisfree/2022/mar/24/countries-covid-trust-damage-pandemic

Lears, J. 2022. 'The forgotten crime of war itself' *NYRB* 21 April: 40–43.

Maki 2022. 'Once mocked by Biden, the rouble emerges from the ashes' SMH https://www.smh.com.au/business/markets/once-mocked-by-biden-russia-s-rouble-emerges-from-the-ashes-20220407-p5abhn.html

Nölke, A. 2022 *Post-Corona Capitalism*. Bristol, UK: Bristol University Press.

Orléan, A. 2014. *The Empire of Value*. Cambridge, MA: MIT Press Books.

Pigeaud, F. and Sylla, N. S. 2021 *Africa's Last Colonial Currency: Ehe CFA Franc Story*, Trans. T Fazi, London, Pluto Press.

Pixley, J. F. 2004 *Emotions in Finance: Distrust and Uncertainty in Global Markets*, Cambridge University Press.

Pixley, J. F. 2018. *Central Banks, Democratic States and Financial Power*. Cambridge University Press.

Polanyi, K. 1957 [1944]. *The Great Transformation*. Boston, MA: Beacon Press.

Ryan-Collins, J. R. 2015. 'Is Monetary Financing Inflationary? A Case Study of the Canadian Economy, 1935–75', *Levy Economics Institute, Working Paper* No. 848, October: 1–51.

Schumpeter, J. A. 1954. *History of Economic Analysis*. New York: Oxford University Press.

Sylla, N. S. 2022 'The Franc Zone, a Tool of French Neocolonialism in Africa' 12/4/22. https://www.jacobinmag.com/2020/01/franc-zone-french-neocolonialism-africa

Ugolini, S. 2011. "What do we really know about the long-term evolution of central banking? Evidence from the past, insights for the present." Working Paper 15. Norges Bank.

Weber, M. (1981 [1927]). *General Economic History*, Tr. F. H. Knight. New Brunswick, NJ: Transaction Books Inc.

Weisbrot, M. 2022. 'Biden's sanctions on Afghanistan' *USA Today*, March 10 https://www.usatoday.com/story/opinion/columnist/2022/03/10/biden-sanctions-afghanistan-humanitarian-crisis/6918023001/ Also see https://peacenews.info/node/10183/tell-biden-not-steal-afghan-people.

Werner, R. 2016. 'A Lost Century of Evidence: Three Theories of banking' *International Review of Financial Analysis* 46 (2016): 361–379.

Wheatcroft, G. 2021. *Churchill's Shadow, an Astonishing Life and a Dangerous Legacy*. London: The Bodley Head.
Wilkins, B. 2019. 'Jimmy Carter on USA as warlike' https://johnmenadue.com/brett-wilkins-jimmy-carter-says-that-the-us-is-the-most-warlike-nation-in-the-history-of-the-world/
Woodruff, D. 1999. *Money Unmade: Barter and the Fate of Russian Capitalism*. Ithaca, NY: Cornell University Press.

3 Central Bank Digital Currencies in the Post-pandemic Era

Dominique Torre and Qing Xu

Introduction

Since the fall of the Bretton Woods agreements, means of payment have transitioned from material to immaterial and digitalized forms, from coins and notes to credit cards and mobile phones. Given such rapid changes, the very nature of money seems likely to evolve in turn. New mechanisms could directly link agents in need of liquidity and central banks through technology using a decentralized clearing system: mechanisms appearing under the name of Central Bank Digital Currencies (CBDCs).

In part, a strictly technological evolution, the fast development of digital innovations and technological advances pushed a fundamental revolution in the banking industry. The rise of cryptocurrencies and stable coins with blockchain utilization, the widespread use of mobile payment, and the global expansion of a cashless economy pose additional challenges for central banks worldwide. Moreover, the COVID-19 pandemic has accelerated the digital transformation of people's work and life, speeding up the adoption of digital payment while heavily decreasing the use of cash in most countries. Depending on countries and continents, this shift promoted FinTech or telephonic operators' services. Simultaneously, Facebook, in partnership with VISA, PayPal, and other partners, announced the stablecoin "Libra" project in June 2019, and rebranded it to "Diem" at the end of 2020 (Chiu *et al.* 2021; Pilkington 2022). Such events could not leave the central banks unaffected.

The taxonomy defines a CBDC as a new digital form of central bank money that serves three essential functions: a medium of exchange, a unit of account, and – to some extent – a store of value, though different from traditional reserves or settlement account balances (BIS, 2018). Around 100 countries are exploring CBDCs (Kristalina 2022); some countries have already issued CBDCs officially, others are conducting research, while some are undertaking extensive pilots and tests for different CBDC projects. Nine countries[1] have already launched CBDCs, and fourteen countries, including China, South Korea, Singapore, Malaysia, and Thailand, currently rest in the pilot stage, preparing for a potential full launch of CBDCs in the future (Atlantic Council 2022).

DOI: 10.4324/9781003323280-4

The second section briefly reviews the different experiences on CBDCs. The next section presents the different types of CBDCs and the technologies which activate them. The fourth section discusses the motivations of central banks. The last section concludes with a discussion on how CBDCs may evolve and influence the international financial system in the future.

The Projects of CBDCs All around the World

In many regions, monetary authorities have kept a close eye on FinTech evolution, aiming to digitalize fiat currency by placing theory into practice. However, most major central banks do not have an immediate plan to issue CBDCs; most ponder whether to launch CBDCs in the near future or issue pilot studies to examine the implications.

As an early example, Finnish commercial banks and the Helsinki University of Technology collaborated on the experiment of pre-funded payment smart cards in 1987. In the 1990s, the Bank of Finland created the Avant smart card, considered the world's first CBDC; however, the card never gained sufficient popularity, only operating until 2003 (Grym 2020). Having faced in 2000s the negative impact of dollarization, starting from 2014, Ecuador issued in parallel with US dollar the Dinero Electrónico (DE), and discontinued the experience in 2018 (Auer & Boehme 2020; Arauz et Garratt 2021; PWC 2021).

The People's Bank of China (PBOC) focused on the research and development of CBDCs, beginning in 2014 by exploring PBOC's internal digital currency, then, two years later, establishing the Chinese Digital Currency Institute. Issued by the PBOC, electronic Chinese Yuan (e-CNY) would constitute a retail CBDC designed to meet people's daily payments needs by adopting a centralized management model and a two-tier operational system[2] (Working Group on E-CNY Research and Development of the People's Bank of China 2021). At the end of 2017, PBOC started working with commercial institutions to further develop and test e-CNY, eventually leading to the launch of a wide range of pilots, testing and assessing the implementation of e-CNY in different cities of China, including e-CNY tests during the 2022 Beijing Winter Olympics (Working Group on E-CNY Research and Development of the People's Bank of China 2021).

Since the early 2010s, two Chinese digital payment giants, Alipay and WeChat Pay, established by Alibaba and Tencent, respectively, provided mobile payment services accepted by most Chinese people as the primary payment method in China (Torre & Xu 2019, 2020; Xu 2022, p. 227). Chinese digital payments continued to grow during the whole decade. By the end of 2021, Chinese banks processed 274.969 billion electronic payments with a total of RMB2976.22 trillion (around USD461 trillion by using the average exchange rate in 2021 of 6.45), including 151.228 billion mobile transactions with a total value of RMB526.98 trillion (approximately USD83.25 trillion), a respective year-on-year increase of 22.73% and 21.94% (People's Bank of China 2022).

Canada represents another pioneer in CBDC research. In March 2016, the Project Jasper was launched by the Bank of Canada and Payments Canada, R3 (a financial innovation firm), and several Canadian financial institutions, for instance, Scotiabank, Bank of Montreal, RBC, National Bank, and HSBC (Payments Canada, Bank of Canada, & R3 2017). For the first time, a central bank investigated a distributed ledger technology (DLT) experiment with private institutions (Bank of Canada 2017). On June 30, 2020, the Bank of Canada and the Bank for International Settlements (BIS) announced that they would establish a BIS Innovation Hub to promote FinTech innovation within the central banking community, strengthen collaboration on digital technologies, and enhance the global financial system (Bank of Canada 2020). On March 16, 2022, the Bank of Canada cooperated with the Massachusetts Institute of Technology (MIT) Media Lab's Digital Currency Initiative team on a twelve-month CBDC research project, exploring the potential design and implementation of a CBDC (Bank of Canada 2022). However, according to the Bank of Canada (Bank of Canada n.d.) and Canadian government, the project to implement a central bank digital currency now seems less urgent.

In December 2016, the European Central Bank & Bank of Japan (2017) announced the cooperation of a joint research project, "Stella" to assess the impact of FinTech/distributed ledger technology (DLT) on central bank roles and financial market infrastructures. Project Stella consists of four phases: phase 1 focuses on large-value payments processing utilizing DLT, phase 2 examines securities delivery-versus-payment in a DLT environment, phase 3 studies cross-border payments, and phase 4 tests the balance between confidentiality and suitability of CBDC within a distributed ledger environment (European Central Bank 2019; European Central Bank & Bank of Japan 2020).

According to the "Report on a digital Euro," the Governing Council of the European Central Bank (ECB) set a High-Level Task Force in January 2020 on CBDCs to strengthen monetary policy and support the Euro system's strategic goals (European Central Bank 2020). Fabio Panetta (2022), a member of the Executive Board of the ECB, presented in his speech that CBDCs would endorse the accessibility and usability of central bank money in a digital world, maintain the coexistence of sovereign and private money, guarantee the smooth functioning of the payments system, and improve the confidentiality of digital payments. Nine months after the publishing of the "Report on a digital Euro," the Euro system launched a two-year investigation of the digital euro project on July 14, 2021, aiming to address key issues about the design and issuance of the digital euro (European Central Bank 2021).

Likewise, in September 2017, the central bank of Sweden, Sveriges Riksbank, launched an e-krona project of the digital complement to cash to promote a secure and efficient payment system in the future (Sveriges Riksbank 2017). Like cash, the e-krona offers a digital version of Swedish central bank currency without credit or liquidity risk, broadly available to the public at any time, all year round (Sveriges Riksbank, 2018). Sveriges Riksbank (2021, 2022) conducted two e-krona pilots: the first one focused on the possible distribution models, transaction process, e-krona storage methods, and legal analysis of technical solutions; the second one continued deeper testing of the use of e-krona, discussed different wallet models and options for off-line payments, providing good support for the Riksbank's research and investigation on the design and requirements for possible issuance of e-krona.

In Japan, the Digital Currency JPY (DCJPY), a yen-denominated digital currency, is designed on a two-tiered structure with the ledger systems of commercial banks (Common Area) and (Business Process Area) (Currency Digital Forum 2021). Since the beginning of 2021, the Bank of Japan (2020, 2022, 2021) initiated experiments on the technical feasibility of the essential functions and characteristics required for CBDC, completed Proof of Concept (PoC) Phase 1 on testing the basic functions of CBDC's issuance, distribution, and redemption in March 2022, and started the PoC Phase 2 experiments in April 2022. However, according to the Executive Director of the Bank of Japan, Uchida (2022), the Bank of Japan currently does not plan to issue CBDC, and it will continue to work on the possible design of CBDC and the way to construct a highly reliable CBDC ecosystem.

The COVID-19 accelerated digital and contactless payments and encouraged CBDCs research, tests, pilots, and issuance in developed and developing countries (BIS 2021b). In 2020, the Bank of England (2020) issued a discussion report on CBDC, focusing on retail CBDCs, presenting an illustrative "platform" model of CBDC, and evaluating both benefits and risks of CBDC. Compared with other countries, research and experiments of CBDCs in the United States still remain in the early stage. Digital dollar foundation (2020) cooperated with Accenture, the leader in enterprise blockchain services for the CBDC research and released its white paper about the Digital Dollar Project. The Federal Reserve's cautious attitude is undoubtedly related to the dollar's status on the international scene. What would the dollar gain from a split that could lead the central banks of many countries to question the form that their reserves should take?

Responsible for encouraging monetary and financial soundness, safety, and efficiency, the Federal Reserve has recently disaggregated the CBDC project in four work packages: "technological experimentation, economic and policy research, stakeholder engagement and outreach, and international collaboration" and collaborated with different institutions as the Massachusetts Institute of Technology's Digital Currency Initiative, Georgia State University, BIS, etc. (BIS 2021a, Board of Governors of the Federal Reserve System 2022). The Federal Reserve now fosters a general and transparent public dialogue about CBDCs, investigating the potential benefits and risks of a U.S. CBDC without a clear intention about whether to officially issue a CBDC (Board of Governors of the Federal Reserve System 2022). Moreover, the Federal Reserve mentions that the implementation of a CBDC would depend on whether or not research results could demonstrate the overall benefits of CBDC exceed the downside risks, thus proving the CBDC as a superior method to alternatives (Board of Governors of the Federal Reserve System 2022).

Different Types of CBDCs and Different Technologies to Activate Them

Different Types of CBDCs

The first classification of CBDCs could distinguish the wholesale CBDCs and retail CBDCs (or general-purpose CBDCs). Financial institutions such as commercial banks use wholesale CBDCs for settling large-value transactions, which replace or complete central bank deposits and reserves, focusing on inter-bank settlements. In contrast, the public uses retail CBDCs or general-purpose CBDCs for day-to-day payment transactions instead of banknotes for a wide range of end users, including both individuals and firms (BIS, 2018; Noriyuki & Hiromi 2019; Bank of Japan 2020; Working Group on E-CNY Research and Development of the People's Bank of China 2021; Banque de France 2021b).

Another possible classification concerns "account-based" CBDCs and "value-based" ones. The "account-based" CBDCs authorize ordinary people to access their accounts directly with a central ledger-keeper, and the "value-based" CBDCs work as a prepaid value stored locally, allowing users firstly charge a certain amount of CBDCs to e-wallet, IC cards, or smartphone applications and then making payments or transferring them with each other without being recorded in the central bank accounts (Sveriges Riksbank 2017, 2018, 2022; Noriyuki & Hiromi 2019; Banque de France 2021a).

Digitalization has multiplied the new means of payment, without crowding out the old ones. Table 3.1 compares the nature and properties of different means of payment available today.

Additionally, a distinction exists between interest-bearing and non-interest-bearing CBDCs. Many central banks, like the Bank of China, the Bank of Japan, and Sveriges Riksbank, agree with the design of non-interest-bearing CBDCs, assuming CBDCs are the same as the physical banknotes under M0 without an interest. While according to the European Central Bank (ECB) (Mersch 2017), CBDCs can remunerate at a certain rate level, for example, at the rate on the deposit facility.

Table 3.1 Means of payment, their nature, and properties

	Widely accessible	*Digital*	*Central bank issued*	*Peer-to-peer*
Bank deposits	×	×		
Cash	×		×	×
Commodity money	×			×
Virtual currency		×		
Cryptocurrency (permissionless DLT)	×	×		×
Cryptocurrency (permissioned DLT)		×		×
Central bank reserves and settlement accounts		×	×	
Central bank deposited currency accounts	×	×	×	
CBDC (wholesale)		×	×	×
CBDC (retail)	×	×	×	×

Source: Self-made according to World Economic Forum (2019)

Table 3.2 Design of CBDCs worldwide

CBDC	*Country*	*officially issued or not*	*Retail or wholesale*	*Account-based or value-based*	*Interest bear or not*	*Application scenarios (domestic or cross-border payment)*
eNaria	Nigeria	Yes	Retail	Account-based	No	Both
Sand Dollar	Bahamas	Yes	Both	Account-based	No	Domestic payments
JAM-DEX	Jamaica	Yes	Both	Value-based	No	Both
e-CNY	China	No	Both	Both	No	Domestic payments
e-krona	Sweden	No	Retail	Both	No	
DCJPY	Japan	No	Both		No	
Digital dollar	US	No	Both	Token-based		
Digital Euro	European Union	No	Both	Both	Could bear interest	Both

Source: self-made.

Table 3.2 represents different designs of CBDCs worldwide.

Based on various possible architectures, three types of CBDC ensue: indirect CBDC, direct CBDC, and hybrid CBDC (Auer & Boehme 2020). First, indirect CBDC presents a claim on financial intermediaries, the central bank keeps records of wholesale transactions, and financial intermediaries handle retail transactions and issue indirect CBDC; second, direct CBDC is a claim on the central bank and is issued by central bank who controls all types of transactions, both wholesale and retail transactions; third, for hybrid CBDC case, the central bank issues CBDC, handles wholesale transactions, and periodically registers retail transactions, while financial intermediaries keep records of retail payments.

Which Technology to Activate a CBDC?

Central banks use a mixture of technologies to realize core characteristics of CDBCs, such as security, privacy, stability, universal availability, etc. Blockchain technology and distributed ledger technology (DLT) are popular technologies when we talk about digital currency or CBDC projects.

DLT

DLT is a broader term than blockchain, encompassing technologies that authorize simultaneous access, verification, and unchangeable record of a synchronized ledger within a network (BIS, 2017; Bains 2020). "Blockchain is a subset of DLT" (Bains 2020, p. 4), and bitcoin is the first to use the "DLT in its blockchain form." Treiblmaier and Clohessy (2020, p. 5) explained that "distributed ledgers are a type of database that is spread across multiple sites, countries, or institutions, and is typically public. Records are stored one after the other in a continuous ledger, rather than stored into block." DLT positively influences the financial industry by "(i) reducing complexity; (ii) improving end-to-end processing speed; (iii) decreasing the need for reconciliation across multiple record-keeping infrastructures; (iv) increasing transparency and immutability in transaction record keeping; (v) improving network resilience through distributed data management; and (vi) reducing operational and financial risks" (BIS 2017, p. 1).

Blockchain Technology

Blockchain could be defined as serially connected blocks in a distributed system[3] containing entire transaction records, using cryptographic techniques and consensus algorithms, with the main features of security, transparency, and immutability (Gad *et al.* 2022; Daskalakis & Georgitseas 2020, pp. 10–11). Blockchain is the fundamental technology of cryptocurrencies, widely used in a variety of domains, for instance payment transactions, smart contracts, logistics and supply chain tracking, big data, public sector, voting, anti-money laundering (AML), know your customer (KYC), sharing economy, etc. (Daskalakis & Georgitseas 2020, p. 17). Many research investigations on CBDC refer to blockchain technology usage, and some even tested blockchain adoption in CBDC (Currency Digital Forum 2021; PWC 2022; Zhang & Huang 2021).

Types of DLT Arrangements and Blockchain

According to BIS (2017), two types of DLT arrangements commonly occur: unrestricted DLT and restricted DLT. Using unrestricted DLT arrangement, participants have full access to the ledger and could use the service and play any role; multiple entities influence the validation and consensus within the network; this unrestricted access model might generate scalability and information security problems (BIS 2017). In contrast, in restricted DLT arrangement, entities have restricted access to the ledger; new participants need permission to access the network. There are three types of restricted DLT arrangement: "(1) one entity maintains and updates the ledger; (2) only approved entities can use the service; entities can be assigned distinct restricted roles; (3) only approved entities can use the service; entities can play any role" (BIS 2017, p. 8).

The classification of blockchains is quite similar to DLT arrangements. According to Gad *et al.* (2022) and Zhang and Huang (2021), three types of blockchains materialize: public blockchains, federated or consortium blockchains, and private blockchains:

- Public blockchains: the highest openness level, completely decentralized, anyone has equal right and access to the complete information of the network without permission.

- Federated or consortium blockchains: built by consortia with multiple organizations, medium openness level, less decentralized compared with public blockchains, the new organization needs permission from consortia to access the network. Corda, Ripple, R3 are examples of consortium blockchains.
- Private blockchains: controlled by a single organization, the lowest openness level, need permission to access the network, less decentralized compared with consortium blockchains, validators need permission from the creator of private blockchains to access the network.

Based on different design features and requirements, permissioned blockchain/DLT (private blockchain or consortium blockchain) could be more appropriate for CBDCs (BIS 2020; Zhang & Huang 2021).

Why Implement CBDCs?

In an early report published in 2017, the *Committee on Payments and Market Infrastructures* of the BIS defined a list of reasons justifying the implementation of CBDCs. Namely, CBDCs should provide a "continued access to central bank money, increase payments diversity, encourage financial inclusion, improve cross-border payments, support public privacy, and facilitate fiscal transfers" (BIS 2017, pp. 10–11). Nothing revolutionary in this extensive list, but rather a series of small benefits. The counterpart to these small advantages is the low costs attached to CBDC aids in encouraging hesitant institutions; "one crucial advantage of an account-based system is that CBDC payments could be practically instantaneous and costless" (Bordo & Levin 2017, p. 8). The pros began to outnumber the cons in 2018. Sixty-three central banks answered in 2018 to a survey proposed by Barontini and Holden (2019). For all types of CBDCs, safety, efficiency, and stability of the payment system seemed to dominate as motives of adoption. In the case of general-purpose CBDCs, financial inclusion constituted an additional objective, as well as possibility to improve cross-border payments for wholesale CBDCs. New motives then emerged in late 2019. CBDCs "ensure public access to legal tender if cash were phased out and improve the efficiency of payment systems [but also organize the] transition towards a less-cash society, and [are in] competition from private e-money" (Ward & Rochemont 2019, pp. 9–10). The still greater pressure exerted by FinTech on banking systems, the emergence of stable coins among cryptocurrencies (Tether, USD coin, etc.) or proposed by Internet major content providers (Libra project), appealed an adapted reaction of central banks. The contactless revolution of the Covid-era appears to have catalyzed the acceleration of such projects, with an updated objective which appeals a detailed analysis.

Starting from 2020, five objectives to issue CBDCs dominate the debate. Two of the five could be considered as classical, each with a negative counterpart: (i) making the payment system more efficient without endangering the banking industry, (ii) improving the security of payments without making the financial system more unstable. The other three objectives, though seemingly of secondary importance, also merit attention, namely (iii) working to promote cross-border payments in domestic currencies,

(iv) answering to the development of private stable coins, and (v) offering also, in partnership with banks, alternatives to the mobile payment solutions developed by FinTech.

Efficiency Gains and Risk of Disintermediation

Almost all central banks promoting the adoption of CBDCs consider that reducing operational costs of the system of payment ultimately increases the efficiency of exchanges and general economic interactions. Such gains represent an appealing proponent to many central banks, such as the Bank of England (Barrdear & Kumhof 2016; Bank of England 2020), the Bank of India (Priyadarshini & Kar 2021, p. 7), or the Bank of Nigeria (Central Bank of Nigeria 2021). Outside central banks, the search for efficiency gains is also considered an essential operational and economic aspect (Bindseil 2019; Barontini & Holden 2019; Náñez Alonso *et al.* 2020; Davoodalhosseini 2021; Assenmacher *et al.* 2021).

If a blockchain activates a CBDC, the role of banks would be bypassed entirely (Priyadarshini & Kar 2021, p. 5). CBDCs could also improve the capacity of central banks to control monetary aggregates and simplify monetary policy; they should have "a disciplining effect on commercial banks" (Berentsen & Schär 2018, p. 101). However, increased fragility of the banking sector would result, creating possible competition between the two forms of the official currencies: a recessionist decrease of the credit multiplier (Bofinger & Haas 2020), and an increase in refinancing cost. These dangers are understood and integrated into the Chinese project through the so-called "two-tiered" system: "the central bank exclusively supplies the public the central bank money or base money (i.e., banknotes and central bank deposits), and commercial banks provide deposits through credit creation based on the base money" (Amamiya, 2018, p. 3). Finally, the Chinese version of CBDC (which currently remains to be a more advanced version compared to other CBDC projects) intentionally limits the role of the central bank. In this system, the central bank "does not have any direct transaction with consumers, and only acts as the lender of last resort for commercial banks, whereas commercial banks act as an intermediary by attracting consumers for deposits and offering financial services based on deposits" (Shen & Hou 2021, p. 4). "The DCEP [Digital Currency Electronic Payment] issued directly by the central bank suggests direct transactions between financial users and the PBOC and hence the disintermediation of financial institutions" (Ibid. p. 6). "In addition, the PBOC has unambiguously required a 100% reserve rate for financial institutions [...]. In other words, the issuance of RMB 1 in DECP is backed by RMB 1 at the PBOC" (Shen & Hou 2021, p. 6). The counterpart in the non-digital currency for each secondary bank that issues in digital currency is 1 to 1 in the Chinese case, which secures the system but does not encourage banks to issue them.

Security Gains and Risk of Instability

Safety and security constitute additional objectives of central banks when planning to implement CBDCs (Auer et al. 2021): "the traceability and potential program ability of a digital currency [...] enhance central bank supervision and the government's control over money flows and financial activities. These two features of DCEP could help combat illicit financial activities, such as corruption, fraud, money laundering, terrorist financing, and tax evasion. However, they may potentially intensify government monitoring of society" (Knoerich 2021, p. 151). Bofinger and Haas (2020) cautiously distinguish the different versions of CBDCs (wholesale versus retail, store of value versus means of payment). The store of value version corresponds to a possible CBDC available for a large public of users, though not admitted in payments. It works as a sort of central bank deposit rather than a currency. This version could offer a safer alternative for storing liquidities, although still dominated in standard time in terms of returns by other secure liquid bonds. However, as attested by the monetary history of the United States during the nineteenth century, the fragmentation of reserves does not make the payment system more secure.

The key question is whether a more secure payment system in normal circumstances remains so in a pre-crisis period, particularly during a banking crisis. Using a theoretical extension of Champ *et al.* (1996) Kim and Kwon (2019) from the Bank of Korea find ambiguous results: "an increase in the quantity of CBDC can increase the likelihood of bank panic by reducing the supply of private credit, which raises nominal interest rate and lowers a commercial bank's reserve–deposit ratio. However, once the central bank can lend all the deposits in CBDC account to commercial banks, an increase in the quantity of CBDC can improve financial stability by reducing the likelihood of bank panic via an increase in the supply of private credit" (Kim & Kwon 2019, p. 5). Kumhof and Noone (2021) study how CBDCs affect the size and composition of commercial bank balance sheets, considering situations in which the provision of credit to borrowers and the provision of liquidity to depositors are not necessarily curtailed. They conclude that the risk of instability could be controlled, though they confirm that the risk is not of secondary importance. Keister and Monnet share the views of Kumhof and Noone. "The incentives of bank creditors to withdraw funding also depends critically on what sort of policy response they expect if a run develops. If the CBDC also allows the policy maker to react more quickly to an incipient crisis, its net effect can increase rather than decrease financial stability" (Keister & Monnet 2022, p. 3). This discussion argues for the adoption of a wholesale CBDC which would remain under the control of banks and central banks and should decrease and not increase the risk of runs.

International Motives

The Central Bank of China, but also the ECB and the Bank of England defend or have defended the idea that implementing CBDCs could improve cross-border payments. Two versions of the same argument are usually presented.

Improving the means of providing domestic currency among competitive international currencies represents a primary motive for central banks. The PBOC announced this objective: China expects to offer trading partners simplified payment methods – that is, direct transactions denominated in RMB can take place without involving a third-party currency exchange (US dollar in this case). Conducting transactions in this way eliminates the need to incur the cost of currency exchange, further streamlining imports and exports for China and its trading partners. In addition, the Chinese government could use its influence in the international market to accelerate the process of dethroning the US dollar. "China is trying to take advantage of a first-mover strategy and leverage its position to promote the invoicing of trade in digital yuan" (Aysan & Kayani 2022, p. 2; Hoffman *et al.* 2020; Shen & Hou 2021; Knoerich 2021). Commercial partners in China could also use DCEP for standard payments and transactions (Lopez 2020; Wang 2022).

The Bank of England prefers to speak of interoperability between different CBDCs at the international level: "Central banks may work together to link domestic CBDCs in a way that enables fast and efficient cross-border payments. Individual domestic CBDCs could have a design conducive to a common set of standards to support interoperability. This might enable 'atomic' transactions between CBDC systems: where the transfer of CBDC in one currency is linked with a transfer of CBDC in another currency, in a way that ensures each transfer occurs if – and only if – the other does" (Bank of England 2020, p. 19). For ECB, a CBDC would be a way to "overcome the existing fragmentation and to recover the ECB's catalytic role in promoting Europe-wide initiatives in a market that is highly dynamic, but mostly at the local level" (Passacantando 2021, p. 120).

Auer and Boehme (2020, p. 9) propose three different scenarios to build an International Central Bank Digital Currency, ranging from providing an additional means to settle transactions among markets to a more advanced integration of international transfers. This last case seems, however, to suppose that the currencies associated with the arrangement would be linked by fixed or quasi-fixed exchange rates, like the Saudi riyal and UAE dirham that they take as examples. In these countries, local currency is anchored to the US dollar at a specific rate and are *de facto* linked by fixed exchange rates. Lastly, literature (Khiaonarong & Humphrey 2022) also points out the role and advantages of CBDC for small cross-border transfers, particularly remittances.

An Alternative to Stable Coins

Standard crypto-assets/currencies are neither competitors nor a danger to central banks: their use is highly appreciated by speculators but few companies accept them as payment and few central banks as reserve currency or asset: their volatility is far too high, just the opposite of what is required of an international reserve currency. But cryptocurrencies ecosystem needed at some point risk-free assets that could neutralize for a few hours or longer the positions of speculative crypto holders. Stable coins were introduced, using various financial hedging strategies to target a stable value against an announced reference, for the most international currencies. Tether (one of the most significant capitalizations of crypto-assets), USD Coin, Binance USD, and Dai belong to this family of crypto-assets. For the moment, though mainly utilized by crypto-asset holders wishing to neutralize their position momentarily, this category of cryptocurrencies, given their relative opacity, could also serve other and various purposes. If sufficiently resilient, stable coins could attract many holders, presenting a possible reserve asset for individuals, financial intermediaries, or institutions reluctant to hold international currencies or sovereign bills and bonds labeled in reserve currencies. Therefore, "the official opinion of the Bank of England [...] is that CBDC should become the response of central banks to the development of stable coins by large technology companies" (Volkova *et al.* 2020, p. 633). Tacitly, protecting the economy against tax evasion and money laundering, as facilitated by cryptocurrencies, represents a primary motive for many institutions. Another would be "to overcome the volatility risks of an asset without backing and without intrinsic value" (Náñez Alonso *et al.* 2020, p. 10).

The defunct Libra/DIEM project promoted by Facebook has posed an even more dangerous competitor for central banks (Allen *et al.* 2022). The holders of Libra/DIEM would have been not mainly speculators attracted by the rapid gains of cryptocurrencies, but a large population interested in the initiatives/commercial offers of Facebook, free of any constraint related to the borders. The conversion of any currency into Libra would not have been a problem for holders of currencies or secondary importance, who are more usually attracted by conversions into dollars or other international currencies. Another problem is that savings accounts and cash managed by digital companies would have given them a systemic financial position. "a wide use of stable coin on a global scale could transform financial stability from a public good into a common-pool resource" (Kuroda 2019. p. 5). A shared view of central bankers and governments was then to regulate private stable coins (Zetzsche *et al.* 2021) and to hurry the implementation of CBDCs, as public substitutes to Libra/DIEM (Shen & Hou 2021; Aysan & Kayani 2022). The Bank of England expressed, "stable coins will only be widely adopted if they provide functionality and efficiency benefits over existing payment systems. But given the risks they could pose; it may be worth asking if CBDC can be designed to better meet those needs" (Bank of England 2020, p. 17).

The FinTech Issue

Stable coins and Libra present a problem for all categories of central banks. FinTech, the success of which has led to immense financial activity, specifically poses a threat for the Central Bank of China. According to the report of Merchant Savvy (2022), China was the leader in mobile payments in 2021, with 87.3% of the population declaring using mobile contactless payment methods, compared with 45.6% of people in South Korea, 34.9% in Japan, 29.1% in Canada, 24.4% in the UK, 21.1% in France, and 19% in Germany. For various motives, including the size of the Alibaba and Tencent groups, the rapid expansion and uneven competition with traditional banking sectors have prompted the Chinese Government to attempt to stifle its growing influence since 2018.

In 2018, the establishment of the NetsUnion Clearing Corporation in China prevented platforms from receiving banks' remuneration for temporarily held payments (Shen & Hou 2021, p. 10). Alibaba accounted for around 11% of the market in China, causing authorities and financial stakeholders to fear that Alibaba could issue its own currency. In this circumstance, the Chinese CBDC would have played the role of an incumbent, with an installed base of service of payment users, aiming to protect the market from the uncontrolled dynamism of new entrants. "Regulation changes requiring Alipay and WeChat Pay deposits to be moved into PBoC accounts mean[t] that the PBoC has already clawed back a fair degree of oversight and control over funds held by those platforms" (Hoffman et al. 2020, p. 17).

In February 2020, "the Shanghai and Hong Kong Stock Exchange suspended the much-anticipated IPO of Ant Financial, following the expression of 'concern about excess leverage and abuse of consumer data' by the government of China, an alleged practice that has surfaced in other jurisdictions, with other organizations and other governments" (Goodell & Al-Nakib 2021, p. 2). From this moment, commentators tended to consider that "the DCEP will be probably used as an instrument for small or medium scale payment in competition with mobile payment internally and with third party online payment externally" (Shen & Hou 2021, p. 10).

Conclusion

Arauz and Garratt (2021) relate in a passionate article the recent monetary history of Ecuador, which experienced severe inflation in the late 1990, peaking at +96% in 2000. The Treasury defaulted on its Brady bonds issues[4] and quickly became short of funds. The government then decided to keep the US dollar as domestic currency in an economy already widely *de facto* dollarized. This choice instantaneously stopped inflation and allowed the country to return to growth and solvency. From 2008, the government began to gain monetary autonomy by various means. First, it issued low-denomination bonds that could be used as payment, but the initiative remained unsuccessful. Then it tried to set up a system of monetizing net claims, which eventually had to be abandoned for legal reasons. The central bank mobile money was the third initiative. The system was launched in early 2014. Creating a digital xeno-dollar had the advantage of avoiding the problems of converting at demand dollar-denominated accounts into bank notes, which requires the country to have a structural balance of payments surplus to provide a sufficient level of liquidity to the market. With a digital currency, the conversion constraint would disappear, and the country would be able to keep the name of dollar for its currency without having to depend on the Fed to obtain cash. Technically speaking, it was decided to use a very low-cost technology, namely, the USSD technology already adopted by Vodaphone and its African competitors to implement m-payment solutions in East African countries. Nevertheless, after a rapid take-off, the system stagnated and finally collapsed abruptly in March–April 2018.

Ecuador was a small country without practical experience of central banking. However, even for major central banks, how to innovate in monetary organization is not obvious. Where none of the motives mentioned in the last section appears to be relevant from a national or regional point of view, the financial authorities still do not consider it reasonable to accelerate the implementation of a CBDC. Accordingly, the Federal Reserve System's Deputy Governor Christopher Waller expressed in Summer 2021: "What problem would a CBDC solve? Alternatively, what market failure or inefficiency demands this specific intervention? After careful consideration, I am not convinced that a CBDC would solve any existing problem that is not being addressed more promptly and efficiently by other initiatives" (Waller 2021, p. 2). But what is the right choice for the dollar and the US financial system is not systematically the right choice for all currencies and all financial systems around the world.

Despite most central banks being engaged in CBDC research and pilots, until now, no major central bank has officially issued a CBDC. Each one still faces challenges in the design of CBDCs and possible technology implications. But for many of them, the decision relies on economic grounds and must solve the trade-off between the benefits of modernizing the payment system, its capacity to respond to private initiatives, and the uncertainties that the new currency would bring to bear on the resilience of the banking intermediation system, particularly if it is not limited to wholesale transactions. China's next moves will provide an important clue to the future of partner banks' initiatives.

Notes

1 The Central bank of Bahamas issued the nationwide CBDC in October 2020, seven countries in the Eastern Caribbean Union created CBDCs in April 2021, and the Central Bank of Nigeria launched e-Naira in October 2021.
2 The PBOC has the right to issue e-CNY; commercial banks and other commercial institutions take charge of exchanging and circulating e-CNY to the public.
3 In the distributed systems, each node has a whole record of transactions, connects directly with all the other network nodes, and is not controlled by a central authority.
4 Brady bonds are bonds backed by US treasury bonds and denominated in US dollars frequently used by Latin American countries during this time.

References

Allen, F, Gu, X & Jagtiani, J 2022, 'Fintech, cryptocurrencies, and CBDC: FinancialStructural transformation in China', *Journal of International Money and Finance*, 124, 102625.

Amamiya, M 2018, 'The Future of Money', Lecture at the Japan Society of Monetary Economics, Tokyo, October 20.

Arauz, A & Garratt, R 2021, 'Dinero electrónico: The rise and fall of Ecuador's Central bank digital currency', *Latin American Journal of Central Banking*, 2(2), 100030.

Assenmacher, K, Berentsen, A, Brand, C & Lamersdorf, N 2021, 'A unified framework for CBDC design: remuneration, collateral haircuts, and quantity constraints', *ECB Working Paper*, July. Working Paper No. 2578

Atlantic Council 2022, 'Central Bank Digital Currency Tracker', viewed 4 April 2022, https://www.atlanticcouncil.org/cbdctracker/

Auer, R & Boehme, R 2020, 'The technology of retail central bank digital currency', *BIS Quarterly Review*, pp. 85–100 March.

Auer, R, Frost, J, Gambacorta, L, Monnet, C, Rice, T & Shin, H S 2021, 'Central bank digital currencies: motives, economic implications and the research frontier', *Annual Review of Economics*.

Aysan, A F & Kayani, F N 2022, "China's transition to a digital currency does it threaten dollarization?, *Asia and the Global Economy*, 2(1), 100023.

Bains, P 2020, 'Blockchain Consensus Mechanisms. A Primer for Supervisors', Etats Unis: International Monetary Fund.

Bank of England 2020, 'Central Bank Digital Currency—Opportunities, Challenges and Design', Discussion Paper, March.

Bank for International Settlements 2017, *Distributed Ledger Technology in Payment, Clearing and Settlement. An Analytical Framework*, CPMI, ISBN 978-92-9259-031-4, https://www.bis.org/cpmi/publ/d157.pdf

Bank for International Settlements 2018, *Central Bank Digital Currencies*, CPMI, Markets Committee Papers, No 174, https://www.bis.org/cpmi/publ/d174.pdf

Bank for International Settlements 2020, *Central Bank Digital Currencies: Foundational Principles and Core Features*, https://www.bis.org/publ/othp33.pdf

Bank for International Settlements 2021a, *Central Banks and the BIS Explore What a Retail CBDC Might Look Like*, press release, September 2021, https://www.bis.org/press/p210930.htm

Banks for International Settlements 2021b, *Covid-19 Accelerated the Digitalisation of Payments*, viewed 12 May 2022, https://www.bis.org/statistics/payment_stats/commentary2112.htm#graph2

Bank of Canada 2017, *Project Jasper Primer*, https://www.payments.ca/sites/default/files/project_jasper_primer.pdf

Bank of Canada 2020, *Bank of Canada Partners with the Bank for International Settlements to Launch Innovation Centre*, https://www.bankofcanada.ca/2020/06/bank-canada-partners-bank-international-settlements-launch-innovation-centre/

Bank of Canada 2022, *Bank of Canada and Massachusetts Institute of Technology Announce Joint Central Bank Digital Currency Collaboration*, viewed 12 April 2022, https://www.bankofcanada.ca/2022/03/central-bank-digital-currency-collaboration/

Bank of Canada n.d., *Central Bank Digital Currency (CBDC)*, https://www.bankofcanada.ca/research/digital-currencies-and-fintech/projects/central-bank-digital-currency/#:~:text=Simply%20put%2C%20a%20CBDC%20is,able%20to%20be%20used%20online

Bank of England 2020, *Central Bank Digital Currency – Opportunities, Challenges and Design*, March 2020, Discussion Paper, https://www.bankofengland.co.uk/paper/2020/central-bank-digital-currency-opportunities-challenges-and-design-discussion-paper

Banque de France 2021a, *Digital Euro Experiment Combined Feasibility – Tiered Model*, July 2021. https://www.banque-france.fr/sites/default/files/media/2021/08/02/821220_digital_euro_en.pdf

Banque de France 2021b, *Wholesale Central Bank Digital Currency Experiments with the Banque de France*, November 2021, https://www.banque-france.fr/sites/default/files/media/2021/11/09/821338_rapport_mnbc-04.pdf

Bank of Japan 2020, *The Bank of Japan's Approach to Central Bank Digital Currency*, https://www.boj.or.jp/en/announcements/release_2020/data/rel201009e1.pdf

Bank of Japan 2021, *Commencement of Central Bank Digital Currency Experiments*, https://www.boj.or.jp/en/announcements/release_2021/rel210405b.pdf

Bank of Japan 2022, *Commencement of Central Bank Digital Currency Experiments (Proof of Concept Phase 2)*, https://www.boj.or.jp/en/announcements/release_2022/rel220325f.pdf

Barrdear, J & Kumhof, M 2016, 'The macroeconomics of central bank issued digital currencies'. *Bank of England Staff Working Paper* No. 605.
Barontini, C & Holden, H 2019, 'Proceeding with caution – A survey on Central bank digital Currency', *BIS Papers*, 101.
Berentsen, A & Schär, F 2018, 'The case for central bank electronic money and the non-case for central bank cryptocurrencies', *Federal Reserve Bank of St. Louis Review*, 100(2), 97–106.
Bindseil, U 2019, 'Central Bank digital currency: Financial system implications and control', *International Journal of Political Economy*, 48(4), 303–335.
Bofinger, P & Haas, T 2020, 'CBDC: A systemic perspective (No. 101)', WEP-Würzburg Economic Papers.
Board of Governors of the Federal Reserve System 2022, 'Money and Payments: The U.S. Dollar in the Age of Digital Transformation', https://www.federalreserve.gov/publications/files/money-and-payments-20220120.pdf
Bordo, M D & Levin, A T 2017, 'Central bank digital currency and the future of monetary policy (No. w23711)', National Bureau of Economic Research.
Central Bank of Nigeria 2021, 'Design Paper for the eNaira', https://enaira.com/download/eNaira_Design_Paper.pdf
Champ, B, Smith, B D & Williamson, S D 1996, 'Currency elasticity and Banking panics: Theory and evidence', *Canadian Journal of Economics*, 29, 828–864.
Chiu, J, Sablik, T & Wong, R 2021, 'Should Central Banks worry about Facebook's Diem and Alibaba's Alipay?', *Richmond Fed Economic Brief*, May, 21–17.
Currency Digital Forum 2021, 'Digital Currency DCJPY White Paper', https://www.decurret-dcp.com/.assets/forum_20211124wp_en.pdf
Daskalakis, N & Georgitseas, P 2020, *An Introduction to Cryptocurrencies: The Crypto Market Ecosystem*. Routledge.
Davoodalhosseini, S M 2021, 'Central Bank digital currency and monetary policy', *Journal of Economic Dynamics and Control*, 104150.
Digital dollar foundation 2020, 'The digital dollar project - Exploring a US CBDC', http://digitaldollarproject.org/wp-content/uploads/2021/05/Digital-Dollar-Project-Whitepaper_vF_7_13_20.pdf
European Central Bank & Bank of Japan 2017, *BOJ/ECB Joint Research Project on Distributed Ledger Technology*, https://www.ecb.europa.eu/paym/intro/news/shared/20170906_stella_report_leaflet.pdf
European Central Bank 2019, *Third Phase of Stella Project Completed*, https://www.ecb.europa.eu/paym/intro/news/html/ecb.mipnews190604.en.html
European Central Bank 2020, *Report on a Digital Euro*, https://www.ecb.europa.eu/pub/pdf/other/Report_on_a_digital_euro~4d7268b458.en.pdf
European Central Bank 2021, *Eurosystem Launches Digital Euro Project*, https://www.ecb.europa.eu/press/pr/date/2021/html/ecb.pr210714~d99198ea23.en.html
European Central Bank & Bank of Japan 2020, *Balancing Confidentiality and Auditability in a Distributed Ledger Environment*, https://www.ecb.europa.eu/paym/intro/publications/pdf/ecb.miptopical200212_01.en.pdf
Gad, A G, Mosa, D T, Abualigah, L & Abohany, A A 2022, 'Emerging trends in blockchain technology and applications: A review and Outlook', *Journal of King Saud University–Computer and Information Sciences*, ISSN 1319-1578, https://doi.org/10.1016/j.jksuci.2022.03.007.
Goodell, G & Al-Nakib, H D 2021, 'The Development of Central Bank Digital Currency in China: An Analysis', Available at SSRN 3906358.

Grym, A 2020, 'Lessons learned from the world's first CBDC', *Bank of Finland Economics Review*, 8.
Hoffman, S, Garnaut, J, Izenman, K, Johnson, M, Pascoe, A, Ryan, F & Thomas, E 2020, '*The Flipside of China's Central Bank Digital Currency*', Canberra: Australian Strategic Policy Institute.
Keister, T. & Monnet, C. 2022, 'Central bank digital currency: Stability and information', *Journal of Economic Dynamics and Control*, 142, 104501.
Khiaonarong, T & Humphrey, D. 2022, 'Falling Use of Cash and Demand for Retail Central Bank Digital Currency', IMF Working Paper 22/27.
Kim, Y S & Kwon, O 2019, 'Central bank digital currency and financial stability', Bank of Korea WP, 6.
Knoerich, J 2021, 'China's New Digital Currency: Implications for Renminbi Internationalization and the US Dollar', in Bilotta, N., & Botti, F. (2021). *The (Near) Future of Central Bank Digital Currencies: Risks and Opportunities for the Global Economy and Society*, op. cit. pp. 145–166.
Kristalina, G. 2022, *The Future of Money: Gearing up for Central Bank Digital Currency*, Washington DC, IMF Speech, February 9, https://www.imf.org/en/News/Articles/2022/02/09/sp020922-the-future-of-money-gearing-up-for-central-bank-digital-currency
Kuroda, H. 2019, 'Payments innovations and the role of central banks: Addressing challenges posed by stablecoins', Speech at the Symposium for the 35th Anniversary of the Center for Financial Industry Information Systems. Bank of Japan. December 4.
Kumhof, M & Noone, C 2021, 'Central Bank digital currencies – design principles for financial stability', *Economic Analysis and Policy*, 71, 553–572.
Lopez, C 2020, 'Digital Currency: A Global Regulatory Framework Is Needed'. In S. Rochemont, *A Cashless Society in 2019*. Institute and Faculty of Actuaries. https://www.actuaries.org.uk/system/files/field/document/A%20Cashless%20Society%20in%202019.pdf
Merchant Savvy 2022, 'Adoption of Mobile Contactless Payments Increased Globally', https://www.merchantsavvy.co.uk/mobile-payment-stats-trends/
Mersch, Y. 2017, *Digital Base Money: An Assessment from the ECB's Perspective*, Speech Helsinki, 16 January 2017, https://www.ecb.europa.eu/press/key/date/2017/html/sp170116.en.html
Náñez Alonso, S L, Echarte Fernández, M, Sanz Bas, D & Kaczmarek, J 2020, 'Reasons fostering or discouraging the implementation of central bank-backed digital currency: A review', *Economies*, 8(2), 41.
Noriyuki, Y & Hiromi, Y 2019, 'Digital Innovation, Data Revolution and Central Bank Digital Currency', Bank of Japan Working Paper Series, No.19-E-2.
Panetta, F 2022, *Central Bank Digital Currencies: Defining the Problems, Designing the Solutions*, Member of the Executive Board of the ECB, to a panel discussion on central bank digital currencies at the US Monetary Policy Forum, 18 February 2022, https://www.ecb.europa.eu/press/key/date/2022/html/ecb.sp220218_1~938e881b13.en.html
Passacantando, F 2021, 'The Digital Euro: Challenges and Opportunities', in Bilotta, N., & Botti, F. *The (Near) Future of Central Bank Digital Currencies: Risks and Opportunities for the Global Economy and Society*, op. cit. pp. 113–130.
Payments Canada, Bank of Canada & R3 2017, 'Project Jasper: A Canadian Experiment with Distributed Ledger Technology for Domestic Interbank Payments Settlement', https://payments.ca/sites/default/files/2022-09/jasper_report_eng.pdf
People's Bank of China 2022, 'The overall operation of the payment system in 2021', http://www.gov.cn/xinwen/2022-04/03/content_5683319.htm

Pilkington, Marc 2022, 'De Libra 1.0 à Libra 2.0 (Diem): entre échec programmé et pertinence renouvelée pour l'économie politique', *Revue d'Economie Politique*, 132–3, 397–420.

Priyadarshini, D & Kar, S 2021, 'Central bank digital currency (CBDC): critical issues and the Indian perspective', IEG Working Paper, N° 444.

PWC 2021, '*Monnaies digitales de banque centrale: vers une adoption mondiale. Enjeux des nouvelles infrastructures monétaires et opportunités pour les entreprises*', viewed 11 April 2022, https://vu.fr/vzUe

PWC 2022, 'PwC global CBDC index and stablecoin overview 2022', https://www.pwc.com/gx/en/new-ventures/cryptocurrency-assets/pwc-global-cbdc-index-stablecoin-overview-2022.pdf

Shen, W & Hou, L 2021, 'China's central bank digital currency and its impacts on monetary policy and payment competition: Game changer or regulatory toolkit?', *Computer Law & Security Review*, 41, 10557.

Sveriges Riksbank 2017, *The Riksbank's e-Krona Project: Report 1*, https://www.riksbank.se/globalassets/media/rapporter/e-krona/2017/rapport_ekrona_uppdaterad_170920_eng.pdf

Sveriges Riksbank 2018, *The Riksbank's e-Krona Project: Report 2*, https://www.riksbank.se/globalassets/media/rapporter/e-krona/2018/the-riksbanks-e-krona-project-report-2.pdf

Sveriges Riksbank 2021, *E-Krona Pilot Phase 1, https://www.riksbank.se/globalassets/media/rapporter/e-krona/2021/e-krona-pilot-phase-1.pdf*

Sveriges Riksbank 2022, *'E-Krona Pilot Phase 2', https://www.riksbank.se/globalassets/media/rapporter/e-krona/2022/e-krona-pilot-phase-2.pdf*

Torre, D & Xu, Q 2019, 'La Chine aux avant-postes de la digitalisation des paiements', *Revue d'économie Financière*, 2019/3(135), 99–114.

Torre, D & Xu, Q 2020, 'Digital payment in China: Adoption and interactions among applications', *Revue d'Economie Industrielle*, 172(4), 55–82, https://doi.org/10.4000/rei.9471

Treiblmaier, H & Clohessy, T 2020, *Blockchain and Distributed Ledger Technology Use Cases: Applications and Lessons Learned*, Germany: Springer International Publishing

Uchida, S. 2022, 'Possible Design Choices of CBDC. Opening Remarks at the Third Meeting of the Liaison and Coordination Committee on Central Bank Digital Currency', *Bank of Japan Speech*, https://www.boj.or.jp/en/announcements/press/koen_2022/ko220413b.htm/

Volkova, T G, Sevryugin, Y V & Firsova, S N 2020, 'Central bank digital currencies as the instrument of national economic sovereignty consolidation'. In *Proc., 2nd Int. Scientific and Practical Conf. 'Modern management trends and the digital economy: From regional development to global economic growth'(MTDE 2020)*, May. pp. 632–637, Yekaterinburg, Russia: Atlantis Press.

Waller, C J 2021, *CBDC: A Solution in Search of a Problem*, Speech at the American Enterprise Institute. August 5. https://www.federalreserve.gov/newsevents/speech/files/waller20210805a.pdf

Wang, H 2022, *China's Approach to Central Bank Digital Currency*, Available at SSRN. https://papers.ssrn.com/sol3/papers.cfm?abstract_id=4036466

Ward, O & Rochemont, S 2019, *Understanding Central Bank Digital Currencies (CBDC)*, Institute and Faculty of Actuaries. https://www.actuaries.org.uk/system/files/field/document/Understanding%20CBDCs%20Final%20-%20disc.pdf

Working Group on E-CNY Research and Development of the People's Bank of China 2021, *Progress of Research & Development of E-CNY in China*, http://www.pbc.gov.cn/en/3688110/3688172/4157443/4293696/2021071614584691871.pdf

World Economic Forum 2019, *Central Banks and Distributed Ledger Technology: How are Central Banks Exploring Blockchain Today?*, http://www3.weforum.org/docs/WEF_Central_Bank_Activity_in_Blockchain_DLT.pdf

Xu, Q 2022, 'East Asia and East Africa: Different Ways to Digitalize Payments'. In Ratajczak-Mrozek M., & Marszałek, P. (eds.), *Digitalization and Firm Performance. Examining the Strategic Impact.*, Palgrave MacMillan.

Zetzsche, D A, Buckley, R P & Arner, D W 2021, 'Regulating Libra', *Oxford Journal of Legal Studies*, 41(1), 80–113.

Zhang, T & Huang, Z. 2021, 'Blockchain and central bank digital currency', ICT Express, ISSN 2405-9595, https://doi.org/10.1016/j.icte.2021.09.014.

4 The Federal Reserve, COVID-19, and the Governance of the International Monetary System

Ayca Zayim

Introduction

The COVID-19 pandemic was a massive shock to the global community. It has claimed over 6 million lives and induced a rapid recession of unseen severity since the World War II (WHO 2022). The global economy contracted by 3.3 percent in 2020 (IMF 2021c, p. 8) and economic activity declined in around 90 percent of countries (World Bank 2022, p. 1). In the first three quarters of 2020 alone, economic recession amounted to a loss of near 500 million full-time jobs (ILO 2020). The World Bank (2020) estimated as many as 150 million people to fall into extreme poverty. As low-income countries endured more persistent and severe problems compared to their high- and middle-income counterparts, inequalities within and between countries have deepened (Ferreira 2021; World Bank 2020). Describing the pandemic as "a crisis like no other," the Managing Director of the International Monetary Fund (IMF) called for policy action in early April, warning, "2020 will be exceptionally difficult… everything depends on the policy actions we take now" (Georgieva 2020a).

Governments and central banks have taken center stage in efforts to contain the economic collapse. Governments introduced fiscal packages encompassing loans to firms, tax cuts/deferrals, healthcare spending, and wage and unemployment subsidies (Alberola et al. 2020). Central banks and financial regulators forcefully supported government action with policies targeted at reducing financial distress and supporting the real economy. The US Federal Reserve (Fed) alone implemented more emergency programs in the four months following the pandemic than it did during the entire global financial crisis (Mosser 2020, p. 191). Around the world, central banks cut policy rates, undertook asset purchase programs, and acted as the lender of last resort by providing liquidity to domestic financial institutions (Cavallino & Fiore 2020; Mosser 2020).

Aside from domestic liquidity, the main source of concern during the pandemic was a shortage of *global* US dollar (USD) liquidity. As investors flew to "safe-haven" currencies and assets such as the US dollar and Treasuries, global dollar funding became scarce and the cost of funding increased. In particular, emerging economies were badly hit. Emerging economies faced portfolio capital outflows at a speed and scale that was unmatched even by the 2008 financial crisis

DOI: 10.4324/9781003323280-5

and the 2013 taper tantrum (OECD 2020). Between mid-January and mid-May 2020, around 103 billion USD was drawn from emerging market economies (ibid). Amounting to a "sudden stop," these flows led to currency depreciation, economic contraction, and financial stress for many banks and businesses with large foreign currency-denominated debts (Akinci, Benigno & Queralto 2020). Moreover, the decline in exports, tourism receipts, and remittances further limited the access of emerging market and developing economies (EMDE) to US dollars (Herrero & Ribakova 2020). In several economies dependent on external financing, central bankers had to scramble to find adequate amounts of dollars to pass onto their governments, domestic banks, and businesses to pay for imports and meet foreign debt obligations. In more fragile economies, limited access to dollar liquidity restricted much needed access to medical equipment and supplies.

The COVID-19 pandemic has revealed that the global distribution of dollar liquidity in times of crisis has very tangible consequences not just for global inequality but for livelihoods around the world. It has also shown the unique position of the Fed in determining *who* got access to US dollars and *how*. The Fed is the only central bank capable of providing an unlimited supply of dollars to the rest of the world. The US dollar is the dominant international currency, overpowering the use of other currencies as a medium of exchange, store of value, and unit of account in the international monetary system (Cohen & Benney 2014). Not only are debts, loans, bank transactions, and global trade disproportionately undertaken in US dollars, but, more strikingly, 61% of foreign exchange reserves are in USD and around 85% of foreign exchange transactions involve the dollar (Davies & Kent 2020). Although the USD no longer acts as the *formal* anchor of the international monetary system, paradoxically, its dominance has grown after the decline of the Bretton Woods system (Gourinchas, Rey & Sauzet 2019). The dollar has remained the "undisputed world's anchor and reserve currency" (ibid, p. 869).

Starting in March 2020, the Fed provided dollar liquidity to other central banks through two key mechanisms: currency swap agreements and a new repo facility known as the Foreign and International Monetary Authorities (FIMA) Repo Facility. Thus, it has acted as the international lender of last resort for the world (Bordo, Humpage & Schwartz 2015; Broz 2015; Helleiner 2014; Sahasrabuddhe 2019). In the literature, the Fed's provision of liquidity has been viewed as a significant mechanism to backstop the dollar-based international monetary system and an expansion of the so-called global safety net (Bordo 2021; McDowell 2019a; Mehrling 2015; Tooze 2018). Other works have examined the motivations of the US and the Fed in acting as the lender of last resort with a focus on its extending swap lines to other central banks (Aizenman & Pasricha 2010; Cassetta 2022; Hardie & Thompson 2021; McDowell 2012; Pape 2022; Sahasrabuddhe 2019).

Notwithstanding expanding research, the implications of the Fed's actions for global inequality remains understudied—a notable exception is Murau, Pape, and Pforr (2022). This chapter aims to address this gap by examining the Fed's actions in relation to global monetary governance and hierarchy. Using public texts and data, the chapter discusses the Fed's role in the governance of the international monetary system and how its swap lines and FIMA facility tend to reflect and reinforce the international monetary hierarchy.

The next section discusses the evolving global financial safety net and how bilateral central bank swap lines have become the main channel of support for crisis-stricken economies during the pandemic. It also highlights the limitations of the IMF and regional financial arrangements (RFAs). Section Three examines the Fed's provision of liquidity through bilateral swap lines and the FIMA repo facility and the political and economic implications of the Fed's actions as the international lender of last resort. The last section concludes.

The Evolving Global Financial Safety Net

Scholarly publications invoke the concept of a "global financial safety net" to highlight a web of financial resources and institutional arrangements that are expected to provide emergency financial support to countries during crises much like the one prompted by COVID-19 (Fritz & Mühlich 2019; Hawkins, Rahman & Williamson 2014; IMF 2016; Mühlich & Fritz 2018; Scheubel & Stracca 2019; Stubbs et al. 2021; Volz 2016; Weder di Mauro & Zettelmeyer 2017). By addressing economic or financial crises that affect a country's "external payments," the safety net supports the stability of the international monetary system. This net principally includes the IMF, regional financial arrangements (RFAs), central bank bilateral swap arrangements, and countries' domestic foreign exchange reserves. Despite the purported potential of this multilayered and fragmented network to provide the EMDEs with dollars in emergency credit as well as to expand their policy space for developmental goals (Grabel 2019; McDowell 2019a), in practice, the "geographically and structurally scattered" safety net proved to be insufficient in granting access to financing during COVID-19 and the access remained highly unequal across countries (Fritz & Mühlich 2019, p. 981; IMF 2016; Mühlich & Fritz 2018; Weder di Mauro & Zettelmeyer 2017). Recent research shows that the majority of countries could not count on a bilateral swap line and had the IMF as their only source for liquidity (Mühlich & Fritz 2018). However, as the following section shows, the IMF funding has not met the immediate liquidity need during the pandemic, leaving several EMDEs out in the cold.

The (In)Effectiveness of the IMF as the Lender of Last Resort

For several decades, the IMF acted as the primary international lender of last resort in the global economy. Under the Bretton Woods system, central banks were required to intervene in currency markets to maintain fixed exchange rates, helped by controls on international capital movements. The IMF played a crucial role in overseeing this system and providing liquidity to member states to "correct maladjustments in their balance of payments without resorting to measures destructive of national or international prosperity" (IMF 2022b). The IMF loans often came with conditionalities such as a reduction in the fiscal deficit that ultimately aimed to protect stable exchange rates (Babb & Kentikelenis 2018). With the US's decision of "closing the gold window," the IMF reconceptualized its mandate, shifting its focus to the institutionalization of "free markets." Throughout the 1990s, the IMF continued to act as the primary international lender of last resort while becoming a fervent supporter of neoliberal reforms and providing loans for structural adjustment (Babb 2003).

The IMF suffered from a dwindling reputation and demand for its loans in the mid-2000 (Momani & Helleiner 2007); yet, the 2008 financial crisis was a turning point. Amidst fears of financial contagion and rampant liquidity shortages, G-20 leaders agreed to triple the IMF's lending capacity to 750 billion USD in 2009 and to reform its governance, thereby reaffirming the IMF's central role in global economic governance and crisis management (Kentikelenis, Stubbs & King 2016). Acknowledging this change, the IMF Managing Director Strauss-Kahn commented that: "You will see that it's the beginning of increasing the role of the IMF, not only as a lender of last resort, not only as a forecaster, not only as an advisor in economic policy and its old traditional role, but also in providing liquidity to the world, which is the role finally and in the end, of a financial institution like ours" (IMF 2009b).

When COVID-19 struck, both the IMF and the UNCTAD estimated that EMDEs were in urgent need of at least 2.5 trillion USD in March 2020 (Georgieva 2020c; UNCTAD 2020). That same month, the IMF and the World Bank issued a joint statement, announcing that "[they] will use [their] available instruments to the fullest extent possible" (Georgieva & Malpass 2020). Between March 2, 2020 and August 31, 2021, the IMF "approved 221 loans and grants to 88 countries for $117.32bn in total, marking the largest-ever increase in demand for its services" (Kentikelenis, Stubbs & Reinsberg 2022, p. 19). However, of the total $117 billion *approved*, almost half of these funds were channeled through the IMF's Flexible Credit Line ($52 billion) (ibid, p.20). Flexible credit line, which was created in 2009 as part of the IMF reforms to its lending practices, aimed to assist countries "facing a cash crunch" (IMF 2021b). While it did not enforce any ex-post conditionality, it *excluded* many economies by restricting funds to "countries with very strong fundamentals, policies, and track records of policy implementation" (IMF 2009a). Between March 2020 and August 2021, only three countries (Chile, Columbia, and Peru) had Flexible Credit Line arrangements in place.

Most countries accessed emergency funds through the IMF's (non-concessional) Rapid Financing Instrument and (concessional) Rapid Credit Facility. For instance, 37 and 48 countries received funding through Rapid Financing Instrument and Rapid Credit Facility, respectively, amounting to $22 billion and $8 billion (Kentikelenis, Stubbs & Reinsberg 2022). Although the IMF temporarily raised annual access limits to these two facilities in April 2020 from 50 to 100% of the quota (IMF 2020), its quota-based lending system and limited new financing options constrained countries' access to additional funds (Stubbs et al. 2021; Volz 2016). When these low- or no-conditionality options were depleted, countries gradually turned to loans that came with conditionalities such as the Stand-By Arrangement or the Extended Credit Facility (Kentikelenis et al. 2022). For instance, Extended Fund Facility, which was approved for 11 countries during March 2020–August 2021, was targeted at "countries experiencing serious payment imbalances because of structural impediments or slow growth" (IMF 2021a). These funds took longer to disperse—not ideal during a crisis—and required countries to implement structural reforms over long periods.

The IMF took two further actions in response to the pandemic. First, it established a new facility named the Short-term Liquidity Line. This facility was intended to provide "swap-like liquidity support" but only to those members with "very strong fundamentals and policy frameworks" (IMF 2022c). Unsurprisingly, the stringent qualification criteria excluded many EMDEs. As of May 2022, only one country (Chile) had been approved (IMF 2022a). Second, the IMF expanded its Catastrophe Containment and Relief Trust in relation to its purported goal of helping low-income countries and approved 29 countries between March 2020 and August 2021 (Kentikelenis, Stubbs, & Reinsberg 2022). While this brought in new funds to EMDEs, it was only for IMF debt service relief and short of these countries' financial needs (Stubbs et al. 2021, p. 5).

Emergence of Bilateral Swap Lines in Response to Liquidity Shortages

Aside from the IMF's own limitations, EMDEs had also been seeking/building alternative sources of liquidity support since the early 2000s. On the one hand, several EMDEs accumulated foreign exchange reserves as a precaution to be deployed during crises, in large part motivated by the Fund's controversial policy interventions and stigma (Duran 2015; Ghosh, Ostry & Tsangarides 2012). Between 1990 and 2008, the share of global reserves held by EMDEs increased from 28% to 65% (Aizenman, Jinjarak & Park 2010, p. 1). Consequently, those countries with large volumes of reserves, such as China, accumulated significant economic and political leverage in the international monetary system and gained independence from the IMF. On the other hand, several countries established RFAs which either took the form of swap agreements (e.g., Chiang Mai Initiative Multilateralization) or credit facilities (e.g., Latin American Reserve Fund) (Gallagher et al. 2021, p. 143). The common feature of RFAs was to provide their members with "balance of payments support with lighter conditionality and/or less political stigma" (Weder di Mauro & Zettelmeyer 2017, p. 4). However, they were left unutilized and contributed very little to ameliorate the EMDEs' dollar shortage during the pandemic. The Chiang Mai Initiative Multilateralization, for instance, did not approve or disburse any funds in the first six months of the pandemic (Stubbs et al. 2021).

In contrast to the IMF and RFAs, bilateral central bank swap lines—also referred to as currency swaps, swap agreements, or swap lines—have proven to be a crucial part of the global financial safety net after the 2008 financial crisis. They have proliferated rapidly, creating an international liquidity network (McDowell 2019a) and replaced RFAs as the most used option for short-term financing. Between 2008 and 2015, for instance, the volume of existing swap agreements for 50 RFA countries was around \$877 billion, while the total financing volume of RFAs was just \$4.9 billion (Fritz & Mühlich 2019, p. 107). The agreed swap amount was also about 16 times larger than the volume of IMF programs (ibid). In 2020, there were 91 bilateral swap lines (Perks et al. 2021), generating cross-border capital flows in excess of the resources governed by the IMF (Bahaj & Reis 2022). According to IMF estimates, the swap network among central banks—*excluding* those covered under regional financial arrangements—was worth $1.4 trillion at the end of 2019, dominated by the permanent lines extended by the Fed ($610 billion) and those among Asian countries ($470 billion) led by China and Japan (Perks et al. 2021, p. 9). In 2020, China alone had 31 bilateral swap lines (ibid, p. 11), but their use was fairly limited during the pandemic. Most other swap lines had not been drawn either (ibid, p.13). By contrast, the swap lines extended by the Fed provided massive amounts of financing. They have often been regarded as a significant step in the evolution of the global financial safety net and a positive development in safeguarding the stability of the international monetary system (Bordo 2021; McDowell 2019a; Mehrling 2015; Tooze 2018). Instead of providing a blanket protection for all, however, the next section demonstrates how the Fed's actions were selective and reinforced existing inequalities in the global financial system.

The Federal Reserve and International Monetary Governance: Swap Lines and FIMA Repo Facility

Background and Workings

There is consensus in the economics literature that central banks act as the lender of last resort in national economies, providing credit to illiquid (albeit solvent) financial institutions during periods when they cannot secure credit from the market (Bagehot 1873). At the international level, it is less clear-cut who should fill this role (McDowell 2012). According to Eichengreen, Lombardi, and Malkin (2018, p. 12), the "lack of an effective, multilateral, universally recognized ILOLR [international lender of last resort]" has been "one of the long-standing deficiencies of the global financial system." While the IMF had typically fulfilled this function until the 2000s, the Fed has increasingly taken over after 2008 as a "global actor" which was "capable of providing hard currency" but had been "unwilling to do so in the 1990s" (Duran 2015, p. 11). Scholarship argues that in addition to acting as the lender of last resort to US financial institutions, the Fed has been acting as the world'*s de facto* lender of last resort, or in McDowell's words (2012) "the sovereign international last-resort lender" since the 2008 financial crisis (Bordo, Humpage & Schwartz 2015; Broz 2015; Destais 2016; Duran 2015; Helleiner 2014). The Fed was suited to this task because it printed the "top currency" in the currency pyramid (Cohen 2015). In the 2008 FOMC meeting, Fed vice-chairman Geithner alluded to the Fed's new role, saying, "what we're doing is a natural extension of what central banks do" (Federal Reserve 2008, p. 35). The scope of the Fed's actions had implicitly been broadened to the outside of the US.

The Fed acted as the international lender of last resort by providing liquidity through bilateral currency swap lines and the FIMA repo facility. A currency swap, swap line, or liquidity swap is a contractual agreement which allows a central bank to borrow foreign currency from another central bank in exchange for its own currency. Central banks swap their currencies—and at times a "hard currency" like

US dollars from their foreign exchange reserves (McDowell 2019b, p. 124)—and commit to reverse the transaction at the initial transaction's exchange rate on a future specified date. The "borrowing" central bank then distributes borrowed currency among financial institutions in its jurisdiction based on its own priorities and criteria. At the end of the swap term, the borrowing central bank returns the borrowed principal amount plus an agreed-upon interest. Typically, it makes no profits from the operation while the issuing central bank makes a modest profit (Bahaj & Reis 2022, p. 1660). Swaps provide immediate short-term access to foreign exchange, often come with no conditionality, and bypass the lengthy and tedious decision-making and lending processes. They are very effective in giving immediate "breathing space to crisis-stricken economies" and "send[ing] positive signals to global financial markets about the capacity of such economies to provide liquidity to their respective banking systems in times of crisis" (Eichengreen, Lombardi & Malkin 2018, p. 11). FIMA repo agreements are similar to swap agreements in that an exchange occurs between two monetary authorities, but financial assets are used as collateral instead of the borrowing central bank's currency (ECB 2022).

Swap lines are not new to central banking. They were frequently used in the 1960s to help central banks stabilize exchange rates that were fixed under the Bretton Woods system (Bordo et al. 2015; James 1996). While the demise of the Bretton Woods rendered currency swaps redundant for funding an exchange rate intervention, the 2008 financial crisis gave them a new purpose.[1] Following the crisis, the Fed established swap lines with 14 central banks to resolve liquidity shortages in offshore markets and stabilize the global banking system (Bahaj & Reis 2022). The Fed's swap partners included ten advanced-economy and four emerging-economy central banks (Brazil, Mexico, Singapore, and South Korea). The inclusion of the four "peripheral" banks was an unprecedented move since the Fed had so far only selected "core" central banks as its swap partners with the exception of Mexico (Federal Reserve 2008). The Fed provided liquidity amounting to $288 billion in September 2008, $534 billion in October, and a peak of $554 billion at the end of December, accounting for over 25 percent of the Fed's total assets (Bertaut & Pounder 2009). The Fed's actions were praised as "one of the most notable examples of central bank cooperation in history" and "a quantum leap in central bank cooperation" (cited in McCauley & Schenk 2020).

The Fed's swap lines expired in February 2010, but the Fed renewed them with five core central banks in May 2010 due to the Eurozone crisis. Eventually, it converted them into permanent standing facilities in 2013. These five central banks were the Bank of Canada, the Bank of England, the Bank of Japan, the European Central Bank, and the Swiss National Bank. With the onset of the COVID-19 pandemic, the Fed lowered interest rates on its standing swap lines and increased their maturity, thereby allowing the select five central banks to borrow US dollars more cheaply and easily. These central banks had access to unlimited dollar funding, because they exchanged their own currency (which they printed) for US dollars. Additionally, the Fed re-established temporary swap lines to nine other central banks in March 2020, including the central banks of Australia, Brazil, Denmark, the Republic of Korea, Mexico, New Zealand, Norway, Singapore, and Sweden. A cap was set at $30 billion for Denmark, Norway, and New Zealand and at $60 billion for the remaining six economies (Choi et al. 2022).

The Financial Times (Jones & Kaminska 2020) described the Fed's currency swap lines as "the most important Fed action thus far" in fighting a "global cash crunch." The Economist (2020) similarly praised the "successes" of the swap lines, noting, "America's central bank shines." In May 2020, swap usage reached $449 billion (Choi et al. 2022). Swap lines alleviated funding pressure, reduced dollar borrowing costs and financial distress, and helped bolster confidence among market participants, thereby positively affecting the currencies and well-being of those countries which had access to them (Bahaj & Reis 2020, 2022; Bordo 2021; Eren, Schrimpf, & Sushko 2020). However, access remained highly unequal. Apart from Brazil and Mexico, EMDEs did not have access to the Fed's swap lines. This meant that they would "need to seek other sources of funding or face shortfalls that could paralyze their economies" (Segal 2020). Especially, those economies that suffered and needed dollar liquidity most were ineligible. Even the IMF admitted that "there may be a need for swap lines to emerging market economies" given that they faced "the largest [capital] outflow they have ever recorded" (Georgieva 2020b).

In addition to the swaps, the Fed established a temporary FIMA repo facility in late March 2020 as "an alternative temporary source of U.S. dollars" (Federal Reserve 2021). It became a standing facility in July 2021. The repo facility had two key differences with the swap network. First, the repo facility was not restricted to a select group of central banks. Most foreign central banks and monetary authorities could access the repo facility any time after opening an account at the New York Fed and being approved for transactions. As the St Louis Fed president Bullard explained, this would increase the availability of dollar funding globally:

> It's always been a question: "Who gets the swap lines?" And: "Why?" And: "Do you want to have this arrangement with every central bank in the world?" And we have not done that, even during the last crisis or during this crisis. But this facility is a way to sidestep that issue and allow quite a bit of liquidity to flow all around the world and allow dollars to be where they're needed around the world.
>
> (Jeffery 2020)

While on the surface the FIMA facility expanded access to dollar liquidity, its conditions were much less generous. In the repo facility, foreign institutions would need to provide US Treasury securities as collateral instead of a national currency. Because foreign central banks cannot print US Treasuries, their borrowing capacity was effectively constrained by the level of US Treasuries held in foreign exchange reserves (Aizenman, Ito & Pasricha 2022, p. 5; Murau, Pape & Pforr 2022). Moreover, borrowing through the FIMA facility was overnight (although it could be rolled over) and requests were made on an *ad hoc* basis (as opposed to pre-approved schedules of swaps). Despite being found to instill confidence among market participants and reduce fire sale of US Treasuries, interestingly, the facility was minimally used in the period soon after its inception and in 2021 (Choi et al. 2022).

The Fed had faced intense public criticism during the 2008 crisis for "going beyond its national mandate" and "covertly bailing out European banks and putting U.S. taxpayers' money at risk" (Prasad 2014, p. 206). The Fed's Open Market Committee (FOMC) had responded by justifying its provision of dollar liquidity as a policy that was mainly in the interests of the US (ibid). Similar to its pronouncements a decade earlier, the Fed emphasized how its actions during COVID-19 benefitted the US economy. Regarding the swaps, the Fed said, "by taking this action to support dollar funding markets abroad, we hope to maintain the flow of credit to U.S. households and firms, reduce dislocations to U.S. financial markets emanating from financial turbulence abroad, and, by supporting foreign growth, maintain exports markets for U.S. producers" (Federal Reserve 2020b). Similarly, the FIMA repo facility would provide "an alternative temporary source of U.S. dollars other than sales of securities in the open market," thereby "support the smooth functioning of the U.S. Treasury market" (Federal Reserve 2020a). According to the Fed, this "helps the U.S. economy by supporting stable and well-functioning U.S. dollar funding markets, as well as by promoting the international role of the dollar" (Federal Reserve 2021).

Moreover, the Fed underlined how these liquidity lines posed no risk to the US taxpayer. In both swap and FIMA repo agreements, the foreign central bank shouldered the credit risk, because it distributed the borrowed dollars among financial institutions in its jurisdiction. The Fed was also protected from any exchange or interest rate risk, because the swap-line interest rate and exchange rate were determined when the contract was signed (Bahaj & Reis 2022). In FIMA repo agreements, the transactions exclusively took place in dollars, similarly posing no exchange rate risk (Federal Reserve 2021). More recently, the Fed compared swaps with the FIMA repo facility, arguing that swaps involved a higher level of credit risk, because "in the event that dollars are not repaid in a swap transaction, the Federal Reserve would be left holding the local currency of the foreign jurisdiction, which may entail a higher risk of value loss" (Choi et al. 2022). While the additional risk might justify the Fed's selectivity of its swap partners, in reality Fed's credit risk associated with the recipient foreign central bank is "negligible" as the foreign central bank's (and thus a country's) reputation is at stake (Bahaj & Reis 2022, p. 1659).

The Fed's Motivations and the Emergent "Apartheid"

What explains the Fed's decision to provide liquidity to the rest of the world? In line with the Fed's public pronouncements, recent scholarship concurs that the Fed mainly acted defensively to shield the US monetary policy and economy from adverse global developments (Cassetta 2022; Hardie & Maxfield 2016; Hardie & Thompson 2021; Helleiner 2014; McDowell 2012; Pape 2022). Based on an analysis of the Fed's swap lines during the 2008 financial crisis, McDowell (2012) argues that the Fed was concerned with spillover threats from world markets in three areas: namely, the exposure of the US financial system to foreign defaults, the Fed's limited control over interest rates, and an adverse change in the dollar's exchange rate. As a result of financial integration and the development of private money markets, a greater share of USD-denominated transactions takes place offshore in the so-called Eurodollar market (Mehrling 2015; Murau et al. 2022). This not only exposed the US financial system to default risk because of its interdependencies with non-US institutions but it also put upward pressure on domestic interest rates and the value of the US dollar. Consequently, the Fed felt pressured to step in and provide dollar liquidity as the international lender of last resort (Hardie & Maxfield 2016; Hardie & Thompson 2021; McDowell 2012, 2017). As Hardie and Maxfield (2016) put it, the Fed "could only serve the interests of the US economy by supporting the global financial system" (p. 602). A more recent study similarly finds swap lines to be integral to the Fed's conduct of monetary policy, helping dampen domestic short-term funding rates in 2020 (Pape 2022). In line with this strand of literature, other researchers contend that the exposures of US banks and the size of the US dollar shortages in big financial centers have influenced the Fed's choice of its swap partners during the 2008 crisis (Aizenman & Pasricha 2010; Allen & Moessner 2010; Broz 2015; McDowell 2012). Yet others focusing on the COVID-19 period point to the financial exposure of US banks as well as the trade exposure to the US as significant determinants of who gets dollar liquidity (Aizenman, Ito & Pasricha 2022). In short, the US was not acting as a "benevolent hegemon" although its actions "created positive externalities" for the international financial system (McDowell 2012).

Formally, the criteria of inclusion in the Fed's swap network have always been opaque. A one-time audit of the Fed's crisis programs by the Government Accountability Office in 2011 announced a set of economic conditions that were used to evaluate swap requests. These conditions included "the economic and financial mass" of a country's economy, its record of sound economic management, its importance as a US trading partner, dollar funding needs, levels of foreign currency reserves, the exposure of US banks to the foreign economy, and whether or not an economy was a global financial center (GAO 2011, p. 118 as cited in Sahasrabuddhe 2019). Nonetheless, scholars cast doubt on the audit's findings, highlighting the discrepancies between the purported selection criteria and the Fed's actual decisions. According to Sahasrabuddhe (2019), the Fed had denied swap requests from at least seven central banks during the 2008 financial crisis (i.e., Chile, the Dominican Republic, Iceland, India, Indonesia, Peru, and Turkey). Based on the levels of US bank exposure—the most agreed-upon criterion—Switzerland and New Zealand ranked low. On the other hand, Brazil and India—two similar economies with a comparable amount of US debt—had opposite results as India's request was denied (ibid). The criterion of being a US trade partner was also challenged empirically (Aizenman & Pasricha 2010; Broz 2015).

Hardie and Thompson's (2021) distinction between countries with systematically important financial systems (e.g., Europe) and those without (most EMDEs) is helpful in unpacking the evident inconsistencies across cases. In the context of the 2008 crisis, Hardie and Thompson (ibid) argue that the Fed "saw little choice but to support European banks" (p. 782), becoming the lender of last resort to Europe, because the US-Europe financial linkages posed a constraint on the Fed's policy space, weakening its "ability to use monetary policy to shape domestic credit conditions" (p. 788). In a sense, the Fed's hands were tied, diminishing its autonomy and monetary power vis-a-vis major European economies. By contrast, the Fed could exercise great monetary power vis-à-vis non-systemic non-European cases. As such, the allocation of swap lines among EMDEs was vastly discretionary with strategic or political concerns often being at work (Bordo 2021; Chey 2012b; Destais 2016; Sahasrabuddhe 2019). For instance, Chey (2012b) found that the US established swap lines with four emerging market economies—Brazil, Mexico, Singapore, and South Korea—during 2008–2009 in order to "reinforce its ties" with them and to "preserve its influence in the new system of global economic governance" (p.2). Building on Chey, Sahasrabuddhe (2019) similarly argues that while economic factors such as capital account openness were influential, politics were determinative; only those countries with economic *and* strategic importance to the US leadership received swap assistance (p. 479). In a recent study, Aizenman et al. (2022) find military alliances to be a significant variable of swap-line selectivity in 2020. Similarly, Cassetta (2022) concludes that political alignment with the US increased the likelihood of receiving a swap line while the exposure of US banks continued to be an important factor in 2020.

The apparent inequalities in accessing dollar liquidity have been part of the public debate even before the pandemic. In 2017, former governor of the Reserve Bank of India starkly described the situation as a "virtual apartheid" (Patel 2017):

> So far, our quest for a robust, equitable and quickly deployable global financial safety net has remained elusive… It is in this context that I would draw your attention to the stark asymmetry prevailing in the provision of swap lines by systemic central banks. In fact, I would go as far as describing the situation as a virtual "apartheid" by which systemic central banks protect themselves and their self-interest. Meanwhile, EMEs that are at the receiving end of global financial turbulence are systematically denied access. The time has come to end this sectarian approach and the access to swap lines be equally available.

Indeed, the implications of the Fed's decisions are profound. Who gets liquidity from the Fed, through which mechanism, and why largely reflect and reinforce existing inequalities in the global financial system (see Cassetta 2022; Mehrling 2015; Murau et al. 2022; Pape 2022). For instance, Murau et al. (2022) highlight the mechanisms through which non-US central banks can access emergency dollar liquidity from the Fed as constitutive of the international monetary hierarchy. While the centrality of the US dollar places the Fed at the apex of this hierarchy, three peripheral and hierarchically distinct layers exist underneath it (ibid). The "first-layer periphery" can access Fed swap lines and thus occupies the most privileged position while the second-layer periphery can utilize the FIMA facility. The third-layer has access to the Fed only indirectly through the Special Drawing Rights system administered by the IMF. Especially important for EMDEs, this is the least desirable option because the process is tedious and access is vetted by the Exchange Stabilization Fund (ibid).

Fed swap lines provide credit to foreign economies in exchange for currencies that can easily be *printed* by their central banks. For a privileged group of advanced economies with standing swap lines, this means unlimited credit and spending power conferred upon by the Fed (Strange 1994). Moreover, a swap agreement with the Fed bestows credibility and trust to its recipient, providing "another layer of protection from wolves in the market, even if the amounts involved were small" (Prasad 2014, p. 208). In contrast to swaps, the FIMA facility not only limits a country's borrowing capacity to its stock of US treasuries, it also shapes market expectations differently. During discussions of the FIMA repo facility in 2008, vice-chair of the Fed Donald Kohn expressed concerns that the repo facility would create a stigma: "Saying that we have enough doubts about these other countries that we need to take collateral—we don't have confidence that their central banks will meet the obligations that they have taken on" (Federal Reserve 2008, pp. 22–23). In a monetary system of fiat currencies where trust is key to maintaining a stable currency, the implied or perceived lack of confidence can quickly become self-fulfilling, potentially heightening capital flight and pressure on those economies with access to the FIMA facility but not to swaps.

What the Economist (2020) dubbed "the swap-envy" has led several EMDEs to seek swap partners alternative to the Fed. In particular, China has opportunistically offered swap lines to countries that were either denied or unlikely to meet the Fed's criteria (Cassetta 2022). Consequently, China has built the world's largest swap network, using swap lines as a tool of "financial statecraft" in order to meet foreign policy objectives, support the internationalization of the renminbi, and create a less dollar-centric global financial system (Chey 2012a; Destais 2016; Eichengreen et al. 2018; Liao & McDowell 2015; McDowell 2019b). Despite the proliferation of swap lines in the last decade, "not all swaps [were] equal" (Mehrling 2015, p. 312). In a financial system that continues to remain dollar based, almost all of the newly established swaps were "local currency swaps"; thus, they have only allowed countries to "economize on existing reserves not to increase global reserves" (ibid, p. 314). Some cases such as Argentina have even used renminbi swaps to get dollar reserves (ibid)—a further testament to the importance of having a swap line to the Fed.

Conclusion

Amidst public fear and rising death toll, a major source of concern in the early days of the pandemic was a growing shortage of global US dollar liquidity. Which countries had access to dollar liquidity was not a trivial issue. It had tangible, serious consequences for macroeconomic and financial stability and individual livelihoods. Starting in March 2020, the Fed provided dollar liquidity through bilateral swap lines and the FIMA repo facility. Reflective of its increasingly central role in global monetary governance after the 2008 financial crisis, it has effectively acted as the world's *de facto* lender of last resort.

"In a world where there is no or little restriction on the currencies in which global financial intermediaries may borrow or lend, and where central banks can create only one currency but in virtually unlimited quantity" (Destais 2016, p. 2257), the Fed's actions have undoubtedly backstopped international money markets by providing money market liquidity. While this has often been seen as a significant development in the governance of the international monetary system and the expansion of the global safety net, this chapter examines how the Fed's decisions around liquidity provision reflect and reinforce inequalities in the global financial system. Sitting at the top of the international monetary hierarchy, the Fed wields great power. It determines who gets dollar liquidity, by how much, and through which mechanism. Similar to how the IMF's governance structure and decisions have long reflected existing global power dynamics, so do the Fed's actions. Some countries benefit from the Fed's actions and are in a privileged position, such as those European economies with systematically important financial systems or countries with political and geopolitical importance to the US.[2] Others rank low in the international monetary hierarchy, scrambling to get dollar liquidity through/from the IMF. It is not surprising that such inequality is described as an "apartheid."

As central banks are increasingly coalescing with political and foreign policy objectives, interestingly, their actions continue to be framed as purely economic decisions and remain largely invisible in the public eye. This is important, because unlike the gold standard and the Bretton Woods systems, there is no clear set of international legal rules by which central banks govern today's international monetary system (Bradlow & Park 2020). As this chapter demonstrates, the Fed's rationale behind its selection of swap partners remains at best opaque. Moreover, the entire swap network among central banks sidelines multilateral arrangements and governance structures such as the IMF. This leaves the current governance infrastructure patchy, distributing the burden of crises unevenly in the global financial system. While it is unknown whether, and if so when, the dominance of the US dollar will be overturned, it seems likely that bilateral swap lines will continue to constitute a key pillar of the global financial infrastructure given the IMF's limitations and the lack of appetite for reforming the global financial system.

Notes

1 McCauley and Schenk (2020) argue that in practice it is difficult to draw the line between different purposes and that some swaps served similar purposes under the Bretton Woods system.

2 Admittedly, the Fed sometimes takes "actions to help out its friends," Cohen, BJ 2015, *Currency power: Understanding monetary rivalry*, Princeton University Press, Princeton, NJ.

Bibliography

Aizenman, J, Ito, H, & Pasricha, GK 2022, 'Central Bank swap arrangements in the covid-19 crisis', *Journal of International Money and Finance*, vol. 122, pp. 1–20.

Aizenman, J, Jinjarak, Y, & Park, D 2010, 'International reserves and swap lines: Substitutes or complements?', *NBER Working Paper Series*, vol. 15804, viewed 21 October 2022, http://www.nber.org/papers/w15804

Aizenman, J, & Pasricha, GK 2010, 'Selective swap arrangements and the global financial crisis: Analysis and interpretation', *International Review of Economics & Finance*, vol. 19, no. 3, pp. 353–65.

Akinci, O, Benigno, G, & Queralto, A 2020, 'Modeling the global effects of the covid-19 sudden stop in capital flows', *FEDS Notes*, viewed 20 October 2022, https://www.federalreserve.gov/econres/notes/feds-notes/modeling-the-global-effects-of-the-covid-19-sudden-stop-in-capital-flows-20200702.html

Alberola, E, Arslan, Y, Cheng, G, & Moessner, R 2020, 'The fiscal response to the covid-19 crisis in advanced and emerging market economies', *BIS Bulletin*, vol. 23, viewed 20 October 2022, https://www.bis.org/publ/bisbull23.pdf

Allen, WA, & Moessner, R 2010, 'Central Bank co-operation and international liquidity in the financial crisis of 2008-9', *BIS Working Papers*, vol. 310, viewed 25 October 2022, https://www.bis.org/publ/work310.pdf

Babb, S 2003, 'The IMF in sociological perspective: A tale of organizational slippage', *Studies in Comparative International Development*, vol. 38, no. 2, pp. 3–27.

Babb, S, & Kentikelenis, A 2018, 'International financial institutions as agents of neoliberalism', in D Cahill, M Cooper, M Konings & D Primrose (eds.), *The sage handbook of neoliberalism*. SAGE Publications, Thousand Oaks.

Bagehot, W 1873, *Lombard street: A description of the money market*, Scribner, Armstrong & Company, New York.

Bahaj, S, & Reis, R 2020, 'Central Bank swap lines during the Covid-19 pandemic', *Covid Economics*, no. 2, pp. 1–12.

Bahaj, S, & Reis, R 2022, 'Central Bank swap lines: Evidence on the effects of the lender of last resort', *The Review of Economic Studies*, vol. 89, no. 4, pp. 1654–93.

Bertaut, CC, & Pounder, L 2009, 'The financial crisis and U.S. cross-border financial flows', *Federal Reserve Bulletin*, vol. 95, viewed 21 October 2022, https://www.federalreserve.gov/pubs/bulletin/2009/pdf/bulletin_article_november_2009a1.pdf

Bordo, MD 2021, 'Monetary policy cooperation/coordination and global financial crises in historical perspective', *Open Economies Review*, vol. 32, no. 3, pp. 587–611.

Bordo, MD, Humpage, OF, & Schwartz, AJ 2015, 'The evolution of the Federal Reserve swap lines since 1962', *IMF Economic Review*, vol. 63, no. 2, pp. 353–72.

Bradlow, DD, & Park, SK 2020, 'A global leviathan emerges: The Federal Reserve, covid-19, and international law', *American Journal of International Law*, vol. 114, no. 4, pp. 657–65.

Broz, JL 2015, 'The politics of rescuing the world's financial system: The Federal Reserve as a global lender of last resort', *The Korean Journal of International Studies*, vol. 13, no. 2, pp. 323–51.

Cassetta, JM 2022, 'The geopolitics of swap lines', *M-RCBG Associate Working Paper Series*, vol. 181, https://www.hks.harvard.edu/centers/mrcbg/publications/awp/awp181

Cavallino, P, & Fiore, FD 2020, 'Central banks' response to Covid-19 in advanced economies', *BIS Bulletin*, vol. 21, viewed 20 October 2022, https://www.bis.org/publ/bisbull21.pdf

Chey, H-k 2012a, 'Can the renminbi rise as a global currency? The political economy of currency internationalization', *GRIPS Discussion Paper*, vol. 11-20, https://www.grips.ac.jp/r-center/wp-content/uploads/11-20.pdf

Chey, H-k 2012b, 'Why did the US Federal Reserve unprecedentedly offer swap lines to emerging market economies during the global financial crisis? Can we expect them again in the future?', *GRIPS Discussion Paper*, vol. 11-18, viewed 25 October 2022, https://core.ac.uk/download/pdf/51221372.pdf

Choi, M, Goldberg, LS, Lerman, R, & Ravazzolo, F 2022, 'The Fed's Central Bank swap lines and FIMA Repo facility', *Economic Policy Review* vol. 28, viewed 21 October 2022, https://www.newyorkfed.org/medialibrary/media/research/epr/2022/epr_2022_fima-repo_choi.pdf

Cohen, BJ 2015, *Currency power: Understanding monetary rivalry*, Princeton University Press, Princeton, NJ.

Cohen, BJ, & Benney, TM 2014, 'What does the international currency system really look like?, *Review of International Political Economy*, vol. 21, no. 5, pp. 1017–41.

Davies, SM, & Kent, C 2020, 'US dollar funding: An international perspective', *CGFS Papers*, vol. 65, viewed 20 October 2022, https://www.bis.org/publ/cgfs65.pdf

Destais, C 2016, 'Central Bank currency swaps and the international monetary system', *Emerging Markets Finance and Trade*, vol. 52, no. 10, pp. 2253–66.

Duran, CV 2015, 'The international lender of last resort for emerging countries: A bilateral currency swap?', *GEG Working Paper*, vol. 108, viewed 21 October 2022, https://www.geg.ox.ac.uk/sites/default/files/WP_108%20-%20The%20International%20Lender%20of%20Last%20Resort%20for%20Emerging%20Countries%20-%20Camila%20Duran_0.pdf

ECB 2022, *Central Bank liquidity lines*. European Central Bank. viewed 21 October 2022, https://www.ecb.europa.eu/mopo/implement/liquidity_lines/html/index.en.html

Eichengreen, B, Lombardi, D, & Malkin, A 2018, 'Multilayered governance and the international financial architecture: The erosion of multilateralism in international liquidity provision', *Global Policy*, vol. 9, no. S1, pp. 7–20.

Eren, E, Schrimpf, A, & Sushko, V 2020, 'US dollar funding markets during the covid-19 crisis – the money market fund turmoil', *BIS Bulletin*, viewed 21 October 2022, https://www.bis.org/publ/bisbull14.pdf

Federal Reserve 2008, *Meeting of the Federal Open Market Committee on october 28–29, 2008*. The Federal Reserve of the United States. viewed 21 October 2022, https://www.federalreserve.gov/monetarypolicy/files/FOMC20081029meeting.pdf

Federal Reserve 2020a, *Federal Reserve announces establishment of a temporary fima repo facility to help support the smooth functioning of financial markets*. United States Federal Reserve. viewed 21 October 2022, https://www.federalreserve.gov/newsevents/pressreleases/monetary20200331a.htm

Federal Reserve 2020b, *Swap lines FAQS*. United States Federal Reserve viewed 21 October 2022, https://www.federalreserve.gov/newsevents/pressreleases/swap-lines-faqs.htm?utm_source=npr_newsletter&utm_medium=email&utm_content=20200420&utm_term=4531919&utm_campaign=money&utm_id=8005577&orgid=554

Federal Reserve 2021, *FIMA repo facility FAQS*. United States Federal Reserve Bank viewed 21 October 2022, https://www.federalreserve.gov/monetarypolicy/fima-repo-facility-faqs.htm

Ferreira, FHG 2021, 'Inequality in the time of Covid-19', *Finance & Development*, vol. June viewed 25 October 2022, https://www.imf.org/external/pubs/ft/fandd/2021/06/pdf/inequality-and-covid-19-ferreira.pdf

Fritz, B, & Mühlich, L 2019, 'Regional financial arrangements in the global financial safety net: The Arab monetary fund and the Eurasian fund for stabilization and development', *Development and Change*, vol. 50, no. 1, pp. 96–121.

Gallagher, KP, Gao, H, Kring, WN, Ocampo, JA, & Volz, U 2021, 'Safety first: Expanding the global financial safety net in response to Covid-19', *Global Policy*, vol. 12, no. 1, pp. 140–48.

GAO 2011, 'Federal reserve system: Opportunities exist to strengthen policies and processes for managing emergency assistance', viewed 25 October 2022, https://www.gao.gov/assets/gao-11-696.pdf

Georgieva, K 2020a, *Confronting the crisis: Priorities for the global economy*. IMF. viewed 20 October, https://www.imf.org/en/News/Articles/2020/04/07/sp040920-SMs2020-Curtain-Raiser

Georgieva, K 2020b, 'Policy action for a healthy global economy', *IMF Blog*, vol. 2022, no. 20 October 2022, viewed 25 October 2022, https://www.imf.org/en/Blogs/Articles/2020/03/16/blog031620-policy-action-for-a-healthy-global-economy

Georgieva, K 2020c, *Transcript of press briefing by Kristalina Georgieva following a Conference call of the International Monetary and Financial Committee*. IMF. viewed 21 October 2022, https://www.imf.org/en/News/Articles/2020/03/27/tr032720-transcript-press-briefing-kristalina-georgieva-following-imfc-conference-call

Georgieva, K, & Malpass, D 2020, 'Joint statement from managing director, imf and president, world bank group', *IMF Press Release* viewed 20 October 2022, https://www.imf.org/en/News/Articles/2020/03/02/pr2076-joint-statement-from-imf-managing-director-and-wb-president

Ghosh, AR, Ostry, JD, & Tsangarides, CG 2012, 'Shifting motives: Explaining the buildup in official reserves in emerging markets since the 1980's', *IMF Working Papers*, viewed 21 October 2022, https://www.imf.org/en/Publications/WP/Issues/2016/12/31/Shifting-Motives-Explaining-the-Buildup-in-official-Reserves-in-Emerging-Markets-Since-the-25683

Gourinchas, P-O, Rey, H, & Sauzet, M 2019, 'The International Monetary and Financial System', *Annual Review of Economics*, vol. 11, no. 1, pp. 859–93.

Grabel, I 2019, 'Continuity, discontinuity and incoherence in the Bretton Woods order: A Hirschmanian reading', *Development and Change*, vol. 50, no. 1, pp. 46–71.

Hardie, I, & Maxfield, S 2016, 'Atlas constrained: The US external balance sheet and International Monetary Power', *Review of International Political Economy*, vol. 23, no. 4, pp. 583–613.

Hardie, I, & Thompson, H 2021, 'Taking Europe seriously: European Financialization and US Monetary Power', *Review of International Political Economy*, vol. 28, no. 4, pp. 775–93.

Hawkins, A, Rahman, J, & Williamson, T 2014, 'Is the global financial safety net at a tipping point to fragmentation?', *Economic Roundup*, vol. Issue 1, https://treasury.gov.au/publication/economic-roundup-issue-1-2014/economic-roundup-issue-1/is-the-global-financial-safety-net-at-a-tipping-point-to-fragmentation

Helleiner, E 2014, *The status quo crisis: Global financial governance after the 2008 meltdown*, Oxford University Press, New York.

Herrero, AGa, & Ribakova, E 2020, 'Covid-19's reality shock for external-funding dependent emerging economies', *Bruegel Policy Contribution*, vol. 10, viewed 22 October 2022, http://hdl.handle.net/10419/237646

ILO 2020, *ILO monitor: Covid-19 and the world of work. Sixth* edition. ILO. viewed 20 October, https://www.ilo.org/wcmsp5/groups/public/---dgreports/---dcomm/documents/briefingnote/wcms_755910.pdf

IMF 2009a, *IMF implements major lending policy improvements*. International Monetary Fund. viewed 20 October 2022, https://www.imf.org/external/np/pdr/fac/2009/032409.htm

IMF 2009b, *IMF survey: G-20 reaffirms IMF'S central role in combating crisis*. International Monetary Fund. viewed 20 October 2022, https://www.imf.org/en/News/Articles/2015/09/28/04/53/sonew040309a

IMF 2016, 'Adequacy of the global financial safety net', *IMF Policy Papers*, https://www.imf.org/en/Publications/Policy-Papers/Issues/2016/12/31/Adequacy-of-the-Global-Financial-Safety-Net-PP5025

IMF 2020, *IMF executive board approves the extension of increased access limits under the rapid credit facility and rapid financing instrument.* International Monetary Fund. viewed 20 October 2022, https://www.imf.org/en/News/Articles/2020/10/05/pr20305-imf-executive-board-approves-extension-increased-access-limits-under-rcf-and-rfi

IMF 2021a, *Extended fund facility (EFF)*. International Monetary Fund. viewed 20 October 2022, https://www.imf.org/en/About/Factsheets/Sheets/2016/08/01/20/56/Extended-Fund-Facility

IMF 2021b, *Flexible credit line (FCL)*. International Monetary Fund. viewed 20 October 2022, https://www.imf.org/en/About/Factsheets/Sheets/2016/08/01/20/40/Flexible-Credit-Line#:~:text=The%20Flexible%20Credit%20Line%20(FCL,countries%20facing%20a%20cash%20crunch

IMF 2021c, *World economic outlook: Managing divergent recoveries*. https://www.imf.org/en/Publications/WEO/Issues/2021/03/23/world-economic-outlook-april-2021

IMF 2022a, *Chile Receives IMF's first short-term liquidity line*. International Monetary Fund. viewed 20 October, https://www.imf.org/en/News/Articles/2022/05/20/pr22164-chile-receives-imfs-first-short-term-liquidity-line

IMF 2022b, *Introduction to the IMF*. International Monetary Fund. viewed 20 October, https://www.imf.org/external/np/exr/center/mm/eng/mm_intro.htm

IMF 2022c, *Short-term liquidity line (SLL)*. International Monetary Fund. viewed 20 October 2022, https://www.imf.org/en/About/Factsheets/Sheets/2020/04/17/short-term-liquidity-line

James, H 1996, *International monetary cooperation since Bretton woods*, Oxford University Press New York.

Jeffery, C 2020, *James Bullard on the Fed's policy review, FSOC and forecasting jobs data*. Central Banking. viewed 21 October 2022, https://www.centralbanking.com/central-banks/financial-stability/7668906/james-bullard-on-the-feds-policy-review-fsoc-and-forecasting-jobs-data

Jones, C, & Kaminska, I 2020, 16 March 2020, 'Why fx swap lines are the most important fed action thus far', *The Financial Times*. https://www.ft.com/content/6a9f9653-5a5e-46a0-9995-c608d74523d6

Kentikelenis, A, Stubbs, T, & Reinsberg, B 2022, 'The IMF and the road to a green and inclusive recovery after Covid-19', *Cambridge Centre for Business Research (CBR) Special Report*, viewed 20 October 2022, https://www.repository.cam.ac.uk/handle/1810/338625

Kentikelenis, AE, Stubbs, TH, & King, LP 2016, 'IMF conditionality and development policy space, 1985–2014', *Review of International Political Economy*, vol. 23, no. 4, pp. 543–82.

Liao, S, & McDowell, D 2015, 'Redback rising: China's bilateral swap agreements and renminbi internationalization', *International Studies Quarterly*, vol. 59, no. 3, pp. 401–22.

McCauley, RN, & Schenk, CR 2020, 'Central Bank swaps then and now: Swaps and dollar liquidity in the 1960s', *BIS Working Papers*, vol. 851, https://www.bis.org/publ/work851.htm

McDowell, D 2012, 'The US as "sovereign international last-resort lender": The Fed's currency swap programme during the great panic of 2007–09', *New Political Economy*, vol. 17, no. 2, pp. 157–78.

McDowell, D 2017, *Brother, can you spare a billion? The United States, the IMF, and the international lender of last resort*, Oxford University Press, New York.

McDowell, D 2019a, 'Emergent international liquidity agreements: Central Bank cooperation after the global financial crisis', *Journal of International Relations and Development*, vol. 22, no. 2, pp. 441–67.

McDowell, D 2019b, 'The (ineffective) financial statecraft of China's bilateral swap agreements', *Development and Change*, vol. 50, no. 1, pp. 122–43.

Mehrling, P 2015, 'Elasticity and discipline in the global swap network', *International Journal of Political Economy*, vol. 44, no. 4, pp. 311–24.

Momani, B, & Helleiner, E 2007, 'Slipping into obscurity? Crisis and reform at the IMF', *Centre for International Governance Innovation Working Paper*, vol. 16, https://www.cigionline.org/publications/slipping-obscurity-crisis-and-reform-imf/

Mosser, PC 2020, 'Central Bank responses to Covid-19', *Business Economics*, vol. 55, pp. 191–201.

Mühlich, L, & Fritz, B 2018, 'Safety for whom? The scattered global financial safety net and the role of regional financial arrangements', *Open Economies Review*, vol. 29, no. 5, pp. 981–1001.

Murau, S, Pape, F, & Pforr, T 2022, 'International monetary hierarchy through emergency US-dollar liquidity: A key currency approach', *Competition & Change*, vol. Online first.

OECD 2020, *Covid-19 and global capital flows*. OECD. viewed 20 October 2022, https://www.oecd.org/coronavirus/policy-responses/covid-19-and-global-capital-flows-2dc69002/

Pape, F 2022, 'Governing global liquidity: Federal Reserve swap lines and the international dimension of US Monetary Policy', *New Political Economy*, vol. 27, no. 3, pp. 455–72.

Patel, UR. (2017, October 15, 2017). 'Financial regulation and economic policies for avoiding the next crisis', in *32nd Annual G30 International Banking Seminar Inter-American Development Bank, Washington, D.C.* https://www.bis.org/review/r171024c.pdf

Perks, M, Rao, Y, Shin, J, & Tokuoka, K 2021, 'Evolution of bilateral swap lines', *IMF Working Paper Series*, viewed 21 October 2022, https://www.imf.org/en/Publications/WP/Issues/2021/08/06/Evolution-of-Bilateral-Swap-Lines-463358

Prasad, ES 2014, *The dollar trap: How the U.S. dollar tightened its grip on global finance*, Princeton University Press, Princeton, NJ.

Sahasrabuddhe, A 2019, 'Drawing the line: The politics of federal currency swaps in the global financial crisis', *Review of International Political Economy*, vol. 26, no. 3, pp. 461–89.

Scheubel, B, & Stracca, L 2019, 'What do we know about the global financial safety net? A new comprehensive data set', *Journal of International Money and Finance*, vol. 99, p. 102058.

Segal, S 2020, *Dollar swap lines: Welcome support but only part of the solution*. Center for Strategic and International Studies. viewed 21 October 2022, https://www.csis.org/analysis/dollar-swap-lines-welcome-support-only-part-solution

Strange, S 1994, *States and markets*, Pinter Publishers, London.

Stubbs, T, Kring, W, Laskaridis, C, Kentikelenis, A, & Gallagher, K 2021, 'Whatever it takes? The global financial safety net, Covid-19, and developing countries', *World Development*, vol. 137, p. 105171.

The Economist 2020, 'The successes of the Fed's dollar-swap lines', *The Economist*, viewed 25 October 2022, https://www.economist.com/finance-and-economics/2020/06/18/the-successes-of-the-feds-dollar-swap-lines

Tooze, A 2018, *Crashed: How a decade of financial crises changed the world*, Allen Lane, New York.

UNCTAD 2020, 'The Covid-19 shock to developing countries: Towards a "whatever it takes" programme for the two-thirds of the world's population being left behind', viewed 21 October 2022, https://unctad.org/system/files/official-document/gds_tdr2019_covid2_en.pdf

Volz, U 2016, 'Toward the development of a global financial safety net or a segmentation of the global financial architecture?, *Emerging Markets Finance and Trade*, vol. 52, no. 10, pp. 2221–37.

Weder di Mauro, B, & Zettelmeyer, J 2017, 'The new global financial safety net: Struggling for coherent governance in a multipolar system', *CIGI Essays in International Finance*, vol. 4, no. January https://ssrn.com/abstract=2946452

WHO 2022, *Who coronavirus (covid-19) dashboard.* viewed 20 October https://covid19.who.int

World Bank 2020, *Covid-19 to add as many as 150 million extreme poor by 2021.* World Bank. viewed 10 October, https://www.worldbank.org/en/news/press-release/2020/10/07/covid-19-to-add-as-many-as-150-million-extreme-poor-by-2021

World Bank 2022, *World development report 2022: Finance for an equitable recovery*, World Development Report, Issue. https://openknowledge.worldbank.org/bitstream/handle/10986/36883/9781464817304.pdf

5 Public Banking for a Public-Financed Post-pandemic Transition: A Proposal for a New Public Bank System in Spain

Jorge Garcia-Arias, Nuria Alonso, Eduardo Fernández-Huerga and David Trillo

Introduction

The twenty-first century has seen three consecutive international events which have had a significant impact on the world's economic and financial stability: the subprime crisis and the subsequent sovereign debt crisis; the economic collapse caused by the COVID-19 pandemic; and, more recently, the invasion of Ukraine. Although different in essence, all have affected the world (and Spanish) economy with no time to consolidate an economic and social recovery in between.

Commercial banks suffered a credit crunch following the 2008 crash and they did not only exhibit their difficulties for self-regulation (before 2008), but also their need for public bailout (in the form of bank restructuring processes, liquidity facilities provided by central banks, or an intensification of funding streams from public banks).

These crises have not only exposed failures in the management of financial risks; they are also an example of how governments implemented bank-rescue policies at the expense of the taxpayers. Meanwhile, the financial restructuring process has resulted in a smaller number of financial entities with more market power, which has led to a higher systemic risk, a considerable staff and office reduction, and an increase in bank fees.

On the other hand, the COVID-19 crisis has highlighted the advantages of public banks (Barrowclough et al., 2020), including their rapid response and their capacity to comply with mandates concerning collective well-being, supply liquidity at reduced interest rates and under preferential reimbursement conditions, and profit from public-public partnerships – for instance, in relation to sovereign wealth funds and public pension funds. In addition, public banks apply financial sustainability policies and criteria that are different from those implemented by private commercial banks.

Regarding their financial capacity, Cull et al. (2017) estimate that public banks proper manage a total of USD 5 billion in assets. Other works – which consider that all financial institutions are public when the State owns more than 50% of their shares, and they are governed by public mandate and subject to public law

DOI: 10.4324/9781003323280-6

(public banks, multilateral banks, pension and sovereign wealth funds, and central banks) – estimate that public banks manage assets that are worth USD 48 billion (Marois, 2021).

The classical discussion on the role, functions, and good (or evil) nature of public banks has been reactivated in the last decades, with two opposing perspectives emerging (Marois, 2021): the '(orthodox) political' and the '(heterodox) developmental' views, both with a clear political component. The first one (La Porta et al., 2002; Frigerio & Vandone, 2020), built on mainstream neoliberal economics, argues that public banks are used by politicians and bureaucrats to pursue their own interests and exert their influence on voters, as well as to generate inefficiencies and create a breeding ground for corruption and underdevelopment. The second one (Andrianova et al., 2012; Duprey, 2015) rests on (development) political economy foundations, and considers that public banks have a very important role in providing the funding that private banks cannot or will not contribute (i.e. infrastructures), in achieving certain socio-economic objectives, and in stabilising the economy and reducing the intensity of the crises (with counter-cyclical policies).

However, from an 'anti-essentialist and dynamic' point of view, the most important aspect of public banks, beyond their form of ownership, is how they carry out their financial activity in relation to the 'structural confines of gendered, racialized, and class-divided capitalist society' (Marois, 2022: 357).

Judging public banks for their behaviour and institutional functions, rather than for their attributes (public vs. private), is especially important in relation to the financialisation, shadow-banking, and market-based finance taking place at a global level. In effect, there is an ongoing debate in the literature about the emergence (or not) of a 'hidden investment state' (Mertens & Thiemann, 2019). The debate is taking place regarding various political geographies but especially in the case of the EU (Mertens et al., 2021), where an apparent confluence of the interests of the European Investment Bank (EIB) – as multilateral development bank of the Union – and the national development banks (NDBs) of the member states, would have (re)activated a policy that would aim at fuelling investment in some key sectors – and theoretically also promoting some socio-economic goals that would go beyond a mere (post-) Keynesian counter-cyclical policy and closer to an 'industrial policy' –, either by channelling their own funds or, more usually, by leveraging resources from other actors, mainly private.

The agency of those 'public development banks' (both the EIB and the NDBs) would have increased during the period following the 2008 crisis, and also with the boost, from 2014 onwards, generated by the Juncker Plan and its European Fund for Strategic Investments (EFSI), which is one of the pieces of the neoliberal and financialised machinery designed to implement a 'capital markets union' (CMU) whose fundamental objective is to promote market-based finance and so-called 'market-based banking', that is, shadow-banking in other words (Braun et al., 2018).

While the European Commission has been the key promoter of this CMU, both the European Central Bank (ECB) and the EIB have played a key role (Engelen & Glasmacher, 2018). Moreover, Mertens and Thiemann (2018) show how the relationships between the CMU, the EFSI, the EIB, and the NDBs have actually fostered a state-led 'financial innovation', mainly in sectors related to infrastructure and financing for small- and medium-sized enterprises (SMEs) that, beyond the goodness of the objective of stimulating European economies on the demand side – in a context of flagrant failure to meet the objectives set to combat the ecological and civilisational crisis which climate change highlights –, has fostered a process of implicit 'securitisation' as an instrument for the achievement of macroeconomic objectives. The implications are severe because, as Braun et al. (2018: 118) point out: 'While facilitating coordination between public and private financial actors, this off-balance-sheet approach to public investment (…) transforms governments into risk managers in the service of private-sector investors'. And, as Griffith-Jones and Naqvi (2020: (1) point out in relation to the role of the EIB, the NDBs, and the EFSI, their financial operations are 'too generous for private investors [and] has in some cases generated excessive "financial risk"'.

In that context, our chapter justifies the implementation of a public bank system in Spain as one of the necessary (and feasible) measures to face the severe (economic and social) consequences of the above-mentioned crises, particularly of the COVID-19 pandemic, but also as an alternative to other NDBs models proposed in Europe (which will contribute to create a financialised and neoliberal framework).

Public banks need not maximise their profit as private banks, but neither can they be conceived as decentralised cash transfer management units, because that is the role of public administration budgets. There needs to be a return on their investment, although the timing and amount of it should not be conditioned by market profitability objectives. Moreover, public banks may contribute to an equitable, solidarity-based, and convivial management of social and political economy objectives for the whole country.

Additionally, it is worth considering whether the credit policy of public banks can generate effects on inflation and reduce the effectiveness of monetary policy. Lima and Setterfield (2010) describe positive variations in prices after contractionary shocks ('price puzzles') that would derive from higher financial costs passed on to consumers by companies that set prices as a surcharge on costs. In this sense, monetary policy faces the dilemma of having to reduce inflation at the expense of production. However, Passos and Modenesi (2021) point out that 'policies promoted by public banks, which increase the maturity of loans and the stability of credit rates, can improve the general objectives of monetary policy in times of financial fragility', so there would be no relevant consequences for the financial stability objectives of the central bank.

The rest of this chapter is organised as follows. In the next section, the differential impact of the pandemic on the Spanish economy is presented. We then examine both the evolution and the current situation of public banks in Spain, before describing some of the key elements of our proposal for a new public bank system in Spain. The chapter ends with some final considerations.

The COVID-19 Crisis in Spain

The outbreak of the COVID-19 pandemic has had worldwide devastating consequences not only on people's health but also on the economy. Particularly, the temporary standstill of most economic sectors or the enforcement of restrictions on movement and gatherings had a direct impact on production and employment, interrupted the supply chains, and led to a strong supply shock. On the other hand, income fall, uncertainty, lockdowns, mobility restrictions, and social distancing had heavy repercussions on consumption and investment that resulted in a demand shock (Chaves Ávila, 2020; De la Fuente, 2021; Hidalgo Pérez, 2021).

Effects of the Crisis in Spain

Some of the factors mentioned, in addition to provoking a global crisis, generated differential impacts in Spain.

Impact on Production

Spain is among the countries whose economic activity has most intensely suffered the consequences of the pandemic: it was the third OECD country with the largest GDP drop during the second quarter of 2020, only behind the United Kingdom and Mexico (OECD, 2022). In 2021, the recovery only involved a 5.1% increase of the GDP, lower than the 5.5% average of all OECD countries (OECD, 2022).

Additionally, the fall in production affected the various production industries and sectors very differently. In 2020, the GVA of the 'Hospitality' sector decreased by 50%, that of 'Artistic, recreational and entertainment activities' by 34%, 'Transportation and storage' by 26%, 'Other services' by 20%, 'Administrative activities and auxiliary services' by 18%, and 'Professional, scientific and technical activities' by 14% (INE, 2022a).

The geographical distribution of the fall has also been uneven because of the production specialisation of each Spanish region and the unequal mobility restrictions imposed by regional governments.

The sharp decline of the GDP occurred despite the implementation of public policies focused on protecting businesses (in addition to employment) and preventing irreversible damage to the production capacity (De la Fuente, 2021). In this sense, the main aim was to respond to the firms' liquidity needs.

For this purpose, in addition to measures intended to postpone the payment of certain taxes and social contributions, EUR 100 billion was initially made available in the form of public guarantees meant to support financial institutions in providing firms and self-employed workers the cash flow required to face their payments. Moreover, the net indebtedness limit initially established by the *Instituto de Crédito Oficial* (ICO) – the only Spanish national public bank –, was increased by EUR 10 billion to provide additional liquidity to the firms, especially to SMEs and self-employed workers. To this, we should obviously add the measures adopted by the European Central Bank (ECB) to inject liquidity into the financial system in order to facilitate access to funding for the real economy. Among these measures, one of those that has had the greatest impact has been precisely the acceptance of loans partially guaranteed by the ICO as collateral for participation in Eurosystem refinancing operations by counterparties (Escolar & Yribarren, 2021).

Impact on the Labour Market

The fall in production was directly reflected on the labour market: the number of employed persons decreased by 1,074,100 between the second quarter of 2020 and the first one of 2021 (INE, 2022b). Unemployment was very unevenly distributed, with temporary workers, most vulnerable groups (women, young people, migrant workers), and economic sectors with greater difficulties in implementing teleworking bearing the largest part of the adjustment.

In any case, the employment adjustment has been less intense than the one carried out during the 2008 crisis, despite the fact that the GDP drop was not as sharp back then. Public policies seem to have significantly contributed to it, especially the possibility of implementing so-called '*expedientes de regulación temporal de empleo*' (ERTE, temporary labour force adjustment schemes) to cushion the impact of COVID-19. These ERTE relieved the firms from the obligation of paying social security contributions and acknowledged the workers' right to receive a contributory unemployment benefit. They have proved useful to preserve the employment relationship, to enable firms to reduce their labour costs and to maintain the income level of the workers affected (De la Fuente, 2021). In addition, an 'extraordinary benefit' was established for self-employed workers who were forced to cease their business activities during the pandemic.

Unemployment data show that the adjustment has been smaller than during the 2008 crisis: the unemployment rate, which had followed a decreasing trend before the pandemic and was at 13.78% during the last quarter of 2019, increased to 16.26% in the third quarter of 2020. However, the activity rate was significantly affected, being 58.74% in the last quarter of 2019 and 55.54% in the second quarter of 2020.

Impact on Inequality, Poverty, and Social Exclusion Levels

The pandemic has brought about increased inequality in most economies across the world (IMF, 2020). In Spain, the problem was aggravated by the initial inequality and poverty levels, which were already higher than those of other countries in Europe. According to the *Survey on Income and Living Conditions* (Eurostat, 2022), the Gini coefficient applied to the equivalised disposable income was 32.1 in 2020 in Spain, which was the sixth highest figure for all EU-27 countries. The AROPE social exclusion indicator shows that in 2020 there were 12,658,000 people in Spain living under poverty and social exclusion conditions (27% of the population).

Although the official statistics do not yet reflect the actual impact of the pandemic on the inequality and poverty levels, the first studies carried out in Spain seem to indicate that the crisis has affected the most vulnerable groups more intensely and caused an increase in those levels (Cáritas, 2020; Fundación FOESSA, 2022).

More than in other countries in the region, public transfers have played in Spain a significant role in softening the impact of the crisis, particularly in the lower part of the income distribution (Cantó et al., 2021; Gómez Bengoechea, 2021). As mentioned before, the Government implemented a series of policies aimed at maintaining family incomes and protecting the most vulnerable households. Moreover, the so-called '*ingreso mínimo vital*' (basic minimum income) was launched, a new social security benefit designed to eradicate extreme poverty and promote social inclusion and the participation in the labour market of persons in vulnerable situations. To this, several other measures destined to protect vulnerable households were implemented: mortgage moratoriums, security of the water and energy supply, or establishment of a guarantee line to provide funding to tenants with difficulties. Nevertheless, the channelling of these benefits corresponded to various administrations that were already overloaded with work before the pandemic, a reality that slowed down the process and hindered the efficient management of the benefits.

Additional Impacts

The pandemic has increased the deterioration of public finances: the increase in expenditure and the fall in income pushed public deficit up to 10.95% of the GDP in 2020 (2.87% in 2019), while public debt picked up to 119.95% of the GDP (95.54% in 2019).

Outside the strictly economic sphere, the pandemic has had additional consequences for two central areas: education and health. It has made explicit a triple gap in the educational system (Mañas Alcón et al., 2021): in access to ICT equipment; in use, due to differences in digital competencies; and between educational centres (public vs. private, and according to their geographical location).

Secondly, the pandemic, the lockdown, and social distancing have affected the (physical and mental) health of many people – due to loss of healthy eating and exercising habits, situations of stress, anxiety –, and have resulted in the neglect of patients with other diseases and in increasing waiting lists (Mañas Alcón et al., 2021; Pinilla Domínguez & González López-Valcárcel, 2021).

Causes of the Differential Impact of the Crisis in Spain

Spain is one of the developed countries where the pandemic has had a greater impact. Multiple reasons may explain this fact. Firstly, the sectoral specialisation of the Spanish economy (Garrido Yserte & Mancha Navarro, 2021). The measures adopted in most countries to combat the effects of the pandemic mostly focused on those sectors considered to be essential, those where mobility or direct social contact cannot be avoided, and those that involve gatherings – tourism, hospitality, transportation, non-essential commerce, personal services, artistic and entertainment activities, etc. The scale of the impact in Spain is related to the relevance that these sectors have in its production structure (Gómez & del Río, 2021), especially because of the centrality of tourism.

Another factor associated with the production structure that explains the differences in the GDP drop among countries is the capacity to implement teleworking. Before the pandemic, Spain was among the countries with the lowest percentage of remote workers (Chaves Ávila, 2020), because it had less jobs capable of being performed online and because it was less prepared for teleworking under lockdown circumstances (Palomino et al., 2020).

An additional factor is the existence of many SMEs within its production structure, which tend to have a more limited financial capacity to face this type of shocks.

The second motive behind the differential effects of the pandemic in Spain is connected to the intensity of the healthcare crisis and the severity of the containment measures implemented. In terms of deaths by number of inhabitants, Spain has been one of the countries most affected. Partly in response to this, measures adopted by the authorities were very stringent. If we observe the Oxford Severity Index (OSI), the indicator for Spain was over 60 points from March 2020 to June 2021 – except for two brief periods –, which places the country among the middle- to top-ranking positions in the world in terms of the stringent policies implemented (Blavatnik School of Government – University of Oxford, 2022).

Various studies have described the relationship between the rigorousness of the mobility restrictions and the fall of the production activity (Gómez & del Río, 2021; Hidalgo Pérez, 2021). Symmetrically, the restrictions were connected to the country's production structure (Battistini & Stoevsky, 2021) in the sense that the impact of those measures was larger where the influence of sectors like commerce, transportation, hospitality, artistic and entertainment activities, etc. was stronger, since those sectors were more elastic to variations in the restriction measures. Both factors, which were very intense in the Spanish case, increased the harshness of the pandemic's impact on the Spanish production structure.

The Need for a Post-pandemic Public Bank System

In the current context of successive crises, strongly aggravated by the pandemic, the debate on the need of a public bank system with ample capacity for action has been revitalised.

'Public banking' may be defined in a broad way: 'A bank can be owned publicly – that is, by a government, public authority or public enterprise; or it can be controlled publicly – that is, governed according to a legally binding public interest mandate, or according to public law, or by meaningful public representation on the governing board, or by some combination of these governance factors. Either or both situate a bank within the public sphere and as a public financial institution' (Barrowclough et al., 2020). Given that the objective of this chapter is not to analyse the operational details or the differences between the various modalities of public banks, we will use the terms 'public bank', 'NDB', 'state-owned bank', or 'government-controlled bank' as equivalents, assuming an expanded definition of the concept as a financial institution that is controlled and mainly funded by a government body in the public interest, rather than by private investors.

The functions of public banks also comprise a wide range of activities, which may focus mostly on economic development – with special emphasis on supporting SMEs –, on exports, on development projects in other countries, etc. It can also have a determining role in the economic and social transformation of the country by channelling public investment or operating in a field that is usually controlled by commercial banks as deposit managers.

Public banks may be sub-national, regional, national, or multilateral institutions – such as the EU's EIB, the Inter-American Development Bank, or the Commonwealth Development Corporation. In the national sphere, the largest public banks are the Chinese ones, which control a total of USD 20.6 billion in assets (Marois, 2019). Among the most important public banks in the rest of the world, which accumulate USD 17 billion in assets, the KFW group in Germany and the State Bank of India, each with more than USD 0.5 billion in assets, must be mentioned. Other examples of large public banks – with assets valued in more than USD 400,000 million – are Sberbank in Russia, the Cassa Depositi e Prestiti in Italy, and the CDC-BPI Group in France.

Public banking can, potentially, perform many functions (Griffith-Jones & Ocampo, 2018; Romero, 2017):

a In times of economic instability, a public bank may counteract the procyclical behaviour of private funding – rationed during economic crises due to the inefficient functioning of the financial markets – by promoting credit (Stiglitz & Weiss, 1981).

 Under instability conditions, problems associated with asymmetric information lead commercial banks to tighten the requirements to access credit. They also cause increments in the risk premium and, consequently, in the cost of finance. As a result, the volume of credit in the financial system is reduced. Public banks may serve as a network that facilitates the recovery of funding by promoting public policies.

 Moreover, the need for public banks to finance SMEs has become more acute since the 2008 crisis. Despite the large increase in money supply and liquidity by the ECB, commercial banks did not significantly increase their financing to SMEs. The ECB (2013) pointed out that in view of the deterioration in the transmission of monetary policy, the European Commission and the EIB explored joint risk-sharing instruments that would combine the resources of the EU budget with the lending capacity of the EIB and the European Investment Fund to finance activities in priority areas of the EU. A good example of this has been the stabilisation policies that have provided credit to businesses during the COVID-19 crisis. Alonso and Trillo (2021) estimate the relative weight of loans and guarantees granted to companies during the pandemic by five public banks in Europe at between 8% and 17% of the GDP of each country analysed.

b Public banks may promote innovation and a change of domestic economic structure – or even at a global level through operations undertaken by multilateral banks.

Public funding is essential for the development of technological research and innovation activities, and may also contribute to the energy transition and to the process of decarbonisation of the economies (Mazzucato & Semieniuk, 2018; Polzin et al., 2021).

The Next Generation EU funds are a good example of public environmental investment policies, financed through the issuance of debt by the European Commission. The implementation of the national recovery and resilience plans associated with this mechanism would require the participation of NDBs.

c Public banks may finance the development of prioritised regions and economic sectors, investment in infrastructures, and exports.

Supporting domestic strategies for the development of specific economic sectors or geographical areas usually involves financing transportation, housing, education, or healthcare projects, as well as the remunicipalisation of common goods such as water (Garcia-Arias et al., 2022; McDonald & Marois, 2022). In addition, it can also be linked to changes in the production structure or to the funding of businesses, particularly SMEs. Likewise, public banks can invest in venture capital.

d They can improve financial inclusion and compensate for the imbalances in the supply or demand of credit that the private sector leaves unattended (Marois, 2021).

NDBs may become involved in rural financing when the markets remain incomplete, implement specific programmes aimed at funding gender-sensitive projects, or provide retail services, including low-fee deposit management.

e Public banks may also play a key role in financing for development in the global South.

The pandemic has exacerbated the needs for development finance; the additional financial needs of countries in the global South derived from the crisis are exceptionally high and will persist in the long term (World Bank, 2020). There are, additionally, cross-financing needs related to the Paris Agreement or the global New Green Pact (UNCTAD, 2019).

The role of public banks is also relevant at the present moment regarding governance, audit, and the financial and parliamentary control of institutions. NDBs may have some advantages in terms of governance, including the active involvement of civil society and of the bank's employees, and the creation of public channels of information about the bank's activities (Romero, 2017). They may also commit to an agreement to protect their management against 'undue pressure from the Government' that is contrary to the mandate of public banking. Finally, they may develop mechanisms to facilitate the participation of stakeholders or to perform independent external audits, as well as complaint procedures.

This may, at the same time, represent a weak spot for public banks since their work, and the very way in which they evolve, are the result of power struggles – inherent to capitalism – between opposing public and private interests (Marois & Güngen, 2016). It is important to take reality into consideration and the fact that markets, institutions, and economic actors may be sceptical in relation to the transformative potential of public policies and see private profit opportunities in their access to public institutions (Fernández-Huerga, 2008). Loans provided by state-owned banks cannot be a new tool for co-optation and/or corruption. It is essential that public banks operate according to professional criteria of accountability and transparency, that their internal financial control system is reinforced with democratic oversight, that they are audited and held accountable for the social efficacy of their credit policies.

On the other hand, the possibility that problems related to political influence may arise is not a good enough reason to claim that public banks are more inefficient than private ones – which are indeed affected by the same difficulties, as the 2008 crisis has made evident. For instance, Chen et al. (2016) analysed a sample of 2,655 banks from 56 countries between 2004 and 2010, and showed that the loans granted by government banks have grown at higher rates than those granted by private banks during the crisis, but also that in countries with low corruption levels the increase of public bank loans is associated with a better banking performance and a better economic recovery after the crisis.

The Spanish Public Bank System

The Evolution of Public Banking in Spain

The Spanish public bank system reached its peak during the 1970s and 1980s, although its history goes back to the end of the nineteenth century when a series of private sectoral banks were created. Those banks were subsequently nationalised as part of a bank reform implemented in 1962, after which they were known as '*entidades de crédito oficial*' (OCIs, official credit institutions). The new bank reorganisation that took place in 1971 included the creation of the *Instituto de Crédito Oficial* (ICO), which became responsible for coordinating and supplying the necessary funds for the OCIs to comply with their obligations in funding the corresponding economic sector.

In 1988, the ICO became a 'state agency' and took over the ownership of the shares representing the capital stock of the OCIs (Casado et al., 1995). However, the reform of the public bank system implemented in 1991 completely changed this structure of public sectoral banks – which allowed much space for intervention – with two main consequences. First, the *Corporación Bancaria de España* (CBE, Spanish Banking Corporation) was created as a public limited society, to be later on privatised. It was the head of a group that also included the *Caja Postal de Ahorros*, which did not belong among the former. The ICO remained independent and separate from the CBE, although no specific tasks were assigned to it at that time. The passing of Royal Decree-Law 12/1995 on urgent measures on budget, fiscal, and financial matters reinforced the ICO's characteristics as a credit entity and its capacity to initiate activities. It was recognised as a 'state financial agency' with the generic objective of 'sustaining and promoting economic activities that contribute to growth and to improving the distribution of national wealth and, in particular, promoting those activities that merit promotion because of their social, cultural, innovative or ecological importance'.

Since 1991, ICO has been the only national public bank in Spain. As such, it plays a central role in relation to the issues addressed in this chapter.

The ICO Nowadays

Currently, ICO's functions are almost the same that were established in the 1995 regulations (ICO, 2021):

1 As a *state financial agency*, it is responsible for performing the financial operations of the State, acting as a broker, billing the costs incurred to the State, and receiving a management fee for the interest rate differential.
2 As a *credit entity*, it is responsible for funding middle- and long-term productive investment projects carried out by firms and social economy organisations, in those financial areas that are considered necessary for the development of certain economic sectors or regions, without entering into competition with private commercial banks. These operations include (i) *direct operations*, for large companies; the ICO usually cofinances these operations with other financial entities in the form of syndicated loans, club deals, project finance, national or international guarantees, issuances in the primary bond market, corporate promissory notes, securitisations, etc.; (ii) *brokerage operations*, channelled through private banks – given that the ICO does not have commercial offices; the ICO provides the funding, while the private banks perform the identification and risk analysis of the beneficiaries, and determine whether the funding will be granted or not, which often causes inefficiencies in the transmission mechanisms; and (iii) *funding operations*, through venture capital funds designed to promote the creation and development of firms throughout the entire life cycle of investment.
3 As a *financial instrument of economic policy*, the ICO channels the various types of resources received from the EU, and collaborates with different public administration bodies to transfer those resources to the businesses to meet the objectives of economic and sectoral policies.

ICO's role after 1991 has been ancillary to the private bank system, partly because of its small size – it employs about 350 staff, and it only has one office in Madrid. The market share that the ICO has maintained over the last decades is about 2% (ICO, 2020), except in the years of the Great Recession, when the credit activity of the ICO greatly intensified to face the needs of both firms and regional and local administrations. The ICO swiftly reacted to the financial crisis by promoting counter-cyclical measures that were implemented between 2009 and 2012, and came together with significant increases in the funding of both the State and the CBE. However, after the crisis, the general funding obligations were drastically

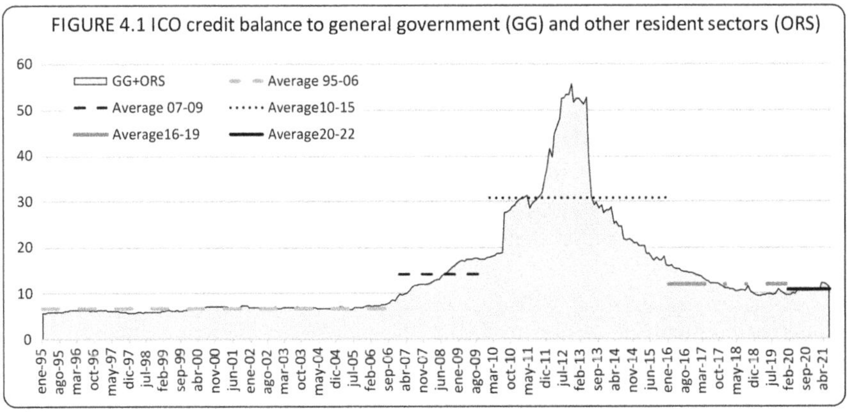

Source: Banco de España (Time series search engine) and own elaboration
http://app.bde.es/bie_www/faces/bie_wwwias/jsp/op/Home/pHome.jsp

Figure 5.1 ICO credit balance to central government and other resident sectors (ORSs)

Source: Banco de España (Time series search engine) and own elaboration http://app.bde.es/bie_www/faces/bie_wwwias/jsp/op/Home/pHome.jsp.

reduced and returned to pre-crisis levels, while the special funds became almost insignificant (Clifton et al., 2021).

Figure 5.1 shows the credit balance between January 1995 and February 2022, and how it behaved differently under economic stability conditions and during the different phases of the financial crisis. It also shows the return to the pre-crisis situation after 2019. In other words, the counter-cyclical capacity of public banks has not been sufficiently exploited.

However, in the crisis caused by the COVID-19 pandemic, the role of the ICO has been mainly supporting businesses, not by increasing its loans but through public guarantee programmes meant to ensure the firms' access to bank loans, thus transferring part of the credit risk and potential credit losses from the banks to the public sector. More specifically, the ICO established a guarantee line of up to EUR 140 billion (Cuadro-Saéz et al., 2020).

In summary, the ICO's activity as a public bank is hardly significant except during crises, when it has counterbalanced the contraction of the private banks' activity. This has reinforced its subsidiary and hardly proactive role, which is the result of its small size and the legal limitations to its autonomy, given that its strategic management as well as the assessment and control of the results of its activity are incumbent upon the Ministry of Economy (RDL 706/1999).

A Proposal for a Reorientation of Spanish Public Banking System

As mentioned before, the current public bank system in Spain is clearly insufficient. In fact, implementing our proposal would require an institutional structure that is currently non-existent. Also, the proposition counters the hegemonic view that favours a neoliberal and financialised public bank system. This view will probably articulate the foreseeable evolution of NDBs within the EU, which is based on a private-public collaboration model characterised by the complementariness with the commercial bank system and the development of shadow-banking and market-based banking, rather than on the provision of a public-public service that may contribute to a change in production or become an instrument to finance 'transitions' and encourage conviviality and social justice.

The main fields of action that we suggest for the public bank system in Spain are as follows:

a Increasing financial support to SMEs. In Spain, there are approximately 3 million SMEs, in contrast with 5,000 large corporations (Ministerio de Industria, Comercio y Turismo, 2021). It is therefore necessary to increase the funding of the production activities of those SMEs that the ICO is presently providing. Among them, digitalisation and the increase of the average size of the firms are essential to improve competitiveness and resilience to the economic cycle.

   The difficulties of Spanish's SMEs to obtain funding are still connected to the requirement of guarantees, high interest rates, and short repayment periods.

b Funding 'transitions', both in terms of energy and towards a sustainable and convivial urban planning (transportation, water, housing, remunicipalisations). All of them are necessary to respond to the climate emergency and the problems concerning justice, equality, and access to commons that the current civilisational crisis is deepening, including the threat of desertification, which is especially serious in Spain, or external fossil fuel-based energy dependence.

c Fighting rural depopulation. The rural-urban population drift is very intense in Spain; there are large rural areas where population density is lower than 10 inhabitants/km^2. It creates a vicious circle of loss of public (and private) services and depopulation that is an obstacle for the economic development of those regions. It limits productivity and hinders the incorporation of human and technological capital, as well as the development of innovative processes, the internationalisation of the firms' activities, or their access to funding (Consejo Económico y Social de España, 2021).

   The European Commission (2021) has asked its member states to seek the support of the EIB to compensate for current deficiencies of investment in rural areas. The connection between the EIB and the new NDB here proposed would therefore be well endorsed and generate positive synergies.

d Promoting financial inclusion and channelling savings. The difficulty to access financial services is a growing problem. Public banks may contribute to solving the problems of geographical exclusion and de-banking caused by the closing down of 50% of the private bank branches in Spain, especially in rural areas, by attracting liabilities in competition with private banks. They should also help avoid the widening of the 'digital divide' – due to lack of resources and digital management tools – and the exclusion from banking services of people whose profile is considered to be of high risk because of their low-income level (EAPN, 2021).

e Promotion of entrepreneurship among women and other groups underrepresented in the business sphere (migrants, rural population, aged people, etc.). This is a cross-cutting area that may contribute to improving effective equality.

 Here again, the synergies with the European public bank system are clear. For instance, the European Commission (2021) has pointed out that supporting women entrepreneurship in rural areas would help improve women's participation in the labour market and combat female depopulation.

f Improvement of development finance. As a state financial agency, the ICO manages the *Fondo para la Promoción del Desarrollo* and the *Fondo de Cooperación para Agua y Saneamiento*, which are instruments for Spanish cooperation for development. However, it could certainly play a more intense role as part of a systemic model of financing for development (Garcia-Arias, 2015).

It is important to note as well that, to the generic objective of promoting a new post-pandemic economic recovery and to improving the distribution of national wealth, particularly those that are socially, culturally, convivial or ecologically relevant, we must add the requirement that the firms that receive funding are respectful of labour rights, gender/age/ethnic equality, and environmental sustainability.

A public bank system that aims to develop the above-described activities needs a large operational structure – with offices, staff, etc. – that enables its functioning and avoids or minimises the intermediation of private banks in credit operations. This would require a network, the cost and implementation of which are a long-term challenge. Nevertheless, in the case of Spain, it could be possible to use the physical and administrative infrastructures that may be available in other public management entities. Firstly, regional public administrations have the capacity to channel funds for industrial, entrepreneurial, or rural development that favours a post-pandemic economic recovery and decent employment. Secondly, the 2,400 branches of the Spanish *Correos* (post office network) have traditionally provided financial services to the citizens, first through the *Caja Postal de Ahorros* (which joined the CBE in 1991) and subsequently through different collaboration agreements with private banks, which have been enhanced and expanded in recent years to compensate the closing down of bank branches, especially in rural and sparsely inhabited areas.

Additionally, the creation of a public bank system as the one here proposed requires well-trained and public-service-oriented professionals, a good financial risk management capacity, a well-designed corporate governance, and accountability mechanisms.

Final Considerations

The COVID-19 pandemic has further aggravated pre-existing problems affecting Spain's economic and social structure, which were exacerbated by the 2008 crisis, but had in fact been dragging on for decades. Among them, the high specialisation of the production structure and the differential functioning of the Spanish labour market – characterised by very high unemployment rates and a high level of temporary employment (Ferreiro & Serrano, 2001).

In addition, Spanish economy has very high levels of private sector indebtedness, mainly since the economic expansion prior to the 2008 crisis, which have affected the capacity of those agents to face the crisis (Garrido Yserte & Mancha Navarro, 2021). To this, we should add the indebtedness of the public sector after the 2008 crisis, which has also limited its capacity for action through fiscal policy in the face of the pandemic.

On the other hand, the austerity policies implemented from 2008 onwards caused the deterioration of the Spanish welfare state, mainly in the spheres of healthcare and education. Additionally, neoliberal policies reduced the redistributive capacity of the public sector, as witnessed by the increase of inequality and poverty, the intensification of regional imbalances in Spanish peripheral areas (depopulation, financial exclusion, reduction of public services), the lack of a policy that actually addresses the energy and sustainable urban planning transitions, or the shrinking financing for development.

The absence in Spain of a public bank acting as a true NDB has only aggravated these problems, hindering an efficient, homogeneous, equitable, and stable channelling of the funds necessary to modify the production structure, combat inequalities, poverty and social, gender and geographical exclusion, finance development, and address indispensable 'transitions'. Moreover, the activity of central banks and the effectiveness of monetary policy improve with the interaction with public banks, since they can focus on credit to SMEs and other economic sectors in stages in which the policy of reducing interest rates fails to achieve its goal of increasing lending activity.

Our proposition for a future public bank system in Spain aims to fill that gap by recommending the reconfiguration of the ICO or the *ex novo* creation of an institution that takes over some of the above-mentioned tasks and builds on a 'dynamic and non-essentialist' public bank model (Marois 2021, 2022), which, beyond its denomination, becomes a key driver for the funding of a more just, solidarity-based, feminist, convivial, and equitable post-pandemic economy, capable of facing the coming challenges without giving in to the temptation of promoting neoliberal and financialised mechanisms like the ones demanded by certain hegemonic groups within the EU.

Bibliography

Alonso, N, & Trillo, D 2021, 'La banca pública como instrumento de estabilización en la crisis del COVID-19', *Papeles De Europa*, vol. 33, no. 2, pp. 79–90.

Andrianova, S, Demetriades, P, & Shortland, A 2012, 'Government ownership of banks, institutions and economic growth', *Economica*, vol. 79, no. 315, pp. 449–69.

Barrowclough, D, Marois, T, & McDonald, D 2020, 'Public banks matter at a time of COVID-19' in D McDonald, T Marois & D Barrowclough (eds.) *Public banks and COVID-19 combatting the pandemic with public finance*, Municipal Services Project, UNCTAD and Eurodad, Kingston, Geneva and Brussels.

Battistini, N, & Stoevsky, G 2021, 'The impact of containment measures across sectors and countries during the COVID-19 pandemic', *ECB Economic Bulletin*, vol. 2.
Blavatnik School of Government – University of Oxford 2022, *Oxford COVID-19 Government Response Tracker*, accessed 28 April 2022, https://covidtracker.bsg.ox.ac.uk/.
Braun, B, Gabor, D, & Hübner, M 2018, 'Governing through financial markets: Towards a critical political economy of capital markets Union', *Competition & Change*, vol. 22, no. 2, pp. 101–16.
Cantó, O, Figari, F, Fiorio, CV, Kuypers, S, Marchal, S, Verbist, G, Romaguera-de-la-Cruz, M, & Tasseva, IV 2021, 'Welfare resilience at the onset of the COVID-19 pandemic in a selection of European countries: Impact on public finance and household incomes', *Review of Income and Wealth*, vol. 68, no. 2, pp. 293–322.
Cáritas 2020, 'La crisis de la COVID-19: el primer impacto en las familias acompañadas por Cáritas', *Observatorio de la Realidad Social*, no. 1.
Casado, JC, Campos, JD, & Chuliá, C 1995, 'La regulación financiera española desde la Adhesión a la Unión Europea', *Servicio de Estudios del Banco de España*, Working Paper no. 9510.
Chaves Ávila, R 2020, 'Crisis del COVID-19: Impacto y respuestas de la economía social', *Noticias De La Economía Pública, Social y Cooperativa*, no. 63, pp. 28–43.
Chen, Y-S, Chen, Y, Lin, C-Y, & Sharma, Z 2016, 'Is there a bright Side to government banks? Evidence from the global financial Crisis', *Journal of Financial Stability*, vol. 26, pp. 128–43.
Clifton, J, Díaz-Fuentes, D, García, C, & Lara Gómez, A 2021, 'Is a European "hidden investment state" emerging in Spain? The role of Instituto de Crédito Oficial', in D Mertens, M Thiemann & P Volberding (eds.) *The Reinvention of Development Banking in the European Union: Industrial Policy in the Single Market and the Emergence of a Field*, Oxford University Press, Oxford, pp. 199–223.
Consejo Económico y Social 2021, *Un medio rural vivo y sostenible*, Informes no. 02|2021, CES, Madrid. https://www.ces.es/documents/10180/5250220/Inf0221.pdf
Cuadro-Sáez, L, López-Vicente, F, Párraga, S, & Viani, F 2020, 'Fiscal policy measures in response to the health crisis in the main euro area economies, the United States and the United Kingdom', *Documentos Ocasionales del Banco de España*, no. 2019.
Cull, R, Martinez Peria, MS, & Verrier, J 2017, 'Bank Ownership: Trends and Implications', *IMF Working Paper*, WP/17/60, Washington, DC.
De la Fuente, A 2021, 'The economic consequences of COVID in Spain and how to Deal with them', *Applied Economic Analysis*, vol. 29, no. 85, pp. 90–104.
Duprey, T 2015, 'Do publicly owned banks lend against the wind?', *International Journal of Central Banking*, vol. 11, no. 2, pp. 65–112.
EAPN (European Anti-Poverty Network) 2021, *Inclusión financiera para el desarrollo sostenible: un enfoque de derechos en el proceso de reconstrucción post pandemia*, https://www.eapn.es/ARCHIVO/documentos/documentos/1637059788_estudio-exclusion-financiera_vfinal.pdf.
Engelen, E, & Glasmacher, A 2018, 'The waiting game: How securitization became the solution for the growth problem of the Eurozone', *Competition & Change*, vol. 22, no. 2, pp. 165–183.
Escolar, J, & Yribarren, JR 2021, 'Las medidas del Banco Central Europeo y del Banco de España contra los efectos del COVID-19 en el marco de los activos de garantía de política monetaria, y su impacto en las entidades españolas', *Documentos Ocasionales del Banco de España*, no. 2128.
ECB 2013, Small and medium-sized enterprises in the euro area: economic importance and financing conditions. *Monthly Bulletin* 07/2013.

European Commission 2021, *A long-term Vision for the EU's Rural Areas - Towards stronger, connected, resilient and prosperous rural areas by 2040*, https://ec.europa.eu/info/strategy/priorities-2019-2024/new-push-european-democracy/long-term-vision-rural-areas_en#documents.

Eurostat 2022, *European Union Statistics on Income and Living Conditions (EU-SILC)*, viewed 25 April 2022, https://ec.europa.eu/eurostat/data/database.

Fernández-Huerga, E 2008, 'The economic behaviour of human beings: The institutional/post-Keynesian model', *Journal of Economic Issues*, vol. 42, no. 3, pp. 709–26.

Ferreiro, J, & Serrano, F 2001, 'The Spanish labour market: Reforms and consequences', *International Review of Applied Economics*, vol. 15, no. 1, pp. 31–53.

Frigerio, M, & Vandone, D 2020, 'European development banks and the political cycle', *European Journal of Political Economy*, vol. 62, p. 101852.

Fundación FOESSA 2022, *Evolución de la cohesión social y consecuencias de la COVID-19 en España*. Fundación FOESSA, Colección de Estudios, 50, Madrid.

Garcia-Arias, J 2015, 'International financialization and the systemic approach to international financing for development', *Global Policy*, vol. 6, no. 1, pp. 24–33.

Garcia-Arias, J, March, H, Alonso, N, & Satorras, M 2022, 'Public water without (public) financial mediation? Remunicipalizing water in Valladolid, Spain', *Water International*, Vol, vol. 49, no. 5, pp. 733–750.

Garrido Yserte, R, & Mancha Navarro, T 2021, 'Principales consecuencias económicas de la COVID-19: Especial referencia al caso español', in FJ de la Mata, P Sánchez-Prieto Borja, E Senra Díaz, & MJ Such-Devesa (coord.), *COVID-19: Un enfoque plural*, Editorial Universidad de Alcalá, Madrid, pp. 241–268.

Gómez Bengoechea, G 2021, 'The impact of the COVID-19 crisis on income distribution under different protection schemes: The case of Spain', *Public Sector Economics*, vol. 45, no. 4, pp. 517–41.

Gómez, AL, & del Río, A 2021, 'El impacto desigual de la crisis sanitaria sobre las economías del área del euro en 2020', *Documentos Ocasionales del Banco de España*, no. 2115.

Griffith-Jones, S & Ocampo, JA, 2018, The Future of National Development Banks, Oxford University Press, Oxford.

Griffith-Jones, S, & Naqvi, N 2020, 'Industrial policy and risk sharing in public development banks. Lessons for the post-COVID response from the EIB and EFSI', *GEG Working Paper 143*, Global Economic Governance.

Hidalgo Pérez, MA 2021, 'El impacto económico del COVID-19 en España'. *Información Comercial Española, Revista De Economía*, no. 923, pp. 91–103.

ICO (2020): Integrated Report 2020, ICO's official webpage, accessed October 2020, https://www.ico.es/documents/77230/77289/Memoria+ICO+2020+EN.pdf/452ce043-b3da-8b0c-0e78-4af98145eefe?t=1628851014782

ICO 2022, *Presentación Institucional*, ICO's official webpage, accessed April 2022, https://www.ico.es/documents/20124/39529/ICO+Presentacion+Institucional+20221205.pdf/86894437-6acf-0711-c9fd-8d6a120577de?t=1670244116224

IMF 2020, *World economic outlook, October*, Washington D.C.

INE 2022a, *Contabilidad Nacional Anual de España: agregados por ramas de actividad*, accessed April 2022, https://www.ine.es/dyngs/INEbase/es/operacion.htm?c=Estadistica_C&cid=1254736177056&menu=resultados&idp=1254735576581.

INE 2022b, *Encuesta de Población Activa*, accessed 26th April 2022, https://www.ine.es/dyngs/INEbase/es/operacion.htm?c=Estadistica_C&cid=1254736176918&menu=resultados&idp=1254735976595.

La Porta, R, Lopez de Silanes, F, & Shleifer, A 2002, 'Government ownership of banks', *The Journal of Finance*, vol. 57, no. 1, pp. 265–301.

Lima, G, & Setterfield, M 2010, 'Pricing behaviour and the cost-push channel of monetary policy', *Review of Political Economy*, vol. 22, no. 11, pp. 19–40.

Mañas Alcón, E, Gallo Rivera, MT, & Fernández Olit, B 2021, 'España ante la COVID-19: Nuevas y viejas brechas sociales', in FJ de la Mata, P Sánchez-Prieto Borja, E Senra Díaz, & MJ Such-Devesa (coord.), *Covid-19: Un enfoque plural*, Editorial Universidad de Alcalá, Madrid, pp. 203–240.

Marois, T 2019, 'Public banking on the future we want' in L Steinfort & S Kishimoto, (eds.) *Public finance for the future we want*, Transnational Institute, The Democracy Collaborative, Change Finance, Focus on the Global South, New Economics Foundation, Fairfin, MOBA Housing Network & Tellus Institute, Amsterdam.

Marois, T 2021, *Public banks: Decarbonisation, definancialisation, and democratisation*, Cambridge University Press, Cambridge, MA.

Marois, T 2022, 'A dynamic theory of public banks (and why it matters)', *Review of Political Economy*, vol. 22, no. 2, pp. 356–71.

Marois, T, & Güngen, AR 2016, 'Credibility and class in the evolution of public banks: The case of Turkey', *Journal of Peasant Studies*, vol. 43, no. 6, pp. 1285–309.

Mazzucato, M, & Semieniuk, G 2018, 'Financing renewable energy: Who is financing what and why it matters', *Technological Forecasting and Social Change*, vol. 127, pp. 8–22.

McDonald, D, & Marois, T 2022, 'public banks, public water: Exploring the links in Europe', *Water International*, vol. 47, no. 5, pp. 673–690.

Mertens, D, & Thiemann, M 2018, 'Market-based but state-led: The role of public development banks in shaping market-based finance in the European Union', *Competition & Change*, vol. 22, no. 2, pp. 184–204.

Mertens, D, & Thiemann, M 2019, 'Building a hidden investment state? The European investment bank, national development banks and European economic governance', *Journal of European Public Policy*, vol. 26, pp. 23–42.

Mertens, D, Thiemann, M, & Volberding, P, (eds.) 2021, *The reinvention of development Banking in the European union: Industrial policy in the single market and the emergence of a field*, Oxford University Press, Oxford.

Ministerio de Industria, Comercio y Turismo 2021. *Retrato de la PYME. DIRCE a 1 de enero de 2021*. Dirección General de Industria y de la Pequeña y Mediana Empresa, Ministerio de Industria, Comercio y Turismo, Madrid.

OECD 2022, *OECD Stats. Key Short-Term Economic Indicators*, viewed 25 April 2022, https://stats.oecd.org/

Palomino, JC, Rodríguez, JG, & Sebastián, R 2020, 'Wage inequality and poverty effects of lockdown and social distancing in Europe', *European Economic Review*, vol. 129, pp. 103564, pp. 1–25.25.

Passos, N, & Modenesi, A 2021, 'Do public banks reduce monetary policy power? Evidence from Brazil based on state dependent local projections (2000–2018)', *International Review of Applied Economics*, vol. 35, no. 3–4, pp. 502–519.

Pinilla Domínguez, J, & González López-Valcárcel, B 2021, 'Impacto de la COVID-19 sobre la sanidad y la economía en España', *Ekonomiaz*, no. 100, pp. 42–59.

Polzin, F, Sanders, M, & Serebriakova, A 2021, 'Finance in global transition scenarios: Mapping investments by technology into finance needs by source', *Energy Economics*, vol. 99, p. 105281.

Real Decreto 706/1999, de 30 de abril, de adaptación del Instituto de Crédito Oficial a la Ley 6/1997, de 14 de abril, de organización y funcionamiento de la Administración General del Estado y de aprobación de sus Estatutos.

Romero, MJ. 2017, *Public development banks: towards a better model*, https://www.eurodad.org/public_development_banks_towards_a_better_model.

Stiglitz, J, & Weiss, A 1981, 'Credit rationing in markets with imperfect Information', *American Economic Review*, vol. 71, no. 3, pp. 393–410.

UNCTAD 2019. *Trade and Development Report 2019. Financing a Global Green New Deal*, accessed September 2020, https://unctad.org/en/PublicationsLibrary/tdr2019_en.pdf.

World Bank 2020, *World Bank Group Launches First Operations for COVID-19 (Coronavirus) Emergency Health Support, Strengthening Developing Country Responses*, accessed October 2020, https://www.worldbank.org/en/news/press-release/2020/04/02/world-bank-group-launches-first-operations-for-covid-19-coronavirus-emergency-health-support-strengthening-developing-country-responses.

6 The Political Economy of Asset versus Consumer Inflation

Christoph Scherrer and Nora Horn

Introduction

From the financial crisis of 2008 until the Russian attack on Ukraine in February 2022, monetary easing had become the norm. The world's major central banks had significantly softened the criteria for debt purchases. Accordingly, their balance sheets have inflated. The willingness to severely increase government debt, already shown during the financial crisis, has become even more pronounced in the pandemic. Even earlier in 2017, drastic tax cuts in the United States had massively increased its government debt. This change of course was driven by the Republican Party that had previously advocated monetary restraint and fiscal austerity. Even in the traditionally fiscally conservative Germany, an increase in government debt in response to the pandemic was carried out under a Chancellor from a conservative party. While the quantitative easing by the European Central Bank (ECB) was much criticized by prominent German economists, the German government tolerated the ECB's loose monetary policies. However, as consumer inflation has accelerated in 2022, calls for fiscal and monetary restraint have gained strength again in both countries.

How can these reversals of positions by parts of the public and politicians be explained?

Given the rather arcane subject of central banking and the relative independence of central banks from governments, public and private attitudes toward central bank policy may not be an important topic for the study of central banks. Yet, they do influence central bank policy and its effectiveness in several ways. The strongest public influence is through fiscal policy, which is in the hands of governments concerned about their reelection. The impact of central bank policy depends on whether fiscal policy supports or counteracts it (Del Negro & Sims 2014). As the recent discussion of anchored inflation expectations shows, central bankers need to consider the public's expectations about future inflation rates when making decisions about anti-inflationary policies (Corsello et al. 2021). Moreover, central bankers are not hermits. Depending on the specifics of their country's constitution, they may have to justify their actions to elected policymakers, and of course, they are in contact with expert audiences, usually composed of economists and financial market practitioners.

Our answer to the reversals of positions is based on a class-analytical perspective that highlights the differential distributional effects of asset and consumer

DOI: 10.4324/9781003323280-7

inflation by class. Loose fiscal and monetary policies may foster increases in asset values or consumer price inflation, or both, depending on circumstances. While higher consumer inflation affects significant portions of the population, whether they own assets or not, asset price inflation benefits those who already own assets and/or have access to cheap financing that allows them to buy assets on credit. Therefore, we hypothesize that the business community will generally support government spending, government debt and accommodative monetary policy if its members are the main beneficiaries and inflation is mainly confined to assets. If one or both conditions are not met, resistance is to be expected from at least large parts of the business community.

This makes the analysis of class interests an indispensable part of the explanation of changing attitudes toward expansionary economic policies. However, "class in itself" does not equal "class for itself". Ideological, cultural and individual differences influence class position. Therefore, we do not exclude other factors like deeply rooted systems of meaning-making on issues of fiscal and monetary policy. Therefore, our contribution examines the plausibility of this hypothesis using the example of United States and German attitudes toward the two types of inflation. Given the postwar tradition of widespread fear of inflation and the recent political mobilization against the ECB's low interest rate policy, the German case may contradict the hypothesis and support a cultural political economy perspective that emphasizes on a deep-seated concern about inflation independent of its actual occurrence.

The chapter is organized as follows. We begin with a brief characterization of financialized asset capitalism and continue with highlighting the differences in asset ownership between Germany and the United States. Next, we discuss the distributional effects of inflation. We commence with an introduction of a class perspective on inflation and continue to differentiate the distributional effects between consumer and asset inflation. An analysis of the societal attitudes toward inflation, distinguished for consumer and asset inflation, follows. The empirical part ends with a presentation of the position on inflation by businesses and central banks. We conclude with a reflection on the differences between Germany and the United States in their attitudes toward the different forms of inflation.

Financialized Asset Capitalism

As the phenomenon of asset inflation is a typical part of financialization, we want to highlight the financialized aspects of today's capitalism. Financialization is understood to mean the vastly expanded role of financial motives, financial markets, financial actors and financial institutions in the operation of domestic and international economies (Epstein 2005). Besides the significantly increased share of corporate profits by financial institutions (Krippner 2005), a conspicuous example of financialization is the securitization of loans taken out for the purchase of assets such as homes, automobiles, and financial products. While traditionally such loans were held in banks until they were repaid, they are now sold as bundles to investors around the world. The degree of financialization varies among countries (Becker et al. 2016; Kaltenbrunner & Painceira 2018).

Our study focuses on the United States of America and the Federal Republic of Germany because their economies are financialized to different degrees. On both dimensions—financialization and asset holdings—the United States exceeds Germany. Therefore, the US is the more pronounced financialized country (Krippner 2005; Detzer et al. 2017; Jayadev et al. 2018). The balance of payment constraints of both countries are, however, comparably low which is insofar important since countries with strong constraints, mostly so-called developing countries, are likely to face a balance of payment crisis in case they pursue a strategy of externally funded public debt and loose monetary policies.

A key feature of a financialized economy is rising asset prices in an economic upswing. By the time the dot.com bubble burst in 2000, stock valuations had risen significantly. In the years leading up to the great financial crisis of 2008, real-estate prices had risen massively. These rising asset prices had macroeconomic effects. Already in 2000, Barry Bluestone pointed out the role of rising stock prices for what he called the "Wall Street model" of economic growth. As owners of stocks feel wealthier, they would spend more. This extra spending would lead to higher output, investment, and employment. The precondition for rising asset prices is a low inflation environment allowing for low interest rates (Bluestone 2000). While direct stock ownership is limited to a small group of citizens (even in the United States only 15%; see below), homeownership is much more widespread. Therefore, when the prices for real estate accelerated in the early 2000, the wealth effect and, thereby, its contribution to economic growth was much more pronounced. Not only the demand for homeownership but also the possibility of homeowners refinancing their mortgages at lower interest rates, thereby increasing their purchasing power, is driving economic growth. As ordinary homeowners have a higher propensity to consume goods and services than investors in stocks, the impact of overall demand is even higher than in the "Wall Street model" (Schwartz 2008, p. 268). The role of real estate in economic growth has led Adkins et al. (2020) to coin the term asset economy for those countries, where homeownership is prevalent. A key driver for real-estate appreciation was the financial innovation of securitizing mortgages besides low interest rates. For the critic of the "Wall Street model", Bluestone, the financialized asset economy is crisis-prone. The financial crisis of 2007/8 has given credence to this critical assessment.

Nevertheless, the hegemony of finance capital survived the financial crisis; it diminished in the United States only slightly. Indicators of its hegemony, as in the Gramscian definition of a mixture of coercion and consent, are its support by the business community, the political class, its penetration into the everyday lives of citizens as measured by their debt levels for housing, education, health, and consumer goods, as well as the prevalence of the capital-based pension system. Except for the immediate aftermath of the financial crisis, no broad popular challenges to the position of finance capital have taken place (Scherrer 2011, 2015). The somewhat less pronounced position of finance capital in Germany can be explained by the presence of a significant public and cooperative banking sector, the comparatively higher number of family-owned businesses (Lehrer & Celo 2016), the pay-as-you-go public pension system, the comprehensive public health insurance and tuition-free higher education (Beck et al. 2005). The financial crisis of 2007/8

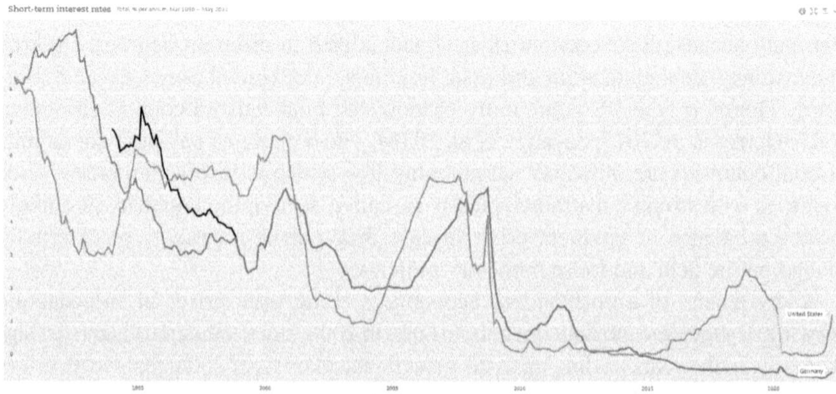

Figure 6.1 Short-term interest rates, Germany and USA, % per annum, March 1990 to May 2022

Source: https://data.oecd.org/interest/short-term-interest-rates.htm.

weakened the German private banking sector. Correspondingly, the role of foreign investment banks and institutional investors, especially from the United States, increased (Nienhüser et al. 2016).

In their response to the financial crisis, the Federal Reserve System (the Fed) as well as the ECB initiated a new round of asset price appreciations with their ultra-loose monetary policies (Figures 6.1 and 6.2), providing the financial actors with

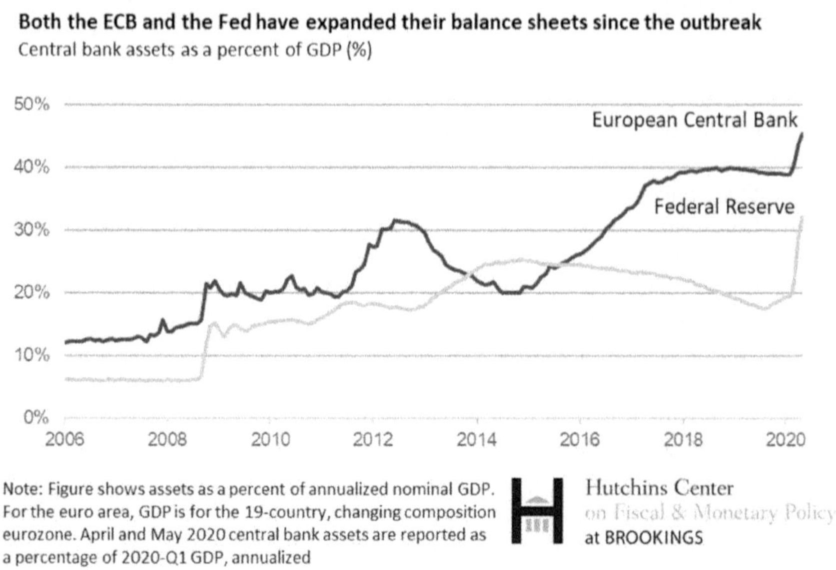

Figure 6.2 ECB and Fed Bank Assets as a percent of nominal GDP

Source: https://www.cmegroup.com/insights/economic-research/2022/fx-in-focus-as-central-bank-policies-diverge.html.

huge liquidity which found its way less into investment for new facilities to produce goods and services and more into different asset classes (Jayadev et al. 2018).

Varieties of Asset Capitalism: United States–Germany

Not only does the extent of financialization between the United States and Germany differ, but also the spread of asset holding. The question is whether these differences explain variations in the attitudes toward economic policies in the two countries. We therefore look at asset holdings that are more widespread in the United States than in Germany. While before the financial crisis of 2008, about 60% of adult Americans owned stocks, according to Gallup surveys, it declined, thereafter, to 55% in 2020. Most of them own stock through their retirement accounts; only 15% own stock directly. For households with a yearly income of more than $100,000, direct ownership of stock is very prevalent (84%); only 22% of those below $40,000 own stock.[1]

In Germany, stock ownership is less prevalent. In 2020, 9.9% of households owned stocks (Suhr 2020). The primary reason for this is that tax-exempted retirement accounts do not allow investments in stocks, but only in funds. Accordingly, ownership of mutual fund shares is more widespread: it increased from 20% in 2014 to 28% in 2021.[2] Another reason is that the generational cohort having the highest net wealth in Germany and comprising persons between 51 to 64 years, seem to be especially skeptical toward stocks. Two-thirds of them consider it to be too risky.[3] Ordinary Germans continue to entrust a significant share of their savings to the low interest bearing savings accounts (the savings account is still the most used form of financial investment by a large margin; Suhr 2020).

Besides the skeptical attitude toward stock ownership, it is limited not the least by institutional factors. Unlike the United States, the German pay-as-you-go retirement system is not complemented by tax exempted 401(k) retirement savings and investment plans that allow investments into stocks. These 401(k) plans have greatly expanded the group of persons owning stocks in the United States. There is a minuscule German equivalent, the so-called Riester pension. Its rules exclude direct investment in stocks, they allow only contributions to investment funds (which amount to about 16% of the overall Riester funds in 2018).[4]

In the United States, the homeownership rate of occupied units declined to 65.4% in 2021, somewhat from the high point of 69.1 before the financial crisis.[5] In Germany, the homeownership rate of occupied housing is considerably lower but slightly growing: from 45.7% in 2010 to 46.5% in 2018 (Statistisches Bundesamt et al. 2021: 262). Again, the German pay-as-you-go retirement system also lowers the propensity to own real estate. Instead of paying for a mortgage during the time of employment to avoid paying rent at old age, the contribution of employed persons to the state pension system is comparatively higher (9.3%)[6] in Germany than that paid in the United States (6.2%; 2022).[7] While the pension contributions leave less disposable income for paying a mortgage, for most retired persons they provide a sufficiently high pension to pay rent for housing. However, the proportion of tenant households with at least one member older than 65 years shouldering a rent burden of more than 30% of their household income increased sharply from 38% in 1996 to 63% in 2016 (Romeu Gordo et al. 2019, p. 468).

Another factor limiting homeownership is the comparably high transaction costs of acquiring a home (4.5% in Germany versus 1.9% in the United States for property/mortgage acquisition of total cost, Schwartz 2008, p. 271)[8] and the more prudent lending standards common among lenders.

Drivers of Inflation

What drives inflation is a controversial issue (Minsky 2008, p. 2; Boissay et al. 2022, pp. 3–4). We take the view that consumer inflation is primarily driven by supply bottlenecks and/or monopolistic market structures. When demand outstrips supply, it is easy for sellers of goods and services to increase the prices of the goods or services. Companies dominating the market can also increase prices in a situation when demand is not stronger than supply. The median markup can go up, as it has in the last decade (Boissay et al. 2022, p. 3). Demand can outstrip supply when wages rise quicker than productivity in a situation of full employment and/or the volume of credit expands faster than supply. The degree of indebtedness depends not only on the level of the interest rate and perceived future prospects but also on institutional factors such as the rules governing access to credit for public bodies, corporations, and households.

Through their policies on interest rates, refinancing conditions, and lending practices, central banks can influence the availability of credit and thereby inflation indirectly. The expansion of the money base faster than production does not necessarily show up as consumer inflation. The additional money can flow into assets that are not part of the consumer basket or into luxury items which are underrepresented in the consumer basket (Schnabl 2015, p. 255).

Furthermore, central banks' exchange rate policies can also influence the level of inflation. Government policies such as wage suppression, fiscal restraint, rigorous antitrust enforcement, and opening borders for goods and migrant labor may dampen inflationary trends, while opposite policies may foster inflation. In other words, many factors must be considered for any analysis of the movement of consumer prices.

Asset inflation is driven by some of these factors, but not all. Assets differ from consumer products by being less reproducible, either by their natural characteristics or actors' decision, and in the main more durable. Building houses takes time and may be limited due to the scarcity of land. Mining gold takes a lot of effort as well. Of course, being less reproducible is not a sufficient condition for being deemed to be a storage of wealth. Time-honored conventions of owning one's home and finding gold attractive secure the social demand for these assets and, thereby, sustain their exchange value beyond their use value. Financial assets such as stocks, bonds, and derivative contracts can not only be reproduced and multiplied easily but also kept in short supply. Their attractiveness depends on the income they are expected to generate and/or the expectation that they will gain in value because many other persons will also buy these assets that are limited by their issuers. In light of the recent cryptocurrency boom, anything can become an asset as long as a sufficient number of people believe that it might function as a store of wealth.

Again, institutional factors influence the price of these assets. Looking at homes, policies such as zoning laws (which limit the number of units that can be built in a given territory), building codes, and infrastructural investments influence their supply. On the demand side, immigration and natalist policies, tax incentives, as well as credit access conditions have an impact on the demand for homeownership among other factors.

Besides the mentioned institutional factors, asset prices are also moved by monetary policy. Loose monetary policies, while intended to stimulate the productive economy, may accelerate investment in real estate and financial products. This has been the case in the aftermath of the financial crisis (Jayadev et al. 2018).

Asset prices and consumer prices are not completely independent of each other. Rising asset prices can stimulate consumer demand through the wealth effect described above. Inflation of consumer prices may incentivize the flight into real estate and other assets deemed to gain in value over time.

A Class Perspective on Inflation

In their work on asset economy, Adkins et al. (2021) differentiate social classes along the line of asset ownership. They argue "that employment and wage-based taxonomies of class are no longer adequate for understanding a process of stratification in which capital gains, capital income, and intergenerational transfers are preeminent" (Adkins et al. 2021, p. 548). In determining life chances, the ownership of assets seems to be more important than employment. Beyond the dichotomy of ownership and non-ownership, they differentiate among the homeowners between those who are investing in real estate, those who own the house outright, and those who have taken out a mortgage to own a home. The group of those who do not own homes are separated in those who are renters and those who are homeless. This analytical class perspective on "class in itself" is a good starting point for theoretical considerations about the interests of these classes. However, one should be careful about any claims concerning the positions that are actually taken by members of these classes. Whether such a "class in itself" transforms into a "class for itself" (Marx 1847, pp. 180–181) remains an open question in search of empirical evidence. In other words, the following deductive reasoning about these classes' interests on monetary issues needs to be complemented by an analysis of the positions taken by organized interests and in randomized surveys.

Distributional Effects of Consumer Inflation

The main economic schools differ in their assessment of the effects of expansive monetary policies. While from a neoclassical perspective, inflation is to be the expected outcome, Keynesian-inspired new central banking thinking comes to the opposite conclusion—that without expansive monetary policies, deflation will occur in an environment of not fully utilized capacities (Williams 2009).

The distributional effect depends on the way the extra liquidity is being spent. If it is used for productive investments, then its benefits might spread throughout the economy. If the additional liquidity fuels asset inflation, then asset holders will be the main beneficiaries.

While galloping inflation is considered to be detrimental to economic growth by all economic paradigms, the Keynesian school views moderate consumer inflation as growth-enhancing (Herr 2009). From that perspective, moderate inflation, in principle, is beneficial for employment seekers. Nevertheless, even moderate inflation can be harmful to the economic well-being of some parts of the population. The negative impact of inflation on households depends on the degree to which household income and assets adjust to inflation. Those living on fixed nominal wages, pensions, transfers, or interests on bonds, will see their purchasing power declining. Owners of companies that cannot pass on higher input costs to consumers will equally lose out in real terms (Jayadev et al. 2018).

The impact of consumer inflation on owners of assets depends on the type of asset. In case of cash balances or saving accounts with low interest rates, inflation diminishes the value of these assets. A common reaction is a shift to less liquid assets such as gold, stocks, and real estate. If such a shift occurs on a large scale, it will lead to an asset price inflation.

For the households servicing a mortgage, consumer inflation carries the risk of interest rate hikes. The extent of the risk depends on the conditions of the mortgage. Households, which have taken out a long-term mortgage with a fixed interest rate, are protected against nominal interest rate hikes for the period of fixed interest rate, as agreed upon. In case their income adjusts to inflation or even exceeds inflation, they may even profit from consumer inflation, as their nominally denominated debt diminishes in real terms. However, in contrast to Germany, adjustable interest rates are common in the United States, though their share of mortgages fluctuates considerably (Moench et al. 2010, p. 2). These mortgage holders will quickly see increased interest payments.

From these considerations of the distributional effects of consumer inflation one can deduct preferences in relation to consumer inflation. Among the homeowners, the ones servicing a flexible rate mortgage are most likely to be inflation averse. They will therefore not only join the ranks of those with nominally fixed incomes but also financial institutions which fear that consumer inflation outpaces their ability to adjust interest rates in compensation of the losses on the principal in real terms.

Distributional Effects of Asset Inflation

In case of rising asset prices, the "investing" households are better positioned to profit from the price rises as they can more easily realize the paper gains by selling their assets. The class of single-unit homeowners are less likely to sell the home in which they live. Even if they want to sell, they will register a profit only if they are not planning to buy another home which of course would also have become more expensive.[9] Because homes require maintenance, paper gains may be eroded by rising maintenance costs at or above the general rate of inflation. In case property taxes are calculated based on periodically assessed market values, as it is common in the United States (Bell & Kirschner 2009, p. 112), real estate inflation will cut into current purchasing power.

Nevertheless, one clear benefit of real estate inflation for homeowners exists, that is, access to a second mortgage becomes easier since the collateral for the mortgage, their home, turns out to be more valuable. They can use it for consumption purposes or for buying a second house as an investment or for their children. It thereby facilitates the intergenerational transfer of wealth. At the same time, it limits the access of the offspring of families not owning homes to real estate. The result is increased inequality in wealth. For mortgagors, real-estate inflation comes with another benefit. In case they can service their mortgage no longer, they are relieved of the anxiety of losing their home and, at the same time, be burdened by debt because they can repay the outstanding sum with the proceeds of having sold their home.

In the United States, the rising housing prices outstripped the usual median weekly earnings for the age group of 15–24 years at least since 1979 (Duarte & Schnabl 2018, p. 627). Thus, it is no surprise that homeownership rates are at 79.6% for those 65 years and older and only 37.8% for the ones under 35 (2021).[10] Households with a family income greater than or equal to the median family income display a homeownership rate of 78.9%; those with less than the median only 51.9%. The homeownership rate of the historically disadvantaged group of black Americans is also much lower at 44.6% than the non-Hispanic whites at 74.2%.[11] The record-low borrowing costs of the 2010s should have made homeownership more accessible for young persons and people of color. Instead, the low interest rates pushed up the prices of homes (Gopal 2021).

In Germany as in the United States, household wealth comes mostly in the form of real estate. Those owning real estate have a much higher individual net worth than those paying rent: 10 times as much for those who have repaid their mortgages, six times as much for those still burdened with a mortgage (Statistisches Bundesamt et al. 2021, p. 252). Falling numbers of first-time buyers, a rising age of first-time buyers, and an increase in the income of first-time buyers, indicate that as in the United States, young people in Germany too are not benefiting from the favorable financing conditions. This is partly due to the increase in equity requirements in proportion to the steep increases in purchase price (Voigtländer & Sagner 2019). Furthermore, ownership of significant real estate not for own use is limited to the ninth and tenth decile of net wealth ownership (Statistisches Bundesamt et al. 2021, p. 249).

Based on the Household Finance and Consumption Survey (HFCS) in the euro area of 2010, a study of the distributional effects of asset price inflation concluded that "the capital gains from bond price and equity price increases turn out to be concentrated among relatively few households, while the median household strongly benefits from housing price increases" (Adam & Tzamourani 2016).

In sum, asset inflation is beneficial for all those households who already own assets and their offsprings except those who face higher property taxation at nominal fixed incomes.

They are joined by the banks in their preference for asset inflation. Banks benefit from asset inflation in a couple of ways: higher loan volume, increased trading activities, more collateral for credit-financed speculation. All of this translates into earning more bonuses, while the losses are borne by the owners of their institutions or the taxpayers (Schnabl 2015, p. 257) or are absorbed by the central bank.

Economic growth driven by asset bubbles also increases tax revenues. This serves as an incentive for government not to rein in on bubbles (Schnabl 2015, p. 258). Workers and their organizations will also not oppose asset inflation as long as it leads to more employment. The bursting of an asset bubble leads, however, to restrictive fiscal policies with negative impact especially on wages in the public sector (Ibid., p. 264).

This deductive reasoning suggests a fairly broad coalition against consumer inflation and a not-so-less broad coalition tolerating asset inflation in the United States and Germany.

Societal Attitudes toward Consumer Inflation

Multiple factors influence people's attitudes toward inflation. Their objective class position, be it according to the Marxian or the above elaborated asset-related definition of class, maybe only one among other factors. A key determinant seems to be one's own experience whereby household expenditure items such as energy or transport whose use cannot be easily adjusted figure most prominently (Benford 2008, p. 153). As older people have experienced bouts of higher inflation, they are more likely to be apprehensive about inflation (Ehrmann & Tzamourani 2012). In most countries, the perception of inflation differs markedly from the officially registered inflation. Respondents to an international survey estimated the inflation rate up to three times higher than the one announced by the statistical offices. Exceptions are the highly educated and the people in managerial roles (European Commission 2009).

Distorted memories of the effects of high inflation (Haffert et al. 2021) and the inability to assess the inflation rate correctly indicate discursive influences on people's attitudes toward inflation. The way the media frames inflation seems to play an important role (Barnes & Hicks 2018). Elite consensus on inflation may contribute to widely shared frames on inflation in the media. While one finds a greater variety of views on inflation in the United States, in Germany, the parties in parliament share more or less an anti-inflationary stand in line with the Bundesbank (Howarth & Rommerskirchen 2013). The support for low inflation cuts across the political spectrum (ibid., p. 10). "Stability Culture" became deeply ingrained into the German political culture. The so-called "Wirtschaftswunder" of the 1950s and 60s in West Germany following the economic hardships and suffering during the hyper-inflations 1921–23 and the pent-up inflation 1936–48 was widely attributed to the ordo-liberal policies at the time of which low inflation was a core element (Kolinsky 1991). Therefore, there lies a certain continuity in the Stability Culture discourse that became present again in the course of the European Debt Crisis from 2009 onwards (Howarth & Rommerskirchen 2013).

Little data exists on attitudes toward inflation differentiated according to one's socio-economic status. An earlier study saw little relationship between inflation aversion and levels of income or education among US citizens over nearly four decades (Fischer & Huizinga 1982; confirmed by Aklin et al. 2022). Based on survey data from Eurobarometer between 2002 and 2009, Berlemann and Enkelmann determined that persons with a higher income and educational attainment are less likely to fear inflation than those with a lower income (2013, p. 5). However, for an earlier period of slightly higher inflation, an international survey revealed for 1996 that "a firm owner is about a fourth more likely to prefer anti-inflation to anti-unemployment policies" and that a person with a pro-business and anti-labor position was highly likely to be also averse to inflation (Jayadev 2008, p. 7). Unfortunately, the phrasing of the survey question posited inflation against unemployment. It is, therefore, to be expected, that those who were less likely to suffer from unemployment were more averse to inflation.

The long period of low inflation in both countries (see Figure 6.3) seems to have left an impact on the public's fear of inflation (Statistisches Bundesamt, 2022; U.S. Bureau of Labor Statistics, 2022). In Germany, inflation remained below the 2% level in 23 of the last 30 years (Statistisches Bundesamt, 2022, p. 5). Accordingly, in surveys between 2017 and 2021, the importance of fighting inflation in relation to other policy goals was ranked at the fourth place (ALLBUS 2018; European Commission 2021, p. 27). In the United States, till 2021, inflation was the most important problem for an insignificant number of respondents only (Gallup 2021). However, in March, 2022 this changed drastically. In the context of the COVID-19 pandemic and the first noticeable effects of the Russian war on Ukraine, the high

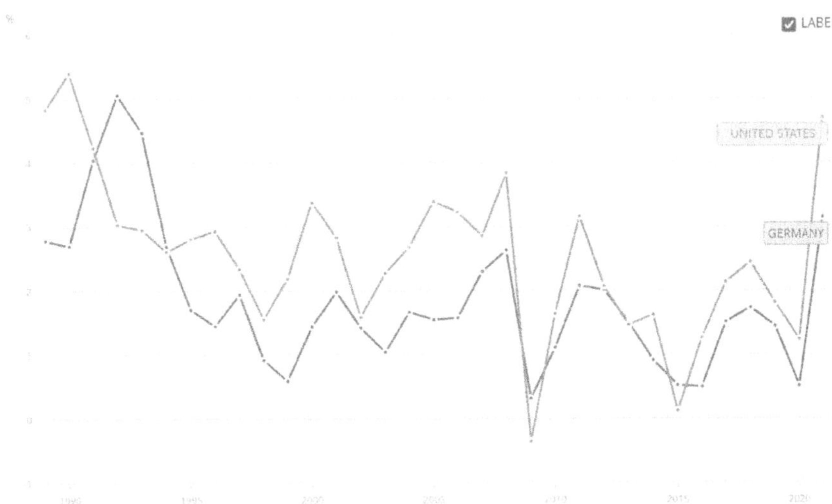

Figure 6.3 Consumer price inflation, annual percent, Germany and United States, 1989–2021

Source: https://data.worldbank.org/indicator/FP.CPI.TOTL.ZG?end=2021&locations=DE-US&start=1989&view=chart.

cost of living/inflation became the most important problem within the category of economic problems, mentioned by 17% of the respondents. Together with the rising fuel and oil prices (4%), roughly one in five Americans considered rising prices as the nation's top problem (Saad 2022). Even more pronounced were the inflation concerns of respondents to a German survey. From January, 2022 to March, 2022, the share of adult respondents becoming very concerned increased from 44% to 53%. In March, almost one in four respondents with a net monthly household income of less than EUR 2,500 said that inflation threatens their livelihood.[12]

Societal Attitudes toward Asset Inflation

Concern about asset inflation shows up in worries expressed with regard to the cost of housing. A survey in the metropolitan areas of the US revealed that 64% of the respondents were very concerned and 22% were somewhat worried about the cost of housing; this concern topped all others that were included in the 2021 survey. The degree of apprehension depended on income. Among the households with an income below US$50,000 per year, 53% rated the affordability of housing as very poor/poor versus 42% of those earning more than 150,000. The difference between these two groups is even more pronounced with respect to the rating "very good/ good": 23% under US$50,000 versus 39% above hundred US$50,000.[13] Younger Americans, urban residents, and those with lower incomes were naturally more likely to express concern about the availability of affordable housing in the survey by the Pew Research Center in October 2021.[14]

In Germany, the concern is more about the rising rents for housing than the prices for homes (Kohl et al. 2019; Thomsen et al. 2019). The increases in rents have benefited the top 10% of the income pyramid. Their rental income increased by 39% from 2010 to 2016 (Grabka et al. 2019). Nevertheless, there is also worry about ever more expensive real estate. A 2022 survey among 1,000 prospective real-estate buyers and purchasers revealed that for 65% of respondents, high real-estate prices act as a deterrent.[15] There seem to be no concerns about stock market appreciations in Germany as there is no recent literature on the issue, indicating lack of interest by those able to commission such surveys.

The Position on Inflation by Businesses and Central Bankers

We find a marked contrast between the position of businesses on consumer inflation and asset inflation. The recent rising consumer inflation has led to widespread warnings among representatives of businesses (Krugman 2022; Kröner 2022).

In contrast to previous bouts of consumer inflation (Lubik & Schorfheide 2004; Arestis & Chortareas 2006), the heads of the Fed and the ECB were very hesitant in acknowledging inflationary tendencies and the need to rein in on them (Dabrowski 2022). They were not quite sure about the origins of the inflationary tendencies. Some argued that the inflationary pressures resulted from supply constraints and, therefore, were a transient phenomenon. However, when confronted with loud warnings about the possibility of an entrenched inflation, the Fed reacted with significant increases of the federal funds rate (Smialek 2022). The ECB reacted more cautiously out of fear for the economic health of some member countries of the Eurozone. The ECB wanted to avoid a recurrence of the euro crisis (Schnabel 2022). Of course, the German Bundesbank had warned about inflationary prospects already a year earlier in its critique of the loose monetary policies (Weidmann 2021).

There are rational grounds to favor anti-inflationary policies. Businesses that cannot pass on higher input prices will experience a profit squeeze, which is compounded in case workers are able to defend their real wages. Money holders or holders of bonds with a longer maturity will also suffer losses (cp. Tooze 2022). Yet, these arguments do not explain the broad spectrum of support for such policies. Paul Krugman argues that the "monetary permahawks are motivated by politics—by the fear that flexible use of the printing press will give too much room for big government" (Krugman 2022).

The critique of asset inflation was much more muted, if at all existing. Famous is a dictum of the long-term chairman of the Fed, Alan Greenspan (1987–2006), that it is better to "clean up the mess" after the bursting of bubbles than to prevent asset price bubbles (Greenspan 1999). A former Director of Research at the Fed of New York, Stephen G. Cecchetti, together with a member of the Bank of England, Sushil Wadhwani, had argued already in the year 2000 in favor of adjusting a central bank's policy instruments to asset prices (Cecchetti et al. 2000, p. xix). Ben Bernanke defended in a much-cited article the policy of not responding to asset prices (Bernanke & Gertler 2001, p. 256). Five years later, in 2006, Bernanke assumed the chair of the Fed, where a few years later he had to clean up after the bursting of the housing price bubble in the United States.

Thus, except for some contrarians (short-sellers betting on falling prices and a few academics), neither financial actors nor corporate elites and central bankers were alarmed about the rising real-estate prices and stock market appreciations before the great financial crisis of 2007/8 (Remmel 2011, pp. 205–206; Brunnermeier & Schnabel 2016, p. 496).

After this crisis, central bankers became more attentive to the occurrence of asset price bubbles. A consensus developed that central banks must deal with asset price bubbles in the framework of macroprudential policies with such tools as margins, reserves, and credit limits (Blinder et al. 2017). Nevertheless, in their attempt to stabilize the financial markets and to avoid deflationary tendencies, the Fed and the ECB provided the markets with massive amounts of liquidity. It was no secret that much of that liquidity was funneled into various asset classes. While between 2009 and 2019 the S&P 500, the stock market index tracking the stock performance of 500 large companies listed on stock exchanges in the United States, increased by close to 400% and US housing prices by about 40%, the consumer price index rose only by 19%.[16]

Conclusion: Asset Holders Prefer Asset over Consumer Inflation

There are no major differences in attitudes toward the two variants of inflation in Germany and the United States. The differences are more a matter of degree. Concerning consumer inflation, the German public as well as the economic policy circles are less tolerant even though the negative experience with inflation was more pronounced in the United States in the late 1970s, i.e., in a period that was personally experienced by the generational cohort that continues to influence policy and public opinion. The specific German postwar discourse about the economic crisis in the interwar period may cast a long shadow. Yet, inflation adversity seems to be reinforced by a higher savings rate as well as a higher propensity to save in interest-bearing financial products that are more likely to lose in real terms by inflation.

Similarly, the German population, business community, and policymakers were less supportive of policies conducive for asset inflation. Both home and stock ownership are significantly more prevalent in the United States. Institutional factors limit asset inflation in Germany, most importantly the pay-as-you-go state-run pension system. On the one hand, it leads to significantly lower financial flows from households to pension funds investing in financial products, on the other hand, it lowers the propensity to own real estate. Attitudes toward inflation are more relaxed in the United States as asset inflation is beneficial for most households already owning assets and their offspring although there are also vast class differences within the US society.

Political culture remains salient for an explanation of the differences between the two countries concerning inflation attitudes. However, the influence of culture is difficult to measure. It also seems to be reinforced by institutional factors that lead to considerable differences in asset ownership. These differences need to be taken into consideration to explain the reversals of positions concerning government debt, monetary easing, and anti-inflation policies.

We showed that analytically, the differentiation between asset and consumer price inflation is necessary to make sense of changing attitudes and reactions toward inflation. Based on this distinction, we highlighted the importance of the different distributional effects of asset and consumer inflation, depending on class. This makes the analysis of class interests an indispensable part of the explanation of diverging (anti-)inflation policies. However, it is no less important for the understanding of class determined by ownership of assets as introduced in this paper that "class in itself" does not equal "class for itself". Ideological, cultural, and individual differences influence class position. Nevertheless, the persisting and eventually widening inequality highlights the essential role of central banks and their partisanship in class conflict which is connected to the differing attitudes and reactions of policymakers and the public toward consumer and asset inflation. Our analysis shows that class matters in making sense of central banking and political economy in general. Class is a question of both: ownership of assets and of production facilities.

Notes

1 https://www.visualcapitalist.com/how-many-americans-own-stocks/
2 https://de.statista.com/statistik/daten/studie/199639/umfrage/formen-der-geldanlage-der-deutschen/

3 https://www.handelsblatt.com/finanzen/anlagestrategie/trends/anlegerverhalten-warum-die-deutschen-angst-vor-aktien-haben/23918372.html?ticket=ST-4645813-xAUoTYtCyaJoUbMJOEud-ap6
4 https://de.statista.com/statistik/daten/studie/1256464/umfrage/beitraege-zur-riester-rente-nach-anbietertypen/
5 Quarterly Residential Vacancies and Homeownership, Second Quarter 2021, U.S. Census Bureau
6 https://www.deutsche-rentenversicherung.de/Rheinland/DE/Presse/Pressemitteilungen/2021/211208_rentenwerte.html
7 https://www.ssa.gov › policy › trust-funds-summary
8 Since 2008, transaction costs have increased faster than other building costs in Germany, especially the real estate transfer tax was significantly increased (Datenreport 2021: 266).
9 Exceptions apply: house flipping or moving to a bigger home with a new mortgage at lower interests.
10 Quarterly Residential Vacancies and Homeownership, Second Quarter 2021, U.S. Census Bureau
11 Quarterly Residential Vacancies and Homeownership, Second Quarter 2021, U.S. Census Bureau
12 Postbank/YouGov cited in https://www.business-on.de/hamburg/postbank-umfrage-die-inflation-kommt-in-der-mittelschicht-an.html
13 https://manhattan.institute/article/metropolitan-majority-the-survey-2
14 https://www.pewresearch.org/fact-tank/2022/01/18/a-growing-share-of-americans-say-affordable-housing-is-a-major-problem-where-they-live/
15 https://www.interhyp.de/ueber-interhyp/presse/studie-zur-leistbarkeit-wohneigentum-halten-viele-fuer-einen-unerreichbaren-traum.html
16 The differences between asset and "real economy" price movements are well illustrated by: https://www.investing.com/analysis/where-is-inflation-hiding-in-asset-prices-200406994

Literature

Adam, K & Tzamourani, P 2016, 'Distributional consequences of asset price inflation in the Euro', *European Economic Review*, vol. 89, no. 2016, pp. 172–192.

Adkins, L, Cooper, M & Konings, M 2020, *The asset economy*, Polity.

Adkins, L, Cooper, M & Konings, M 2021, 'Class in the 21st century – Asset inflation and the new logic of inequality', *EPA: Economy and Space*, vol. 53, no. 3, pp. 548–572.

Aklin, M, Arias, E & Gray, J 2022, 'Inflation concerns and mass preferences over exchange-rate policy', *Economics & Politics*, vol. 34, no. 1, pp. 5–40.

ALLBUS 2018, Variable report, *GESIS Studien*, Nr. 5270 (v2.0.0).

Arestis, P & Chortareas, G 2006, 'Monetary policy in the euro area', *Journal of Post Keynesian Economics*, vol. 28, no. 3, pp. 371–394.

Barnes, L & Hicks, T 2018, 'Making austerity popular: The media and mass attitudes toward fiscal Policy', *American Journal of Political Science*, vol. 62, no. 2, April 2018, pp. 340–354.

Beck, S, Klobes, F & Scherrer, C (eds) 2005, *Surviving globalization? Perspectives for the German economic model*, Berlin, Springer.

Becker, J, Ćetković, P & Weissenbacher, R 2016, 'Financialization, dependent export industrialization, and deindustrialization in Eastern Europe', in Cozzi, G, Newman, S & Toporowski, J (eds) *Finance and industrial policy: Beyond financial regulation in europe*, Oxford, Oxford University Press, pp. 41–64

Bell, ME & Kirschner, C 2009, 'A reconnaissance of alternative measures of effective property tax rates', *Public Budgeting & Finance*, Summer, pp. 111–136.

Benford, J 2008, 'Public attitudes to inflation and interest rates', *Bank of England Quarterly Bulletin*, vol. 2008, no. Q2, pp. 148–156.

Berlemann, M & Enkelmann, S 2013, ',Die „German angst "– inflationsaversion in ost- und Westdeutschland', *Ifo Dresden Berichtet*, vol. 20, no. 2, pp. 3–9.

Bernanke, BS & Gertler, M 2001, 'Should Central banks respond to movements in asset prices?, *The American Economic Review*, vol. 91, no. 2, pp. 253–257.

Blinder, A, Ehrmann, M, de Haan, J & Jansen, D 2017, 'Necessity as the mother of invention: Monetary policy after the crisis', *Economic Policy*, vol. 32, no. 92, pp. 707–755.

Bluestone, B 2000, 'The battle for growth with equity in the 21st century', *International Politics and Society*, 3.

Boissay, F, De Fiore, F, Igan, D, Pierres-Tejada, A & Rees, D 2022, 'Are major advanced economies on the verge of a wage-price spiral?' *BIS Bulletin*, vol. 53, no. 4 (May), Bank for International Settlements.

Brunnermeier, MK & Schnabel, I 2016, 'Central Banks at a crossroads: What can we learn from history?', New York, Cambridge University Press, pp. 493–562.

Cecchetti, SG, Gensberg, H, Lipsky, J & Wadhwani, S 2000, 'Asset prices and Central bank policy', *Geneva Reports on the World Economy*, vol. 2, CEPR.

Corsello, F, Neri, S & Tagliabracci, A 2021, 'Anchored or de-anchored? That is the question', *European Journal of Political Economy*, vol. 69.

Dabrowski, M 2022, 'Central banks have been too slow in responding to higher inflation', *Opinion*, vol. 6 (July), Brussels, Bruegel.

Del Negro, M & Sims, C 2014, 'When does a central bank's balance sheet require fiscal support?', *Staff Report*, No. 701, Federal Reserve Bank of New York, New York, NY

Detzer, D, Dodig, N, Evans, T, Hein, E, Herr, H & Prante, FJ 2017, *The German financial system and the financial and economic crisis*, Springer.

Duarte, P & Schnabl, G 2018, 'Monetary policy, inequality and political Instability', *The World Economy*, vol. 42, no. 2, pp. 614–634.

Ehrmann, M & Tzamourani, P 2012, 'Memories of high inflation', *European Journal of Political Economy*, vol. 28, no. 2, pp. 174–191.

Epstein, GA (ed) 2005, *Financialization and the world economy*, Cheltenham, U.K. Northampton, Massachusetts, Edward Elgar Pub.

European Commission 2009, *Eurobarometer 2009: Poverty and Social Exclusion, Social Services, Climate Change, and the National Economic Situation and Statistics*, vol. 72, no. 1, ZA no. 4975.

European Commission 2021, *Standard Eurobarometer 94 – Winter 2020–2021 – Public opinion in the European Union.*

Fischer, S & Huizinga, J 1982, 'Inflation, unemployment, and public opinion Polls', *Journal of Money, Credit and Banking*, vol. 14, no. 1.

Gallup 2021, *Most important problem*, https://news.gallup.com/poll/1675/most-important-problem.aspx

Gopal, P 2021, *First Time Homebuyers Are Getting Crushed in a Cutthroat US Housing Market*, https://www.bloomberg.com/news/articles/2021-09-29/home-prices-jump-american-dream-of-buying-a-house-is-getting-crushed

Grabka, MM, Goebel, J & Liebig, S 2019, 'Wiederanstieg der Einkommensungleichheit', *DIW Wochenbericht*, vol. 19, pp. 343–353.

Greenspan, A 1999, *Testimony of Chairman Alan Greenspan before the Committee on Banking and Financial Services*, U.S. House of Representatives, 22 July.

Haffert, L, Redeker, N & Rommel, T 2021, 'Misremembering Weimar: Hyperinflation, the great depression, and German collective economic memory', *Economics and Politics*, vol. 33, no. 3, pp. 664–686.

Herr, H 2009, 'The labour market in a Keynesian economic regime: Theoretical debate and empirical findings', *Cambridge Journal of Economics*, vol. 33, no. 10, pp. 949–965.

Howarth, D & Rommerskirchen, C 2013, 'A panacea for all times? The German stability culture as strategic political Resource', *West European Politics*, vol. 36, no. 4, pp. 750–770.

Jayadev, A 2008, 'The class content of preferences towards anti-inflation and anti-unemployment policies', *International Review of Applied Economics*, vol. 22, no. 2, pp. 161–172, DOI: 10.1080/02692170701880643.

Jayadev, A, Mason, J & Schröder, E 2018, 'The political economy of financialization in the United States, europe and India', *Development and Change*, vol. 49, pp. 353–374.

Kaltenbrunner, A & Painceira, JP 2018, 'Subordinated financial integration and financialisation in emerging capitalist economies: The Brazilian Experience', *New Political Economy*, vol. 23, no. 3, pp. 290–313.

Kohl, S, Sagner, P & Voigtländer, M 2019, 'Mangelware Wohnraum: Ökonomische Folgen des Mietpreisbooms in Deutschen Großstädten', *FGW-Studien: Integrierende Stadtentwicklung*, vol. *18*.

Kolinsky, E 1991, 'Socio-economic change and political culture in West Germany' in J. Gaffney & E. Kolinsky (eds), *Political culture, France and Germany*, Routledge, pp. 34–68.

Krippner, GR 2005, 'The financialization of the American economy', *Socio-Economic Review*, vol. 3, no. 2, pp. 173–208.

Kröner, A 2022, '"Gift für die Gesellschaft": Deutsche-Bank-Chef warnt vor Folgen der Inflation', *Handelsblatt*, 4 July.

Krugman, P 2022, 'The coming rage of the money hawks', *New York Times*, 27 May.

Lehrer, M & Celo, S 2016, 'German family capitalism in the 21st century: patient capital between bifurcation and symbiosis', *Socio-Economic Review*, vol. 14, no. 4, pp. 729–750.

Lubik, TA & Schorfheide, F 2004, 'Testing for indeterminacy: An application to U.S. Monetary Policy', *The American Economic Review*, vol. 94, no. 1, pp. 190–217.

Marx, K 1847, '*Das Elend der Philosophie*', *Marx-Engels- Werke*, vol. 4, pp. 63–182.

Minsky, HP 2008, *John Maynard Keynes*, McGraw-Hill.

Moench, E, Vickery, J & Aragon, D 2010, 'Why is the market share of adjustable-rate mortgages so low?' Federal Reserve Bank of New York, *Current Issues in Economics and Finance*, vol. 16, no. 8.

Nienhüser, W, Peetz, D & Murrayet, G 2016, 'Wem Gehören die Großen Unternehmen? Restrukturierung des Eigentums Während der Finanzkrise in Deutschland und den USA', *WSI Mitteilungen*, vol. 8, pp. 584–593.

Remmel, N 2011, 'Zwischen Selbstregulierung, Staat und Markt: Eine Systemische Perspektive auf Governance-Strukturen des Finanzsektors im Lichte der Finanzkrise 2007–2009' in Kessler, O (ed.), *Die Internationale Politische Ökonomie der Weltfinanzkrise*, VS Verlag, pp. 199–226.

Romeu Gordo, L, Grabka, MM, Alcántara, AL, Engstler, H & Vogel, C 2019, 'Immer Mehr ältere Haushalte Sind von Steigenden Wohnkosten Schwer Belastet', *DIW Wochenbericht*, vol. 86, no. 27, pp. 467–476.

Saad, L 2022, 'Inflation Dominates Americans' Economic Concerns in March', https://news.gallup.com/poll/391220/inflation-dominates-americans-economic-concerns-march.aspx

Scherrer, C 2011, 'Reproducing hegemony: US finance capital and the 2008 crisis', *Critical Policy Studies*, vol. 5, no. 3, pp. 219–247.

Scherrer, C 2015, 'Auspolierte Kratzer. Das US-Finanzkapital: Durch Mehr Regulierung Weiter Hegemonial?, *PROKLA. Zeitschrift Für Kritische Sozialwissenschaft*, vol. 45, no. 2, pp. 257–276.

Schnabel, I 2022, United in diversity – Challenges for monetary policy in a currency union, Commencement speech, Panthéon-Sorbonne University, Paris, 14 June.

Schnabl, G 2015, 'Die Gefährliche Missachtung der Vermögenspreisinflation. Zur Wirkungslosigkeit von Inflationszielen als Geldpolitische Regelmechanismen', *Leviathan*, vol. 43, no. 2, pp. 246–269.

Schwartz, H 2008, 'Housing, global finance, and American hegemony: Building conservative politics one brick at a time', *Comparative European Politics*, vol. 6, pp. 262–284.

Smialek, J 2022, 'Federal Reserve Takes Swing at Inflation With Largest Rate Increase Since 1994', *New York Times*, 15 June.

Statistisches Bundesamt (Destatis) 2022, *Preise – Verbraucherpreisindizes für Deutschland – Lange Reihen ab 1948*.

Statistisches Bundesamt (Destatis), Wissenschaftszentrum Berlin für Sozialforschung (WZB) & Bundesinstitut für Bevölkerungsforschung (BiB) (eds) 2021, *Datenreport 2021: Ein Sozialbericht für die Bundesrepublik Deutschland*, Wiesbaden.

Suhr, F 2020, '*Die Beliebtesten Geldanlagen der Deutschen*', https://de.statista.com/infografik/23656/die-beliebtesten-geldanlagen-der-deutschen/

Thomsen, SL, Vogt, D & Brausewetter, L 2019, 'Wohnungsmarkt und Wohnungspolitik in Deutschland: Situation und Optionen' in (eds) *Hannover economic papers (HEP)*, Leibniz Universität Hannover, Wirtschaftswissenschaftliche Fakultät, Hannover.

Tooze, A 2022, 'Why inflation and the cost-of-living crisis won't take us back to the 1970s', *The New Statesman*, 7 February.

Voigtländer, M & Sagner, P 2019, *Eine Analyse von Mieten und Wohnnutzerkosten für 401 Kreise*, Köln, IW-Gutachten.

Weidmann, J 2021, Geldpolitik und die Rolle der Notenbanken – ein Ausblick, Speech presented at Freundeskreis der Ludwig-Erhard-Stiftung, 01 July, Frankfurt, Bundesbank

Williams, JC 2009, 'The Risk of Deflation', *FRBSF Economic Letter*, no. 2009-12, Federal Reserve Bank of San Francisco.

7 The Effects of Institutional Independence on Initial Central Bank Responses to the COVID-19 Crisis

Ioannis Glinavos

Introduction

Has central bank institutional independence functioned as an asset, or did it inhibit initial economic policy responses to the COVID-19 pandemic? This chapter seeks to answer this question, by looking at responses to the COVID-19 emergency, focusing on the actions of central banks in the US, the Eurozone, and Britain. This presentation demonstrates how central banks used tools developed during the financial crisis of 2008 and adapted them alongside new ones to combat the economic whirlwind created by the pandemic. The chapter then reflects on the quality of integration of policy-making by monetary and fiscal authorities. The chapter argues that an unprecedented level of cooperation between monetary and fiscal authorities led to high policy coordination that had beneficial effects on the global economy as the crisis developed in the course of 2020. The chapter uses this conclusion to enquire whether independence is responsible for the positive outcomes or whether it acted as an impediment to improved outcomes. The conclusion reached is that independence, to say the least, did not inhibit effective response. The chapter then moves on to consider whether – because of what we experienced in 2020 – institutional independence is under threat (in the US, Eurozone, and the UK?). The conclusion is that dangers to independence from the actions taken during the pandemic are more theoretical than real. The commonality of interest between monetary and fiscal authorities means that there was no actual threat of subordination of central bankers to politicians, and such a threat may not emerge as their interests are likely to remain aligned for the near future. As the chapter demonstrates, the evils that independence was meant to fight, inflation and the command of economic policy by an electoral timetable were not present at the beginning of the pandemic. What was present however was the danger that real economic collapse, on a global level, would wipe away theoretical constructs faster that we could anticipate. The key message emerging from the chapter therefore is that monetary and fiscal policy will be intertwined in the post-pandemic world, even when that means that central banks become the permanent guarantors of liquidity to both private economic activity and the funders of public expenditures and state debts. (Is this the case for the US, Eurozone, and UK only?)

DOI: 10.4324/9781003323280-8

The chapter also addresses the question of whether monetary and fiscal policies are as distinct as theory suggests they are. It is argued here that despite oft-repeated arguments in favour of policy discretion for governments and independence for central banks, the boundaries between fiscal and monetary, demand and supply side are not as clear cut as economic textbooks suggest. In a contemporary setting where globally inflationary pressures were low, with interest rates also low, growth was subdued, and employment was high – at least on pre-pandemic data – one could argue that the relevance and importance of monetary policy are less than it used to be. Strict divides between policy domains, therefore, may need to be rethought, or reworked in practice, if not in theory. As in most areas of contention, crisis leads to change. Impetus for change came after the financial crisis of 2008 (Glinavos, 2013) and currently stems from the challenges of the COVID-19 pandemic (and the supply chain disruptions, shocks exacerbated by the war between Russia and Ukraine?). As the following discussion demonstrates, the pandemic necessitated coordinated responses from monetary and fiscal authorities, with fiscal measures and guarantees to liquidity and credit provision supporting central bank actions. This chapter examines how divides between monetary and fiscal policy, amongst central banks and governments, amid theory and practice stretch and adjust in crisis. The chapter draws from the experiences of the financial crisis to offer a reflection on the resilience of institutional arrangements and regulatory regimes during the pandemic. The aim is to reflect on whether the idea of central bank independence itself has been an asset to policymaking during the crisis of 2020, or an impediment, and also to enquire whether the institutional independence of central banks is being threatened – or is likely to be threatened – in the post-pandemic political economy.

Central Bank Response to the Pandemic

The split of monetary from fiscal policy became accepted, almost universally (Nordhaus, 1975:169), on the understanding that political control over monetary policy makes the business cycle dependent on the political-election timetable, with politicians trying to manipulate economic performance to gain short-term political gain. It is worth articulating the key distinction between monetary and fiscal policy more clearly before proceeding further. Fiscal policy and supply-side interventions are the premises of governments. Monetary policy is the domain of central banks. In the context of the pandemic-defined political economy we are discussing in this chapter, we can note that central banks, specifically in advanced economies, but also universally, reacted to COVID-19-induced disruption by deploying the full range of crisis tools stocked in their armouries. Initial responses to the crisis that enveloped the world in the spring of 2020 focused on ameliorating financial stresses and ensuring the continuation of the provision of credit to the real economy. Asset purchases also helped contain the costs of fiscal expansions by acquiring material share of public debt at the respective central banks. Similar patterns emerged in relation to the banks' prudential functions. In response to the pandemic, and perhaps in this instance unlike the experience of the financial crisis response as we will see later in the chapter, prudential policies adjusted to adopt a complementary role to that performed by fiscal and monetary authorities (Borio 2020).

There is little point in exalting the importance and impact of the pandemic on the world economy. All readers of this chapter will have experienced the personal, professional, and wider effects of this truly global phenomenon. Inevitably, uncertainty about economic activity caused by border shutdowns and national lockdowns, alongside myriad restrictions on personal movement and transactional capacity have created financial conditions that are similar and to a significant degree more dangerous than those prevalent during the financial crisis of 2008. The initial consequences of the pandemic on the real economy were unusually sudden and severe in many jurisdictions. For example, unemployment in the United States rose to levels reminiscent of the Great Depression (Casado et al, 2020). Although the causes of the COVID-19 crisis were quite unlike those of the financial crisis a decade ago, many of the consequences raised the same challenges. There was a marked flight to safer assets leading to many financial intermediaries shedding riskier investments and running towards government bonds. Responses to these challenges were also comparable. Central banks, however, were quicker off the mark and implemented solutions to the developing problems rapidly, benefiting from their hard-gained experience with unconventional policies after the events of 2008. Crucially, the current crisis was characterised by close cooperation between fiscal and monetary authorities, in ways that were not in evidence during the response to the financial collapse of 2008. The success of initial responses however carries within it several dangers. One particular concern is that the high degree of cooperation and coordination between monetary and fiscal authorities threatens to retain central bank independence in the post-pandemic world (Adrian, 2020).

What have central banks done in response to the pandemic? Central bankers alongside regulatory and prudential authorities have played a key role in shaping responses to the economic impacts of the pandemic, both in the immediate stabilisation phase in mid-2020 and subsequently. In the spring of 2020, the COVID-19 pandemic caused an economic crisis, impacting commercial and investment activity in equal measure (Adrian, 2020). Most states and almost the totality of the private sector faced the gravest health emergency of modernity, with financial markets seizing up, for the second time this century, bringing back fears of a repeat of the 2008 credit crunch (Glinavos, 2010:539). The world's financial institutions were better prepared to respond to this shock, however, precisely because of the experiences of the financial crisis (Bradlow & Park 2020:657). At the initial stages of the pandemic, in March 2020, central banks in developed and emerging economies acted together to cut interest rates, purchase government debt, and launch new lending and funding programs. The consequence was significant intervention in domestic and foreign economies and financial markets amounting to trillions of dollars in asset purchases (Winck, 2020). Many central banks also extended collateral frameworks to broaden both the variety and quality of assets that could be purchased. Quantitative easing programmes were also expanded (or introduced for the first time) and many additional financing and purchase facilities were thrown in the fight of propping up asset prices and maintaining financial sector liquidity (Dikau et al., 2020).

One feature of the pandemic that differs from the challenges of the financial crisis of 2008 was the need to support the flow of credit to households and non-financial corporations. This need was the result of the severe disruption to the real economy, which was impacted before financial institutions in the case of the COVID-19 pandemic. The causal flow of stress in 2008 was the opposite of what we experienced in 2020, with stress in the financial system migrating to the real economy and ultimately transitioning to sovereign debt markets (Glinavos, 2013). For this reason, support this time had direct and far-reaching impacts on households and corporates to support consumer spending. Consequently, liquidity support to the financial sector has played a much more limited role during the initial response to the COVID-19 pandemic (Alwazir, 2020). The way in which central banks addressed the economic effects of the pandemic on the real economy was by expanding funding for lending schemes. This is built frequently on existing mechanisms (Sachs et al, 2019:81) established in the aftermath of the financial crisis. For example, in the US, the Fed used its Main Street Lending Program, to provide multi-year loans to firms that were in good financial standing before the crisis (Cavallino & De Fiore, 2020). We now turn to look in some more detail at the tools deployed by central banks in response to the economic emergency spawned by the pandemic in the first stage of the crisis from the spring to the summer of 2020.

The Fed

The Federal Reserve in the United States is a natural place to start in examining central bank responses to the initial stage of the pandemic, and its actions have

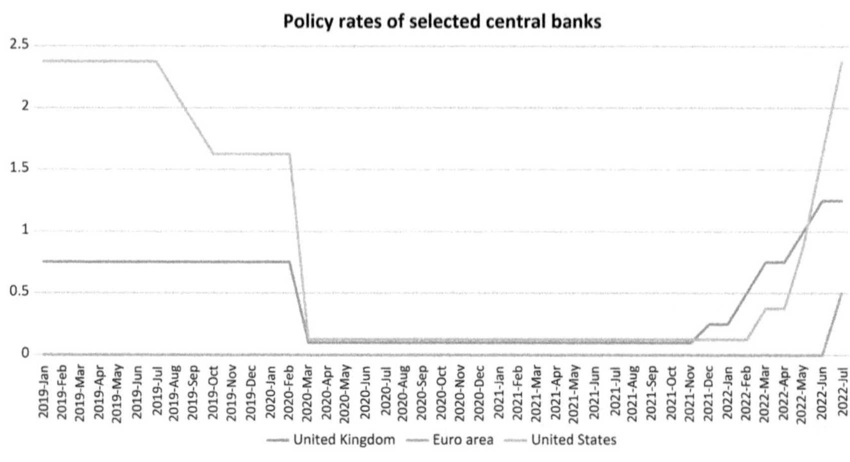

Figure 7.1 Data from BIS https://www.bis.org/statistics/oth_ind.htm?m=2680

Source: © free illustration.

attracted the attention of most commentators. In keeping with its role as trendsetter in global central banking, the Fed reacted quickly to economic disruption and exploding unemployment numbers in the spring of 2020 by deploying a broad array of lending facilities aiming to enhance the flow of credit to private and public financial actors in the domestic context (Smialek and Ewing, 2020). Broadly, the Fed built on lending programs that were developed after the crash in 2008 and acted to help public and private financial actors, in effect purchasing most qualifying loans made by banks to small and middle-sized companies. It lowered the cost of discount window lending and through the Commercial Paper Funding Facility enabled the continuing issuance of commercial paper by companies and municipal issuers, even in an environment of stress in financial markets. Other tools deployed included the Primary Dealer Credit Facility (to provide financing to the Fed's primary dealers), the Money Market Mutual Fund Liquidity Facility (to provide loans to depository institutions for the purchase of assets from prime money market funds), the Primary Market Corporate Credit Facility (to purchase new bonds and loans from companies), the Secondary Market Corporate Credit Facility (to provide liquidity for outstanding corporate bonds), the Term Asset-Backed Securities Loan Facility (to facilitate the issuance of asset-backed securities), the Paycheck Protection Program Liquidity Facility (to provide liquidity to financial institutions that originate loans to incentivise small businesses to maintain employment), the Main Street Lending Program (to purchase new or expanded loans to small and medium enterprises) and the Municipal Liquidity Facility (to purchase short-term notes directly from state local governments) (Wade, 2020). At their end, US Federal banking supervisors assisted these efforts by mandating that holdings of US Treasury Securities and deposits at the Federal Reserve Banks could be temporarily excluded from the calculation of supplementary leverage ratios and lowered community bank leverage ratios. Both measures are designed to increase liquidity in an environment of stress.

In the international context, actions aimed at increasing dollar liquidity and helping other central banks maintain credit lines by establishing a repurchase agreement facility for foreign central banks and enhancing US dollar liquidity swap lines with a select number of other central banks (Economist (2), 2020). Examples of actions in coordination with other central banks were the institution of the Foreign and International Monetary Authorities Repo Facility, which allowed central banks to borrow US dollars against US sovereign bonds held as foreign exchange reserves (Fed (1), 2020). The Fed also built on tools established after the 2008 financial crisis by enhancing currency swap arrangements with the aim of allowing other central banks to deal with credit lines with the Fed denominated in US dollars at the same rate as domestic operators (Conti-Brown & Zaring 2019:693). One could argue that by enabling foreign central banks to swap their own currencies for US dollars, the Fed ceded its function of acting as lender of last resort to foreign central banks (Baker, 2013). However, this complaint is more theoretical than real. This was a move that was bold but enabled some degree of stabilisation in global markets, by ensuring the continuation of dollar liquidity, avoiding a credit crunch from becoming entrenched as in 2008.

What happened to the traditional instrument of policy, interest rates, was perhaps less impressive when compared to the actions detailed above. The Fed cut the policy interest rate to a range of 0–0.25% and promised that rates would stay low for as long as necessary (Klebnikov, 2020). All this was welcomed in the United States and internationally, but there is concern that the size of interventions underway in 2020 will cause problems of both a political and economic nature. The crisis of 2008 taught us that there are limits to public borrowing expansion. A limit will inevitably be reached when creditors will start worrying about the sustainability of public debt. A rerun of the 2010 European debt crisis on a global level would not be conducive to post-pandemic recovery. There are also limits to the ability of central banks to prop up government spending through expanding their balance sheets. How far can central banks maintain initiatives such as quantitative easing before they transition from temporary emergency response measures to permanent tools used to inflate state debts away? The need to maintain the integrity of debt markets will need to be balanced against the reality of taxpayers having to be asked to serve their government's debts again. This of course is a question of global significance, as the presentation of the experiences of the ECB below shows.

ECB

At the early stages of the pandemic in Europe, the role of the ECB was recognised as central to a European and specifically Eurozone response (Demertzis, 2020). Because of COVID-19, real gross domestic product (GDP) declined by 11.8% during the second quarter of 2020 in the Euro area and was estimated by ECB staff to decline by 8% for 2020, turning to a growth of 5% in 2021 and 3.2% in 2022 (Marmefelt, 2020). The shock to the financial system inflicted by the country-wide lockdowns in the spring of 2020 and worrying turbulence in government bond spreads forced central bank action before the situation gained unstoppable momentum. The peculiarities of the eurozone system mean that the ECB is tasked with providing liquidity to the financial system, but it is not in control of all measures thaw (that?) can affect economic activity across all participating member states. The summer of 2020 was tensions developing in markets highlighting the need for enhancing liquidity, including dollar availability. The ECB was particularly concerned that COVID-19-induced economic shocks could lead to major distress in euro-area sovereign bond markets and reignite the euro sovereign debt crisis that has plagued the currency area since 2010. The only adequate remedy to stress in sovereign debt markets was an increase in Eurosystem bond purchase programmes. The ECB however is not a single or federal state central bank, and its discretion can only be exercised within the outer boundaries set by the Treaties. The ECB cannot directly fund member states (Glinavos, 2016a), and even in the case of corporate markets asset purchases are limited by constraints to the ECB Quantitative Easing programme. The latter could not be stretched indefinitely, and in early 2020, it was already quite close to limits in several countries, yet Christine Lagarde overruled objections from Germany and the Netherlands to adopt a no-limits commitment to supporting the European economy (Canepa & Koranyi, 2020). While perhaps there was little scope for monetary policy stimulus, the ECB still had a range of tools available to use in effecting liquidity provision.

Looking more specifically at the policy tools at the ECB's disposal, the bank expanded the range of eligible assets under the corporate sector purchase programme, and relaxed collateral standards for Eurozone refinancing operations. These initiatives were assisted by the expansion of the scope of the additional credit claims framework to include public sector guaranteed loans. The cumulative effect of such measures were additional asset purchases of €120 billion under the Asset Purchase Programme and €750 billion of private and public sector securities under the Pandemic Emergency Purchase Program (ECB, 2020a). These actions were supplemented around supervision by changes in classification requirements and expectations on loss provisioning for non-performing loans, a major problem in certain eurozone member states even before the COVID-19 emergency. Supervisors also allowed banking institutions to operate temporarily below bank capital conservation buffers and adjusted the prudential floor to banks' current minimum capital requirement to increase financial system liquidity.

Arguably, Eurozone institutions responded to current developments with strongly complementary monetary and fiscal policies. One could argue that the ECB navigated the crisis remaining within its Treaty mandates and maintained its policy and action independence via using unconventional monetary policy measures to reach price stability. However, while the massive coordinated monetary and fiscal expansion presented above helped prevent the serious socioeconomic problems that would stem from an economic collapse in Europe and hopefully help secure future economic growth, they have also led to increases in public deficits and public debts (Gramlich, 2020). While central banks have resorted to purchases of government bonds to maintain monetary transmission, with the ECB stepping on the line of its authority to do 'whatever it takes' (Glinavos, 2016b), with interest rates close to the zero lower bound many are worried about an emerging monetary-fiscal nexus. EU commenced its own fiscal policy as a response to the current crisis, contrary to what was done in the aftermath of 2007–08. However, if fiscal policy now drives ECB decisions, could it continue to dominate after the immediate emergency has passed? The ECB faces some serious policy trade-offs and in a federalised system that lacks a fiscal counterpart, euro's central bank may find it difficult to maintain its monetary independence (Marmelfelt, 2020:11).

The Bank of England

In the UK, the Bank of England (BoE) presents an interesting example of a central bank free from the legal constraints imposed on the constitutionally enshrined Fed, and the severely Treaty-constrained ECB. The BoE operates based on traditional legal powers that can be more easily amended than those that motor its counterparts. This could be a benefit in allowing increased flexibility in policy-making, but also present a danger of government encroachment on the bank's independence. The BoE, like other central banks acted quickly in the spring of 2020 to enhance liquidity in the economy. For example, it launched together with the Treasury the COVID-19 Corporate Financing Facility which, together with the Coronavirus Business Loans Interruption Scheme, can make £330bn, equivalent to 15% of GDP, of loans and guarantees available to businesses. This facility came hand in hand with expanding by £200 billion the bank's portfolio of UK government bonds and non-financial corporate bonds. The Treasury and the BoE agreed to extend temporarily the use of the government's overdraft account at the BoE to provide a short-term source of additional liquidity to the government as and when needed. A new Term Funding Scheme was used to boost the effect of interest rate cuts using extra incentives for lending to small and medium enterprises. In terms of supervision, the UK saw similar moves to other jurisdictions, with the Prudential Regulatory Authority (PRA) adjusting capital requirements to ease the pressure on bank balance sheets (Hill, 2020). The UK countercyclical buffer rate was reduced, and reporting requirements were eased. For example, the PRA allowed a delay to the publication of results of the 2019 Insurance Stress Tests and postponed the next Insurance Stress Test until 2022 (BoE (1), 2020).

The actions of the BoE and the Treasury represent a radical departure from traditional behaviours of British authorities. After all, Conservative administrations after the financial crisis highlighted the need for balanced budgets and reductions in public debt, despite the significant disruption brought by repeated campaigns at implementing austerity measures in the public sector (Glinavos, 2015). The controversial history of purse tightening was quickly reversed in 2020 with public spending now being considered a first-strike tool in preventing job losses and economic stagnation. The British government in 2020 exhibited unheard of enthusiasm for committing money to a range of policies designed to keep the economy afloat during the pandemic and (perhaps conveniently) to mask the effects of Brexit. The government took it upon itself to underwrite the employment costs of millions of workers through its Job Retention Scheme, it funded several state aid packages and arranged for guarantees to some business loan programmes. Most of these initiatives were renewed at the time of the UK's third successive lockdown at the beginning of 2021 when the discovery of a new variant of the virus and trade disruption at the end of the Brexit transition period threatened to derail economic stabilisation (Elliott, 2021). At the same time, the BoE dropped interest rates to 0.1%, as well as bringing the total amount of government debt on its balance sheet to £635bn (Whisker & Buller, 2020).

Considering the developments described above, one wonders whether a distinction between fiscal and monetary policy persists in the UK and if it does not, whether the degree of coordination evident in 2020 poses a threat to the Bank's identity. Such concern is particularly acute in Britain, which has seen vocal opposition to the idea of central bank independence from the right and the left of the political spectrum that is perhaps matched only by opposition to institutional independence by the former Trump administration in the US (Glinavos, 2020). The BoE is not unaware of these risks but as the new governor Andrew Bailey made clear, it takes the view that institutional safeguards ensure the preservation of its independence from political decision-making. Nonetheless, the Bank's willingness to directly finance additional government spending by expanding the government's overdraft limit through the Ways and Means facility raises concerns about the degree to which coordination with ministers is starting to bleed into command and control.

Discretion on ministers on using and repaying this overdraft raises for many the possibility that the BoE will participate in an inflationary public spending spree reminiscent of the 1970s. That would be quite the reversal for one of the first central banks to attain and legally entrench its independence, won precisely on the back of these experiences of the pre-independence era (King, 2005). Arguably, an unlimited extension to the amount of government bonds the Bank could hold would allow the Treasury to bypass bond markets in meeting its spending needs (Economist (3), 2020). Would legislated mandates contain such dangers? The Bank is currently legally required to deliver price stability, and under Quantitative Easing, it is the Monetary Policy Committee that decides when and how much government debt to purchase. While under the temporary facilities described above, ministers have discretion on how they use them, the Debt Management Office has accepted that the government will only operate its overdraft as a temporary and short-term cash-flow management tool. One could argue that the government can be believed in its constraint, as a similar extension to the Ways and Means account was allowed in 2008, without becoming a permanent feature of government financing techniques (Whisker & Buller, 2020). On the other hand, the government of Cameron and Osborne (2010–2016) was not the same type of government as the one of Johnson and Sunak.

Conflating Fiscal and Monetary Policy

The classic explanation of the function of a central bank is that it operates as a lender of last resort (Bindseil, 2014). True as that may be, a lender of last resort is not the same as the underwriter of the entire economy. Nonetheless, arguably, one of the legacies of the 2008 financial crisis has been the gradual assumption by central banks of precisely the role of a backstop – and possibly an underwriter – to the entire financial system. Central banks, the Fed being a central example, did not suddenly assume the role of state-wide economy underwriters suddenly at the time of the financial crisis, however. One could argue that the Fed was set along this trajectory following the global stock market crash of 1987, reinforced its direction during the dot-com crash of the 1990s, and finally solidified its role in 2008. The response to COVID-19 is consistent with this view of central banks as the Atlases of the financial world. What this Atlas uses to prop the world is of course liquidity provision. Such liquidity is commonly injected by interventions in the market for government debt. The mirror image of intervention is low or even negative interest rates. When central banks engage in the purchase of large amounts of private debt, they drive up the prices of corporate bonds prices and depress returns (Tooze 2020).

Stimulus and expanding balance sheets are the central banks' way to prevent a slide into a deflationary spiral. Does this addiction to stimulus though mean that central banks are now the drivers of economic policy, encroaching on the fiscal space reserved for governments, or can we still maintain that this globe of interventions is still held on-top of monetary policy institutionally entrusted to central bankers? One could argue that lowering the cost of borrowing is precisely the point of monetary policy. 2020 could be the year that economic theory finally breaks free from economic need. Perhaps the classic paradigm of inflation-fighting independence is obsolete and cannot address current problems such as the threat of deflation, the stability of the financial system, and the weakness of fiscal policy to save economies in a COVID-19 freefall. Conceivably, the way to interpret the changing role of central banks is not to perceive a shift from monetary to economic policy but to understand what is happening as a shift from restraining inflation to preventing deflation or stagflation under current circumstances?. Such a role sees central banks escape from their legislated narrow policy objective of inflation targeting and allows them to act as dealers of last resort providing a backstop to the entire financial system. All this could even be legally compliant, depending on the jurisdiction you are looking at, as well as practically necessary.

During times of acute crisis, like in the context of the COVID-19 pandemic, fiscal policy should have and has indeed taken the lead. This is natural as fiscal policy is mandated by governments with democratic mandates and has the tools to respond to the consequences of lockdowns and social distancing measures that depress incomes by making direct interventions through tax breaks of direct transfers (Woodford, 2020). One could even look forward to some of that famous helicopter money (Blommesten & Turner, 2012) whereby the government directly credits individual and corporate accounts (Reis & Tenreyro, 2022). Monetary policy, on the other hand, has traditionally been focused on keeping interest rates low. Inflation targeting is not necessarily compatible with the large-scale corporate bond and state debt purchases that have been taking place during the crisis. For their part, government debt holdings are a legitimate and justifiable monetary policy tool, but it would be remis to pretend that they do not also blur the line between the role of central banks and the interests of fiscal authorities. These conflicts between government support and legislated mandates have been particularly pronounced in the context of the EU, where the lender of last resort protects a currency, but not a state. For the ECB, holdings of government, member state debt, mean mutualising sovereign liability risks through central bank balance sheets, and this is precisely the reason why they were difficult to accept during the European debt crisis (Acharya et al, 2018). If European parliaments and governments were unable to agree on euro-bonds when it looked like the eurozone was on the brink of braking up, they are not likely to embrace them quickly now, and certainly, they are not likely to derogate a decision to accept them to the central bank (Weidmann, 2020), even to one designed in the image of the Bundesbank. As Jens Weidmann, the Bundesbank president, noted, it is important that monetary policy is not placed at the service of fiscal policy. If a different impression is created, it can place both central bank independence and its credibility at risk.

There are also clear links between the central banks assumed role as backstop and oversight of the financial sector and prudential functions. Emerging from the financial crisis, prudential functions became a progressively larger part of central bank responsibility, aiming to bolster financial stability (ECB, 2010). Our presentation above has shown the complementarity between monetary actions and adjusting prudential oversight to allow leeway to the financial sector in adjusting to shock. Keeping an eye on inflation, deflation, stagflation? financial stability, and oversight over the financial sector necessitates coordinated moves by policymakers and prudential authorities. This has been evident in the response to the economic effects of the pandemic and will have lasting effects on the institutional design of policy frameworks and directly affect an understanding of the function and effects of institutional independence (Restoy, 2020).

But is independence something that is worth preserving in a global political economy defined by crisis? We can also think of this question in the context of the trade disruption and energy crisis born of the Russia-Ukraine conflict of 2022. The question institutional actors need to answer now is whether independence helps central banks to respond to emergencies, or whether it creates barriers to their communication with governments and other state institutions, leading to information gaps undermining policy effectiveness in fast-moving situations. It was always challenging to balance various policy instruments on allocating monetary, macro-prudential and micro-prudential responsibilities to different agencies, but this is a much more pressing issue in the context of a pandemic-defined world (Restoy, 2020:7). The initial regulatory response to Covid-19 offers evidence that adjustments can and should be explicitly adopted to contain effects on everyday economic activities. That represents clear recognition that macroprudential tools do matter, for both financial stability and economic stability (ECB, 2020b). One possible takeaway could be that financial stability and macroprudential policies should not be conducted by separate institutions in the absence of effective coordination mechanisms (Restoy, 2020:5). Which begs the question, have there been effective coordination mechanisms in evidence during this crisis?

It does seem that such coordination mechanisms operated effectively with central banks and fiscal authorities working together (Alberola-Ila et al. 2020). Fiscal authorities supported central banks' actions in a variety of ways. For example, as detailed earlier in this chapter, the US Treasury provided support to various Fed projects in 2020 (Cox, 2020). The UK Treasury, similarly, amongst many other actions, also offered guarantees to commercial debt acquired by the BoE. In several jurisdictions, including the Eurozone, governments extended guarantees to private non-financial sector loans. The idea behind such interventions was that by alleviating default risks, fiscal support went hand in hand with monetary policies maintaining the money supply and liquidity support for the real economy helping central banks expand their provision of credit to borrowers. Central bank responses to the COVID-19 shutdown made them partners of governments, without however subsuming them to the commands of fiscal authorities. The need to support liquidity, helped overcome legacy programmes from the financial crisis, with lending no longer restricted to financial institutions, as was the case in 2008 (Bowmaker & Wachtel, 2020).

It is safe to argue that the COVID-19 crisis and the ensuing conflict between Russia and Ukraine pushed central banks to break away from traditional ways to support the economy and placed monetary and financial policy at the heart of government responses often doing away with the distinction between central bank lending and government expenditures. This is a particularly controversial issue, especially in the European context, where member state central banks have been indirectly supporting the fiscal expansion of many governments. Actions such as interest rate cuts, expanding lending operations and public asset purchase programmes were all parts of a larger effort to reduce the cost of bearing both private and public debt. Was this all consistent with legal frameworks? In the case of the ECB, the bank's objectives are determined by its mandate as defined in the European treaties and so long as bond purchases make economic sense, central bank credibility is not at risk and nor is independence (Zeitung, 2020). Without central bank support, a large-scale issuance of government bonds to finance fiscal expansion would risk impairing the proper functioning of sovereign bond markets (Fischer, 2011).

Does this relatively 'new' function (or rather the return to an old function) of central banks, subsidising government borrowing and propping up the wider economy in the guise of crisis response, herald trouble in the long run? One could argue that if governments get 'addicted' to this form of fiscal policy piggybacking on central bank actions, they will not envisage a return to stricter inflation-targeting mandates. Monetizing government debt and engaging in credit allocation, central banks risk sacrificing monetary control and their independence (Dorn, 2020). It is argued that a situation in which the central bank would be forced by the government to change its reaction function and accept to inflate the government debt away at the expense of its price-stability objective could destroy the credibility of the central bank and of the value of the money which it defends (Claeys, 2020:13). In the words of Charles Plosser, former CEO, and president of the Federal Reserve Bank of Philadelphia, independence is drifting away and after this crisis, it will be easier and easier for politicians to seek bank participation in off-budget fiscal actions (Dorn, 2020). This is perhaps a lesser danger in the context of the EU, but a more visible threat in other jurisdictions, for example developing countries (Glinavos, 2020) and the newly 'independent' UK. Unconventional monetary policy may have shifted the monetary-fiscal policy interaction from monetary dominance with independent central banks to fiscal dominance (Marmefelt, 2020:22), where the central bank is forced to support fiscal policy and where fiscal dominance is measured by the fraction of government debt that needs to be backed by monetary policy (De Haan & Eijffinger, 2016). Perhaps however these concerns belong to a different time. A time where economic Armageddon born of a worldwide pandemic was not threatening the very existence of the global economy. What would be the point of maintaining the theoretical construct of independence if the result is sub-optimal policies leading to widespread failure?

Conclusion

This chapter has presented the actions of central banks in the initial phase of response to the COVID-19 pandemic with two key aims. The first was to examine the degree to which monetary policy complemented the reactions of fiscal authorities to determine whether independent institutions can effectively work in tandem with political authorities in responding to emergencies of this magnitude. The second was to assess whether independence has been an asset or an impediment to policy-making in times of crisis. The main conclusions are that indeed monetary and fiscal authorities worked effectively together both in developed and emerging economies. Institutional independence and policy autonomy did not inhibit this cooperation, and the results so far have been positive, in the sense that a global economic collapse was avoided even as the pandemic and its effects on the global economy were worsening.

There is no robust evidence to suggest that independence was a hindrance, with the only problems identified being those put in place by rigid legal frameworks (like in the case of the ECB), not with the exercise of autonomy. Another conclusion of this analysis however was less expected. This was the realisation that a challenge to independence may not stem from power-grabbing politicians in the US, Eurozone, and the UK that may exploit our current predicaments, but from the conflation of monetary and fiscal policy arising from circumstances themselves. The message of the chapter in outline is that state interference is more likely when the task is controlling inflation. The covid response was geared towards keeping deflation at bay and propping up economic systems that we cannot envisage collapsing. The post-covid environment characterised by resurgent inflation due to the Russian war in Ukraine (and the trade disruption and energy crisis it caused) is rekindling political appetites for monetary intervention as evidenced in the UK in the dying days of the Johnson government (James, 2022).

The core rationale for central-bank independence emerged from inflationary episodes of the 1970s, when the danger according to leading economists was economic destabilisation stemming from rising prices at the behest of politicians trying to keep unemployment under control. The covid crisis demanded action on unemployment, but not for party political reasons. What we need going forward is central banks helping states salvage employment and the real economy. And for this to happen it is not even necessary to formally subject institutions to political control. The banks themselves, as they have shown with their initiatives during the crisis are very much aware of the needs of governments and they are fully committed to meeting them. Information presented in this chapter does not show any evidence of central banks being tricked or pushed into actions they were not fully willing to take themselves, and while central bankers warned politicians to stay away from the realm of independent institutions, there is no suggestion that they felt threatened on a practical, as opposed to a theoretical sense.

The pandemic demonstrates that even taboo issues up till recently, like direct monetary financing of state debts which merges monetary and fiscal policy is a tool to be debated, not a chimera to be avoided. Where legal regimes allow central banks to ease government debts through actions like making their loans interest-free and irredeemable, or through purchasing perpetual sovereign bonds, these actions should be considered. They could alleviate the need for fiscal measures to be brought in to subsidise public expenditure. Coordinated monetary and fiscal policy will remain a feature of governance and will be employed, not because politicians leaned on central bankers, but because this is what the interests of nations require. It is likely that some will christen this post-pandemic reality 'the end of independent central banks', but should we really be afraid of this (Crook, 2020)? The above reflection is by no means meant to negate the lengthy scholarship supporting the idea that monetary policy must be kept separate from fiscal policy (Warburton, 1966). It is well-established and empirically validated that to effectively design monetary policy, central banks must maintain a high level of independence from governments and have the means to support and reinforce that independence. A post-pandemic reality of cooperation between monetary and fiscal domains does not mean that banks should lose their budgetary independence or the ability to allocate credit across different sectors of the economy as needed. It does mean however that the objects and means to implement monetary and fiscal policies are closer together than ever before. As the experience of 2020 has shown, coordination does not induce ineffective or less appropriate policy-making (Broaddus & Goodfriend 2001:7). The momentous events of 2020 suggest that Modern Monetary Theory (MMT), the idea that governments can and should freely print and spend their own currency (Ehnts, 2017), has finally become mainstream (Dmitrieva, 2018).

References

Acharya, V. et al Real effects of the sovereign debt crisis in Europe: Evidence from syndicated loans (August 2018) Vol 31, The Review of Financial Studies, Issue 8, p. 2855

Adrian, T. Monetary and financial stability during the coronavirus outbreak (11.3.2020) IMF Blog https://blogs.imf.org/2020/03/11/monetary-and-financial-stability-during-the-coronavirus-outbreak/ accessed 12.1.2021

Alberola-Ila, E. et al The fiscal response to the Covid-19 crisis in advanced and emerging market economies (17.6.2020) BIS Bulletin No 23 https://www.bis.org/publ/bisbull23.htm accessed 12.1.2021

Alwazir, J. Central bank support to financial markets in the coronavirus pandemic (2020) IMF Special Series on COVID-19 https://www.imf.org/~/media/Files/Publications/covid19-special-notes/en-special-series-on-covid-19-central-bank-support-to-financial-markets-in-the-coronavirus-pandemic.ashx accessed 12.1.2021

Arslan, Y. et al, Central bank bond purchases in emerging market economies (2.6.2020) BIS Bulletin, no 20 https://www.bis.org/publ/bisbull20.htm accessed 12.1.2021
Baker, C. (2013) 'The federal reserve's use of international swap lines', Arizona Law Review 603, vol. 55, p. 607.
Bank of England, Bank of England measures to respond to the economic shock from Covid-19 (11.3.2020) Press Release https://www.bankofengland.co.uk/news/2020/march/boe-measures-to-respond-to-the-economic-shock-from-covid-19 accessed 12.1.2021
Bindseil, U. (2014) Monetary Policy Operations and the Financial System, Oxford University Press
Blommesten, H. & Turner, P. Threat of Fiscal Dominance? (May 2012) BIS Papers No 65 https://www.bis.org/publ/bppdf/bispap65.pdf accessed 12.1.2021
Borio, C. The prudential response to the Covid-19 crisis (30.6.2020) Speech at BIS AGM, https://www.bis.org/speeches/sp200630a.htm accessed 12.1.21
Bowmaker, S. & Wachtel, P. The federal reserve's biggest success during the coronavirus crisis: keeping itself out of politics (11.7.2020) Business Insider https://www.businessinsider.com/federal-reserve-independence-pandemic-covid-19-recession-2020-7?r=US&IR=T accessed 12.1.2021.
Bradlow, D. & Park, S. (2020) 'A global leviathan emerges: the federal reserve, COVID-19, and international law', American Journal of International Law, vol. 114, no. 4, p. 657
Broaddus, A. & Goodfriend, M. (2001) 'What assets should the federal reserve buy?', Federal Reserve Bank of Richmond Economic Quarterly, vol. 87/1, p. 7
Canepa, F. & Koranyi, B. ECB's Lagarde overruled German and Dutch resistance to 'no-limits' pledge (19.3.2020) Reuters https://www.reuters.com/article/uk-health-coronavirus-ecb-exclusive/exclusive-ecbs-lagarde-overruled-german-and-dutch-resistance-to-no-limits-pledge-sources-idUKKBN21625K accessed 12.1.2021
Casado, M. et al The effect of fiscal stimulus: evidence from COVID-19 (2020) NBER Working Paper 27576 http://www.nber.org/papers/w27576 accessed 12.1.2021
Cavallino, P. & De Fiore, F. Central banks' response to Covid-19 in advanced economies (5.6.2020) BIS Bulletins https://www.bis.org/publ/bisbull21.htm accessed 12.1.2021, p.4
Claeys, G. The European Central Bank in the COVID-19 crisis: whatever it takes, within its mandate (2020) Policy Contribution 09/2020, Bruegel https://www.bruegel.org/2020/05/the-european-central-bank-in-the-covid-19-crisis-whatever-it-takes-within-its-mandate/ accessed 12.1.2021, p.13
Conti-Brown, P. & Zaring, D. (2018) 'The foreign affairs of the federal reserve,' The Journal of Corporation Law 665, vol. 44, p. 693
Cox, J. Federal reserve unveils details of $2.3 trillion in programs to help support the economy (9.4.2020) CNBC https://www.cnbc.com/2020/04/09/federal-reserve-unveils-details-of-its-much-anticipated-main-street-lending-program.html accessed 12.1.2021
Crook, C. Central bank independence may not survive the coronavirus (20.4.2020) https://www.bloomberg.com/opinion/articles/2020-04-20/central-bank-independence-may-not-survive-the-coronavirus accessed 12.1.2021
De Haan, J. & Eijffinger, S. The Politics of Central Bank Independence (2016) European Banking Center Discussion Paper Series No. 2016-004, https://ssrn.com/abstract=28879311 accessed 12.1.21
Demertzis, M. An effective economic response to the coronavirus in Europe (1.3.2020) Bruegel Policy Contribution, issue nr. 6(1), p. 8–9
Dikau, S. et al A Toolbox for Sustainable Crisis Response Measures for Central Banks and Supervisors (23.11.2020) INSPIRE Briefing Paper, p. 6 https://www.lse.ac.uk/

granthaminstitute/publication/a-toolbox-of-sustainable-crisis-response-measures-for-central-banks-and-supervisors-second-edition/ accessed 12.1.2021

Dmitrieva, K. A Hedge Fund Guy Lefties Can Love (11.10.2018) Bloomberg Businessweek https://www.bloomberg.com/news/articles/2018-10-11/a-hedge-fund-guy-lefties-can-love accessed 12.1.2021

Dorn, J. COVID-19: Implications for Monetary Policy and Fed Independence (20.4.2020) Cato Institute https://www.cato.org/blog/covid-19-implications-monetary-policy-fed-independence accessed 12.1.21

ECB, ECB announces €750 billion Pandemic Emergency Purchase Programme (PEPP) (18.3.2020a) Press Release https://www.ecb.europa.eu/press/pr/date/2020/html/ecb.pr200318_1~3949d6f266.en.html accessed 12.1.21

ECB, ECB Banking Supervision provides temporary capital and operational relief in reaction to coronavirus (12.3.2020b) Press Release https://www.bankingsupervision.europa.eu/press/pr/date/2020/html/ssm.pr200312~43351ac3ac.en.html accessed 12.1.2021

ECB, The Great Financial Crisis (May 2010) ECB Colloquium https://www.ecb.europa.eu/pub/pdf/other/greatfinancialcrisisecbcolloquiumpapademos201206en.pdf accessed 12.1.2021

Editor, The Covid-19 pandemic is forcing a rethink in macroeconomics (25.7.2020a) The Economist, https://www.economist.com/briefing/2020/07/25/the-covid-19-pandemic-is-forcing-a-rethink-in-macroeconomics accessed 12.1.21

Editor, The successes of the Fed's dollar-swap lines (18.6.2020b) The Economist https://www.economist.com/finance-and-economics/2020/06/20/the-successes-of-the-feds-dollar-swap-lines accessed 12.1.21

Editor, Britain's budget and the bond markets (5.3.2020c) The Economist https://www.economist.com/britain/2020/03/05/britains-budget-and-the-bond-markets accessed 12.1.21

Ehnts, D. (2017) Modern Monetary Theory and European Macroeconomics, Routledge

Elliott, L. Rishi Sunak unveils £4.6bn relief package for UK retail and hospitality sectors (5.1.2021) The Guardian https://www.theguardian.com/politics/2021/jan/05/rishi-sunak-unveils-46bn-relief-package-for-uk-retail-and-hospitality-sectors accessed 12.1.2021

Federal Reserve, FIMA Repo Facility FAQs (31.3.2020) Press Release https://www.federalreserve.gov/newsevents/pressreleases/fima-repo-facility-faqs.htm accessed 12.1.2021

Fischer, P. Interactions of sovereign debt management with monetary conditions and financial stability (2011) Committee on the Global Financial System, CGFS Papers No 42. https://www.bis.org/publ/cgfs42.pdf accessed 12.1.2021

Glinavos, I. Necessity vs legality: is the ECB running or ruining Europe? (16.9.2016a) Oxford Business Law Blog https://www.law.ox.ac.uk/business-law-blog/blog/2016/07/challenging-emergency-liquidity-assistance-decisions-international accessed 12.1.2021

Glinavos, I. Whatever it takes vs whatever is legal: the ECB's problematic relationship with the rule of law (2016b) SSRN http://dx.doi.org/10.2139/ssrn.2798692 accessed 12.1.21

Glinavos, I. (2013) Redefining the Market State Relationship, Routledge, p. 50

Glinavos, I. (2020) Institutional Metamorphosis: The Backlash Against Independent Central Banking, Chapter in Political Economy of Central Banking in Emerging Economies, Routledge

Glinavos, I. Law's Empire of Austerity (2015) Transnational Institute, Recommended Reading for State of Power Report 2015, https://www.tni.org/files/download/laws_empire_of_austerity.pdf accessed 12.1.21

Glinavos, I. (2010) 'Regulation and the role of law in economic crisis', *European Business Law Review*, vol. 21, no. 4, p. 539

Gramlich, J. Coronavirus downturn likely to add to high government debt in some countries (29.4.2020) Fact Tank, Pew Research Center https://www.pewresearch.org/fact-tank/2020/04/29/coronavirus-downturn-likely-to-add-to-high-government-debt-in-some-countries/ accessed 12.1.2021

Hill, C. et al COVID-19: response from the Bank of England and Prudential Regulation Authority (10.12.2020) Taylor Wessing https://www.taylorwessing.com/zh-hant/insights-and-events/insights/2020/07/covid19-response-from-the-bank-of-england-and-prudential-regulation-authority accessed 12.1.21

IMF, The IMF's Response to COVID-19 (28.10.20) Q&A, IMF https://www.imf.org/en/About/FAQ/imf-response-to-covid-19 accessed 12.1.21

James, H. Can truss be trusted with the Bank of England? (2.9.2022) Project Syndicate, https://www.project-syndicate.org/commentary/liz-truss-bank-of-england-central-bank-independence-by-harold-james-2022-09 accessed 9.9.2022.

King, M. (2005) 'Epistemic communities and the diffusion of ideas: central Bank reform in the United Kingdom', West European Politics, vol. 28, no. 1, p. 94.

Nordhaus, W. (1975) The political business cycle', The Review of Economic Studies (1975) vol. 42, no. 2, p. 169

Klebnikov, S. Federal reserve says it will keep interest rates near zero until 2023 (16.9.2020) Forbes https://www.forbes.com/sites/sergeiklebnikov/2020/09/16/federal-reserve-says-it-will-keep-interest-rates-near-zero-until-2023/?sh=611f1f97798d accessed 12.1.2021

Marmefelt, T. COVID-19 and economic policy toward the new normal: a monetary-fiscal nexus after the crisis? (November 2020) European Parliament, Monetary Dialogue Papers https://www.europarl.europa.eu/RegData/etudes/IDAN/2020/658193/IPOL_IDA(2020)658193_EN.pdf accessed 12.1.21, p.8

Marmelfelt, T. COVID-19 and economic policy toward the new normal: a monetary-fiscal nexus after the crisis? (November 2020) European Parliament, Monetary Dialogue Papers https://www.europarl.europa.eu/RegData/etudes/IDAN/2020/658193/IPOL_IDA(2020)658193_EN.pdf accessed 12.1.21, p.11

Reis, R. & Tenreyro, S. Helicopter money, what is it and what does it do? (Feb 2022), LSE Working Paper, https://personal.lse.ac.uk/tenreyro/helicopter.pdf accessed 9.9.22

Restoy, F. Central banks and financial stability: a reflection after the Covid-19 outbreak (August 2020) BIS Occasional Paper No 16, https://www.bis.org/fsi/fsipapers16.pdf accessed 12.1.21, p.1–2

Sachs, J. et al (2019) Springer Handbook of Green Finance: Energy Security and Sustainable Development 81, Springer Singapore

Smialek, J. & Ewing, J. Central bankers have crossed bright lines to aid economies (9.6.2020) *The New York Times* https://www.nytimes.com/2020/06/09/business/economy/central-banks-coronavirus-economies.html accessed 12.1.2021

Tooze, A. The death of the Central Bank myth (13.5.2020) foreign policy https://foreignpolicy.com/2020/05/13/european-central-bank-myth-monetary-policy-german-court-ruling/ accessed 12.1.2021

Wade, T. Timeline: The federal reserve responds to the threat of coronavirus (2.11.2020) *American Action Forum: Insight* https://www.americanactionforum.org/insight/timeline-the-federal-reserve-responds-to-the-threat-of-coronavirus/ accessed 12.1.2021

Warburton, C. (1966) Depression, Inflation, and Monetary Policy: Selected Papers, 1945–1953, The Johns Hopkins Press

Weidmann, S. Too close for comfort? The relationship between monetary and fiscal policy (6.11.2020) Speech at the OMFIF Virtual Panel https://www.bis.org/review/r201106d.htm accessed 12.1.21

Whisker, B. & Buller, J. COVID-19 and the Bank of England (28.5.2020) University of Sheffield, Speri http://speri.dept.shef.ac.uk/2020/05/28/covid-19-and-the-bank-of-england/ accessed 12.1.2021

Winck, B. The world's major central banks bought $1.4 trillion of assets in March (21.4.2020) Markets Insider https://markets.businessinsider.com/news/stocks/central-banks-buy-trillion-financial-assets-g7-march-federal-reserve-2020-4-1029113160 accessed 12.1.2021

Woodford, M. Effective Demand Failures and the Limits of Monetary Stabilization Policy (2020) NBER Working Paper, No. 27768 https://www.nber.org/papers/w27768 accessed 12.1.2021

Zeitung, I. The ECB's independence in times of mounting public debt (10.10.2020) ECB, Interview https://www.ecb.europa.eu/press/inter/date/2020/html/ecb.in201010~438af28894.en.html

8 Open Banking on Different Sides of the Atlantic: A Comparative Study between Brazil and the United Kingdom

Vinícius Klein and Rodolfo Rodrigues da Costa Farias

Introduction

The digitalization of markets is changing the way products and services are created and made available to the public, preparing a variety of new business arrangements with the intensive use of technologies such as Artificial Intelligence (AI) and Machine Learning (ML).

Financial Industry is also undergoing intense transformation with the entry of new competitors that seek to use innovative ways to meet desires and needs of the financial consumer (Palmieri and Nazeraj, 2021, p. 220). On the other side, financial regulation must evolve to be effective in this new reality.

In the case of Brazilian financial regulation access to credit is problematic, there is a recent effort of the Brazilian Central Bank ("BCB") to reduce costs and simplify its regulation to support entrepreneurship and economic development through new entrants. The digitalization of financial markets is an opportunity and a tool available for BCB to enhance financial inclusion and reduce credit spread costs.

So, the implementation of Open Banking ("OB") by the BCB is aimed to reduce the cost of credit and improve financial inclusion in Brazil, in a different context as in the response to a specific competition problem of market concentration found in the financial sector of other countries such as the United Kingdom.

The OB can be defined as a series of technological standards that enable the sharing of data on products, services and the financial history of a given customer mainly between regulated financial entities, with the customer's consent. In practice, it is a new way of sharing data within financial systems that allow participants to reduce existing informational asymmetries – which, in practice, is an informational advantage – among themselves for the benefit of competition, making players more capable of offering products and services adapted to the consumption needs of their customers.

There has been a change in the way of thinking about capturing and using customers' financial data, especially for their benefit. In the previous paradigm, each institution managed the data captured from its clients in an isolated and protective way, restricting the ability of this consumer to transmit information to other financial institutions due to the high switching costs in doing so (OECD, 2006, 2014). In that scenario, an incoming institution will face asymmetric transaction costs to

DOI: 10.4324/9781003323280-9

distinguish risky consumers, leading to a higher cost of credit and less competition (Nakane and Alencar, 2004, p 6).

In addition to these considerations, OB also creates new opportunities in the market, due to innovative solutions, mainly: (i) data aggregator, allowing the customer to access and manage their financial information in different providers in a single application; (ii) credit assessment, with greater data availability, it is possible to establish more accurate profile analysis algorithms, improving scoring and pricing for each risk level; (iii) product comparison, presenting a financial marketplace to the consumer in a single application, making it easier to compare financial offers; (iv) identity verification, sharing data between providers facilitates the onboarding process and verification of new customers; and, depending on the scope of each Open Banking (OB) jurisdiction, (v) interoperability in payments, creating new interoperable frameworks for instant payments, in example.

Regardless of the scope given to OB in each jurisdiction, it remains a way of exercising the rights that are being granted to holders of personal data around the world, whose informative self-determination encourages the individual to decide with whom and when to share your data. In this context, OB is the externalization of data rights, presented in legislations such as the General Data Protection Regulation ("GDPR") in Europe,[1] approved in 2016 and, in Brazil, as the *Lei Geral de Proteção de Dados* ("LGPD"), approved in 2018, as explained in Mourão and Silva (2020) and Jarude et al (2020).

The question is also addressed by antitrust authorities aiming to increase competition in the banking markets and reducing concentration in some segments, such as the credit market in Brazil and personal accounts and services for small and medium-sized companies in the United Kingdom. As a measure to solve this problem and improve the efficiency and healthy expansion of the credit supply,[2] the doctrine points to a consensus that the sharing of consumer banking data would increase competition (Casoria, 2021, p. 8).

This point has special relevance in the credit market since it can reduce transaction costs by reducing the asymmetry of information between the supplier and the borrower (Bag, 2013). The existence of this asymmetry constitutes an important barrier to entry in this market, making it more difficult for new entrants to compete efficiently, as they have no other way of accessing the credit history of potential customers and, consequently, the customer's ability to pay, as opposed to incumbents (De la Mano and Padilla, 2018, p. 503).

For this comparative analysis, the approach developed by Julia Black will be used to analyze the movements of regulation in Brazil and the United Kingdom. In this sense, regulation can be considered not exclusively emanating from the State, but also diffused throughout society, given its government-society and intra-society nature (Black, 2002). The concepts of Black's writings on regulation will be applied to analyze the process of OB regulation and its outcomes.

These chapters will perform a comparative study of the different implementation and governance structures of OB carried out in the United Kingdom and Brazil. The choice of the United Kingdom and Brazil is due to: (i) United Kingdom being the first country to adopt OB in 2018 and became a benchmark for other countries;

(ii) the Brazilian model has a wide scope of data and services compared to other countries, including profile and transactional data, as well as services, such as payment initiation and forwarding a credit proposal (BCB, 2021b, p.117); (iii) In 2020, the United Kingdom, via the UK Market Access Fund, became BCB's partner in the Open Banking Implementation project in Brazil (BCB, 2020c, p. 57); (iv) the Governor of the Central Bank of Brazil, in a presentation on the subject, pointed out that the implementation of a single standard, defined by a central governance authority, was a lesson learned and incorporated by the Brazilian OB (BCB, 2021c, p.6). In this sense, while the efforts in Brazil were made by the Monetary Authority, in the United Kingdom they were led by the Competition Authority.

It will be explored how both jurisdictions are behaving in the process of decentralized regulation of OB and the governance structure has been implemented. Therefore, in addition to this introduction, the chapter presents, in the first and second sections, respectively, the implementation history of OB in the United Kingdom and Brazil; in the third section, the regulation and governance process in both countries; the fourth section on how this public policy relates to the post-pandemic world and, in the fifth section, the conclusions identified in the study.

Open Banking in the UK

In May of 2022 more than 30 countries (Propague, 2020, p. 3) have been actively involved in some projects to implement OB. The United Kingdom was a pioneer in starting the process of implementing OB and became a reference point for projects around the world.

UK´s OB project was initiated by a public consultation (HM Treasury, 2013) aimed to "increase access to credit data for small and medium-sized companies ("SMEs") to stimulate competition in the credit market for SMEs". The scenario in the United Kingdom at the time was a high concentration rate in the market for this business segment of around 85%, which could potentially be harmful to customers and companies.

As a result of the consultation (HM Treasury, 2014a) a framework to allow the sharing of data from SMEs was developed and ratified by a Regulatory Impact Study (HM Treasury, 2014b) that culminated in an amendment (HM Treasury, 2014c) to address the problem. Later, its predictions were part of the *Small Business Enterprise & Employment Act (SBEEA),* a series of legal measures to reform and encourage the business environment for SMEs, the first part focused on the financial subject, with data sharing obligations to certain financial agents, depending on its market size.

This law was also responsible for the establishment of the *Commercial Credit Data Sharing (CCDS)*, a way for sharing data that allows decision-making on granting credit based on the records coming from *Credit Reference Agencies* that operate, comparatively, like a credit *bureau*, covering companies with revenue of up to GBP 25 million. Under this flow, the nine largest banks were obliged, with the consent of SMEs, to share their financial data with competitors in the financial market.

This British reform coincides with an important change that took place in the European market: the *Payment Service Directive 2 (PSD2)*, directive no. 2015/2366 of the *European Parliament and the Council of the European Union* (2015), aimed to modernize the payment market guidelines and create the legal framework for *Payment Initiation Service Providers* (PISP) and *Account Information Service Providers* (AISP).

These important innovations[3] created two types of service provisions in the financial market based precisely on the possibility of sharing customer data, either to carry out a payment order via a third party in the case of PISP, or to aggregate financial information that may be dispersed in different providers, in the case of AISP, using pre-defined standards that allow interoperability between systems through APIs. The incorporation of the European Union Directives happened through the *Payment Services Regulations* (United Kingdom, 2017), promoting an update of the *Payment Systems and Services and Electronic Money* policy.

These legal changes were crucial for the Competition and Markets Authority (CMA) to create the basic structure of the OB in the United Kingdom. CMA is a UK non-ministerial independent government department and the leading competition and consumer protection authority (CMA, 2022a), whose main responsibilities are (i) investigating mergers between organizations to ensure they do not reduce competition; (ii) investigating entire markets if there are indications suggesting competition or consumer problems, with emphasis on actions against cartels or anti-competitive behavior; (iii) protecting consumers from unfair commercial practices; (iv) encouraging the government and other regulators to use competition to the benefit of consumers.

In this context, CMA investigated the competition in the banking products and services market, mainly to individuals and SMEs (CMA, 2016). The main finding was that market concentration was harming the consumer. It was highlighted that large and traditional banks did not compete strongly to serve customers and new entrants were having difficulties accessing the market. As a result, CMA issued an Order for the nine largest account providers in the region[4] to finance and actively create the *Open Banking Implementation Entity ("OBIE")*, a structure responsible to implement OB according to the first principles and rules established by the CMA.

It is at this point that CCDS, PSD2 and OB connected to provide standardized channels to allow consumers and SMEs to authorize third parties to access their financial data and make payments based on the explicit consent of the customers, from an organized and interoperable structure with the major players established in the market.

Despite the good intentions for implementing the project, a survey carried out by KPMG (2018) consulting 1000 SMEs showed that 47% of respondents would not engage in sharing their data and another 25% would not share their data with third-party providers under any circumstances.

The CMA (2021) has already indicated that the project has been greatly expanded, with the current participation of more than 330 regulated companies, representing more than 95% of current banking accounts.

Given this context, it is important to know the implementation history for Brazil to compare models, governance structures and expected results.

Brazilian Open Banking

Since 2016, Brazil has been undergoing an intense regulatory agenda to modernize its financial system (SFN). The major actor has been the Brazilian Central Bank (Banco Central do Brazil, "BCB") and the reforms have been carried out by legal[5] and infra-legal rules.

The legal attributions of the BCB are provided by Law no. 4.565/65, with the following attributions highlighted: (i) control of inflation via monetary policy instruments, especially in controlling the basic interest rate and the amount of money in circulation; (ii) efficiency and security of the SFN, through the regulatory and supervisory activity of Financial and Payment Institutions; (iii) Government Bank, holding the most important government accounts and depositary of international reserves; (iv) Bank of Banks, controlling the Institution's deposits, and; (v) Money Issuer, ensuring the adequate supply of cash.

BCB modernization Agenda started in 2016 is committed to five areas of action: (i) Financial Citizenship; (ii) Legislative Modernization; (iii) SFN (National Financial System) Efficiency, (iv) Cheaper Credit and, more recently; and (v) Sustainability.

In the Open Banking Workshop Opening (BCB, 2019) BCB Governor stressed the crucial moment for the financial markets regarding the ability to process, store, organize and interpret information, which results in democratization, digitization, debureaucratization and demonetization of the market. These characteristics culminate in a strategy of modernizing the SFN, reducing the cost of credit and increasing competition among market agents. The recent history of Brazil demonstrates that the influence of the BCB is important for increasing social welfare through competition and equally possible through regulation (Murta Filho, 2006).

The diagnosis promoted by BCB is that the banking sector needed to be reviewed for at least three aspects: (i) high interest rate spread; (ii) high banking ROE; (iii) the concentration in the credit market with just five Commercial Banks.

The data on Brazilian interest rate spread[6] shows that in 2015 the banking interest spread in Brazil was 31.34%, positioning the country as the second highest in the world, just behind Madagascar, which had a rate of 42.05% (World Bank, 2015). The BCB agenda 2021 data shows that the spread remains high, with the country occupying the third position and a spread of 25.67%, just behind Zimbabwe, with 37.42% and Madagascar, with 34.53%. The reduction of the spread is relevant since there is a significant correlation between market concentration and credit spread (Jorgensen and Apostolou, 2013; Zeidan, 2020). Due to market power, the incumbents could exert pressure on prices to keep them high.

The five largest commercial banks in Brazil[7] concentrated 81.8% of the stock of credit operations until 2020 (BCB, 2020a). This entire framework leads to the belief that high concentration and high spread converge in a way that Brazilian banks have the highest return on equity (ROE) among banks with assets above

US$100 billion, which add up to 453 institutions around the world, according to a study carried out by Economatica (2019).[8]

Those three factors: high-interest spread, high ROE of banks and banking concentration have a negative effect on economic development. This happens because, when the spread is low, individuals and companies can borrow at reasonable rates to stimulate economic growth (Dwumfour, 2019, p. 139).

On the other hand, these aspects point to the inefficiency of the Brazilian credit market, affecting the overall ability to save. After all, low returns discourage savers, which reduces deposits and the capital allocation in the form of a credit. In consequence, credit access to productive projects is reduced, as borrowers stop using available credit lines due to their high cost (Brock and Rojas Suarez, 2000, p. 140).

In this scenario, in addition to the inefficient production of financial services, we have (Claessens, 2009): (i) less innovation, behold it makes entry barriers high and new contestants rare, (ii) less well-being of consumers, who pays more for a service that, in a scenario of increased competition, would pay less and, theoretically, would receive a better-quality service. When one considers the concentration of capital raising for investments through the banking market, instead of the capital market, its negative influence on economic development becomes even more evident, as it portrays the hardship to access the needed capital to invest in new projects which can contribute to economic growth.

In response, BCB started in 2019 to lead the implementation of OB with the "objective of increasing efficiency in the credit and payments market in Brazil, by promoting a more inclusive and competitive business environment, preserving the security of the financial system and consumer protection" (BCB, 2019).

In the next section, the foundations of OB and the governance process of implementation is analyzed, aiming to identify similarities, differences, best practices and expected results among Brazil and UK experiences.

Open Banking Regulation and Governance

In the United Kigdom and in Brazil inefficiencies of the financial market drove the implementation of OB and the main tool is data sharing between institutions to reduce information asymmetries was a major goal of OB. However, each jurisdiction adopted a specific model of OB regulation with specific governance and implementation structures.

A regulatory reform as the OB can be implemented by a fully state regulation based on a command-and-control model, by voluntary self-regulation or a diversity of hybrid models. In this sense, only within the scope of self-regulation, Black (1996, p. 27) points out four options: (i) mandatory self-regulation, in which self-regulation is based around a mandatory content defined by state regulation; (ii) sanctioned self-regulation, in which the content is formulated by private agents but its validity depends on prior state approval; (iii) coerced self-regulation, in which the content and imposition are of private agents but in response to the achievement of goals and objectives defined by the State and which must be achieved under threat of imposition of state regulation; (iv) voluntary self-regulation, in which the state has no direct or indirect involvement with the content and enforcement of self-regulation.

In the Brazilian case, as in other countries, the choice of the regulatory model was based on complex institutional factors and not just in terms of unique optimal global standards. After all, the framework of Brazilian banking regulation, the strength of the interest group of financial institutions already established in the Legislative and at the BCB, the technical and political legitimacy of BCB and the political context itself affect the choice of a regulatory model, as in the case of OB.

UK decisions were for mandatory self-regulation, while Brazil chose the sanctioned self-regulation or, as called by the entity, assisted self-regulation.[9]

It is this context the first aspect that draws attention is the differences in the competences of the main Authorities involved in promoting the implementation in each region.

While in the United Kingdom it was carried out by the Competition and Markets Authority (CMA), in Brazil it was conducted by the Monetary Authority, the BCB.

In the case of the United Kingdom, the CMA ordered the nine largest English banks to participate in the Open Banking project and, with that, carry out the data sharing required by PSD2, in addition to bearing the costs of creating the implementing entity, called OBIE, a private nature entity in which, although financed by the banks, had its composition and budget rules established by the CMA.

Since OBIE's implementation, it was up to the entity to define software standards and general guidelines for the behavior and organization of agents to promote interoperability between market participants, fundamental to allow the desired sharing of data and services.

The leadership of the OBIE is carried out by a Trustee, appointed by the CMA, who makes the decisions on the implementation rules and manages the funds received from the CMA to implement this policy. This figure has two support groups: (i) the Trustee's Office, responsible for monitoring and supervising compliance with the rules and (ii) the Implementation Entity Steering Group, a group formed later to bring together a multiplicity of representatives (CMA, Information Commissioner's Office, FCA, Treasury, Pay.UK, Payment System Authority and CMA9), whose main function is to advise the Trustee. Connected to this structure is the Executive Committee, which carries out the daily demands and work, including technical standards and working groups to improve initiatives and support the Trustee's decisions.

In the case of Brazil OB, it was born with a broader scope, as defined by the Resolution n. 1/2020 (BCB, 2020b). The implementation process demanded the inclusion of data on products and services beyond the banking scope, such as investment and insurance, even though the legitimacy of the BCB or the National Monetary Council could be discussed here regarding such an expansive scope.

To implement the self-regulation strategy the BCB determined mandatory participation for the larger financial Institutions.[10] The Institutions that have exposure or total assets in relation to GDP greater than 1% would be forced to participate, which represented twelve Institutions, with the voluntary participation of the other SFN members. But, when a voluntary institution decides to participate, they should respect the reciprocity principle, that is, for the right to receive data from other entities, they must share the data of their own customers, based on their request and consent.

To organize the development of the implementation, BCB determined the first general set of rules and resolved that a definitive structure must be deliberated by June 30, 2022.[11] Until then, a transitional implementation structure was created, composed by associations representing market agents,[12] divided into six groups.

The aforementioned transitional structure has three levels: (i) the Deliberative Council, which, in addition to the representatives of the six groups of entities, has an Independent Councilor, with the attributions of making strategic implementation decisions; (ii) the Secretariat, with the attribution of coordinating activities and works and; (iii) the Technical Groups, defined by topics whose definitions are necessary for the implementation of the policy, such as systems architecture, infrastructure, fraud prevention, among others, with the objective of subsidizing with studies and technical proposals the decision-making by the Deliberative Council.

The decisions made by the Board are supervised by the Central Bank, which has the prerogative, even, to deny a certain decision if it deems in disagreement with its objectives. On the other hand, if they agree, the definitions taken are brought into the regulatory framework.

Given the different structures between the two countries, the process of decision-making and approval of the themes also follows a different process. In the case of the OBIE, the decision is taken centrally by the Trustee, while in Brazil it is taken collectively by the Council and, later, ratified by the Central Bank. This validation officially does not take place in the British model.

Table 8.1 summarizes the different governance aspects of each location (Propague, 2020). As was evident, a large part of the structuring of OB on both sides of the Atlantic was built in parallel with the state, by private entities. This characteristic is present both in regulatory decentralization, co-regulation and incentive-based regulation models.

These diverse choices of regulatory design can be analyzed by the following characteristics: complexity, fragmentation, power and control, autonomy of actors, interactions and interdependence, collapse of the distinction between public and private (Black, 2001, p. 106). Complexity comes from the interdependence of interactions between different social actors that make regulatory decisions. Fragmentation stems from the asymmetry of information between the various agents and the impossibility of any one of them – including the regulator – having all the information needed to solve the problem. Power and control derive from the recognition that control and power are fragmented between social actors and between them and the state. This characteristic is directly connected to the autonomy of actors, which clarifies that social actors will continue to act according to their own desire in the absence of regulatory intervention. The next aspect comes from the interactions and interdependencies between social actors and these towards the State in the regulatory process, including the regulator and those directly regulated.

Table 8.1 Comparison between the Brazilian Regulatory Model and the English one

	Initial project scope	*Institution that led the project*	*Institutions involved in regulation*	*Was a specific body created?*	*Creation of technical standards*	*Inspection process*
United Kingdom Self-Regulation Model	Banking Sector	CMA	CMA (originally). Second phase: Treasury, FCA	Yes, the OBIE, an entity financed by CMA9, with a governance structure and budget defined by CMA, with the participation of CMA, FCA and Treasury.	Data structure and security architecture were developed by OBIE, with the participation of private institutions and regulators in the debate.	The system is overseen by OBIE, which is responsible for managing disputes. The OBIE reports to the CMA, FCA and Treasury. The overseers are also subject to relevant financial and data protection regulations. Participants need to register with FCA.
Brazil Assisted Self-Regulation Model	Financial System	BCB	CMN, BCB, CVM, SUSEP	Yes, the Governance Structure as a temporary body which will be replaced by a permanent body	The Governance Structure is responsible for suggesting technical standards that must be approved by the BCB and then standardized.	The BCB oversees the process to ensure compliance with established standards. Participants need to be authorized by the BCB and are also subject to specific financial and data protection regulations. The BCB oversees the process to ensure compliance with established regulations.

Source: Propague, 2020

Finally, regulation is seen as a product of interactions and not exclusively as the exercise of the formal power of the state as a public entity.

Thus, the vision of systemic and centralized regulation cannot account for this reality. In contrast, decentralized regulation prescribes indirect regulation focused on coordinating, directing, influencing and balancing actions between actors and systems, to establish new patterns of interaction for actors and systems to reorganize.

This complexity of elements should be reflected in the procedural and organizational structure built for OB both in Brazil and in the United Kingdom. Although adopting different models of self-regulation, both projects fail to absorb the complexity in the formation of the decision-making process that would involve other market agents.

It is worth remembering that both jurisdictions clearly share the main objective of promoting mechanisms to increase efficiency in their markets, via data sharing and, therefore, competition. In this way, producing an increase in consumer welfare.

However, by failing to observe the complexity of interactions, CMA and BCB relegate the success of the project to a restricted system of a single sector. Although both have conducted public consultations prior to the implementation effort, in both cases there is no knowledge of the participation of other sectoral entities that could share their knowledge and competence to complement and counterbalance the decisions taken.

Taking Brazil as an example, the interrelationship of competences with the National Data Protection Agency (ANPD) is evident, which has not been part of the implementation effort and is not represented in the Deliberative Council of the OB.

Moreover, it has the same aspect in relation to the competition. Although BCB has legal attributions to address competition concerns, Law 12.529/2011 (BRASIL, 2011), which instructs the Brazilian System for the Defense of Competition, entrusts the Economic Monitoring Secretariat with the promotion of competition in government bodies and in society, has not actively participated in the Open Banking policy.

Regulatory designs such as these tend to lose the expertise concentrated in such bodies at the expense of the difficulty of coordinating incentives that are not, a priori, aligned. It is precisely the reflection of the non-observance of the characteristics set out above, such as the notion of fragmentation, the disregard between the forces that exercise power and control and how they influence the autonomy of the actors.

For the system to remain in constant motion and allow new organizations to take place, there must be some tension between the parties involved, which would be more possible with the integration of these distinct agents, or their representatives, currently excluded from the implementation process.

The maturity of UK Open Banking demonstrates that this is the way forward. After the conclusion of an investigation conducted by Alison White[13] in 2021, the CMA opened a public consultation for stakeholders to present their visions for the addressable next steps. At the consultation conclusions and in response to White's investigation, the authority published a report (CMA, 2022b) indicating the next steps, including: (i) a succession plan for the activities performed by the OBIE, including creating another entity; (ii) the division of OB supervision with the CMA, the Treasury, the FCA and the PSR, as components of a Supervisory Committee; (iii) the inclusion of new stakeholders in the decision-making process, namely consumers and companies, or some of their representatives; (iv) the evolution of Open Banking to Open Finance.

The transition to the Open Finance model represents a greater breadth in the data and services that are shared within the scope of Open Banking to cover new aspects of our financial lives. In the case of the United Kingdom, going beyond the original scope of data about transactional accounts provided by PSD2 to, similarly to the Brazilian case, encompass the sharing of data and services that involve a series of other products that are beyond the shelves of Banks, in example, capitalization, insurance and private pension products, in other words, it is the same logic of sharing data and financial services of other types that are not exclusively banking.

Therefore, the evolution of UK OB led to an increase in the participation of other stakeholders in the process, in line with the decentralization theory explored in this chapter.

After understanding the creation and implementation of OB the next section will deal with the relation between OB and the COVID-19 pandemic.

Effects of Open Banking in a Pandemic World

The implementation process of OB is contemporaneous with the COVID-19 pandemic. In this sense, it is important to correlate both events.

The pandemic has certainly been a catalyst for the digitalization of financial transactions, whether for purchase or for receiving government aid. For the latter, in addition to the social benefits of the measure, it influenced financial inclusion. As a World Bank Study (2021, p. 5) points out that 13% of those who have a bank account worldwide opened their first account to receive a salary, government benefits or the sale of agricultural products, which will generate the maintenance of this individual within of the formal financial system.

When looking at payment transactions used to make retail purchases, the UK Finance study (UK Finance, 2021) reflects that in 2020, the share of card payments reached 52% among all payments made, because of merchants encouraging the use of contactless payment or online purchases. In the opposite direction, the period of 2020 delivered a 35% decrease in the use of money compared to 2019.

On the other side of the Atlantic, in relation to measures to support the population, Brazil used the state bank *Caixa Econômica Federal* to enhance the distribution of "*coronavoucher*"[14] via digital bank accounts opened in this bank to the beneficiaries. Altogether, the program benefited around 68.3 million people, of which it is estimated that 14 million have carried out their first formal operation within the financial system through the mandatory adoption of the account (World Bank, 2021, p. 10). The result is, due to digital measures for distributing the financial benefit, the unbanked Brazilian population decreased by 73% (Americas Market Intelligence, 2020, p. 13)

Also in this context, the pandemic coincides with BCB launching the infrastructure to allow instant payments, called PIX. This new system lets payments and transfers to happen 24 hours a day, 7 days a week, in an interoperable way, either between financial institutions or between other payment service providers.

Data targeted at payment transactions will certainly be greatly influenced by the interoperability and efficiency-enhancing agendas promoted at the heart of Open Banking's objectives. The success of the PSD2 in the United Kingdom and the PIX in Brazil demonstrates this will be a path of no return and whose movement can contribute to economic growth, the reduction of inequalities and the effectiveness of macroeconomic policies (Sahay et al. 2020).

In terms of credit, it is certain the disruption of supply and demand for goods and services increased uncertainty and has reduced the appetite of financial institutions in granting new operations. So, an increase in the interest rate is an expected response to the increase in risk and can lead to the rationalization of credit supply (Stiglitz and Weiss, 1981). In that scenario, people and companies access less credit, either because of the lower supply of banks, higher costs, or tougher conditions. As a result, access to the financial system is reduced (Pérez and Titelman, 2018, p. 40 – 42).

These observations help explain the high consumption in the United Kingdom during the pandemic. Experian (2021) suggests 57% of borrowers in the period between May 2020 and May 2021 adopted the technology in the period. Even so, the World Bank (2017, p. 31), estimates around 162 million SMEs around the world have a possible unmet credit demand of US$5.2 trillion.

In Brazil alone, the SMEs segment[15] corresponds to about 17.3 million Brazilian enterprises and, only for the first three months of the pandemic (March, April and May/2020), an unmet demand was estimated between $35 and R$79 billion Brazilian Reais[16] (Gonzales, Barreira and Ridolfo, 2021).

The technologies promoted by OB encourage the digitization of financial services and, notably, electronic transactions and data transfer. The greater access to financial services can boost economic recovery and align with the goals of sustainable development (UNSGSA, 2018), including the reduction of inequalities and the strengthening of institutions.

After the most serious phase of the pandemic has passed, economic recovery implies the effort of Governments and Financial Institutions to adequately support and promote access to services, increasing the efficiency of their payment systems and their ability to offer access to credit in a way that transaction costs can be reduced.

Other measures, according to Plaitakis and Staschen (2020) are pointed out as options for this new post-pandemic world with an OB context: (i) smoothing the effects of volatile financial income; (ii) reduction in domestic bill fees; (iii) overcoming the lack of documentation to contract banking products and services; (iv) promote healthy financial habits; (v) responsible credit expansion; (vi) support in debt rehabilitation and (vii) avoid the use of inappropriate credit products.

The advancement of such initiatives may represent a good path for other countries. The pandemic has demonstrated that digitization of financial services is a necessary way to increase financial inclusion. However, other infrastructure barriers need to be addressed, such as access to connectivity and smartphones, in addition to developing skills to browse and consume financial products and services online.

Conclusions

This article describes the economic and competitive context of the Brazilian and UK banking markets, elucidating the need for intervention in each jurisdiction and, given the authority that carried it out, how the intervention has been conducted and the expected effects based on its competencies. It is important to note that Open Banking, as a regulatory intervention, has importance for financial systems as a modern measure in response to the need identified in both countries to increase competition in the banking market, notably for the service of accounts for SMEs in the United Kingdom and, in the case of Brazil, the credit market.

Despite the different economic and institutional contexts in Brazil and the United Kingdom, the regulation of OB in both has similarities like the goal of ensuring efficiency and completeness of financial markets. The models of regulatory decentralization were different: in the United Kingdom the choice was of mandatory self-regulation and in Brazil sanctioned self-regulation.

Within the scope of the regulatory decentralization process, the complexity of the interaction between agents is a central point, which is quite relevant in the case of Open Banking. After all, there is an interaction between financial, data and competition regulation at the same time and confined within the scope of public agents. Furthermore, the interaction between traditional financial institutions, new entrants, consumers, economic agents that own data and other agents must be properly addressed. Thus, the organizational structure must be able to address all these interests and have adequate governance to produce adequate regulatory decisions.

The two studied models had chosen to escape from extreme models of voluntary self-regulation and pure state regulation. However, there are relevant differences that were highlighted throughout this study.

The centralization of the state portion of regulation in the financial authority and the absence of representatives with a specific interest in data regulation is a deficiency in the Brazilian organizational structure and governance process. After all, the fragmentation of regulation and regulatory asymmetry makes it unlikely that the BCB will be able to produce adequate regulation, without a diversity of members in the organizational structure adopted by Brazil. The technical legitimacy of the Central Bank is not projected for markets other than the financial market.

Movements such as Open Banking demonstrate a change in the position that Central Banks occupy in the supervision of financial markets and the challenges faced with the digital evolution as new business dynamics can generate or exacerbate market failures. As a result, the basic role of a Central Banks that provides financial and banking services to the government and commercial banks, in addition to implementing monetary policy and cash control, is being challenged to assume new contours and characteristics.

Above all, Regulation Agencies and Central Banks are called to act proactively, as catalysts for changes in favor of innovations such as, in example, the provision by the BCB of the necessary infrastructure for instant payments in an integrated manner with the Open Banking strategy.

Such innovations will demand, as proposed by the theory of decentralized regulation, better coordination between sectorial entities, like those being created to address privacy and personal data protection, to deeply understand and address the modern problems the digital economy presents.

Even so, the implementation of the OB took place at the critical moment of the COVID-19 pandemic, which was marked, whether in Brazil or in the United Kingdom, by the accelerated digitization of banking services, especially payment services. The technological standardization promoted by the OB and the acculturation to electronic transactions were important aspects to highlight the influence of this policy in the recovery of the economy in a post-pandemic world.

Notes

1 Also, on the interconnection of themes, the *European Data Protection Board* (EDPB, 2020), an independent European body that contributes to the application of data protection rules throughout Europe, presented specific guidelines that connect the GDPR and the PSD2. The latter, as will be shown, is the legislation that underpins the implementation of Open Banking in the United Kingdom.

2 In a logic that the sharing of data would reduce the rationalization of credit in imperfect information markets, affecting the model foreseen in STIGLITZ and WEISS (1981).

3 It is worth highlighting the standardization promoted by the directive, to make all the European electronic payments market more efficient.

4 As known as CMA9, these are: AIB Group UK, Bank of Ireland, Barclays Bank, HSBC Group, Lloyds Banking Group, Nationwide Building Society, NatWest Group, Danske Bank and Santander UK

5 With special emphasis on Act 12.865/2013 (BRAZIL, 2013b), which defined relevant aspects for the payment market and was able solve a problem related with legal. This law is an important legal milestone in the structural transformation that the Brazilian payment market is undergoing.

6 Interest rate spread can be defined as: "the difference between the interest rate charged to borrowers and the rate paid to depositors" (Dwumfour, 2018, p.140) and can be perceived as an indicator for the cost of intermediation and the market efficiency (Brock and Rojas Suarez, 2000, p. 114).

7 These are Caixa Econômica Federal, Banco do Brasil, Itaú Unibanco, Bradesco e Santander. It is worth mentioning that the first two are state-owned.

8 Banco Santander Brasil with a ROE of 19.25% leads the list, followed by ItauUnibanco with 18.59%, Bradesco with 17.97% and Banco do Brasil with 17.71%. Only in fifth position is a non-Brazilian bank, which is the Royal Bank of Canada, with 16.13%.

9 As stated by the Deputy Director of Regulation, Otávio Damaso, *see* BANCO CENTRAL DO BRASIL. **Após regulamentação, BC se prepara para implementar primeira fase do Open Banking**. BCB homepage. May 21 2020. Available at: <https://www.bcb.gov.br/detalheticia/454/noticia>. Access on May 28. 2022

10 Defined by its size, the international activity and Conglomerate of Financial and Non-Financial Institutions profile risk and size.

11 According to the most recent standard on the subject, BCB Resolution No. 152, of October 6, 2021.

12 They are: i) Brazilian Federation of Banks (FEBRABAN), representing the large banks; ii) Brazilian Association of Banks (ABBC), representing medium and small banks; iii) Organization of Brazilian Cooperatives (OCB), representing credit unions; iv) Brazilian Association of Credit Card Companies and Services (Abecs), mostly representing incumbent payment processors; v) Coalition formed by the Brazilian Association of Payment Institutions (Abipag), the Brazilian Internet Association (Abranet) and the Brazilian Chamber of Electronic Commerce (Câmara-e.net), mostly representing new entrants to electronic payment processors; v) Brazilian Association of Digital Credit (ABCD) and Brazilian Association of Fintechs (ABFintechs), representing fintechs in general as new entrants.

13 The investigation was initiated after receiving a complaint against the management of OBIE for, among other problems, the failure to address potential conflicts of interest of the organization and the market and in its corporate governance. *In* WHITE, 2021

14 Public policy coverage data can be monitored at:<https://aplicacoes.mds.gov.br/sagi/vis/data3/index.php?g=2>

15 Considering i) Individual Microentrepreneur (MEI); ii) Microenterprise (ME); and iii) Small Business (EPP).

16 The equivalent of approximately US$6.5 and US$14.7 billion in the Brazilian Real to US Dollar conversion on September 28, 2022.

References

Americas Market Intelligence. (2020). The acceleration of financial inclusion during the COVID-19 pandemic: Bringing hidden opportunities to light. Mastercard. https://www.mastercard.com/news/media/j41fhoyr/mastercard_financial_inclusion_during_covid_whitepaper_external_20201012.pdf

Bag, D. 2013, *Transaction Costs and Efficiency in Intermediation*, Journal of Services Research, Volume 13, Number 1, April–September 2013, https://ssrn.com/abstract=3770422

Brazil 2013, *Lei n° 12.529, de 30 de novembro de 2011*, viewed 12 April 2022, *http://www.planalto.gov.br/ccivil_03/_ato2011-2014/2011/lei/l12529.htm*

——— 2013b, *Lei n° 12.865, de 9 de outubro de 2013,* viewed 12 April 2022, *http://www.planalto.gov.br/ccivil_03/_ato2011-2014/2013/lei/l12865.htm*

Black, J., 1996, *'Constitutionalizing Self-Regulation'*, The Modern Law Review Limited 1996 (MLR 59:1, January).

———, 2001 '*Decentring Regulation: Understanding the Role of Regulation and Self-Regulation in a 'Post-Regulatory' World'*, Current Legal Problems.

———, 2002, *'Critical Reflections on Regulation'*. Centre for Analysis of Risk and Regulation. London School of Economics and Political Science. viewed 28 September 2022, <http://eprints.lse.ac.uk/35985/1/Disspaper4-1.pdf.

Brock, P. L., & Rojas Suarez, L., 2000, Understanding the Behavior of Bank Spreads in Latin America. Journal of Development Economics, 63(1), 113–134. https://doi.org/10.1016/s0304-3878(00)00102-4

Casoria, M., 2021, *'The Relationship Between Open Banking And Competition Law: A Novel European Saga'*, 16th Annual ASCOLA Virtual Conference on Competition and Innovation in Digital Markets Porto, 1–3 July 2021.

Central Bank of Brazil (BCB), 2019, *'Comunicado N° 33.455, de 24 de Abril de 2019'*, viewed 06 May 2022, https://www.in.gov.br/web/dou/-/comunicado-n%C2%BA-33.455-de-24-de-abril-de-2019-85378506

——— 2020a, *'Relatório de Economia Bancária – 2020'*, viewed 07 May 2022, https://www.bcb.gov.br/publicacoes/relatorioeconomiabancaria

——— 2020b, *'Resolução BCB n° 1 de 12/8/2020'*, viewed 07 May 2022, https://www.bcb.gov.br/estabilidadefinanceira/exibenormativo?tipo=Resolu%C3%A7%C3%A3o%20BCB&numero=1

——— 2020c, *'Relatório Integrado do Banco Central, RIg 2020'*, viewed 28 September 2022, https://www.bcb.gov.br/content/publicacoes/rig/rig_2020.pdf

——— 2021a, *'Resolução BCB n° 152 de 6/10/2021'*, viewed 28 May 2022, https://www.bcb.gov.br/estabilidadefinanceira/exibenormativo?tipo=Resolu%C3%A7%C3%A3o%20BCB&numero=152

——— 2021b, *'Relatório de Cidadania Financeira'*, viewed 28 May 2022, https://www.bcb.gov.br/content/cidadaniafinanceira/documentos_cidadania/RIF/Relatorio_de_Cidadania_Financeira_2021.pdf

——— 2021c, *'Apresentação do Presidente do Banco Central, Roberto Campos Neto, no Seminário Open Banking, realizado pela Folha de S.Paulo e Embratel'*, viewed 29 September 2022, https://www.bcb.gov.br/conteudo/home-ptbr/TextosApresentacoes/Apresenta%C3%A7%C3%A3o%20RCN_Open%20Banking_vpub.pdf

Claessens, S., 2009, *'Competition in the Financial Sector: Overview of Competition Policies'* IMF Working Paper, Research Department, viewed 27 September 2022, https://www.imf.org/external/pubs/ft/wp/2009/wp0945.pdf

Competition and Markets Authority (CMA), 2016, *'Retail banking market investigation, Final report'*, viewed 14 May 2022, https://assets.publishing.service.gov.uk/media/57ac9667e5274a0f6c00007a/retail-banking-market-investigation-full-final-report.pdf

——— 2021, *'Corporate report: Update on Open Banking'*, viewed 14 May 2022, https://www.gov.uk/government/publications/update-governance-of-open-banking/update-on-open-banking#fnref:8

——— 2022a, *'The future oversight of the CMA's Open Banking remedies, Response to consultation'*, viewed 14 May 2022, https://assets.publishing.service.gov.uk/government/uploads/system/uploads/attachment_data/file/1063319/Consultation_response.pdf>

——— 2022b, *'Competition and Markets Authority Annual Plan 2022/23'*, viewed 14 May 2022, https://assets.publishing.service.gov.uk/government/uploads/system/uploads/attachment_data/file/1062414/Final_Annual_Plan_for_2022_23.pdf

De la Mano, M., & Padilla, J. 2018, *'Big Tech Banking'*, *Journal of Competition Law & Economics*, 14(4), 494–526, https://doi.org/10.1093/joclec/nhz003

Dwumfour, R. A., 2019, *'Explaining banking spread'*, *Journal of Financial Economic Policy*, 11(1), 139–156. https://doi.org/10.1108/JFEP-02-2018-0031

Economatica, 2019 *'Bancos Brasileiros têm a Maior Rentabilidade Sobre Patrimônio ENTRE Bancos Com Ativos Acima de US$100 Bilhões. ITAU Unibanco Perde A Liderança Para O Santander Brasil'*, Economatica Insights, viewed 21 September 2021, https://insight.economatica.com/bancos-brasileiros-tem-a-maior-rentabilidade-sobre-patrimonio-entre-bancos-com-ativos-acima-de-us-100-bilhoes-itauunibanco-lose-the-leadership-to-santander-brasil/

European Data Protection Board (EDPB), 2020, *'Guidelines 06/2020 on the interplay of the Second Payment Services Directive and the GDPR Version 2.0*, viewed 09 April 2022, https://edpb.europa.eu/sites/default/files/files/file1/edpb_guidelines_202006_psd2_afterpublicconsultation_en.pdf

Experian, 2021, *'Open banking demand triples during Covid-19 pandemic'*, viewed 09 April 2022, https://www.experianplc.com/media/latest-news/2021/open-banking-demand-triples-during-covid-19-pandemic/

HM Treasury 2013, *'Competition in banking: improving access to SME credit data'*, viewed 15 May 2022, *https://www.gov.uk/government/consultations/competition-in-banking-improving-access-to-sme-credit-data/competition-in-banking-improving-access-to-sme-credit-data*

______ 2014a, *'Improving access to SME credit data: summary of responses'*, viewed 15 May 2022, https://assets.publishing.service.gov.uk/government/uploads/system/uploads/attachment_data/file/323318/PU1681_final.pdf

______ 2014b, *'Improving access to SME credit data: regulatory impact assessment'*, viewed 15 May 2022, https://assets.publishing.service.gov.uk/government/uploads/system/uploads/attachment_data/file/323318/PU1681_final.pdf

______ 2014c, *'The Small and Medium Sized Businesses (Credit Information) Regulations 2015: draft secondary legislation'*, viewed 15 May 2022, https://assets.publishing.service.gov.uk/government/uploads/system/uploads/attachment_data/filc/389204/DraftRegulations_12_12_14_1111__2_.pdf

Jarude, J., Vita, J., & Wandscheer, L., 2020, *'O Sistema Financeiro Aberto (Open Banking) Sob a Perspectiva Da Regulação Bancária e Da Lei Geral De Proteção De Dados'*, Revista Brasileira De Filosofia Do Direito, 6(1), 78–95, viewed 17 May 2022, https://www.indexlaw.org/index.php/filosofiadireito/article/view/6455

Jorgensen, O., & Apostolou, A., 2013, *'Brazil's bank spread in international context: From macro to micro drivers'*, Policy Research Working Paper Series 6611, World Bank, viewed 16 May 2022, https://openknowledge.worldbank.org/bitstream/handle/10986/16839/WPS6611.pdf?sequence=1&isAllowed=y

KPMG 2018, *'Is Open Banking open for business? UK entrepreneurs outline what they want from Open Banking services'*, viewed 17 May 2022, https://assets.kpmg/content/dam/kpmg/uk/pdf/2018/11/is-open-banking-open-for-business.pdf

Mourão, C., & Silva, L., 2020, *'A Proteção De Dados Pessoais à Luz Do Direito concorrencial'*, Revista De Defesa Da Concorrência, 8(2), 31–53, viewed 29 May 2022 https://revista.cade.gov.br/index.php/revistadedefesadaconcorrencia/article/view/649/350

Murta Filho, M., *'Reformas Regulamentares e Concorrência: O caso da Indústria Brasileira'*, Prêmio SEAE: monografias em defesa da concorrência e regulação econômica: 2006, Ministério da Fazenda, Secretaria de Acompanhamento Econômico., p. 167–230.

Nakane, M., & Alencar, L., 2004, *'VIII - Análise de fusões e aquisições horizontais no setor bancário: uma reflexão a partir da experiência internacional'*, Seminário de economia bancária e crédito, 2004, viewed 27 September 2022, https://www.bcb.gov.br/pec/semecobancred2004/port/paperVIII.pdf

Organization For Economic Co-Operation And Development (OECD), 2006, 'Competition and Regulation in Retail Banking', Policy Roundtables, viewed 27 September 2022 https://www.oecd.org/daf/competition/39753683.pdf

______, 2014, 'Competition role in financial consumer protection', Issues Paper by the Secretariat, viewed 27 September 2022, https://one.oecd.org/document/DAF/COMP(2014)6/en/pdf

Palmieri, A., & Nazeraj, B., 2021, *'Open banking and Competition: an Intricate relationship'*, EU and Comparative Law Issues and Challenges Series (ECLIC), 5, 217–237, viewed 29 May 2022, https://hrcak.srce.hr/ojs/index.php/eclic/article/view/18822

Pérez, E., & Titelman, D., 2018. *'La inclusión financiera para la inserción productiva y el papel de la banca de desarrollo'*. Santiago de Chile: Cepal. https://web.bndes.gov.br/bib/jspui/bitstream/1408/22030/1/14-BNDES-Revista56-Inova%c3%a7%c3%b5esServi%c3%a7osFinanceirosOpenBanking.pdf

Plaitakis, Ariadne, and Stefan Staschen. 2020. 'Open Banking: How to Design for Financial Inclusion.' Working Paper. Washington, D.C.: CGAP.

Propague, I., 2020, *'Open Finance. Modelos de Governança em diversos países'*, Carta Propague, 5th edition. viewed 29 May 2022, https://institutopropague.org/wp-content/uploads/2022/04/Open-Finance-modelos-de-governanca-em-diferentes-paises-Carta-Propague-5.pdf

Sahay, R., von Allmen, U. E., Lahreche, A., Khera, P., Ogawa, S., Bazarbash, M., & Beaton, K., 2020, 'The Promise of Fintech: Financial Inclusion in the Post COVID-19 Era'. International Monetary Fund. Monetary and Capital Markets Department. Departmental Paper No. 2020/009. ISBN/ISSN: 9781513512242/2616-5333. Washington, D.C.: International Monetary Fund.

Stiglitz, J., & Weiss, A., 1981, *'Credit Rationing in Markets With Imperfect Information'*, The American Economic Review, 71(3), 393–410, viewed 08 May 2022, http://www.jstor.org/stable/1802787

The European Parliament And The Council Of The European Union 2015, *'Directive (EU) 2015/2366, Payment Service Directive 2'*, viewed 18 May 2022, https://eur-lex.europa.eu/legal-content/EN/TXT/?uri=celex%3A32015L2366

The World Bank, 2015, *'Interest rate spread (lending rate minus deposit rate, %)'*, viewed 07 May 2022, https://data.worldbank.org/indicator/FR.INR.LNDP?view=map&year=2021

——— 2017, *'MSME Finance Gap: Assessment of the Shortfalls and Opportunities in Financing Micro, Small, and Medium Enterprises in Emerging Markets'*. Washington, DC. © International Finance Corporation, viewed 07 May 2022, https://openknowledge.worldbank.org/handle/10986/28881

——— 2021, *'The impact of COVID-19 on digital financial inclusion'*, Global Partnership for Financial Inclusion, viewed 07 May 2022, https://www.gpfi.org/sites/gpfi/files/sites/default/files/5_WB%20Report_The%20impact%20of%20COVID-19%20on%20digital%20financial%20inclusion.pdf

United Nations Secretary-General's Special Advocate For Inclusive Finance For Development – UNSGSA 2018. *'Igniting SDG progress through digital financial inclusion'*, viewed 17 April 2022, https://www.unsgsa.org/sites/default/files/resources-files/2020-09/SDG_Compendium_Digital_Financial_Inclusion_September_2018.pdf

United Kingdom, 2017, *'The Payment Systems and Services and Electronic Money (Miscellaneous Amendments) Regulations 2017'*, Statutory Instruments, viewed 16 April 2022, https://www.legislation.gov.uk/uksi/2017/1173/contents/made

UK Finance, 2021, 'UK Payment Markets Summary 2021', viewed 16 April 2022, https://www.ukfinance.org.uk/sites/default/files/uploads/SUMMARY-UK-Payment-Markets-2021-FINAL.pdf

White, A., 2021, *'Investigation of Open Banking Limited. Independent report by Alison White'*, viewed 18 May 2022, https://assets.publishing.service.gov.uk/government/uploads/system/uploads/attachment_data/file/1022451/Independent_report.pdf

Zeidan, R., 2020, *'Why Is Bank Credit in Brazil the Most Expensive in the World?*, Brazilian Review of Finance, 18(4), 1–22, 20 May 2022, https://bibliotecadigital.fgv.br/ojs/index.php/rbfin/article/view/81507/78702

9 Central Banking in Russia, Ukraine, and Belarus in the Face of Pandemic, War, and Sanctions

Cornelia Sahling

Introduction

In the first years of transition, post-Soviet governments expected their central banks (CBs) to function as something close to the Soviet Gosbank, in its subservience to leadership. Until 1995, monetary financing was commonly used for budget balancing. But gradually, new standards were introduced. The idea of autonomous CBs was also promoted by the International Monetary Fund (IMF). Constant modernization efforts and several monetary policy (MP) regime changes seemed to implement a new culture of central banking and to guarantee financial and macroeconomic stability. Modern MP instruments and more flexible exchange rates (floating or free-floating) aimed to set formal rules and to increase the CB credibility and policy predictability.

With the declared MP goals, the implementation of modern MP instruments in Eastern Europe promoted Western standards of central banking and improved financial supervision. Recent developments, however, have caused us to question the outcome of the modernization efforts. Against the government's increasing involvement in central banking, this chapter examines measures undertaken by the Central Bank of Russia (CBR), the National Bank of Ukraine (NBU), and the National Bank of the Republic of Belarus (NBRB) during the pandemic (2020–2022) and Russia's military invasion of Ukraine starting from February 24th, 2022. This investigation identifies how the MP changed under coronavirus-related restrictions and the war and how the CBs managed to maintain stability.

A focus on CB autonomy and on supporting stability (as often promoted by the IMF) can be effective in some cases, but other models may be suitable for particular countries. The relationship between the CB and the government is very complex and depends on the political realities in a country. Discrepancies between de jure and de facto CB autonomy in Eastern Europe (Kißmer & Wagner 2004, pp. 123–124) complicates the understanding of actual independence. Traditional (formalized) indexes mainly consider legal constraints on central banking. But external influence (as through the IMF), training for central bankers, the experience of developed states, and mainstream monetarism in Western countries combined with internal (political and economic) pressures to reform and regional peculiarities (the unsuccessful experience of the Ruble zone[1])

DOI: 10.4324/9781003323280-10

explain how the development of central banking was promoted in transition economies (for a discussion see Hartwell 2020). In Eastern Europe, an autonomous CB may be useful to achieve secondary policy goals such as stimulating investments and improving the standard of living. As the CBR (since 2014) and the NBU (since 2016) introduced inflation targeting and the NBRB inflation targeting with elements of monetary targeting (since 2015), more political and economic independence could have been achieved. However, this investigation shows a tendency towards less CB autonomy. This observation is based on a broader understanding of autonomy than formalized criteria of traditional indexes on CB independence and reflects political and economic independence of a CB in conducting their policy.

This paper extends the existing literature on the overall development of central baking in Eastern Europe (e.g., on the CBR, see Johnson 2018, Nakamura 2019, Korhonen & Nuutilainen 2016) with reflections on MP during crises. The paper provides early reflections on MP responses to COVID and to the war in Ukraine. As the war in Ukraine is ongoing when this chapter was finished (September 2022), this investigation is limited by the first monetary policy reactions to the war and related sanctions for Russia and Belarus (February–September 2022). This chapter argues that Russia's economic and political isolation is growing and the CBR tries to adapt to the new financial realities, while Belarus' dependence on Russia is growing and the pressure on the NBRB to promote MP harmonization with Russia (in the "Union State" of Russia and Belarus) is increasing. For Ukraine, the dependence on foreign creditors and the IMF is significant; a longer period for regaining financial stability and more international financial assistance will be necessary to function properly. Central banking cannot be separated from political developments and the overall environment, as the pandemic and its controversial outcomes have shown. During times of war, monetary policy is used as one of the instruments in the service of governments, and geopolitical developments cannot be understood without the role of CBs.

Monetary Regime Transformations in Russia, Ukraine, and Belarus and CB Autonomy

In the process of transforming former regional branches of the Soviet Gosbank (State bank) and developing a new two-tier banking system, both external and internal influence factors on the new national CBs were of importance. In general, the history of Russian, Soviet, and post-Soviet central banking reveals contentious attempts of political interference into central banking. The role of the State Bank of the Russian Empire (created in 1861) differed from other European CBs (that were also under political influence) in terms of the open control by the Ministry of Finance and the widespread involvement in loans to the private sector to support industrial development (Garvy 1972, p. 873). In the Soviet monetary system, Gosbank had a subordinate position, and served communist party-state interests, and goals provided by Gosplan (State Planning Committee). The gradual liquidation of commercial banks enabled central control of monetary relations in the Union of Soviet Socialist Republics (USSR) and the use of loans was managed by the government. In addition, the monopoly status of the savings bank system and lacking alternatives for spending or investing money facilitated the quasi-usage of household savings for state interests. These historical legacies of central banking and expectations of central bankers influenced the development of a contemporary culture of central banking in transition economies. In the first years after the dissolution of the USSR, key positions at the CBs were held by former Soviet servants. These central bankers were trained in the USSR. The first governor of the NBRB, N. Omelianovich, considered the difficulties of staff adaptation as one of the problems in the transformation of the CB. After a long time of working under the control of the central government, the staff was used to implement regulations and instructions from above (Omelianovich 2013, p. 69).

The CBR, NBRB, and NBU have developed a modern legal framework. But de facto political influence is apparent in the frequent changes of the CB governors in the 1990s in Russia, Ukraine, and Belarus (see Table 9.1). Trunin et al. 2010 calculated the GMT (Grilli, Masciandaro, and Tabellini)-Index for post-Soviet and Eastern European countries. They showed that Belarus and Ukraine had the lowest index among the investigated countries and Russia was ranged in the middle (Trunin et al. 2010, pp. 55–60). In the case of the CBR, the amendments to the CB law in 2002 lowered formal (legal) CBR's independence (Trunin et al. 2010, pp. 25–33).

Table 9.1 Terms of office of CB governors

CBR	*NBRB*	*NBU*
1990–92 – G. Matyukhin	1991 – N. Omelianovich	1991–1992 – V. Matwijenko
1992–94 – V Gerashchenko	1991–1995 – S. Bogdankevich	1992 – V. Hetman
1994–95 – T. Paramonova (acting chairperson)	1996–1997 – T. Vinnikova	1993–2000 – V. Yushchenko
Nov 1995 – A. Khandruyev (acting chairperson)	1997–1998 – G. Aleynikov	2000–2002 – V. Stelmakh
1995–1998 – S. Dubinin	1998–2011 – P. Prokopovitch	2002–2004 – S. Tigipko
1998–2002 – V. Gerashchenko	2011–2014 – N. Yermakova	2004–2010 – V. Stelmakh
2002–2013 – S. Ignatiev	Since 2014 – P. Kallaur	2010–2012 – S. Arbusov
Since 2013 – E. Nabiullina		2013–2014 – I. Sorkin 2014 – S. Kubiv 2014–2017 – V. Hontareva 2018–2020 – Y. Smoliy 2020–2022 K. Shevchenko Since October 2022 – A. Pyshnyy

Sources: CBR, NBRB, NBU.

Recent history of Russian central banking showed a process of modernization. Not only new MP instruments were implemented. The usage of mathematical models and foreign analytical resources became a new standard for the research department (Reiter & Lyutova 2022). Important MP changes were related to the switch to free-floating exchange rate regime (introduced since the 10 November 2014) after the annexation of Crimea, imposed sanctions and Russian counter measures. Before that, from 1999 until 2014, managed floating (since February 2005 with a dual currency basket) was used by the CBR. The abandonment of the operational band in November 2014 and a market-determined ruble exchange rate enabled a sharp devaluation of the Russian exchange rate (Figure 9.1). In 2014, the CBR implemented an inflation targeting regime with a goal of 4.0%. In the period prior to inflation targeting, the CBR's monetary policy framework was classified by the IMF as "other" (neither monetary targeting nor exchange rate anchor) as the CB had no stated nominal anchor and used various indicators for its monetary policy framework (IMF 2005, p. 16). At the same time, the CBR had been preparing for the inflation-targeting regime and elements of an exchange rate anchor were apparent.

In general, capital outflows, high exchange rate fluctuations after the introduction of free-floating, banking supervision, and financial sanctions (since 2014) were important MP challenges. Since the 2000s (V. Putin's first presidential

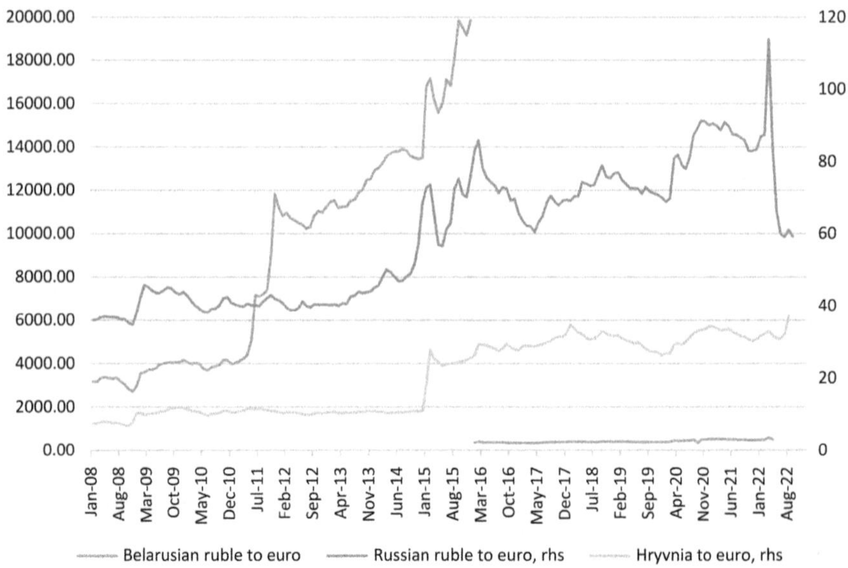

Figure 9.1 Official exchange rates to the euro (monthly geometric mean)

Source: CBR, NBRB, NBU.

Note: In 2016, there was a currency denomination by a factor of 10,000 in Belarus. Before that, the Belarusian exchange rate is shown on the left-hand scale.

term) the idea of monetary sovereignty was promoted by the government as an important goal for economic policy (Johnson 2008). This was a long-term de facto government interference into the CBR's policy framework, as the idea of "protecting" the national financial system from external influence was used to reinforce state's sovereignty over monetary relations. The CBR increased monetary sovereignty from the West to face possible financial sanctions and deeper economic isolation. This policy change functioned as an important precondition for the achievement of foreign policy goals for the government, but lowered CB independence without formal legislation amendment. In general, strengthening financial nationalism (understood as the usage of financial and monetary policy to support nationalist policy goals) is usually with lower CB autonomy (Johnson & Barnes 2015, p. 539).

The NBRB is still working towards the goal of full inflation targeting. In 2015, the NBRB introduced managed floating after a long period of a pegged arrangement. In the following year (July 2016), new Belarusian rubles were introduced at the rate of 1:10,000.[2] This third denomination (two others took place in 1994 and 2000) was also the biggest in the country's monetary history after gaining independence with the dissolution of the USSR. Understanding the MP regime in Belarus requires the comparison of de facto and de jure regimes (Table 9.2). The legal framework in 2005-2008 suggested an official peg to the Russian ruble (within a narrow band), but de facto, the NBRB pegged the exchange rate against the US dollar. This discrepancy between proclaimed exchange rate regime and actual working conditions can be understood as a political pressure on the NBRB. As the Belarusian President determines the main directions of MP, the choice of a peg to the Russian currency is politically motivated to get support from Russia. This motivation can be explained through the dependence of the Belarusian economy on subsidized prices for Russian oil and gas. In addition, Russia is the biggest trading partner for Belarus. However, Belarus is not Russia's main trading partner.

A new law on the NBRB was introduced in 1994 with the aim to ensure CB independence (at least formal). But after the election of A. Lukashenko as president, pressures on the NBRB increased and the banking system was used as an instrument to direct credits close to a command economy (Barisitz 2000, pp. 87–88). In 1998, a presidential decree allowed the president to appoint and remove the CB governor. Contemporary CB law still enables the president to remove the governor[3]. In such conditions, an independent decision-making process cannot be ensured. Indices of higher CB independence would be autonomous MP formulation and little authority of the government to appoint (or dismiss) the CB governor/ staff members (Cukierman et al. 1992, p. 357). In the case of the NBRB, neither autonomous policy formulation nor the independent appointment of the chairperson and board is provided. Due to high exchange rate fluctuations and the problems with maintaining a stable inflation within the medium target of 5%, the degree of dollarization remains high. A lack of trust leads citizens to prefer holding savings in dollars or other foreign currencies after the

Table 9.2 NBRB's policy framework for 2005–2021

Time period	*Exchange rate regime*		*MP regime*
	De facto classification of the IMF	*De jure classification*	
2005–2008	Fixed peg arrangement to the US dollar	peg to the Russian ruble within a band	Exchange rate anchor
Since 04/2008	Stabilized arrangement (since 04/2008 – reclassification of the IMF methodology)		
Since 01/2009	de facto pegged exchange rate within horizontal bands	Pegged exchange rate within horizontal bands (since 01/2009 the Belarusian ruble is pegged to a basket of currencies: the euro, the US dollar, and the Russian ruble)	
Since 05/2010	Since 05/2010 – de facto stabilized arrangement against the US dollar		
2011	other managed arrangement (since 05/2011 – IMF reclassification)	managed floating regime since 10/2011	
2012–2014	Crawl-like arrangement (IMF reclassification since 09/ 2012)		Switch to other regime (abandonment of the euro-dollar currency basket as monetary anchor)
2015–2019	Other managed arrangement (IMF reclassification since 01/2015)		Since 01/2015 – monetary aggregate target (base money as an operational target)
2020	Floating (de facto and de jure)		

Source: NBRB; IMF: Annual Reports on exchange arrangements and exchange restrictions, for 2005–2018 and 2020.

experiences of crises, high inflation, and currency denominations. Household deposit dollarization was about 70% in 2018 and loan dollarization for corporates was about 65% (IMF 2018, p. 4). Also, multiple currency practices were common in Belarus until 2002.[4] According to the IMF, other important problems to be solved are NBRB credibility in CB independence and better CB communication[5] (IMF 2021a).

For Ukraine, the IMF[6] and the EU influence is apparent. The NBU implemented a floating rate in 2014 and an inflation targeting in 2016. As in the case with the NBRB, some discrepancies between de jure and de facto regimes and lacking CB independence caused problems. In 2005–2008 the NBU carried out a conventional peg to the US dollar (de jure crawling band) with an exchange rate anchor and, after that in 2009–2013, a stabilized arrangement (de jure floating with no predetermined path) under a monetary targeting regime (Ignatyuk et al. 2020, pp. 131–132; Annual Reports on exchange arrangements and exchange restrictions). The overall development of central banking in a country should be considered in the context of the general macroeconomic conditions and peculiarities of the national economy. Ukraine suffered from low economic growth (−0.2% annual growth rate for 1990–2017), shrinking population (−0.5% was the average annual population growth in 1990–2017), and low investment rates (average of 20% of GDP in 1990–2017) (Ari & Pula 2021, p. 4). The low investments are partly caused by the absence of strong institutions, corruption, and monopolization (Ibid., p. 5). The overall macroeconomic development was challenging, and the Ukrainian economy could not rely on economic benefits from Russia, as it is the case with Belarus. Resulting problems with balancing the government budget were solved through external funding and indirect monetary financing. Direct monetary financing to the government is prohibited[7]. However, monetary financing through the purchase of government bonds on the secondary market is not limited by the CB law (this is also true for the CBR and NBRB as for many Western CBs). Official data suggests that the share of domestic government bonds in circulation held by the NBU decreased from 54.8% in December 2011 to 33.2% in December 2021 (Figure 9.2).

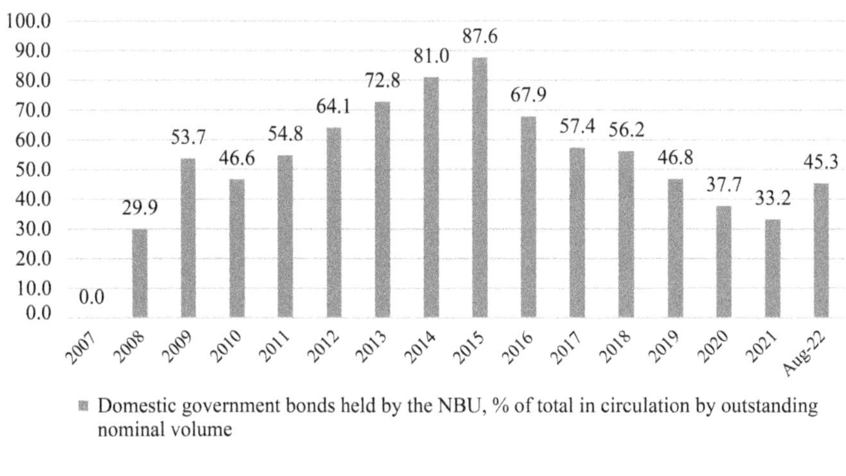

Figure 9.2 Indirect monetary financing in Ukraine

Source: NBU.

Note: The data are taken as of the end of December for each year.

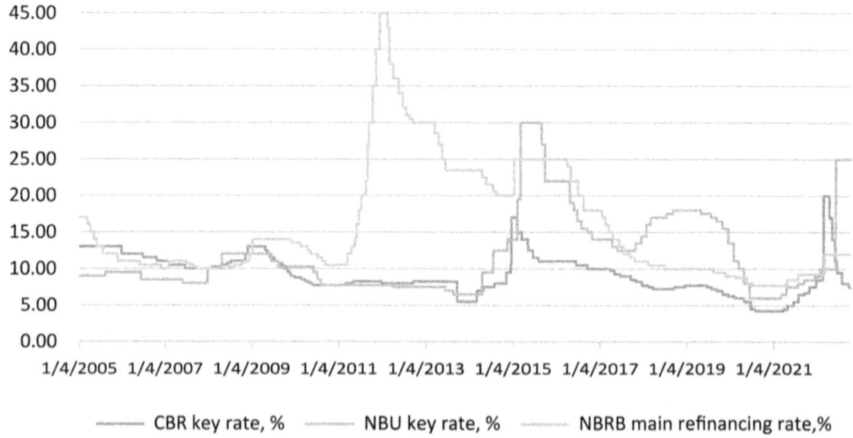

Figure 9.3 The key rates/ main refinancing rates

Source: CBR, NBRB, NBU.

Note: In Russia, the key rate was introduced in September 2013, before that the main financing rate is shown.

Prior to coronavirus restrictions and the war in February 2022, several crises were apparent in these three countries. For all of them, the global financial crisis of 2008 influenced their economies and monetary policies. Belarus[8] and Ukraine applied for IMF support. For Russia, a currency crisis was caused in 2014/2015 by the switch to free-floating (and the resulted ruble devaluation). The Belarusian economy was hit by a currency crisis in 2011 (sharp devaluation of the Belarusian ruble and a high CPI) and by the Russian crisis of 2014/15. Adjustment of the key rate/ main refinancing rates to the crisis can be used to explain CB monetary policy responses (Figure 9.3). Macroeconomic data that illustrates the economic consequences of these crises is provided in Table 9.3.

Monetary Responses to the Pandemic

The deep fall in economic activities after several lockdowns required monetary policy and regulatory measures addressing the financial problems in each country. This section considers only monetary measures and some selective amendments of financial regulation; fiscal measures are not considered. In transition economies, the MP measures in response to COVID-19 restrictions and to provide liquidity differed from developed economies: the expansion of the CB balance sheets was less than in the leading developed economies and liquidity injections were lower (Mironchik et al. 2021). Table 9.4 illustrates the growth of the monetary base in the three countries. CBs can influence the monetary base through their policy (e.g., changing reserve requirements). The exchange rates were much more volatile than for hard currencies (see also Figure 9.1).

Table 9.3 Selected macroeconomic evidence in Russia, Belarus, and Ukraine for 2008–21

	2008	*2009*	*2010*	*2011*	*2012*	*2013*	*2014*	*2015*	*2016*	*2017*	*2018*	*2019*	*2020*	*2021*
Economic growth, % of GDP														
Russia	5.2	−7.9	4.5	4.3	4.0	1.8	0.7	−2.0	0.2	1.8	2.8	2.0	−3.0	4.7
Belarus	10.2	0.2	7.7	5.5	1.7	1.0	1.7	−3.8	−2.5	2.5	3.1	1.4	−0.9	2.3
Ukraine	2.2	−15.1	4.1	5.5	0.2	0	−6.6	−9.8	2.4	2.4	3.5	3.2	−3.8	3.4
External debt, bln USD														
Russia	480.5	467.2	488.5	538.9	636.4	728.9	600.0	518.5	511.8	518.5	455.1	491.5	467.6	482.1
Belarus	15.2	22.1	28.4	34.0	33.8	39.6	40.0	38.3	37.5	39.8	39.3	40.7	42.0	41.9
Ukraine	101.7	103.4	117.4	126.2	134.6	142.1	125.3	117.7	112.5	115.5	114.7	121.7	125.7	129.7
International reserves, bln USD														
Russia	455.73	447.67	483.06	510.91	528.24	515.59	418.88	364.71	385.23	431.64	462.10	542.03	582.68	622.50
Belarus	3.78	4.59	5.71	7.36	8.21	6.46	5.82	4.58	4.84	7.41	7.44	9.12	7.38	8.47
Ukraine	32.74	27.29	33.54	32.41	25.38	18.81	9.97	13.15	15.27	18.93	17.71	21.93	26.14	30.60
CPI growth, %														
Russia	14.1	11.7	6.9	8.4	5.1	6.8	7.8	15.5	7.0	3.7	2.9	4.5	3.4	6.7
Belarus	14.8	13.0	7.8	53.2	59.2	18.3	18.1	13.5	11.8	6.0	4.9	5.6	5.6	9.5
Ukraine	25.2	15.9	9.4	8.0	0.6	−0.2	12.1	48.7	13.9	14.4	11.0	7.9	2.7	9.4
Direct investments (netto inflows), bln USD														
Russia	74.8	36.6	4.2	55.1	50.6	69.2	2.0	6.9	32.5	28.6	8.8	32.0	9.5	40.5
Belarus	2.3	4.8	5.6	13.3	10.4	11.1	10.2	7.2	6.9	7.6	8.5	7.2	6.0	6.6
Ukraine	10.9	4.8	6.5	7.2	8.4	4.5	0.4	−0.3	4.1	3.7	4.7	6.0	−0.4	6.6

Source: CBR, NBRB, NBU, Rosstat, Belstat, World Bank.

Notes: International reserves for Russia and Belarus are shown as of December 1st of the current year and for Ukraine as of the beginning of the following year.

Table 9.4 Monetary base: Total amount (nominated in national currency) and annual growth

	CBR		*NBRB*		*NBU*	
	RUB bln	*Annual growth, %*	*BYR bln*	*Annual growth, %*	*UAH bln*	*Annual growth, %*
01.01.2016	11043.80	−2.5	4.1	11.4	335.08	2.6
01.01.2017	11882.70	7.6	4.0	−2.1	362.00	8.0
01.01.2018	14701.50	23.7	6.2	55.4	392.33	8.4
01.01.2019	16,063.40	9.3	7.4	18.6	428.92	9.3
01.01.2020	16,822.10	4.7	8.8	18.8	469.76	9.5
01.01.2021	18,472.40	9.8	11	25.6	612.70	30.4
01.01.2022	20,338.90	10.1	12.4	12.2	692.83	13.1

Source: CBR, NBRB, NBU.

Note: The CBR uses monetary base within its broad definition (currency in circulation, required reserves deposited with the CB, bonds issued by the CB, credit institutions' deposits and correspondent accounts with the CB). For Belarus, data is shown as a monthly average for January of the respective year. The NBU includes currency in circulation, transferable deposits of other deposit-taking corporations and transferable deposits of other sectors of economy into the monetary base.

For the case of Russia, monetary policy responses to COVID-19 (see Table 9.5 for a comparative overview) had to deal not only with the "usual" economic consequences of the pandemic, but also with a sharp decrease in oil prices in March-April 2020.[9] Some differences compared with policy responses in developed countries are the following. One important aspect is that the CBR hasn't purchased assets, as this was not common in the pre-Covid policy era of the years before (Yudaeva 2021, p. 277). Also, monetary policy easing was limited both in time and scope and since March 2021 the CBR has again increased its key rate after inflationary pressures and ruble depreciation (Figures 9.1 and 9.3).

For Belarus, not only the general dependence on Russia is crucial, but the growing isolation from other countries. After the large-scale and violent oppressions in 2020 in the context of falsifications in the presidential elections,[10] Western countries imposed restrictive measures on Belarus, starting in October 2020. In June 2021, new economic sanctions (including restricted access to EU financial markets) were implemented.[11] The political crisis and loss of confidence influenced financial markets, and sanctions hit the economic system. The NBRB had to side out the effects of the political crisis and sanctions in addition to the pandemic in 2020–22. External funding was used: loans from Russia (USD 1 bln in 2021) and the Eurasian Fund for Stabilization and Development (EFSD) (USD 500 mln to support the state budget in October 2020[12]). The additional issue of SDR for Belarus (USD 0.9 bln in 2021) under a new SDR allocation of USD 650 bln from the IMF contributed to a recovery of the foreign reserves. A part of the reserves was spent for FX interventions in 2020, to repay FX liabilities and stabilize the national currency. The SDR were provided without any political conditions, as this program was designed for emerging countries to overcome the recession after the outbreak of COVID-19. In 2020, Belarus applied for a loan from the IMF, but no agreement

Table 9.5 Main monetary measures in response to the pandemic (selection for 2020–21)

Measures	*CBR*	*NBRB*	*NBU*
Liquidity providing/ support of the banking sector	Monthly and annual repo auctions; lower costs of collateralized liquidity lines	Limited Monthly auctions of loans (6 months), credit auctions (loans for 7 days at interest rate competitions) Extended maturity of NBRB's refinancing loans	Interest rate swaps with banks, long-term refinancing up to 5 years (from July 2021 up to 3 years) (both until Sept 2021) Maturity of short-term refinance loans in weekly tenders was increased (90 days instead of 14 days; from October 2021: 30 days)
FX operations	Rule-based (depending on oil prices; additional FX sales with prices below $25/barrel), but limited amount	Interventions to stabilize the national currency in 2020	Interventions on the FX market, but no FX swaps
Asset purchases	Not used	NBRB's share on the bonds market is low, and the NBRB conducts purchases and sales of bonds in a very limited amount (in 2021, only 0.004 bln BYR, see Ministry of Finance of the Republic of Belarus 2022, p. 14)	Secondary market purchases (see Figure 9.2)
Regulatory amendments	Extensively implemented different kinds of reduced requirements for credit institutions (e.g., easing liquidity coverage ratio, postponed enactment of the large exposure concentration ratio until Jan 2022, reduced risk weights on some investments)	Changes to prudential requirements: coverage ratio (80% instead of 100%) capital conservation buffer (2% from April 2020, from March 2.25% instead of previous 2.5%); capital adequacy ratio (for systemically important borrowers 100%; with Government guarantees 20% for debt/securities nominated in foreign currency and 0% for debt/ securities nominated in national currency); lowering asset classification requirements	Loose reserve ratios
Interest rate level (Figure 9.3)	Policy easing at the beginning of the pandemic (gradual decrease of the key rate from 6.0% in February/March 2020 to its lowest amount of 4.25% in July 2020 to March 2021), after that increase of the key rate	Gradual decrease of the main refinancing rate from 9% in February 2020 to 7.75% in July 2020; since April 2021, the NBRB started to increase the rate	Monetary easing in 2020: gradual cuts of the key rate from 13.5% in January 2020 up to 6% in June 2020 to March 2021 (then the NBU started to raise the key rate), narrowed interest rate corridor

Source: Yudaeva 2021, CBR 2022, NBRB, NBU.

could be reached. As the access to international financial markets is limited in the context of sanctions, Russia is the main creditor among China and the EFSD. At the same time, a big share of government debt consists of FX liabilities and a high share of FX loans in the banks' assets is also problematic. The NBRB was not involved in big asset purchases.

The overall liquidity injections to the banking sector in Belarus were moderate compared to Western economies, and liquidity was not sufficient. Banks issued new loans during the pandemic in a limited amount and often at high interest rates. More than a half of the Belarusian banks are state-owned and credit state-owned enterprises. Government-directed lending in the country contributes to a higher credit risk due to uncertainty of loans (with a probably high share of low quality) and inefficient credit allocation (Barisitz 2022, p. 64). This fact requires a tightening of banking supervision in Belarus to avoid bank recapitalization. As for the interest rate policy, the main refinancing rate was decreased at the beginning of the pandemic (from 9% in February 2020 to 7.75% in July 2020) and since April 2021 the NBRB started to increase the rate to fight inflationary pressures and Belarusian ruble depreciation. The policy easing with a low decrease in the main refinancing rate was moderate compared with Ukraine.

Looking at policy responses in Ukraine, we must consider financial assistance from international partners (the IMF, the World Bank, and the EU). A new Stand-By Arrangement (SBA) for over USD 5 bln (or 3.6 bln SDR) for 18 months was approved in June 2020 by the IMF. In August 2021, 2.7 bln SDR were provided under the issue of additional SDR for emerging countries. After the government change in March 2020, the new regime preferred minimal reforms, and most reform measures were promoted by the IMF (Åslund 2021). One important issue among the necessary reform measures was the strengthening of the NBU independence. This was one of the conditions of the 2020 SBA.[13] Particularly illustrative for lacking de facto independence is that the former governor Y. Smoliy resigned due to systematic political pressure on the NBU (on the 1 July 2020 just after the negotiation of the new agreement with the IMF).[14] In the first review of the arrangement (November, 2021) IMF staff appreciated legal improvements in CB independence[15] (IMF 2021b), but the law is not able to completely regulate the complex and controversial relationship between the government and the CB (and this is true for any country). Informal arrangements between central bankers and government officials, the personality of important decision makers, and the policy recommendations provided by the research department at the CB influence the CB independence (Cukierman et al. 1992, p. 355).

Important emergency monetary measures during the pandemic also include interest rate swaps and long-term refinancing for banks and changes to banking regulation as looser reserve ratios (Table 9.2). But the banks used a big part of the additional liquidity provided by the NBU to purchase government bonds. The high share of state-owned banks (46.7% in 2021, see NBU 2021, p. 36) explains the focus on government bonds. As a result, commercial banks didn't increase lending to the economy and preferred government bonds that were categorized as low-risk financial instruments with good interest rates. At the beginning of the spread of

COVID in Ukraine, the NBU launched monetary easing and decreased the key rate from 11% in March 2020 to 6% in June 2020 in several steps (Figure 9.3). On 5 March 2021, the key rate was increased again (6.5%) and later several times the rate was increased (up to 9% in December 2021).

The initial monetary policy responses to the pandemic in all three investigated countries were introduced in March 2020. These measures were related to cuts in interest rates, looser prudential regulation, and liquidity injections to the banking sector. At the same time, liquidity operations were applicable, but not all commercial banks made use of them in the possible amounts (especially in the case of Russia). Asset purchases haven't been used as a policy instrument by the CBR; ensuring stability and compensating for a sharp decrease in oil prices at the beginning of the pandemic were more important targets. Generally, FX interventions were important for Russia and Ukraine. The CBs started to exit monetary easing in March–April 2021 after an economic stabilization and inflationary pressures were apparent. Expectations for economic recovery in the next years could have been realistic, but after February 2022 the situation has changed.

MP Responses to the War and Sanctions

The official recognition of Donetsk and Luhansk oblasts, the deployment of Russian troops to these areas and the following military invasion into Ukraine in February 2022[16] was the occasion for the implementation of sanctions that included, among others, financial sanctions, sectoral import and export bans, and investment restrictions. A first set was adopted by the EU on February 23, then on 25 and 28; later several amendments and additional sanctions were adopted[17]. Other (mainly Western) countries also imposed sanctions. These measures were taken in addition to the sanctions implemented after the annexation of Crimea (2014) and after oppressions in Belarus in 2020 (both packages are still valid). The first packages of financial sanctions mainly affected systemically important Russian banks. Several banks (both Russian and Belarusian) were disconnected from SWIFT[18]. Also, the CBR's and NBRB's assets are frozen by Western countries. But reserves held in Russia (and in Belarus) and securities nominated in non-Western foreign currencies were not affected (for Russia, about one-half of the total international reserves were frozen). Bonds issued by the Russian or Belarusian government, or their CBs (after 12 April 2022) were prohibited to purchase. Any transaction in general with the CBR and NBRB were prohibited in Western countries. The political and economic isolation of Russia and Belarus from the West is growing, but many important emerging countries (as China, India, and Türkiye) continue their partnership with Russia, at least in many important sectors.

The overall economic impact of sanctions is not limited to formal restrictions. Attempts to withdraw investments from Russia and to limit new investments as well as reluctance of trade relations were apparent even in non-sanctioned sectors (for examples see Götz 2022, p. 203). These responses were based on the unwillingness of former trading partner/investors to support the current political regime in Russia (even in an indirect way), the high degree of uncertainty, possible expropriations, and expectations of further sanctions. The long-term effects of sanctions can be compensated through developing import and export substitutions. But one of the remaining problems is the integration into global value chains and the related dependence on imported equipment, technology, and components (Yakovlev 2022, p. 8). The already imposed sanctions have affected more Russia's imports than exports (and the current account surplus contributed to ruble appreciation) and created welfare losses due to limited imports (Itskhoki & Mukhin 2022, p. 148). Higher prices for commodities made in Russia but with foreign components were also a result of the adopted sanctions.

The financial sanctions (especially the frozen CB assets) limit possible MP responses. In general, the effectiveness of sanctions can be questioned (both political and economic outcomes). In any case, damage to the economic system for sanctioned countries (and for the countries imposing sanctions[19]) can be expected, but without a guarantee of political change in the desired direction (for a discussion see Peterson & Schwab 2022). The effects of sanctions differ regarding the macroeconomic conditions in a country, the international "solidarity" of imposing sanctions, the possibilities of import substitutions, alternative markets for exports, and the overall duration of the sanction regime (Ibid.). The Russian internal market is big, some non-Western allied countries such as China and India don't support the sanctions, the richness of different resources and the obvious value for other countries of these exports, previous experience with economic isolation, and sanctions undermine the effectiveness of the sanction regime. For Belarus, the imposed sanctions increase the dependence on Russia. At the same time, the implemented sanctions are far-reaching and difficult to handle over a longer period.

To limit capital outflows, fight inflationary pressures, and restore financial stability, the CBR introduced unconventional measures. As these measures were adopted within a presidential order[20], the CBR's autonomy seems to be more limited since the end of February 2022. This is not surprising (even if this war was officially declared as a "special military operation" by the Russian government). On February 28, 2022, the CBR increased the key rate from 9.5% to 20% (see Figure 9.3) after a sharp depreciation of the Russian ruble (113.71 RUB/EUR as a monthly average in March 2022, see Figure 9.1). Later, the rate was decreased again (to 17% since 11 April, 14% since 4 May, 11% since 27 May, 9.5 since 14 June, 8% since 25 July, and 7.5% since 19 September) after an appreciation of the Russian currency (in May 2022 the average exchange rate with 65.82 RUB/EUR was lower than in the pre-war period at the end of 2021). In May, yoy inflation was 17.1% (with an initial target of 5%). Some capital controls (e.g., the requirement to convert 80% of foreign exchange revenues from exports to rubles) and limited ruble convertibility (restrictions to buy foreign currency, a fee in the amount of 12% on purchases of EUR, USD, and GBP from March 04 to April 12, 2022) were introduced. The imposed financial sanctions with frozen CBR's assets also had a stabilization effect on the exchange rate. Domestic demand on foreign currency was limited due to capital controls and restrictions on the purchase of foreign currencies (the CBR could not sell foreign currency to stabilize the ruble and had limited access to its reserves) and the high key rate (and high interest rates on ruble deposits[21]) encouraged people to store their money in rubles at banks (Itskhoki & Mukhin 2022, p. 149). After this stabilization, some measures were loosened again (no restrictions on foreign currency purchases with the exemption of USD and EUR; mandatory sale of FX revenues was first cut to 50% in May, and since June this share is determined by a government commission). Some other measures have been extended. The ruble appreciation decreased foreign currency revenues from oil and gas exports for the government budget. These factors (ruble appreciation and budget pressures, more optimistic inflation scenario) contributed to the decision to remove a part of capital controls and ruble convertibility restrictions.

In Belarus, the NBRB introduced measures in March 2022 (until the end of 2022) to support the banking sector that was affected by sanctions and the growing isolation. For credit risk classification and for building special reserves, differences in exchange rates (after the beginning of February 2022) shouldn't be considered and, for estimating the sufficiency of foreign currency revenues, a bank can use RUB and CNY.[22] Inflation pressures are apparent (yoy inflation was 18.1% in July 2022), but the interest rate hike was moderate: the NBRB increased the main refinancing rate from 9.25% to 12% on March 1, 2022.[23]

The central role of relations with Russia and Eurasian partners characterizes expectations for the economic development in Belarus. Opportunities are assumed with the development of a Union State of Russia and Belarus.[24] This integration project regains importance in a context of ongoing sanctions and after Lukashenko needed help to ensure power after the post-election oppressions in 2020. As part of the general strategy towards a Union State of Russia and Belarus, the goals of harmonization of MP, FX regulation, and macro-prudential regulation and of integration of payment systems were anticipated in the 28-point framework (Roadmap) for deeper economic integration (an agreement was reached in September 2021). Earlier, even the idea of a common currency was discussed. Adopting measures for MP harmonization with Russia and the implementation of full inflation targeting in 2022 was an initial composite of the reached agreement. Consequently, there is the threat of losing Belarusian monetary sovereignty. Possible double dependence on the Belarusian President and on the CBR lowers NBRB autonomy, and possibly conflicting interests can lower the MP effectiveness. The imposed sanctions seem to be followed by growing Belarusian dependence on Russia and on its willingness to subsidize the Belarusian economy. If a full integration of Belarus into the Union State takes place, then the NBRB can become once again something like a Belarusian "regional branch" (as in Soviet times with the Gosbank). The CBR would be leading in decision-making in the case of a full MP harmonization.

High numbers of refugees (and internally displaced persons), involvement of the population into military operations, damaged infrastructure and production facilities, disrupted logistics, and problems with supply of basic goods in occupied zones were among the important problems in Ukraine, to say nothing of the numerous victims and humanitarian crisis caused by the war. The economic consequences of the military invasion in Ukraine are grave. Unbalanced labor supply and demand (more jobseekers than vacancies), higher inflation (22.2% yoy in July 2022[25]), lower wages (as many companies cut wages or send their staff on unpaid leave) and a higher budget deficit should be taken into consideration by the NBU to ensure financial and price stability. In April-May 2022, the economic activity remained below the pre-war period (NBU 2022a). Currency interventions contributed to lower international reserves (USD 25.1 bln in May 2022 and USD 22.4 bln in July 2022; a decrease by around USD 5 bln compared with December 2021). A part of decreased reserves was compensated by international financial assistance. The IMF approved financing support in the amount of USD 1.4 bln under the rapid financing instrument in March 2022[26]. The high budget deficit was financed by external borrowings and war bonds issued by the government. These bonds are nominated in UAH, USD, or EUR, and from June their yields are linked to the key rate. The NBU purchased a total of UAH 190 bln as of June 10, 2022[27]. Before February 2022, the NBU provided only indirect monetary financing (purchases of government bonds on the secondary market) and after the introduction of material law, the NBU started to provide direct monetary financing (for that purpose Art. 54 of the Law on the NBU was waived temporarily by the Verkhovna Rada). Monetary financing is natural for the period of material law, but this undermines the NBU autonomy and creates inflationary pressures and depreciation pressures on the hryvnia.

The NBU tied the exchange rate to the USD (as of February 24, 2022) and implemented some capital controls and restrictions on FX operations. One important policy instrument was FX interventions to maintain a stable exchange rate and to absorb monetary financing (in March to April 2022 a monthly average of USD 2 bln foreign currency was sold by the NBU and in May USD 3.4 bln[28]). The NBU raised the key rate to 25% from 2 June 2022 and widened the interest corridor up to ±2% (23% on certificates of deposit and 27% on refinancing loans).[29] Previous measures were not sufficient to stop capital outflows, withdraws from bank deposits (nominated in UAH) and the melting of international reserves. Resulting higher interest rates on bank deposits and on government bonds nominated in UAH (before the interest hike, the yields were lower than the current inflation) should increase the demand for these assets and decrease pressure on the UAH exchange rate (NBU 2022b, pp. 37-38).

Conclusions

Economic consequences of lockdowns during the pandemic and emergency measures required the reconsideration of the role of MP and stressed the need of reacting quickly in countries all over the world. The CBR's, NBRB's, and NBU's MP responses were not the same as in major Western economies that adopted large-scale quantitative easing programs to ensure economic recovery. Liquidity injections in Eastern Europe were less generous than in the West, where these injections were accompanied by wide-reaching fiscal measures. Typical problems such as currency fluctuations, capital outflows, risk of inflation, and a lack of CB credibility required a different model of central banking. Before the epidemiological crisis, political tensions in Eastern Europe have been apparent (oppressions in Belarus, financial and political problems in Ukraine, and Russia's tendency towards more isolation from the Western world). After the Russian military invasion into Ukraine on February 24, 2022, Western sanctions against Russia and Belarus were adopted. The financial sanctions included the disconnection of selected banks from SWIFT and the freeze on CBR and NBRB international reserves.

The beginning of the war has affected not only security considerations in Europe, but it also changed the financial systems and policy frameworks in the related countries. The idea of modern and autonomous CBs in Eastern Europe should be reconsidered. When the war is ongoing, it is not possible to evaluate all consequences of war and sanctions, and these questions will be of central importance for future research. The investigated initial policy responses to the war and sanctions show the following directions. In the case of Russia, the CBR reintroduced capital controls (before, in 2001–2007, most formal capital controls were abandoned in Russia), tightened access to foreign currency, extended liquidity-providing operations, amended the reserve requirements and raised the key rate up to 20% in March 2022. A part of these measures was removed later, and the key rate was decreased again. The CBR is de facto acting as a government servant that circumvents the sanction regime and ensures the functioning of the financial system during the war. Increasing monetary sovereignty and preparing for times of economic sanctions and isolation were CBR policy goals set by the government before the war. Depending on the development of the war, the CBR may start to support the government by direct monetary financing. At the moment, the CBR is working on the further development of alternative systems to replace SWIFT. The country is also strengthening its political and economic relations with other developing economies, especially with BRICS countries and Eurasian countries. In Belarus, the interest rate hike as a reaction to the war (from 9.25% to 12% in March 2022) was moderate compared with Russia. Other measures to maintain stability in the banking sector after the implementation of new sanctions were adopted (as regulatory amendments). In general, Belarus is now getting closer to Russia. This is not only a result of the adopted sanctions, as the country was dependent on Russia before the new realities in Eastern Europe, but the sanction regime accelerated this process. MP harmonization with the CBR could lead to something close to a regional branch of the Soviet Gosbank, with double dependence on the Belarusian President and the CBR. The loss of NBRB's autonomy would be significant. The NBU adopted a large scope of measures to compensate for such negative effects of war as higher inflation and lower economic activity. The NBU provided FX interventions, tied the exchange rate to the USD, hiked the key rate up to 25%, and introduced capital controls. But the NBU is also losing its autonomy. The IMF tried to address this problem through their loan arrangements, but most changes were related to improvements of legal constraints of CB autonomy. Indirect monetary financing was a problem before February 2022. The introduction of war bonds and some legal amendments enabled direct monetary financing. A reintroduction of a more autonomous bank will be difficult and the dependence on external funding may remain for a long time.

This chapter showed that these developments undermine modernization efforts in central banking over the past few years and CB autonomy in Eastern Europe. This uneven process of moving towards modern central banking, and the growing isolation of Russia and Belarus, is of importance for the reconsideration of Eastern European policy frameworks. There is the risk to get back to pre-reform central banking in Eastern Europe, with capital controls and direct monetary financing. In all three countries, the achievement of higher CB autonomy does not seem to be of high importance. This may serve as an example to other transition economies and influence central banking in other emerging countries.

Acknowledgment

I thank Mustafa Yağcı, Andrei Vernikov, Dóra Piroska, and Kevin Axe for very helpful comments.

Notes

1 For an overview over the introduction of national currencies after the dissolution of the USSR and the participation in the Ruble zone, see Dabrowski 2022.
2 The denomination was fixed in the edict no. 450 of the President of the Republic of Belarus, 4.11.2015 (Ukaz № 450 «O provedenii denominatsii ofitsial'noi denezhnoi edinitsy Respubliki Belarus'»).
3 According to Statute of the NBRB, chapter 1, §3: „…the President … appoints, with the consent of the Council of the Republic of the National Assembly of the Republic of Belarus, the Chairperson and Members of the Board of the National Bank, and removes them from their positions notifying the Council of the Republic of the National Assembly … accordingly…".
4 The number of effective exchange rates in Belarus was changing over time. In 2002, the auction exchange, interbank, and cash rates were officially recognized in the country (see IMF 2002, p.95 and IMF reports of the previous years).
5 Much information on NBRB's policy is still difficult to access or not published in English; CB communication could be improved in this sense.
6 Ukraine applied for financial assistance several times and thirteen agreements were reached: 1995 Stand-By, 1996 Stand-By, 1997 Stand-By, 1998 EFF, 2004 Stand-By, 2008 Stand-By, 2010 Stand-By, 2014 Stand-By, 2015 EFF, 2018 Stand-By, 2020 Stand-By, and 2022 rapid refinancing instrument (two agreements: one in March and one in October). See IMF: Ukraine: History of Lending Commitments. URL: https://www.imf.org/external/np/fin/tad/extarr2.aspx?memberKey1=993&date1key=2021-03-31.
7 Law on the NBU, Article 54, Ban on Lending to the State: "The NBU must not grant loans in the national or foreign currency, both directly and indirectly, through a public institution or other legal entity whose property is state-owned, with the purpose of financing the expenses of the State Budget of Ukraine. The NBU must not purchase in the primary market any securities issued by the Cabinet of Ministers of Ukraine, a public institution or other legal entity whose property is state-owned."
8 Belarus received a Stand-By arrangement with the IMF in 2009.
9 Since mid-2021 a gradual recovery of world oil prices has occurred and since the beginning of 2022 a sharp price increase can be observed.
10 The official election results, declaring Lukashenko to be the re-elected president with 80% of the vote, were unlikely, and the election did not meet minimum standards for democratic elections. Key facts on the oppressions and promised reform agenda in 2020-21 are summarized in Rohava (2021).

11 For details, see Council of the EU: EU imposes sanctions on the Belarusian economy. URL: https://www.consilium.europa.eu/en/press/press-releases/2021/06/24/eu-imposes-sanctions-on-belarusian-economy/

12 The project documentation on that loan is available at the EFSD website. URL: https://efsd.org/en/projects/belarus-financial-credit-budget-support-and-or-balance-of-payments-support/

13 According to the IMF: „Ukraine's IMF supported economic program aims to help the authorities address the effects of the COVID-19 shock, sustain the economic recovery, and move ahead on important structural reforms to reduce key vulnerabilities. In particular, under the agreed policy priorities the Ukrainian authorities are committed to … (ii) safeguarding central bank independence and focusing monetary policy on returning inflation to its target; …" (IMF 2021b, p. 1).

14 NBU: The head of the National Bank, Yakiv Smoliy wrote a letter of resignation due to systematic political pressure. URL: https://bank.gov.ua/ua/news/all/golova-natsionalnogo-banku-yakiv-smoliy-napisav-zayavu-pro-zvilnennya-cherez-sistematichniy-politichniy-tisk.

15 The legal improvements to strengthen CB independence include the following amendments:

- "better describing the role of the NBU Council and its relationship with the Management Board to mitigate interference with the Board's mandate;
- reducing the number of NBU Council and audit committee meetings in line with their mandate;
- introducing an ex ante cooling-off period for Council members to become Management Board members and further clarifying the applicability of existing ex post cooling-off period to Council members;
- clearly formulating the tenure of NBU deputy governors and improving the appointment and dismissal criteria for the members of Council and Management Board without undermining the status of current members;
- strengthening conflict of interest rules for NBU officials; and
- improving legal protections accorded to these officials, including former NBU officials" (IMF 2021b, p. 73).

In addition to these amendments, the NBU Board composition was changed in June 2021, and an additional deputy governor was introduced (IMF 2021b, p. 76). After the amendments, the Board consists of seven members: the Governor, first deputy governor and five deputy governors.

16 It should be mentioned that in these regions, war has been ongoing for eight years before that invasion. This chapter refers only to the war since February 2022, and not previous or ongoing conflict in these regions.

17 The detailed investigation of all EU sanctions is beyond the scope of this study. A complete overview with the latest updates is accessible on the official website: European Commission: Sanctions adopted following Russia's military aggression against Ukraine. URL: https://ec.europa.eu/info/business-economy-euro/banking-and-finance/international-relations/restrictive-measures-sanctions/sanctions-adopted-following-russias-military-aggression-against-ukraine_en

18 In March 2022 (the third EU package of sanctions) the Russian banks: Bank Otkritie, Novikombank, Promsvyazbank, Bank Rossiya, Sovcombank, Vnesheconombank (VEB) and VTB Bank were disconnected, in June 2022 (sixth package of sanctions) – Sberbank, Credit Bank of Moscow, and Russian Agricultural Bank; among Belarusian banks in June 2022 *Belagroprombank*, *Bank* Dabrabyt, the Development Bank *of the Republic of* Belarus were cut off and in June – ***the*** Belarusian Bank for Development and Reconstruction was likewise cut off.

19 An import embargo of Russian oil and gas causes serious economic damage due to higher prices on energy resources and inflationary pressures, difficulties of important diversification, and uncertainty about realistic possibilities to decrease energy consumption. For an analysis, see Götz 2022, pp. 205-218.

20 The executive order No. 79 "On Imposing Special Economic Measures in Connection with the Hostile Actions of the United States in League with Other Foreign States and International Organizations" was signed by the Russian President on February 28, 2022. Later, additional decrees were signed.
21 According to Reiter & Lyutova (2022), not market mechanism alone resulted in higher deposit rates, but the CBR's top managers influenced the bankers' decision.
22 BelTA: Central bank takes additional steps to secure stable operation of Belarusian banks. March 11, 2022. URL: https://eng.belta.by/economics/view/central-bank-takes-additional-steps-to-secure-stable-operation-of-belarusian-banks-148514-2022/
23 In addition to MP measures, the Belarusian government introduced a new system of price regulation on consumer goods in October 2022 (Resolution of The Council of Ministers of the Republic of Belarus of October 19, 2022, no. 713, "About the system of price regulation") to fight inflation. However, the reintroduction of more elements of central planning and possible distorting effects on the Belarusian economy were criticized in Belarus.
24 The initiative of a Union state aims to achieve deeper political and economic integration of Russia and Belarus. In December 1999 an Agreement on the creation of the Union State was signed.
25 NBU: NBU July 2022 Inflation Update. August 11, 2022. URL: https://bank.gov.ua/en/news/all/komentar-natsionalnogo-banku-schodo-rivnya-inflyatsiyi-v-lipni-2022-roku
26 IMF: IMF Executive Board Approves US$1.4 Billion in Emergency Financing Support to Ukraine. March 9, 2022. URL: https://www.imf.org/en/News/Articles/2022/03/09/pr2269-ukraine-imf-executive-board-approves-usd-billion-in-emergency-financing-support-to-ukraine
27 UAH 135 bln were issued in March-April 2022 of which UAH 70 bln were purchased by the NBU (NBU 2022b, p. 29), in May the NBU purchases additional UAH 50 bln and at the beginning of June further UAH 70 bln. See NBU: NBU Purchases War Bonds Worth UAH 70 billion and Emphasizes the Need to Increase Borrowing from the Market. June 9, 2022. URL: https://bank.gov.ua/en/news/all/nbu-zdiysniv-vikup-viyskovih-ovdp-na-70-mlrd-grn-ta-nagoloshuye-na-neobhidnosti-aktivizatsiyi-rinkovih-borgovih-zaluchen
28 NBU: NBU Raises Key Policy Rate to 25%. 2 June 2022. URL: https://bank.gov.ua/en/news/all/natsionalniy-bank-ukrayini-pidvischiv-oblikovu-stavku-do-25
29 Ibid.

Bibliography

Ari, A, & Pula, G 2021, 'Assessing the macroeconomic impact of structural reforms in Ukraine', *IMF Working Paper*, vol. 21/100, p. 37.

Åslund, A 2021, 'Policy reactions to the covid-19 in Russia and Ukraine', *CESifo Forum 6/2021*, vol., November, Volume 22, pp. 22–26.

Barisitz, S 2000, 'The development of Banking sectors in Russia, Ukraine, Belarus and Kazakhstan since Independence', *Focus on Transition*, vol. 1/2000, pp. 67–99.

Barisitz, S 2022, 'The Belarusian banking sector (2016-2021): From timid recovery to renewed crisis?', *Focus on European Economic Integration*, vol. Q1/22, pp. 55–69.

CBR 2022, Measures of the Bank of Russia to Mitigate the Effects of the Coronavirus Pandemic. URL: https://www.cbr.ru/vfs/finstab/plan_limit_covid_eng.pdf

Cukierman, A, Webb, SB, & Neyapti, B 1992, 'Measuring the independence of Central banks and its effect on policy Outcomes', *The World Bank Economic Review*, vol. 6, no. 3, pp. 353–398.

Dabrowski, M 2022, 'Thirty years of economic transition in the former Soviet Union: macroeconomic dimension', *Russian Journal of Economics*, 8(2), pp. 95–121.

Garvy, G 1972, 'Banking Under the tsars and the Soviets', *The Journal of Economic History*, vol. 32, no. 4, pp. 869–893.

Götz, R 2022, 'Sanktionen und Reaktionen. Auswirkungen auf die Wirtschaft Russlands', *Osteuropa*, vol. 72, no. 1–3, pp. 197–218.

Hartwell, CA 2020, 'Central Banks and institutional evolution in transition', in M Yağcı (ed.), *The political economy of Central Banking in emerging economies*, Routledge, New York, pp. 39–55.

Ignatyuk, A, Osetskyi, V, Makarenko, M, & Artemenko, A 2020, 'Ukrainian Hryvnia under the floating exchange rate regime: Diagnostics of the USD/UAH exchange rate dynamics', *Banks and Bank Systems*, vol. 15, no. 3, pp. 129–146.

IMF 2002, Annual Report on exchange arrangements and exchange restrictions 2002. IMF, Washington, D.C.

IMF 2005, Annual Report on exchange arrangements and exchange restrictions 2005. IMF, Washington, D.C.

IMF 2018, Republic of Belarus: Selected Issues. Prepared by Dora Benedek, December 17, 2018.

IMF 2021a, Republic of Belarus: Staff Concluding Statement of the 2021 Article IV Mission, Mission Concluding Statement, December 20.

IMF 2021b, Ukraine: First review under the Stand-By Arrangement, Requests for extension and rephasing of access of the Arrangement, waivers of nonobservance of a performance criterion, financing assurances review, and monetary policy consultation – press release; Staff report; and statement by the Executive Director for Ukraine. IMF Country Report No. 21/250, November 2021.

Itskhoki, O, & Mukhin, D 2022, 'Sanctions and exchange Rate', *Intereconomics*, vol. 57, no. 3, pp. 148–151.

Johnson, J 2008, 'Forbidden fruit: Russia's uneasy relationship with the US Dollar', *Review of International Political Economy*, vol. 15, no. 3, pp., At Home Abroad? The Dollar's Destiny as a World Currency, p. 379–398.

Johnson, J, & Barnes, A 2015, 'Financial nationalism and its international enablers: The Hungarian experience', *Review of International Political Economy*, vol. 22, no. 3, pp. 535–569.

Johnson, J 2018, 'The bank of Russia: From Central planning to inflation Targeting', in Conti-Brown, P & Lastra, Rosa Maria (eds), *Research handbook on Central Banking*, Edward Elgar, Cheltenham and Northampton, pp. 94–116.

Kißmer, F, & Wagner, H 2004, 'Central Bank independence and macroeconomic performance: A survey of the evidence', in Healey, N & Harrison, B (eds), *Central banking In Eastern Europe*, Series: Routledge international studies in money and banking, Routledge, London, pp. p. 107–140.

Korhonen, I, & Nuutilainen, R 2016, 'A Monetary Policy Rule for Russia, or Is it Rules?', *BOFIT Discussion Papers* N° 2.

Ministry of Finance of the Republic of Belarus 2022, January-December 2021. Belarus: Economic Summary. URL: https://www.minfin.gov.by/upload/gosdolg/vneshniy/Belarus_Macroeconomic_Snapshot_2021.pdf

Mironchik, N, Demidenko, M, & Shcherba, E 2021, 'Central Banks' Balances Expansion and Inflation: Conclusions for the Monetary Policy', *Bank Bulletin Magazine*, NBRB, Minsk, pp. 3–12 (in Russian).

Nakamura, Y 2019, 'Money and Finance', in Kuboniwa, M, Nakamura, Y, Kumo, K, & Shida, Y (eds): Russian economic development over three centuries. Palgrave Macmillan, Singapore, pp. 221–249.

NBU 2021, Annual Report 2021.

NBU 2022a, Monthly Macroeconomic and Monetary Review. June 2022.

NBU 2022b, Monthly Macroeconomic and Monetary Review. May 2022.

Omelianovich, N 2013, 'Reforming the Banking system of the byelorussian SSR', *Bank Bulletin Magazine*, vol. 4, no. 585), NBRB, Minsk, pp. 67–69 (in Russian).

Peterson, T, & Schwab, T 2022, 'Handelssanktionen – Wirkungen und Nebenwirkungen', *Wirtschaftsdienst*, vol. 102, no. 5, pp. 354–360.

Reiter, S, & Lyutova, M 2022, 'The banker's dilemma How Elvira Nabiullina and her team have tried to save Russia's economy amid war and sanctions', Meduza. URL: https://meduza.io/en/feature/2022/07/07/the-banker-s-dilemma.

Rohava, M 2021, 'Politische Krise und vertagte Verfassungsreform in Belarus', *Religion und Gesellschaft in Ost und West*, vol. 4–5, pp. 16–17.

Trunin, PV, Kniazev, DA, & Satdarov, AM 2010, 'Analysis of independence of the central banks of the Russian Federation, the CIS and East European countries', Institute of transition economies, Moscow (in Russian).

Yakovlev, A 2022, 'Russia's economy: Between a crash and a Hard Landing', *Russian Analytical Digest: Political and Economic Consequences of Russia's War Against Ukraine*, no. 283, 14 April 2022, pp. 7–9.

Yudaeva, K 2021, 'Bank of Russia policy during the covid-19 pandemic', in English, B, Forbes, K, & Ubide, A (eds): Monetary policy and Central Banking in the covid era. CEPR Press, Centre for Economic Policy Research (CEPR), London, pp. 271–279.

10 Climate Change on the Policy Agenda of Central Banks in Central and Southeast Europe

Tatjana Jovanić

Introduction

Although the emerging energy crisis and soaring inflation have slowed down initiatives undertaken to promote the recognition of climate-related risks in the mandates of central banks, there is an undeniable need to design new policy instruments and adjust the existing policy tools aimed to avoid the destabilising effects of climate change. Financial system regulation is one of the policy areas that governments have to tackle in combating climate change. Therefore, central banks are coming under pressure to become involved in the fight against climate change. Central bankers around the world have understood that climate-related risks are a challenge to financial stability and are slowly adjusting their mandates to fit the new reality. Central banks in Central Europe (CE) and Southeast Europe (SEE) are even more called out, as the predominant source of energy are fossil resources. Some of them have had a history of price volatility and economic instability, and are thus aware of how climate change may affect commodity prices, climate-sensitive economic sectors, overall price stability and financial stability.

Although most central banks and financial regulators have recognised climate change-related risks, some have gone beyond simply raising public awareness of their effects and taken the first steps in promoting the assessment, disclosure and management of climate-related risks. Some central banks did this in a more intrusive way, by employing policy tools to mitigate climate risks in the prudential framework and 'greening' their monetary policy.

This paper briefly outlines the drivers of climate-related risk recognition by central banks, as well as emerging strategies that include climate-related risks in the regulatory and supervisory frameworks. Given that the dominant public policy instruments – not only in the countries of Central and Southeast Europe but also at the global level – are voluntary and mandatory instruments of information regulation, the paper presents an analysis of the informational tools contained in the published strategic and reporting documents of the central banks. Such tools range from central bank declarations and pledges, dedicated programmes, analytical commentaries and reports, to supervisory expectations based on non-binding guidelines, and formalised disclosure of climate risk exposure and risk management.

DOI: 10.4324/9781003323280-11

This paper aims to contribute to the emerging literature on modalities of incorporation of 'green' factors into the policy toolboxes of central banks, proposing a classification of informational tools into five subgroups, and presenting landmark examples of climate change initiatives on the policy agenda of the central banks in new EU Member States and countries aspiring to join the EU, located in Central and Southeast Europe. In most definitions, the new EU Member States from Central Europe are Poland, the Czech Republic, Slovakia, Slovenia and Hungary, whereas Croatia, Romania and Bulgaria are usually considered part of Southeast Europe. Albania, Bosnia and Herzegovina, Montenegro, North Macedonia and Serbia are non-EU SEE countries aspiring to join the EU.

Climate Change Recognition by Central Banks and Climate-Related Risk Impact on Central Bank Mandates

Climate change may be the greatest market failure seen in the world (Stern 2008, p. 1). Emerging research suggests that climate-related damages could potentially also affect the stability of the financial system (Dafermos et al. 2018; Lamperti et al. 2019; Pereira da Silva 2019). Central banks and financial supervisors are called on to extend their powers and assess financial institutions and their risk management, as well as to provide guidance on risk assessment and management (HLEG 2018; NGFS 2020; EBA 2020). The necessity to extend the mandates of central banks and financial supervisors to incorporate climate risk has been recognised and debated in the academic literature and scientific papers (NGFS 2019a; Batten et al. 2016; Schoenmaker and van Tilburg 2016; Campiglio et al. 2018; Chenet et al. 2021; D'Orazio and Popoyan 2019; Dafermos et al. 2018; Volz 2017). Despite the fact that the extension of central banks' mandates could eventually jeopardize monetary and financial stability and rise questions of governance, climate crisis has brought the notion of the market neutrality of monetary policy under intense scrutiny (Dikau and Volz 2021, p. 18).

Whilst central banks in high-income countries have preferred to adopt a market-neutral approach, central banks in a number of emerging markets are responding to environmental challenges by considering climate change as a threat to financial stability (Dikau and Volz 2020), especially due to the fact that low-income countries are more exposed to the risk of climate change (D'Orazio and Popoyan 2019). Although there are wide differences on the policy approaches, central banks in emerging economies are among the most engaged in green financial policymaking (Dikau and Ryan-Collins 2017; Dikau and Volz 2021; D'Orazio and Thole 2022; Forstater et al. 2016).

Countries in Central and Southeast Europe – whether new EU Member states or aspiring candidates – adjusted the definition of the mandates of their central banks in line with the Statute of the European System of Central Banks. This means that the standard legal definition of the legislative mandates of central banks in the new EU Member States, as stipulated in national laws on central banks – in addition to promulgating the price stability as a primary goal – specified that a central bank will support the general economic policies in the European Union with a view to contributing to the achievement and objectives of the Union, as laid down in Article 3 of the Treaty on European Union. Even when sustainable development as a concept is not explicitly mentioned in the legal definition of the central bank's mandate, the reference to the aforementioned article of the TEU implies that the central banks support sustainable economic development. Custom definitions of central bank's mandates in Bulgaria, Croatia, Poland, Romania, Slovakia and Slovenia include price stability as a main objective and some definitions recognize that, in pursuing the primary objective, the central bank will strive for financial stability and provide that, without jeopardising the main objective, it will support general economic policy in accordance with the objectives set in the TEU. The definitions of central bank mandates in the group of non-EU countries of this region (Albania, Bosnia and Herzegovina, Macedonia, Montenegro and Serbia) are similar. However, Czech and Hungarian central banks are explicitly entitled to support the general economic policies of the Government leading to sustainable economic growth.

Environmental, social and governance (ESG) factors and risks shape the definition of both sustainable economic growth and sustainable finance. Whereas 'sustainable finance' is considered to be the process of taking due account of ESG considerations when making investment or financing decisions, 'green finance' is a narrower concept, confined to climate and environment protection (ICMA 2020; Berrou et al. 2019). It is, therefore, an even more precise way of defining the role of the central bank. Following the decision of the National Assembly on 28 May 2021, the mandate of Magyar Nemzeti Bank's statutory objective was extended to support the Government's policy on environmental sustainability, making it the first EU central bank to be granted a green mandate.[1]

The case for assigning an environmental mandate to central banks in emerging economies of Southeast Europe may even be stronger, as environmental regulation is often weakly implemented by other public institutions, while central banks are often among the most powerful public players. Due to their strong institutional standing, expertise and involvement in transnational networks, central banks could promote best practices in sustainability-oriented reforms (Dikau and Volz 2021, p. 18; Volz 2017, p. 12).

Emerging Strategies and Policy Tools for Including Climate Risk in the Regulatory and Supervisory Framework

In promoting green finance, central banks and financial supervision authorities could incorporate sustainability factors into financial policy and regulation through a number of different policy instruments (Dikau and Volz 2020). Policy motives include the aim to tackle climate change by directly influencing the allocation of financial capital (*promotional*), and the desire to ensure the stability of the financial system in the face of climate-related challenges to mitigate climate-related risks (*prudential*) (Baer et al. 2021). Emerging academic literature and policy papers issued by central banks and financial regulators around the world attempt to define the taxonomy of tools available to regulators for coping with climate change and the low-carbon transition (Campiglio et al. 2018; D'Orazio and Popoyan 2022;

Dafermos et al. 2018; Dikau and Volz 2018; Dikau and Volz 2021; Schoenmaker and van Tilburg 2016; Steffen 2021). Following the categorization of policy instruments suggested by Baer et al. (2021), policy instruments can be categorised as tools aimed at expanding climate-related information available to market actors (*informational*), policies introducing monetary incentives to make low-carbon strategies more convenient (*incentive-based*), and direct controls on credit allocation (*quantity-based*).

The cautious approach of many central banks in high-income countries focuses on the assessment of climate-related risks, mainly from a systemic perspective. More proactive strategies are based on prudential and credit policy tools, contributing to facilitating green financing through disclosure and management of risk exposures. Central banks and financial regulators may undertake or promote activities to improve the capacity of financial markets to take into account climate-related risks. Additionally, central banks may reframe their monetary policies from 'conventional' to 'green'. Climate-related factors could be included in the risk assessment of central banks' own portfolios, considered when determining the eligibility of assets for their asset purchase programmes, or as collateral in market operations.

The central banks in Central and Southeast Europe have commenced to address climate change and sustainability issues. The majority of them are in the early stages, involved in institutional learning and capacity building. Exchanges among peers, especially through coordinated supervisory review activities within the Single Supervisory Mechanisms (SSM) and memberships in regulatory communities foster peer learning and contribute to enhancing regulatory capacity and expertise (Augoyard et al. 2021, p. 30). The central banks in Central and Southeast Europe are members of the Network for Greening the Financial System, as the most important transnational regulatory network, which assists central banks and financial supervisors in the integration of climate risks into financial stability monitoring and provides a platform for capacity building and technical assistance.

In line with expert recommendations for the development of policies on greening the financial system in developing countries, central banks and financial supervisors should build internal capacities to better manage and mitigate climate-related financial risks, undertake bottom-up reviews of the major financial institutions to assess their climate risk frameworks, and feed such findings into climate risk stress-testing assumptions and other potential policy tools (Augoyard et al. 2021, p. 30).

Central banks in Central and Southeast Europe have undertaken efforts towards recognising the implications of mounting climate-related risks to economic and financial stability. However, at the moment, many of them are developing their climate policies and contributing to the intended climate objectives in an informal way. Such efforts are useful because they would signal the importance of the problem to financial intermediaries and respectively other state authorities (Chandavarkar 1987, p. 4).

The up-to-date practices of central banks in Central and Southeast Europe, based on official documents and reports, have led to the general conclusion that the central banks in these countries do not significantly differ from their peers. The situation in most new EU Member States and aspirant countries mirrors the overall assessment of the character of the applied instruments for greening the financial system in the EU, where policies are mostly, if not exclusively, based on informational measures aimed at achieving both prudential and promotional purposes (Baer et al. 2021). Incentive and quantity-based policies, as forms of more intrusive intervention, are underdeveloped in the regulatory frameworks of the assessed countries, Hungary being an exception.

Based on the analysis of annual reports and financial stability reports of central banks in the observed countries, in addition to Hungary as the leader, the issue of climate change is high on the agendas of the central banks of Romania, Slovenia, Croatia, North Macedonia, followed by Montenegro, Serbia and Albania. While identifying and measuring the impact of climate risks on the financial sector, the central banks of Poland and the Czech Republic are on the other side of the spectrum. The Governor of the Narodowi Bank Polski has expressed his position in public stating that 'tools in the field of climate policy lie mainly on the side of government, not the central bank… NBP does not see the legitimacy of actively influencing the directions of banks' lending policy at this stage'.[2] In a similar way, top Czech monetary official said that central banks shouldn't try to fight climate change, as doing so could endanger financial stability and undermine their independence.[3]

In addition to benefits from joining networks such as the Network for Greening the Financial System and following international and European Central Bank initiatives, central banks are developing their own research capacities. Good examples are Hungary and Romania. In addition to conducting its own research activities, Magyar Nemzeti Bank has established active cooperation with universities, instituted the Green Finance Academic Council and established the Green Finance Science Awards (MNB 2022a). Following the decision of the General Board of the National Committee for Macroprudential Oversight of October 2020, the National Bank of Romania coordinated representatives of public authorities, financial intermediaries and private companies from relevant industries, with a view to prepare an in-depth report on solutions to support green finance and mitigate the potential negative effects of climate risk, that was released to the general public in June 2021 (NBR 2022).

Climate Finance Initiatives, Soft Powers and Information-Based Policy Tools

Central Bank Declarations, Pledges and Strategic Frameworks on Climate-Related Risks

Encouraged by the activities of other central banks, especially within networks such as the Network for Greening the Financial System, central banks in Central and Southeast Europe have begun not only to recognize the importance of climate change risks but also to declare it a new area of concern. Some of the first steps of illustrating interest in the field were reports and publications presenting the activities carried out at the level of systemically important banks, notably stress tests undertaken at the EU-wide level.[4] Similarly, the central banks often publicly announce joining the Network for Greening the Financial System.[5]

To emphasize the importance of climate-related risks and announce their monitoring role and potential future activities, some central banks have published declarations or pledges, reiterating collective commitments such as the NGFS Glasgow Declaration (NGFS 2021) and the ECB's 2021 pledge on climate change action (ECB 2021a). For example, the Climate Pledge of the National Bank of Slovakia[6] and the Climate Declaration of the Central Bank of Croatia,[7] both published in November 2021, express the determination to contribute to the global response to climate change and commit to increasing awareness and monitoring climate change-related issues. The document of the Central Bank of Montenegro published in March 2022 under the title 'Central Bank of Montenegro policy related to climate change challenges' has similar contents. This policy shall be implemented through the Action Plan, scheduled to be adopted by the end of 2022 (Central Bank of Montenegro 2022).[8] The Strategic Plan 2022–2024 of the National Bank of the Republic of North Macedonia proclaimed climate change as one of its nine strategic objectives (NBRNM 2021).

A particularly good example is the Green Programme by the Central Bank of Hungary (MNB 2019). After explaining the concept of climate risk and its manifestations, and an analysis of the comparative practice of central banks in climate risk management, this document clarifies the relationship with the National Strategy on Climate Change, portraying the implementation of international initiatives in this area and indicating the measures that the central bank itself will undertake in areas of information and risk management, especially in the context of monetary policy implementation. Furthermore, the foundations of the MNB's new central banking approach were laid by the Green Central Banking Policy Instrument Strategy announced on 6 July 2021.

Disclosure and Reporting on Climate-Related Risks in Central Banks' Reports

Since 2015, the predominant approach of many central banks in addressing climate change has been financial risk measurement and disclosures. Financial stability reports and annual reports of central banks, in addition to various forms of announcements, declarations and strategic documents, analytical commentaries and reports, represent another level of information provision. While many EU Member States publish reports and/or strategies outlining the long-term impact of climate change on their national economy, some central banks publish specific reports on climate risks. The NGFS reports and the ECB Guide on climate-related and environmental risks (ECB 2020) seem to have had a major impact on the understanding and presentation of climate change risks.

Following the initiative of the National Committee for Macroprudential Oversight, the working group coordinated by the National Bank of Romania published an in-depth report in June 2021. The report contains 16 proposals of recommendations to the authorities, covering three groups of activities: (1) to sustainably increase the financing of green projects, (2) to support structural changes in the economy towards generating higher value-added and (3) to enhance transparency and raise awareness about the impact of climate change on the economy and the financial system (NBR 2022).

Analytical commentaries are reports in which, in addition to the possible theoretical framework and presentation of the types of risk, the economic sectors that have the greatest impact on climate risk and are most affected by this risk are identified at the national level. For instance, in Slovakia such analytical commentaries present and evaluate the degree of distribution of portfolios of larger banks in key economic sectors in terms of the climate risks (National Bank of Slovakia 2021). Similarly, Banka Slovenije has published a specific research report on climate risks in Slovenia in 2020 (Bank of Slovenije 2020). Since 2019, the National Bank of Romania has launched several research papers on how climate change is affecting Romania's economy, outlining the potential threats to the financial stability, while the Bank's first Climate Risk Dash Board for the Banking Sector in Romania was launched in 2021 (Bank of Romania 2021).

Since 2019/2020, some central banks in the referent group of countries have expanded the scope of their financial stability analysis to include risks associated with climate change. In its Financial Stability Report for 2021, Bank of Slovenije (2022a) repeated the findings of the above-mentioned specific report and presented a detailed review of how transition risks are monitored through the indicators of carbon footprint, carbon intensity and carbon loan intensity. Another example of a more comprehensive analysis of the impact of the climate factor is the Croatian Financial Stability Report (Central Bank of Croatia 2022). In its latest Financial Stability Report, Czech National Bank presented the methodology of a banking sector stress test focused on the impact of climate risks (Czech National Bank 2022). In some countries, such as Serbia, the policy agenda on climate risks is presented in more detail in annual reports. In accordance with the National Bank of Serbia's Annual Report for 2021, the Financial Stability Report for 2021 defines the impact of climate change as both key external and key internal risk, provides an analysis of the impact of climate change and defines pre-emptive and risk mitigation measures (National Bank of Serbia 2022(a), 2022(b)).

In addition to annual reports and reports on financial stability, the implications of climate change on the financial system and financial stability may also be presented in a separate official report on green finance. The Green Finance Report by the Hungarian central bank is the best example again. The main objective of this report is to provide a comprehensive annual overview of the Hungarian financial sector's exposure to environmental sustainability risks and the financing actions promoting sustainability, as well as the related sustainability programmes of Magyar Nemzeti Bank (MNB 2022a).

Supervisory Engagement Activities and Supervisory Expectations

In their reports and statements, many central banks articulated the need to increase awareness of ESG risks and the need for building the capacity of the supervised institutions to engage in climate risk assessment and risk management. While the publication of guides on climate-related and environmental risks presupposes the establishment of standards on how central banks and financial supervisors expect financial institutions to prudently manage and disclose such risks, prior to publishing ESG guidelines and setting supervisory expectations, the first steps regulators have undertaken are supervisory engagement activities. Most supervisors in Central and Southeast Europe consider themselves still in the initial phase of dialogue. It is expected that such a dialogue, followed by the associated publications, studies and reports by central banks, which precede the inclusion of climate change into prudential supervision, would prepare financial intermediaries to develop an understanding and initiate the first steps towards financial risk disclosure and management.

One of the ways of defining supervisory expectations is questionnaires that are created by central banks. For example, in early 2001, the Croatian National Bank asked banks, in the form of a questionnaire, whether they were aware of the existence of climate risks and their impact on business, and whether they had identified them in their portfolios and analysed them qualitatively or quantitatively.[9] Questionnaires can be distributed to banks in order to obtain information about the structure of internal stress testing of climate risks. At this moment, such exercises are primarily aimed at raising awareness and identifying weaknesses. For instance, in relation to climate risk stress tests for the largest European banks, in March and April 2022, along the lines of the ECB SSM model, Banka Slovenije conducted both a survey and calculation of the banks' income from carbon-intensive sectors. Whereas the ECB conducted climate risk stress tests for the largest European banks this year, the survey performed by Banka Slovenije also included less significant banks.[10] The results indicate that the majority of banks face a shortage of high-quality data.

Although stress testing is considered a part of central banks' prudential policy toolbox, a holistic assessment of the resilience and continuity of the big financial intermediaries and the overall financial system to climate-related risks is one of the best ways to signal to financial intermediaries that they have to assess the climate risks of their counterparties and their activities and build frameworks to manage their exposures to climate risk (Augoyard et al. 2021, p. 27). It can be expected that the recommendations of the NGFS (2022), which set the basis for the ECB climate stress tests, the activities of the ECB Banking Supervision towards large financial institutions and the European Banking Authority's proposals on management and supervision of ESG risks will influence the future practices of central banks in the new EU member states and candidates for admission.

Promoting Disclosure: From Non-Binding Guidelines and Recommendations towards Mandatory Taxonomies

To clarify the new concepts of socially responsible business, central banks and financial regulators publish guides, best practices, instructions and recommendations on ESG risks, or specifically on climate-related and environmental risks. Their purpose is twofold. Such non-binding documents are softer forms of promotional activities by central banks, aimed at raising awareness of the importance of climate-related risks and promoting engagement with the industry. At the same time, sustainable finance guidelines establish a yardstick for setting up supervisory expectations and usually define frameworks for environmental risk assessment and incentive schemes for green financing. At the global level, ESG risk measurement approaches and management are at an early stage of development, due to a lack of a common definition of ESG risk, little offered guidance, and underdeveloped quantitative and qualitative metrics. Therefore, some supervisors are communicating elements of the risk management approach through guidelines, issuance of good practices, while others are awaiting the outcome of EU regulatory initiatives. Prior to the completion of mandates of the EBA, supervisors may promote European Banking Authority's recommendations on risk management related to credit risk policies and procedures.

Based on already published guides in developed economies,[11] and notably the ECB Guide on Climate-Related and Environmental risks (ECB 2020), central banks and financial regulators in CE and SEE could encourage supervised entities to understand supervisory expectations, as well as rationales for new supervisory tools, by providing practical guidance on how to address climate risks within financial institutions and describing good practices.

Of all the countries observed, only the Central Bank of Hungary has prepared detailed recommendations. In line with the practice of the European Central Bank, the MNB sets out prudential requirements in its Guide, with a focus on identifying, quantifying and managing sustainability and climate risks and integrating them into their business operations. [12] The Guide sets out expectations for managing financial risks arising from climate change and other environmental causes under four headings: business model and strategy, corporate governance, risk management and disclosures (Magyar Nemzeti Bank, 2022a, p. 37).

Helping banks to develop their capacities for environmental risk assessment and systematic environmental risk analysis is often the first step before green policies evolve from principle-based approaches to standardised frameworks with compulsory elements and mandatory evaluation mechanisms. Taxonomies represent standardised frameworks for labelling sustainable and non-sustainable activities. Although there is no widely agreed-upon criteria for the assessment of 'greenness', 'brown' assets are associated with the financing of emission-incentive activities (UN and World Bank 2017, p. 42). The initiatives at the EU level would significantly define central bank green strategies in CE and SEE. For instance, in defining its capital requirement discounts for loans supporting energy efficiency in real estate, the Central Bank of Hungary based its definition of green property on the report of the Technical Expert Group on the EU Taxonomy of June 2019.

Strengthening the Disclosure of Climate-Risk Exposures and Climate Risk Management

The disclosure of climate-related risks is important as improved transparency enables a more appropriate pricing of risk and, therefore, provides the basis for prudential regulation and climate-related stress testing. Disclosure is also important from the perspective of the central bank's portfolio, as inclusion of carbon emissions disclosure as a requirement in asset purchase programmes has been proposed as a one of the first central bank climate-oriented activities (Dikau et al. 2021).

At the global level, the Taskforce on Climate-related Financial Disclosure (TCFD), created by the Financial Stability Board, promotes the development of climate-related disclosure methods. Disclosure requirements for central banks, financial institutions and companies issuing public debt or equity have been recommended in the very first group of TCFD recommendations (TCFD 2016), with a view to improve the information available to investors and facilitate the inclusion of those factors in decision making. Albeit voluntary, a number of countries have made TCFD disclosures mandatory. Central banks and financial supervisors recommend or expect disclosures in the annual financial statements of the regulated financial institutions, based on four TCFD disclosure pillars (TCFD 2021) (Table 10.1) and the best practices of disclosing climate-related financial risks and opportunities, in line with the TCFD framework.

Given the fact that there are differences in the application of the TCFD recommendations, due to the fact that definitions, data and assessment methodologies are constantly evolving (Kyriakopoulou et al. 2022), the efforts of the central banks in CE and SEE countries will have to follow the progressive improvements in the quantity and quality of disclosures. In this regard, Hungary is again the best example. Magyar Nemzeti Bank's Climate-Related Financial Disclosure is a report focused on the recognition and management of climate risks by the central bank, prepared fully in accordance with the TCFD recommendations (MNB 2022b). Apart from this, central banks may also prepare sustainability-related disclosures on sustainable and responsible investments, as proposed by the UN Principles for Responsible Investments (NGFS 2019b). Furthermore, central banks may develop specific disclosures on their sustainable investment practices, such as carbon footprint.

Table 10.1 TCFD disclosure pillars

Pillar I: Governance	*Pillar II: Strategy*	*Pillar III: Risk management*	*Pillar IV: Metrics and targets*
Disclosing the organisation's governance regarding climate-related risks and opportunities.	Disclosing actual and potential impacts of climate-related risks and opportunities on the organisation's businesses, strategy and financial planning, if such information is material.	Disclosing the way that the organisation identifies, assesses and manages climate-related risks.	Disclosing the metrics and targets used to assess and manage relevant climate-related risks and opportunities, if such information is material.

The EU initiatives on the 'greening' of prudential regulation and rules on disclosure regulation will have a significant impact on central banks in CE and SEE. Namely, both the latest banking regulation package (revised rules on capital requirements CRD V/CRR II),[13] and the corresponding legislation for investment firms, require large financial institutions to publicly disclose their exposures to ESG and climate risks, as well as their mitigating actions. As an initiative to revise the Non-Financial Reporting Directive, the European Financial Reporting Advisory Group has prepared a set of EU sustainability reporting standards (EFRAG 2021). Central banks in EU member states and candidate countries are following the work and guidance of the European Banking Authority on prudential disclosures on ESG risks (EBA 2021). As the EBA's mandate on the prudential treatment of ESG risks is due to be fulfilled by 2025, the integration of ESG risks into national regulatory requirements will probably be influenced by a specific guide for supervisors for integrating climate-related and environmental risks into prudential supervision, issued by the NGFS (2020).

Considerations on Green Prudential Tools

The literature on the existing climate-related macroprudential financial policies highlights the fact that climate-oriented macroprudential measures related to capital requirements, leverage ratios and liquidity requirements for systemically important institutions in G20 countries are currently widely debated, but almost unimplemented in practice (D'Orazio 2022; Campiglio et al. 2018; Lamperti et al. 2021). In its Guide for Supervisors, the NGFS has proposed using discretionary interventions in managing high exposures to environmental risks and suggested measures such as stringent limits on risk concentration, limits or prohibitions on the financing of certain categories of activities or sectors, and mandatory deleveraging of certain risks (NGFS 2020). While central banks and prudential authorities are calibrating prudential instruments, a shift from voluntary to mandatory disclosure has been the first manifestation of tightening the policy stance. A more proactive option would be to adjust macro- and micro-prudential regulations in order to take into account climate-related financial risks, by limiting systemic financial risk, and incorporating specific tools, including reserve and capital requirements, caps and ceilings, and measures encouraging lending to climate-friendly activities (Alexander 2014; Schoenmaker and van Tilburg 2016).

In line with proposals for the active use of capital adequacy rules and prudential exposure limits (Miller and Dikau 2022; Schoenmaker and van Tilburg 2016), the imposition of risk weights sensitive to environment-related risks, as 'penalising factor', and introduction of capital buffers to internalise the potential impact of their activities on the financial system, has been apprised in the European Commission's Sustainable Finance Action Plan, released in March 2018. However, the majority of central banks and financial supervisors were of the opinion that financial policies should be neutral, not interfere in the flow of credits, and not discriminate between low- and high-carbon financial assets (Baer et al. 2021; Dankert et al. 2018). Central banks and financial regulators in more developed economies are still hesitating to adjust prudential regulations to avoid potential conflicts with short-term prudential policy objectives (Campiglio et al. 2018).

The majority of national authorities have not yet undertaken straightforward measures to include climate-related financial risks in the prudential capital framework (BCBS 2020). However, even if the epidemic and the current geopolitical situation in East Europe had not halted climate finance initiatives, the majority of central banks in the EU countries would have opted to await the outcomes of the EBA's initiatives related to the implementation the Action Plan on Sustainable Finance, therefore avoiding to take premature actions. Therefore, most central banks in new EU Member States and aspiring countries seem to have adopted a 'wait and see' approach, awaiting further legislative and regulatory developments in the EU, especially the results of the EBA's mandates on the revision of capital requirements and technical standards on ESG risk disclosures.[14]

The use of a green supporting factor has been advocated by Magyar Nemzeti Bank, which was the first central bank in Europe to introduce a preferential capital requirement programme under Pillar 2 of the banking regulatory framework for green lending, by introducing preferential capital treatment for energy-efficient ('green') housing loans.[15] Banks must comply with the complementary green reporting requirement. This initiative to encourage the renovation of properties aimed at improving energy efficiency was promulgated as a national interest, with the potential of increasing awareness and developing financial markets. Following the Hungarian example, banking regulators in some neighbouring countries have voiced proposals to ease regulatory lending requirements for house renovation loans.

Monetary Policy Adjustments and Green Credit Allocation

In order to guide the allocation of capital, the regulators in emerging economies usually maintain a higher systemic control of the macro-financial environment (Dikau and Ryan-Collins 2017). As the central banks in the former Eastern Bloc, many central banks in Central and Southeast Europe were known to selectively target and encourage certain industries and activities. Some central banks in developing countries have designed interventionist climate policies and introduced measures aimed at promoting the allocation of capital, especially credit allocation. Such credit policy instruments in some Asian countries are predominantly designed to support green activities, and not to discourage the financing of activities of unsustainable sectors (Dikau and Volz 2018). Some examples of targeted green refinancing operations in Europe include the Funding for Lending Scheme of the Bank of England and the Magyar Nemzeti Bank's Funding for Growth Scheme (FGS). As a part of the MNB's Green Toolkit Strategy, FGS helps people purchase and build new, energy-efficient homes with a favourable loan that has a fixed rate until maturity, indirectly encouraging builders to construct energy-efficient residential buildings. The Hungarian example shows that given this lending support is also part of the investment policy, encouraging lending as a policy option would also imply the synergy of central banks with other state bodies, such as the ministries responsible for finance, economy and infrastructure. The role of loans in financing energy efficiency projects – based on the idea that the banking sector provides clients with loans with lower interest rates and/or fees – remains to be seen, as a large number of funds will be required to finance energy efficiency projects (Desalegn et al. 2022).

In addition to green credit allocation tools, green monetary policy instruments have an important role in the transition towards a climate-neutral economy. As part of their operational procedures, central banks determine the criteria or requirements for assets and collateral to be eligible for use in monetary policy operations. The greening of monetary policy operations involves steering the eligibility criteria towards low-carbon assets (Schoenmaker 2021). Quantitative easing and refinancing operations are generally considered a violation of the market neutrality principle. However, large-scale purchases of collateral have made the collateral framework a tool for addressing climate change. Adapting the collateral framework, in terms of defining the criteria for the assets that could be pledged to get liquidity from the central bank, could make climate-friendly financial assets relatively more attractive to banks. Both 'brown' collateral haircuts and 'green hair growth' are found to increase carbon-neutral investment, while decreasing carbon-intensive investment and emissions (McConnell et al. 2022).

By articulating climate change as one of the most critical implications for its primary policy objective, the ECB has announced an ambitious roadmap to incorporate climate change into its monetary policy framework (ECB 2021b). It may be expected that the inclusion of climate risks in the conduct of monetary policy operations and collateral frameworks in the Eurosystem will promote the greening of monetary policy and incentivize central banks in the observed countries.

Several examples from the region should be pointed out. The Magyar Nemzeti Bank was among the first central banks in the world to introduce a green bond portfolio within its foreign exchange reserves. Since 2020, MNB had purchased mortgage bonds that qualify for green bond status. In August 2021, the MNB launched the Green Mortgage Bond Purchase Programme, under which it purchases, on the primary and secondary market, fixed-rate, forint-denominated mortgage bonds with a green certificate satisfying international standards and issued with a maturity of at least 5 years. A share of international reserves managed by the Central Bank of Croatia was made up of the sustainable investments, green bonds, and social and sustainability bonds, whose share in total reserves amounted to 1.2% at the end of 2021(Central Bank of Croatia 2022). Banka Slovenije increased the scope of investments in green, socially beneficial and sustainable bonds, excluded investments in firms involved in corruption and firms causing major environmental harm or breaching human rights, and continued to follow the exclusion list created by the pension fund operated by Norges Bank Investment Management (Bank of Slovenije, 2022b, p. 67.)

Conclusion

Central banks and financial supervisors face the challenging task of ensuring a shift to a low-carbon economy, while striving to maintain price and financial stability. The macroeconomic environment we are now experiencing has been changing, as countries are facing inflationary pressures and an energy crisis. As energy- and food-related issues are the key issues in the overall rise of inflation in the eurozone, possibly resorting to fossil fuels could further undermine the initiatives on greening financial markets.

The central banks in Central and Southeast Europe are voicing the issue of risk related to climate finance, and some of them are promoting and measuring the performance of sustainable finance activities to some extent. In order to integrate green finance measures without jeopardising the primary mandate and responding to climate-related challenges, central banks require capacity building and training. However, the lack of expertise is not a key problem here. The constraint is the availability of data, coupled with the absence of clear methodologies and taxonomy. Although there are pioneering efforts by central banks in developing countries, especially in Asia and South America, it cannot be said that the models of instruments and measures applied by central banks have been developed, nor is it still possible to measure the effectiveness of the undertaken measures.

Considering the membership or orientation towards membership in the EU, the priorities of the central banks in CE and SEE will, evidently, be aligned with the priorities set by the European financial sector regulators, notably with the priorities in banking supervision within the Single Supervisory Mechanism and the EBA's requirements for banks to include ESG risks in their internal governance and risk management. Although the SSM supervisory priorities are primarily focused on the significant institutions under the ECB direct supervision, the national central banks participate in the identification of risks and priority-setting process, through the Joint Supervisory Teams, and translate SSM priorities into their supervisory plans. Through SSM priorities and the coordinated activities of supervisory authorities supporting the Supervisory Review and Evaluation Process, the national supervisors are learning about key issues and tools, thereafter setting their own priorities for the supervision of less significant institutions in a similar way. Translated into strategic objectives, the central banks should encourage and monitor the way supervised institutions have incorporated climate-related and environmental risks into their business strategies and their governance and risk management frameworks.

With the exception of Hungary, in most countries the primary focus seems to be on disclosure and participation in coordinated activities within the Supervisory Review and Evaluation Process. It seems that intervention would predominantly rely on informational policy instruments in achieving both promotional and prudential objectives, in contrast to central banks in some emerging economies, which employ incentive or quantity-based instruments (Baer et al. 2021).

Based on the above, it could be concluded that the Climate Change on the Policy Agenda of Central Banks in Central and Southeast Europe will extend through five stages. The first stage involves the strengthening of promotional activities and the publication of analytical commentaries on the importance and impact of climate-related risks, as well as the publication of voluntary guidelines and recommendations on the disclosure and management of ESG risks. The second stage would entail expanding the scope of their financial stability analyses to include risks associated with climate change and the introduction of climate stress tests, and policy-learning following the initiatives of the ECB, EBA, NGFS and international initiatives. The third stage is a follow-up to the coordinated activities within SREP, further alignment of the disclosure practices of central banks and regulated financial institutions, monitoring risk management, and adherence to supervisory expectations. Pending an agreement on methodologies, regulatory and supervisory instruments at the EU level, some countries, similarly as Hungary, will introduce incentives such as credit policy measures and prudential requirements, which would represent the fourth level. The final stage assumes harmonisation of regulatory and supervisory approaches, at the EU level, to setting standards and monitoring compliance with upcoming regulatory requirements related to the review of bank strategies, governance and risk management frameworks.

Notes

1 The amendment of Act CXXXIX of 2013 on Magyar Nemzeti Bank, Art. 1.3.(2): 'Without prejudice to its primary objective, the MNB shall support the maintenance of the stability of the system of financial intermediation, the enhancement of its resilience, its sustainable contribution to economic growth; furthermore, the MNB shall support the government's economic policy and its policy related to environmental sustainability, using instruments at its disposal.'

2 NBP monitoruje ryzyka związane ze zmianami klimatu, *Rzeczpospolita,* 5. 01. 2022, viewed 10 September 2022, https://www.rp.pl/banki/art19291331-glapinski-nbp-monitoruje-ryzyka-zwiazane-ze-zmianami-klimatu

3 Central Banks Can't Fix Climate Change, Czech Policy Maker Says, Bloomberg, 18. 02. 2021, viewed 15 September, 2022. https://www.bloomberg.com/news/articles/2021-02-18/central-banks-can-t-fix-climate-change-czech-policy-maker-says?leadSource=uverify%20wall

4 For instance, the Croatian National Bank published a note on ECB stress testing exercise in July 2022, viewed 30 October 2022, viewed, 30 October 2022, https://www.hnb.hr/-/banke-se-moraju-u-vecoj-mjeri-usredotociti-na-klimatski-rizik-pokazalo-je-nadzorno-testiranje-otpornosti-na-stres-koje-je-proveo-esb

5 For example, in its announcement on joining the NGFS, the Bank of Slovenia gives a brief overview of the activities of this network and points to new sets of risks in connection with climate change. Bank of Slovenia, Press Release 11. May 2020, viewed 30 October 2022, https://www.bsi.si/en/media/1569/banka-slovenije-joins-the-network-for-greening-the-financial-system.

6 National Bank of Slovakia (2021). Climate Pledge of the National Bank of Slovakia. https://nbs.sk/en/news/climate-pledge-of-the-national-bank-of-slovakia/

7 National Bank of Croatia (2021). Klimatska deklaracija. https://www.hnb.hr/o-nama/funkcije-i-struktura/hnb-i-klimatske-promjene/klimatska-deklaracija

8 Central Bank of Montenegro policy related to climate change challenges (2022). https://www.cbcg.me/slike_i_fajlovi/eng/fajlovi/fajlovi_o_nama/cbcg_and_climate_changes/cbm_policy_related_to_climate_change_challenges.pdf

9 National Bank of Croatia (2021). Financijska podrška projektima koji se poduzimaju radi tranzicije na niskougljično gospodarstvo. https://www.hnb.hr/-/financijska-podrska-projektima-koji-se-poduzimaju-radi-tranzicije-na-niskougljicno-gospodarstvo

10 Bank of Slovenia (2021). Inclusion of climate risks in stress tests at banks and savings banks, Press Release, 7 August. https://www.bsi.si/en/media/1874/inclusion-of-climate-risks-in-stress-tests-at-banks-and-savings-banks

11 Austria – Financial Market Authority (FMA) 2020, Guide for Handling Sustainability Risks (Guidelines); Autorité de contrôle prudentiel et de resolution (ACPR) 2020,

Governance and Management of Climate-Related Risks by French Banking Institutions: some good practices (Good Practices); De Nederlandsche Bank (DNB) 2020, Good Practice: Integration of climate-related risk considerations into banks' risk management (Good practices); European Banking Authority (EBA) 2019, EBA Action plan on sustainable finance (Action plan,); Federal Financial Supervisory Authority (BaFin) 2019, Guidance Notice on Dealing with Sustainability Risks (Guidance); Prudential Regulation Authority (PRA) 2019, Enhancing banks' and insurers' approaches to managing the financial risks from climate change (Supervisory statement SS3/19).

12 Magyar Nemzeti Bank, Recommendation No 5/2021 on climate change and environmental risks and the integration of environmental sustainability considerations in the activities of credit institutions.

13 Regulation (EU) 2019/876 amending Regulation (EU) 575/2013 as regards the leverage ratio, the net stable funding ratio, requirements for own funds and eligible liabilities, counterparty credit risk, market risk, exposures to central counterparties, exposures to collective investment undertakings, large exposures, reporting and disclosure requirements and Regulation (EU) 648/2012, O.J. 2019, L 250/1 (CRR II); and Directive (EU) 2019/878 amending Directive 2013/36/EU as regards exempted entities, financial holding companies, mixed financial holding companies, remuneration, supervisory measures and powers and capital conservation measures, O.J. 2019, L 150/253 (CRD V).

14 The EBA's mandate is outlined in Article 449a of CRR2, which requires the disclosure of ESG-related physical and transition risks.

15 The capital requirement discount is set at 5% of the relevant discount base in the case of renovation, building or purchasing a property with a BB energy rating, and 7% in the case of building or purchasing a property with at least an AA rating. To safeguard financial stability, the discount cannot exceed 1% of the total risk exposure amount of banks.

Bibliography

Alexander, K, 2014, *Stability and sustainability in banking reform: Are environmental risks missing in Basel III?*, UNEP-FI and University of Cambridge Institute for Sustainability Leadership, viewed 5 September 2022, www.unepfi.org/fileadmin/documents/StabilitySustainability.pdf

Augoyard, S, Durrani, A, Fenton, A, & Volz, U, 2021, *Assessing the Effectiveness and Impact of Central Bank and Supervisory Policies in Greening the Financial System across the Asia-Pacific – Findings from the Second APAC Central Bank Sustainability Survey 2021*, International Conference on 'Statistics for Sustainable Finance', 14-15 September 2021, Paris, France, viewed 5 July 2022, https://www.bis.org/ifc/publ/ifcb56_06.pdf

Baer, M, Campiglio, E, & Deyris, J 2021, 'It takes two to dance: Institutional dynamics and climate-related financial policies', *Ecological Economics*, vol. 190, p. 107210.

Bank of Slovenia, 2020, Report on Climate Risks in Slovenia 2020. Discussion Paper No. 3, viewed 15 September 2022, https://bankaslovenije.blob.core.windows.net/publication-files/report_climate_risks.pdf

Bank of Slovenia 2022a, *Financial stability report*, October 2022, Banka Slovenije, Ljubljana.

Bank of Slovenia 2022b, *Annual report for 2021*, Banka Slovenije, Ljubljana.

Basel Committee on Banking Supervision – BCBS, 2020, *Climate-related financial risks: a survey on current initiatives*, viewed 10 June 2022, https://www.bis.org/bcbs/publ/d502.pdf

Batten, S, Sowerbutts, R, & Tanaka, M 2016, *Let's talk about The weather: The impact of climate change on Central banks*, Technical report, Bank of England, London.

Berrou, R, Ciampoli, N, & Marini, V 2019, 'Defining green finance: Existing standards and main challenges' in M Migliorelli & P Dessertine (eds.) *Rise of green finance in Europe: Opportunities and challenges for issuers, investors and marketplaces*, Palgrave, London.

Campiglio, E, Dafermos, Y, Monnin, P, Ryan-Collins, R, Schotten, G, & Tanaka, M 2018, 'Climate change challenges for central banks and financial regulators', *Nature Climate Change*, vol. 8, no. 6, pp. 462–468.

Central Bank of Croatia 2022, *Financial stability report*, CNB, Zagreb.

Central Bank of Montenegro 2022, *Central Bank of Montenegro policy related to climate change challenges*, CBM, Podgorica.

Chandavarkar, AG 1987, *Promotional role of central banks – Beyond monetary policy and regulatory functions*, International Monetary Fund, Washington.

Chenet, H, Ryan-Collins, J, & van Lerven, F 2021, 'Finance, climate-change and radical uncertainty: Towards a precautionary approach to financial policy', *Ecological Economics*, vol. 183, pp. 1–14.

Czech National Bank 2022, *Financial stability report*, December 2022, CNB, Prague.

Dafermos, Y, Nikolaidi, M, & Galanis, G 2018, 'Climate change, financial stability and monetary Policy', *Ecological Economics*, vol. 152, pp. 219–234.

Dankert, J, van Doorn, L, Reinders, HJ, & Sleijpen, O, 2018, A Green Supporting Factor—The Right Policy?, SUERF Policy Note No 43, viewed 10 October 2022, https://www.suerf.org/policynotes/3473/a-green-supporting-factor-the-right-policy/html

Desalegn, G, Fekete-Farkas, M, & Tangl, A 2022, 'The effect of monetary policy and private investment on green finance: Evidence from Hungary', *Journal of Risk and Financial Management*, vol. 15, no. 3, pp. 1–18.

Dikau, S, & Ryan-Collins, J, 2017, *Green central banking in emerging market an developing country economies*, New Economics Foundation, London, viewed 20 June 2022, https://neweconomics.org/uploads/files/Green-Central-Banking.pdf

Dikau, S, & Volz, U, 2018, Central Banking, Climate change and green finance, *ADBI working paper 867*, Asian Development Bank Institute, Tokio.

Dikau, S, & Volz, U, 2020, 'Central Bank mandates, sustainability objectives and the promotion of green finance', *SOAS working paper no. 232*, SOAS, London.

Dikau, S, & Volz, U 2021, 'Central Bank mandates, sustainability objectives and the promotion of green finance', *Ecological Economics*, vol. 184, pp. 1–20.

Dikau, S, Robins, N, & Volz, U, 2021, *Climate-neutral central banking – How the European System of Central Banks can support the transition to net-zero*, Policy report, viewed 20 June 2022, https://www.lse.ac.uk/granthaminstitute/wp-content/uploads/2021/05/Climate-Neutral-Central-Banking_website.pdf

D'Orazio, P, & Popoyan, L 2019, 'Fostering green investments and tackling climate-related financial risks: Which role for macroprudential policies?, *Ecological Economics*, vol. 160, no. C, pp. 25–37.

D'Orazio, P, & Popoyan, L 2022, 'Realising Central Banks' climate ambitions through financial stability mandates', *Intereconomics*, vol. 57, no. 2, pp. 103–111.

D'Orazio, P, & Thole, S 2022, 'Climate-related financial policy index: A composite index to compare the engagement in green financial policymaking at the global level', *Ecological Indicators*, vol. 141, p. 109065.

D'Orazio, PP 2022, 'Mapping the emergence and diffusion of climate-related financial policies: Evidence from a cluster analysis on G20 countries', *International Economics*, vol. 169, pp. 135–147.

European Banking Authority – EBA 2020, On management and supervision of ESG risks for credit institutions and investment firms, *EBA Discussion Paper*, EBA/DP/2020/03, EBA, Paris.

European Banking Authority – EBA 2021, *Draft implementing technical standards on prudential disclosures on ESG risks in accordance with article 449a CRR*, EBA, Paris.
European Central Bank 2020, *Guide on climate-related and environmental risks (supervisory expectations)*, ECB, Frankfurt am Main.
European Central Bank 2021a, *Pledge on climate change action*, ECB, Frankfurt am Main.
European Central Bank, 2021b, Climate change and monetary policy in the euro area, ECB strategy review, *Occasional paper series*, 271, ECB, Frankfurt am Main.
EFRAG, 2021, *Final Report: Proposals for a relevant and dynamic EU sustainability reporting standard-setting*, viewed 10 September 2022, https://www.efrag.org/Assets/Download?assetUrl=%2Fsites%2Fwebpublishing%2FSiteAssets%2FEFRAG%2520PTF-NFRS_MAIN_REPORT.pdf
Forstater, M, Halle, M, & Zadek, S 2016, *Green finance for developing countries - needs, concerns and innovations*, UN Environment Inquiry into the Design of a Sustainable Financial System, Geneva.
High-Level Expert Group on Sustainable Finance – HLEG, 2018, *Financing a sustainable European economy – Final report 2018*, European Commission, viewed 30 June 2022, https://finance.ec.europa.eu/system/files/2018-01/180131-sustainable-finance-final-report_en.pdf
International Capital Market Association – ICMA, 2020, *Sustainable Finance High-level definitions,* viewed 10 June 2022, https://www.icmagroup.org/assets/documents/Regulatory/Green-Bonds/Sustainable-Finance-High-Level-Definitions-May-2020-110520v4.pdf
Kyriakopoulou, D, Antonakaki, T, Bekiari, M, Kartapani, A, Paisiou, K, & Rapti, E, 2022, Central banks and climate-related disclosures: applying the TCFD's recommendations, *The INSPIRE Sustainable Central Banking Toolbox, Policy Briefing Paper No. 3.*
Lamperti, F, Bosetti, V, Roventini, A, & Tavoni, M, 2019, The public costs of climate-induced financial instability, *LEM Papers Series*, no. 2019/42, Laboratory of Economics and Management (LEM), Sant' Anna School of Advanced Studies, Pisa.
Lamperti, F, Bosetti, V, Roventini, A, Tavoni, M, & Treibich, T 2021, 'Three green financial policies to address climate risks', *Journal of Financial Stability*, vol. 54, p. 100875.
Magyar Nemzeti Bank – MNB, 2019, *MNB green programme*, MNB, Budapest, viewed 10 October 2022, https://www.mnb.hu/letoltes/mnb-green-program-en.pdf
Magyar Nemzeti Bank – MNB, 2022a, *Green finance report*, Budapest, viewed 10 October 2022, https://www.mnb.hu/letoltes/20220718-green-finance-report-2022-3.pdf
Magyar Nemzeti Bank, 2022b, *The Magyar Nemzeti Bank's climate-related financial disclosure*, viewed 10 October 2022, https://www.mnb.hu/letoltes/tcfd-jelente-s-2022-en.pdf
McConnell, A, Yanovski, B, & Lessmann, K 2022, 'Central Bank collateral as a green monetary policy instrument', *Climate Policy*, vol. 22, no. 3, pp. 339–355.
Miller, H, & Dikau, S 2022, *Preventing a 'climate minsky moment': Environmental financial risks and prudential exposure limits - exploring the case of the bank of England's prudential regime*, Grantham Research Institute on Climate Change and the Environment.
National Bank Of Serbia, 2022a, *Annual report*, NBS, Belgrade.
National Banko of Serbia, 2022(b), *Financial stability report*, NBS, Belgrade.
National Bank of Slovakia, 2021, Analytický komentár Ohrozuje boj proti klimatickej zmene finančnú stabilitu?, viewed 15 October 2022, https://www.nbs.sk/_img/documents/_komentare/analytickekomentare/2021/ak104_climate_risk_vs_financial_stability.pdf
National Bank of the Republic of North Macedonia – NBRNM, 2021, Strategic Plan 2022-2024, NBRNM, Skopje, viewed on 25 September 2022, https://www.nbrm.mk/content/Strategic-Plan-NB-2022-2024.pdf

National Bank of Romania – NBR 2021, *Climate risk dashboard for the Banking sector in Romania 2021*, NBR, Bucharest. https://www.bnr.ro/PublicationDocuments.aspx?icid=31984

National Bank of Romania – NBR 2022, *Annual report for 2021*, NBR, Bucharest.

Network for Greening of Financial System – NGFS, 2019a, *A call for action – climate change as a source of financial risk*, First comprehensive report, viewed 10 September 2022, https://www.ngfs.net/sites/default/files/medias/documents/ngfs_first_comprehensive_report_-_17042019_0.pdf

Network for Greening the Financial System – NGFS 2019b, *A sustainable and responsible investment guide for Central Banks' portfolio management*, Central Banks and Supervisors Network for Greening the Financial System, Paris.

Network for Greening the Financial System – NGFS, 2020, *Guide for supervisors – Integrating climate-related and environmental risks into prudential supervision*, NGFS, viewed 10 September 2022, https://www.ngfs.net/sites/default/files/medias/documents/ngfs_guide_for_supervisors.pdf

Network for Greening the Financial System – NGFS, 2021, *Glasgow Declaration – Committed to action*, Glasgow, viewed 10 October 2022, https://www.ngfs.net/sites/default/files/ngfsglasgowdeclaration.pdf

Network for Greening the Financial System – NGFS, 2022, *NGFS Climate Scenarios for central banks and supervisors*, viewed 5 October 2022, https://www.ngfs.net/sites/default/files/medias/documents/ngfs_climate_scenarios_for_central_banks_and_supervisors_.pdf.pdf

Pereira da Silva, LA 2019, *Research on climate-related risks and financial stability: An 'epistemological break'*?, BIS speech, Paris, 17 April 2019, viewed 10 November 2022, https://www.bis.org/speeches/sp190523.htm

Schoenmaker, D, & van Tilburg, R 2016, 'What role for financial supervisors in addressing environmental risks?, *Comparative Economic Studies*, vol. 58, no. 3, pp. 317–334.

Schoenmaker, D 2021, 'Greening monetary policy', *Climate Policy*, vol. 21, no. 4, pp. 581–592.

Steffen, B 2021, 'A comparative analysis of green financial policy output in OECD Countries', *Environmental Research Letters*, vol. 16, no. 7, p. 074031.

Stern, N 2008, 'The economics of climate Change', *American Economic Review*, vol. 98, no. 2, pp. 1–37.

Task Force on Climate-Related Financial Disclosures – TCFD, 2016, *Recommendations of the Task Force on Climate-related Financial Disclosures*.

Task Force on Climate-Related Financial Disclosures – TCFD, 2021, *Implementing the Recommendations of the Task Force on Climate-related Financial Disclosures*, viewed 30 June 2022, https://assets.bbhub.io/company/sites/60/2021/07/2021-TCFD-Implementing_Guidance.pdf

United Nations Environment Inquiry into the Design of a Sustainable Financial System and the World Bank, 2017, *Roadmap for a Sustainable Financial System, Inquiry Design of a Sustainable Financial System*, November 2017, viewed 30 June 2022, https://sustainabledevelopment.un.org/index.php?page=view&type=400&nr=2451&menu=1515

Volz, U, 2017, On the role of central banks in enhancing green finance, *UN Environment Inquiry Working Paper 17/01*, UN Environment Inquiry/CIGI Research Convening, viewed 10 August 2022, https://www.unep.org/ar/node/8951

11 Crises of Authoritarian Financialization: Monetary Policy in Hungary and Türkiye in the Polycrisis

David Karas and Pinar E. Dönmez

Introduction

Emerging market economies (EMEs) were prominent casualties in the 2020–22 polycrisis: the COVID-19 shock birthed a "liquidity tsunami" in 2020–21 before morphing into a liquidity crisis in 2022 as the Federal Reserve tightened monetary policy after Russia's invasion of Ukraine. Inflation and capital flight destabilized currencies and political orders in EMEs: many tackled financial instability by ramping up political interventions beyond orthodox monetary policy via price controls for instance (Pyrkalo, 2022). Some EMEs however entered the 2020–22 cycle with already politicized monetary regimes, where the visible hand of the state had presided over the social allocation of money.

In this chapter, we examine the impacts of the 2020–22 period on central banking and monetary policy under authoritarian financialization (AF) in EMEs: We focus on Hungary and Türkiye, both of which pursued debt-based growth strategies under authoritarian regimes where the executive branch had expanded control over monetary policy, financial supervision, and retail banking before 2020. We distinguish between defensive and offensive forms of financial statecraft in EMEs to explain the conflicting rationales for centralized political control over money: the former seeks to enhance the state's relative financial autonomy under structural subordination in global currency hierarchies, whereas the latter aims to harness credit-based growth as a tool of political pacification and governmentality.

We interpret authoritarian financialization as a state capitalist fix to finance-based growth strategies in EMEs under structural financial subordination. Following critical Marxist state theories (Offe, 1974; Poulantzas, 2014), we argue that instead of delivering financial stability, easing monetary policy transmission, and improving credit conditions, the expansion of centralized executive control over monetary policy and finance internalized political and class conflicts within the state apparatus. These tensions were actualized in Hungary and Türkiye in 2022 as political conflicts between the Central Bank and the executive, torn between the objectives of price stability and fiscal solvency on the one hand, and the financialization of the private sector favored by incumbents on the other. When global credit conditions contracted, expanded political control over the social allocation of money precipitated a dual crisis of accumulation and legitimation, pointing to

DOI: 10.4324/9781003323280-12

the limits of authoritarian financialization as a strategy of political and economic stabilization.

Whereas the two countries entered the 2020 COVID-19 period with similar strategies to boost a finance-real estate nexus with low interest rates as a strategy of growth and political cooptation, their policies diverged under the global liquidity squeeze of 2022: When it became impossible to simultaneously manage sovereign and private debt, Hungary prioritized the former and Türkiye the latter. We explain this divergence with differences in debt profiles, social blocs, and external financing conditions.

Literature Review

While multiple operationalizations of financialization in EMEs exist (Karwowski, 2020), we focus here on credit-based growth strategies which target households and non-financial corporations (NFCs). Credit-based accumulation was long treated as an autonomous ideal type, but recent contributions highlighted its key role in both export-led and domestic demand-led growth regimes (Ban and Helgadóttir, 2022), especially in EMEs confronted with the developmental bottlenecks of industrial upgrading (Bonizzi et al., 2022). The state of the art on the relationship between financialization and the state in EMEs is both underdeveloped and contentious (Lapavitsas and Soydan, 2022).

The first generation of a literature on subordinate financialization often reified the view of EME states disempowered by financialization: finance-based growth was described as limiting the sovereignty of EME states occupying a subordinate position in the global currency hierarchy by constraining their monetary policy space and enhancing financial risk for public and private actors alike (Kaltenbrunner and Painceira, 2018; Bonizzi et al., 2020; Alami et al., 2022). Financialization was furthermore viewed as an externally driven process, which reproduced asymmetries between Core reserve currency economies and a Periphery submitted to an external agency.

Both arguments were nuanced as it became apparent that instead of merely eroding statecraft, exposure to global liquidity- and exchange rate volatility actually forced the "*uneven emergence of specific forms of state power in emerging markets in relation to the operations of capitalist finance*" (Alami, 2020). A literature on the Financialization of Housing (FoH) additionally showed that instead of passive rule-takers, EME policymakers played a key role in recycling globally mobile capital by channelling it into domestic real estate sectors in pursuit of growth and political stability (Rodrigues et al., 2016; Pósfai and Nagy, 2017; Ergüven, 2020; Yeşilbağ, 2020; Fernandez and Aalbers, 2020; Feng et al., 2021; Garcia and Martinez Lopez, 2021; Cordeiro Santos, 2022; Gagyi and Mikuš, 2022).

The view of sovereignty-limiting and externally driven financialization was most problematic for a subset of EMEs such as Hungary and Türkiye where centralized political control over monetary policy and finance dramatically increased after the Global Financial Crisis (GFC): re-politicized Central Banks were only the most visible part of this process (Dönmez and Zemandl, 2019; Yağcı, 2018; Sebők, 2018; Piroska, 2021).

One interpretation saw statist interventions as countermovements (Scheiring, 2021) seeking to contain the most destabilizing features of financialization via financial repression and de-financialization (Gabor, 2010; Carney, 2015; Ban and Bohle, 2020). This didn't explain however why credit-driven asset price bubbles boomed in the late 2010s in parallel to an expansion of political control over money in the very same countries. A large literature on statist-neoliberal hybridity debated whether authoritarian statism was meant to sustain neoliberal forms of accumulation (Ban et al., 2021; Bruff, 2016; Callison & Manfredi, 2020; Tansel, 2017), or if it was neoliberalism which was repurposed to sustain authoritarian-statist political projects (Fabry, 2019, p. 137).

Rather than viewing statist-authoritarian political interventions in monetary policy and credit conditions as eradicating financialization or reproducing it, we analyze them instead as precarious attempts at fulfilling contradictory political and economic objectives. Politically, they use centralized state control over credit as a mode of authoritarian governmentality to stabilize rentier social contracts (Bedirhanoğlu, 2020; Büdenbender and Lagna, 2020; Mattioli, 2020; Karas, 2021; Apaydin and Çoban, 2022b). Economically, they play a comparable role to shadow banking in advanced economies (AEs); Braun and Gabor described how shadow banking in AEs emerged to solve the three problems of financing sovereign debt, enhancing monetary policy transmission and fuelling asset prices as a strategy of growth (Braun and Gabor, 2020). In financially subordinate EMEs without reserve currencies and without deep financial markets, centralized political control over monetary policy and retail banking played a functionally similar role by forcing banks to simultaneously hoard the sovereign and boost lending. Unlike in reserve currency economies; however, a trade-off always existed between the sustainability of sovereign and private debt: this tension was only masked by the long global liquidity glut which tapered in 2022.

Theoretical Framework

AF is an authoritarian mode of EME financialization where the executive directly shapes monetary and macro-financial policy by imposing interest rates (Yağcı, 2018), and macroprudential regulations (Piroska, Gorelkina, & Johnson, 2020) to re-politicized Central Banks (Dönmez and Zemandl, 2019), as well as using moral suasion (IMF, 2022a), or outright nationalizing retail banks (Voszka, 2018) compelled to lend both to the public and private sectors. Under AF, the executive develops a "financial vertical" which uses formal and informal instruments to control the entire circuit of money (Mishura and Ageeva, 2020; Karas, 2021).

We observe two rationales for the consolidation of AF: centralized executive control over monetary policy and banking might be pursued to enhance the state's relative financial autonomy from global capital markets and improve monetary policy transmission (Ban and Bohle, 2020; Ban et al., 2021). Conversely, it may also be an instrument to financially starve political opposition forces and engineer asset price bubbles as a basis for rentier social contracts (Karas, 2021) between an authoritarian regime and households or factions of capital dependent on credit provisioning by the domestic banking sector (Apaydin and Çoban, 2022b).

Table 11.1 Defensive and offensive financial statecraft

	Objectives	*Policy Instruments*
Defensive Financial Statecraft	*a. Reduce exposure to global capital markets* *b. Build buffers against future financial shocks* *c. Control monetary transmission*	1. *Deleverage debt* 2. *Reduce FX % of sovereign and private debt* 3. *Reduce non-resident % of sovereign bonds* 4. *FX Reserve accumulation* 5. *Re-politicize Central Banks* 6. *Nationalizations in banking* 7. *Macroprudential regulations* 8. *Capital controls* 9. *Moral suasion & subsidized retail bonds*
Offensive Financial Statecraft	*a. Enhance financialization as a growth strategy* *b. Enhance financialization to sustain rentier social contracts*	1. *Low interest rates* 2. *Subsidized credit to NFCs, SMEs and households* 3. *Macroprudential Interventions* 4. *Asset purchase programs of corporate equities and bonds* 5. *Public guarantees in PPP & blended finance investments*

We adapt the concepts of Defensive Financial Statecraft (DFS) and Offensive Financial Statecraft (OFS) to distinguish these objectives (Armijo and Katada, 2014): DFS targets sovereign debt and foreign capital inflows to contain the risks of exposure to exchange rate and global liquidity volatility while enhancing government control over monetary policy transmission. OFS interventions force lending by financial intermediaries to NFCs and households (Khmelnitskaya, 2014; Büdenbender and Lagna, 2020; Yeşilbağ, 2020; Mishura and Ageeva, 2020; Karas, 2021) (Table 11.1).

Crisis Tendencies of Authoritarian Financialization

AF illustrates Marxist theories of the state which expect statist attempts at solving accumulation bottlenecks to produce new crises (Alami and Dixon, 2021; Bedirhanoğlu, 2021; Bonefeld, 2014: 2, 91, 157–58; Borchert and Lessenich, 2016: 6; Offe, 1974; Clarke, 1991; Holloway and Picciotto, 1991; Burnham, 1994: 47–49). Transposing the arguments of Poulantzas and Offe to subordinate financialization, we argue that by making the executive the key nodeover the social allocation of money, AF internalizes the tension between DFS and OFS objectives within the state, and makes it vulnerable to distributive conflicts between diverse groups (Poulantzas, 2014). Executive centralization spurs accumulation and legitimation dilemmas for the state (Offe, 1974) when DFS and OFS objectives become incompatible. These contradictions manifest as intra-elite conflicts between the Central Bank and the executive, a degradation of monetary policy transmission, and a trade-off between sovereign debt and domestic lending which pose contradictory but interlinked demands on monetary policy, as the former is a key collateral for the latter (Eichacker, forthcoming; Gabor, 2010).

Case Selection

After converging on similar AF models, monetary policy in Türkiye and Hungary diverged during the 2022 polycrisis, illustrating different crisis trajectories. In both countries, financial liberalization in the 1990s resulted in systemic political-economic crises (in 2001 and 2008, respectively). Post-crisis stabilization was undertaken in both countries by nationalist hegemonic parties (AKP and Fidesz) which fused neoliberal and statist elements (Ban et al., 2021): deleveraging combined with FX reserve accumulation and a reliance on banks and households to finance public debt improved financing conditions for the state as interest rates followed a secular decline after AKP's 2001 reforms and Fidesz reforms after 2010 (Figure 11.1).

In parallel, real estate bubbles sustained with cheap credit stabilized rentier social contracts between authoritarian governments, crony capital groups in construction and real estate, as well as middle-class homeowners who benefited from inflating housing prices (Adaman et al., 2014; Yeşilbağ, 2020; Karas, 2021; Güngen, forthcoming) (Figure 11.2).

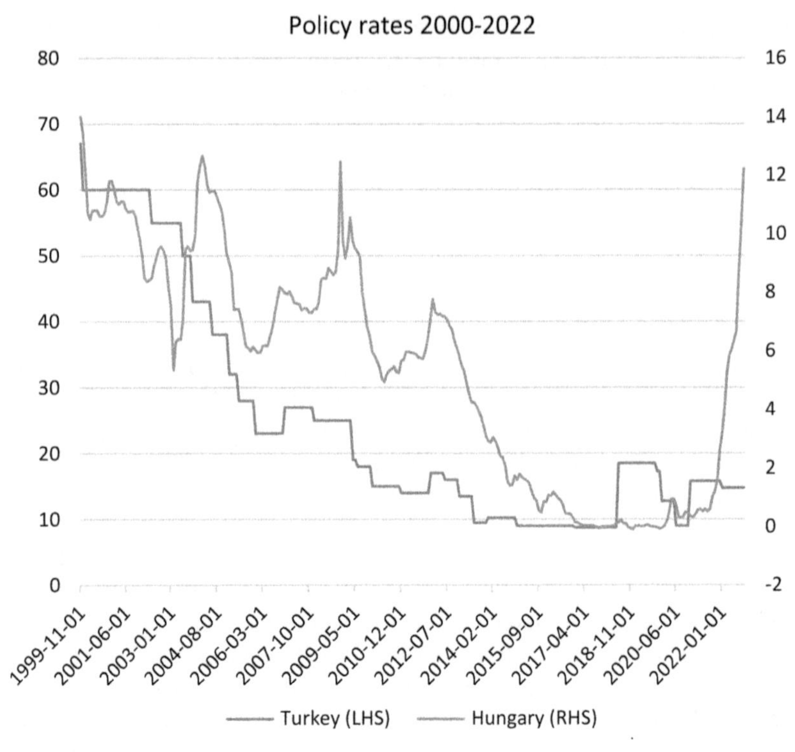

Figure 11.1 Long-term interest rates

Source: Federal Reserve Economic Data (FRED).

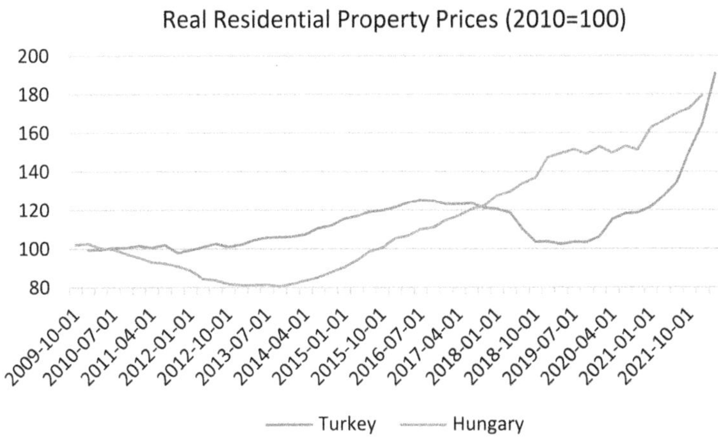

Figure 11.2 Real estate bubbles

Source: Federal Reserve Economic Data (FRED).

This second wave of financialization was accompanied by an expansion of executive control over monetary policy, banking authorities, and retail banks which forced banks to simultaneously finance sovereign debt and deepen the financialization of housing.

The Crises of Authoritarian Financialization in Hungary and Türkiye

The global liquidity glut created by Core central banks in 2020–21 convinced Hungary and Türkiye to deepen OFS interventions and boost credit-based growth. During the 2022 liquidity squeeze; however, the limits of AF as a strategy of political and economic stabilization became apparent: both countries faced a dual crisis of accumulation and legitimation albeit their monetary policies diverged. Türkiye prioritized private debt and embraced an increasingly coercive cycle of OFS and DFS interventions: It maintained record negative real interest rates even amidst inflation above 180% (Thomas, 2022) to shore up an alliance between AKP and firms in export-oriented industries and construction. The cost was a rapid deterioration of public finances, the proletarianization of households and the dollarization of 54.4% of deposits (Bloomberg, 2022), which in turn compelled the government to impose indirect capital controls and appropriate private FX deposits to contain the pressure on the exchange rate. Hungary by contrast retreated from both OFS and DFS objectives to safeguard the exchange rate and stabilize sovereign bond markets: the Central Bank raised interest rates from 0.6% to 18%, while phasing out subsidized credit instruments for households and corporates. A disinflationary interest coalition prevailed between the state's need to stabilize financing for the sovereign on one hand, and the interests of non-tradable domestic capital factions and households hurt by inflation on the other. We explain this divergence in monetary policies with differences in debt profiles, social blocs, and external financing conditions.

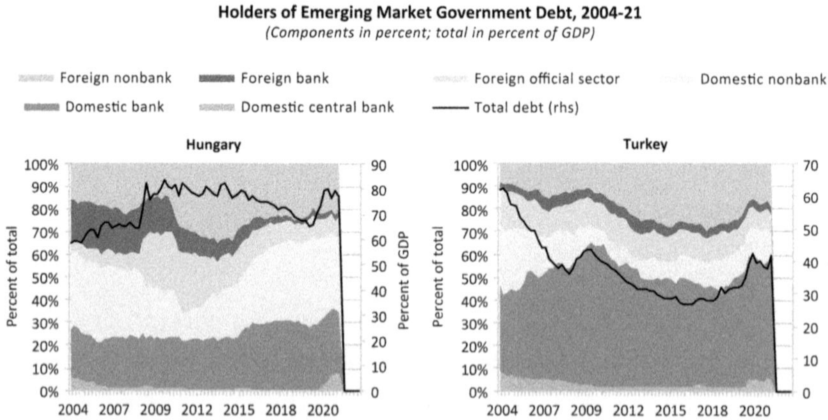

Figure 11.3 Sovereign debt

Source: IMF (2022c).

Debt Profiles

After their respective crises in 2001 and 2008, both AKP and Fidesz deleveraged public debt and relied on domestic banks and households to finance government debt (Figure 11.3).

However, debt stabilized at a high level in Hungary at 78% of GDP in 2022 compared with Türkiye's 42%: public debt, fiscal deficits and social transfers (Table 11.2) remained important for pacifying post-Socialist masses excluded from the labor market (Bohle and Greskovits, 2012). Türkiye deleveraged more radically: under IMF-approved fiscal reforms, government debt to GDP declined from 75.5% in 2001 to 42% in 2022 (Figure 11.3).

After the GFC, Hungary attempted to ringfence sovereign debt from global capital markets: under the Central Bank's guidance, bank reserves were channelled into sovereign bonds whose overall share in total bank assets doubled from 10% to 21%, even as they halved in Türkiye from 28% to 14% (IMF, 2022a). The combination of high levels of public debt and a deep sovereign-bank nexus backfired in 2022 when inflation and depreciation hit EMEs: In Hungary, fiscal and monetary consolidation appeared necessary to improve both the state's fiscal solvency but

Table 11.2 Debt profiles

	Hungary	*Türkiye*
Government debt to GDP	77% (2022)	42% (2022)
Fiscal deficit to GDP	−6.8% (2021)	−3.51% (2021)
Social protection benefits to GDP	18% (2020)	12.8% (2020)
Share of sovereign bonds in bank assets	21% (2020)	14% (2020)

Sources: European Bank Federation, Eurostat (gov_10dd_edpt1), Eurostat (spr_exp_gdp) (IMF, 2022c)

also the portfolio of a nationalized banking sector deeply exposed to the sovereign (Buljan et al., 2020; Boitan and Marchewka-Bartkowiak, 2021; Deghi et al., 2022).

The Composition of Rentier Social Contracts

Periodic capital outflows after 2013 questioned the sustainability of credit-led growth in Türkiye: financialization failed to sustain a broad social bloc and became skewed towards corporates. The share of households in total bank credit to the private sector declined from 33% to 23% between 2012 and 2020 while that of NFCs rose from 46% to 53% (Apaydin and Çoban, 2022a). Conversely, in Hungary, the co-optation of middle classes via subsidized credit accelerated: the share of household debt in private sector debt doubled from 17.9% to 41.6% between 2010 and 2021 (MNB, 2022d). Whereas Turkish export-oriented SMEs were a core constituency for AKP (Buğra and Savaşkan, 2014; Apaydin and Çoban, 2022a; Akçay and Jungmann, 2022), Hungarian domestic capital reliant on state-controlled finance were concentrated in import-intensive and non-tradable sectors, while foreign multinationals dominated export sectors (Vakhal, 2020). By 2022, a disinflationary interest coalition prevailed in Hungary between incumbents, non-tradable domestic capital factions, and households hurt by inflation. In Türkiye, a narrow coalition between incumbents, export-oriented SMEs, and the construction sector maintained a loose monetary policy against misgivings by the Central Bank and households facing proletarianization and dispossession.

External Financial Conditions

The 2022 global liquidity squeeze accelerated a politicization of transnational capital mobility (Vaughn, 2019; Cassetta, 2022), which affected Hungary and Türkiye differently: Hungary entered a stalemate with the EU Commission over systemic corruption which blocked access to 7.5 billion euros in EU funds. The role of EU transfers in sustaining AF in Hungary by augmenting FX reserves and subsidizing the real estate and construction bubbles (KPMG, 2017) was revealed as blocked transfers put unprecedented pressure on the exchange rate and the sovereign but also depressed the construction sector which was earmarked to receive 61.25% (Government_of_Hungary, 2021). Türkiye also faced capital flight, yet FX reserves nominally increased thanks to swap agreements with China, Korea, Qatar and Saudi Arabia alongside an inflow of $28 billion "net errors and omissions" attributed to Russian capital seeking to evade US sanctions (Ashworth, 2022): politicized foreign capital inflows convinced the Turkish presidency that augmented FX reserves could patch up current account deficits and stabilize the lira without monetary tightening (Sonmez, 2022).

Part I: The Consolidation of Authoritarian Financialization

Hungary

During Hungary's first era of financialization before the GFC, public and private debt served political pacification: deficits and sovereign debt ballooned as social transfers were used to pacify masses excluded from a deindustrializing post-Socialist job market mired in unemployment (Bohle and Greskovits, 2012; Scheiring and Szombati, 2020). FX household debt was a pressure valve (Bohle, 2013; Bohle, 2017) in a wage-repressing, export-oriented growth model with high interest rates (Nölke and Vliegenhart, 2009; Gabor, 2010). In 2008, depreciation (Buchholtz, 2020) pushed FX-indebted households to default. The debt crisis unravelled a Socialist-Liberal coalition, and Fidesz won a two-thirds majority in 2010 by promising deleveraging without austerity. The consolidation of AF under Fidesz can be broken down into two periods (Figure 11.4): between 2010 and 2015, DFS interventions prioritized the state's relative financial autonomy. After 2015, OFS interventions engineered a real estate bubble that stabilized a rentier social contract.

After 2010, DFS interventions followed three objectives: deleveraging to improve the state's external financing conditions, domesticating sovereign and household debt by converting FX to forint instruments and enhancing government control over monetary transmission.

Deleveraging was constitutionalized as a budgetary principle in Article 36 of the 2011 Fundamental Law: Between 2009 and 2017, gross external debt was reduced from 150% of GDP to 84.6% (IMF, 2018). Fiscal restraint reassured the EU Commission and ECOFIN which lifted an Excessive Deficit Procedure in 2013 (Ministry_of_National_Economy, 2013): in turn credit rating agencies and foreign investors rallied, easing spreads on credit default swaps (Government_of_Hungary, 2012; Benczúr and Kónya, 2015; Johnson and Barnes, 2015).

The domestication of private debt for FX-indebted households was achieved with a swap scheme between 2011 and 2015 (Beckmann, 2017): The Central Bank

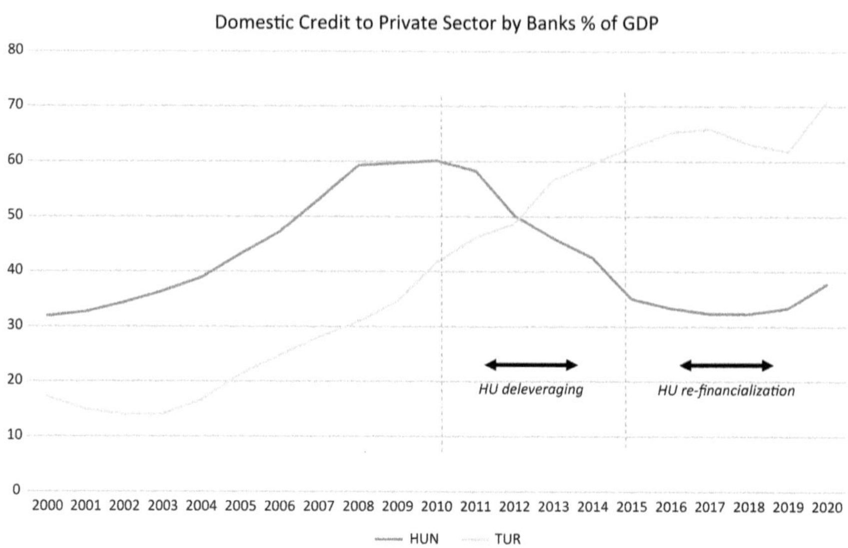

Figure 11.4 Post-GFC deleveraging

Source: World Bank [FS.AST.PRVT.GD.ZS].

(MNB) provided 9.1 billion euros for banks to close their Swiss franc positions (Kolozsi et al., 2015). To domesticate sovereign debt, MNB created a market for local currency bonds by setting a quantitative limit on bank reserves accepted into the three-month deposit policy rate instrument: thus forcing excess reserves into HUF-denominated bonds (András and Motyovszki, 2016; Nagy and Kolozsi, 2017). As fiscal consolidation improved external financing conditions, MNB reduced the base rate from 7% to 0.9% between 2012 and 2016, terminating the pre-GFC sterilization games (Matolcsy and Palotai, 2018). Between 2011 and 2019, the share of non-resident bondholders decreased from 40% to under 25% and FX debt dropped from 48% to 18% (IMF, 2019): foreign bondholders were marginalized as tax-free, subsidized bonds restricted to households financed public debt with domestic savings (Figure 11.5). The state gained in financial autonomy while middle-class bondholders became a rentier class.

Executive control over monetary transmission targeted the Central Bank and foreign retail banks. In 2013, Orbán nominated his Minister of Economy György Matolcsy as Governor of the Central Bank, cementing government control over monetary policy and launching MNB's mission creep (Sebők, 2018; Dönmez and Zemandl, 2019; Piroska, 2021): MNB incorporated the Financial Supervision Authority in 2013 and acquired the Budapest Stock Exchange in 2015. It also steered the renationalization of retail banking. After the GFC, foreign banks, which had controlled 80% of Hungarian banking assets, were gradually nationalized.

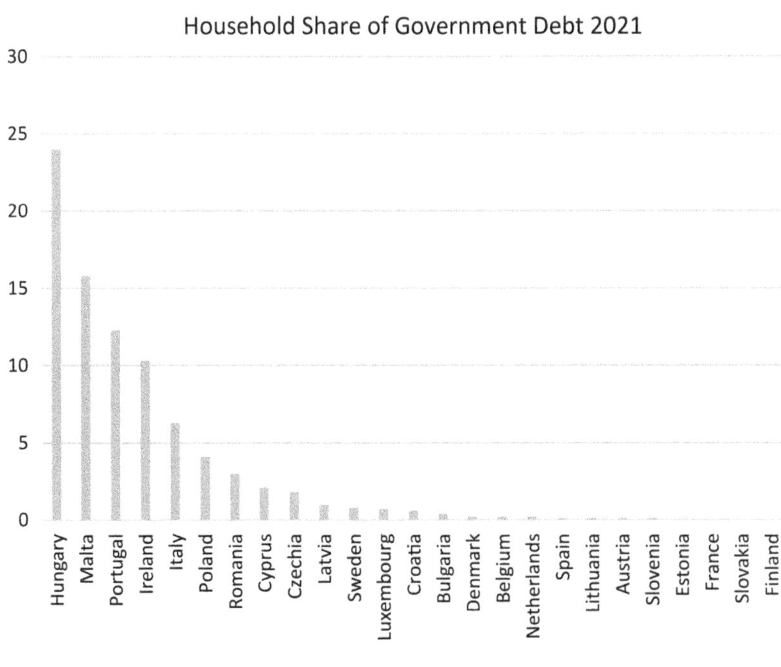

Figure 11.5 Self-financing

Source: Eurostat [GOV_10DD_GGD].

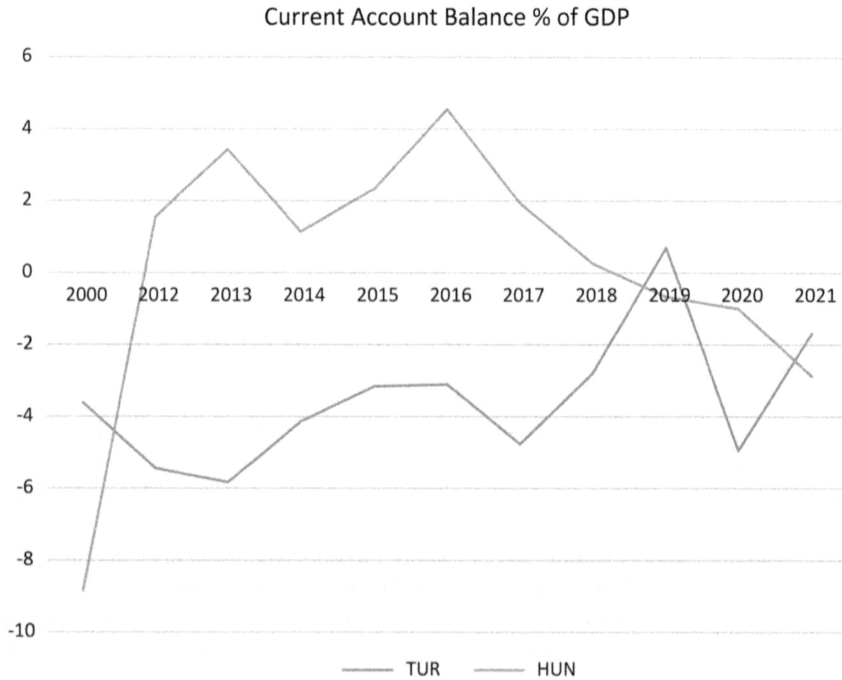

Figure 11.6 Hungary's export competitiveness crisis

Source: World Bank [BN.CAB.XOKA.GD.ZS].

The largest transfer saw MNB become the direct owner of Hungary's fifth largest bank MKB bought from Bayern LB in 2014: MNB cleaned the non-performing loans (NPL) portfolio of MKB before reprivatizing it to Fidesz-aligned oligarchs (Sebők, 2018). By 2017, 50.5% of banking was domestically owned, two-thirds directly by the state (EBF, 2018).

After 2015, an export-competitiveness crisis emerged: current account surpluses began to melt (Figure 11.6), wages and inflation rose and domestic suppliers to MNC-controlled export sectors lobbied for deregulating labor rights to maintain their profitability (Karas, 2021). The executive responded by restricting labor rights and using its new monetary-financial arsenal to revive lending (Figure 11.7).

MNB launched the Funding for Growth Program in 2013, offering banks interest-free refinancing for SME lending with a capped premium of 2.5%: by 2016, 40 000 SMEs had benefitted from the scheme (Matolcsy and Palotai, 2018). This was followed by the Market-based Lending Scheme (MLS) in 2016, which offered preferential interest rate swaps (LIRS) to retail banks conditional on increasing SME lending (MNB, 2018). MNB also launched a Family Housing Allowance (CSOK) program in subsidized credit which accounted for 16% of total loan issuance and 57% of residential loans between 2016 and 2018 (Banai et al., 2018). A natalist "prenatal baby support loan" scheme followed in 2019, offering subsidized

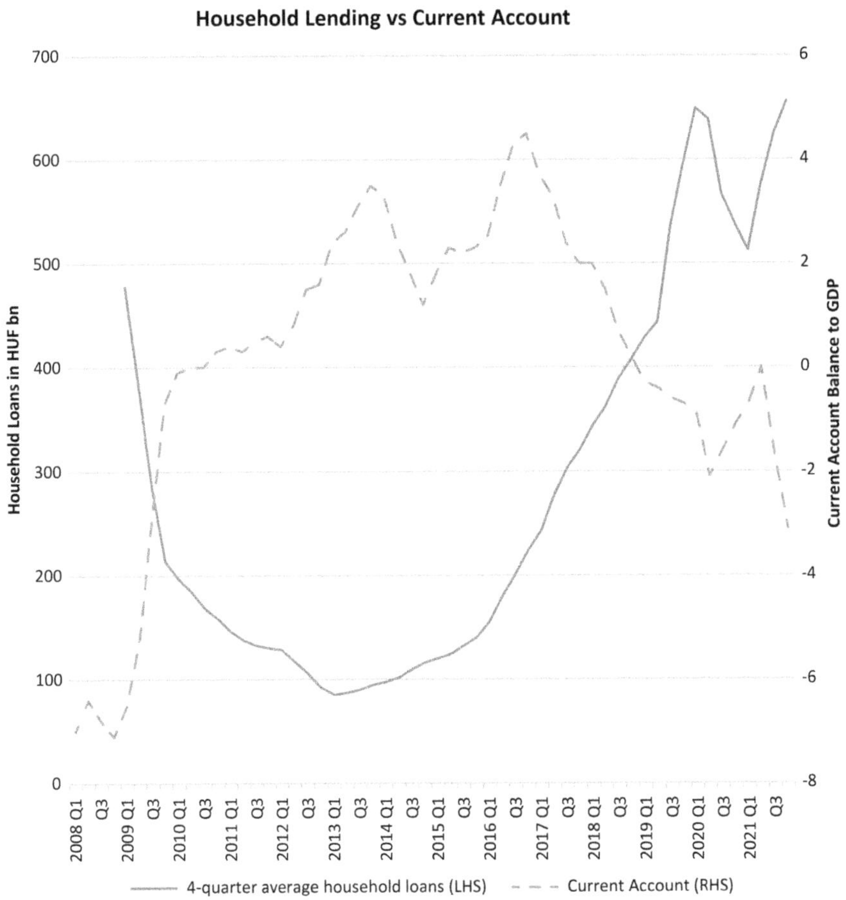

Figure 11.7 Negative correlation in lending and exports

Source: MNB (2022a; 2022c).

housing credit for couples promising to deliver future births: this scheme accounted for 17% of household lending by 2021 (MNB, 2022d). MNB's subsidized lending instruments combined with low base rates fuelled corporate and household lending, and an inflation in real estate prices (see Figure 11.8).

This second, authoritarian mode of financialization reduced sovereign debt, the share of FX debt, the role of foreign bondholders and foreign banks. It fuelled credit-based growth with low interest rates (Gabor, 2010). It also reconciled an authoritarian executive governing society through finance with the material interests of private actors: household savings financed government debt against subsidized yields, improving the state's relative financial autonomy. NFCs and middle-classes enjoyed subsidized credit and assetization via a state-engineered real estate bubble benefitting homeowners and construction firms.

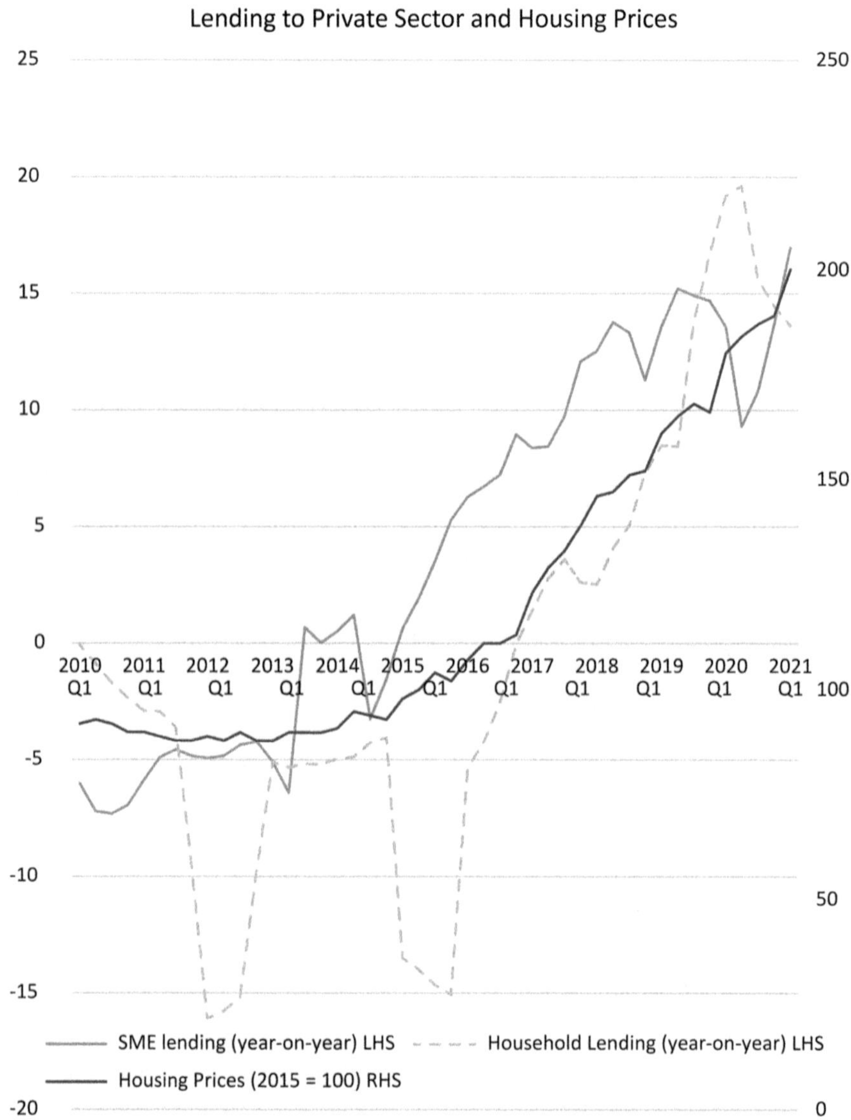

Figure 11.8 The finance-real estate nexus

Source: KSH (2022) and MNB (2022d).

Türkiye (2001–18)

Following a wave of financial crises, AKP's 2001 IMF-endorsed restructuring program laid the ground for OFS strategies which consolidated a finance-led "jobless" growth trajectory (Orhangazi and Yeldan, 2021: 462, 467–8, 481–3) as well as a governing strategy to co-opt and discipline subordinated classes, and fuel dispossession and proletarianization (Bahçe and Köse, 2016: 8; Bryan et al., 2009: 461, 470; Karacimen, 2015: 763).

Prior to the GFC, this process was led by bank lending, household debt, and unprecedented issuance of credit cards (Aslan and Dincer, 2018: 147, 149; Karacimen, 2016: 253). After the GFC, the QE programs of Core reserve currency Central Banks provided an uninterrupted supply of capital inflows while contributing to the long-term real appreciation of the lira – which was as high as 70% between 2001 and 2008 (Orhangazi and Yeldan, 2021: 472). Similar to Hungary before the GFC, the relative appreciation of the lira eased external borrowing conditions in the corporate sector, reduced its reliance on domestic borrowing and banks, and expanded its activities in consumer lending- a trend that was reversed in the post-GFC context (Erol, 2019: 729; Yeldan and Ünüvar, 2016: 22, 26). The overall impact on the industrial circuit of capital was import-dependency given the low value-added, assembly line character of industrial production, rising current account deficits, de-industrialization and declining contribution of industrial production to employment (Orhangazi and Yeldan, 2021: 481; Yeldan and Ünüvar, 2016: 20–22).

What became distinctive after the GFC was a more direct, government-led expansion of OFS: policies such as domestic credit provision to SMEs, the construction sector and households, attempts to re-politicize central banking as well as politicized public procurement consolidated the nexus of finance, real estate and construction. The construction sector appeared viable to generate employment, growth, and attract foreign direct investment without endangering the IMF stabilization programme. It experienced unprecedented growth rates between 2010 and 2014 (Erol and Unal, 2015: 18, 23–24, see also Demiralp et. al., 2016; Yesilbag, 2021: 7–8). Gradually, the pattern of export-led accumulation following trade liberalization in the early 1980s based on lira depreciation shifted towards debt- and construction-led growth during the 2000s.

This period was marked by internal disputes between economic policymakers (cabinet ministers as well as the central bank) and deepening intra-class struggles within the power bloc, namely between the internationalized capital groups, which could finance themselves on global markets and favoured stricter monetary policy, and export-oriented SMEs which relied on cheap domestic credit (Akçay, 2020; Dönmez and Zemandl, 2019; Yağcı, 2018).

The pre-GFC real estate-finance nexus in Türkiye was sustained by the post-2001 macroeconomic recovery, the creation of the housing credit market, the growth of mortgage lending following a 2007 legislation[1] (Aslan and Dincer, 2018: 148–49) and the Mass Housing Administration (TOKI) placed under the office of Prime Ministry after 2003 (Erol, 2019: 728, Tansel, 2019; Yesilbag, 2021). Further "government-led reregulation" from 2010 to 2014 included urban legislative reform, large-scale urban regeneration and infrastructure projects promoting financialization and housing demand (Erol, 2019: 725, 730, 732). These policies actively reshaped state-capital hybridity (Alami and Dixon, 2021) in the housing and construction sector by creating urban rents and commodification, consolidating financialization as a strategy to discipline and manufacture consent, while also deepening the indebtedness of NFCs (CBRT, 2017: 17–18, 20; CBRT, 2018: 20–22)

(Figure 11.2). In March 2022, the combined share of corporate and SME loans within total bank lending was 81% compared to 67% in 2012 whereas the share of consumer loans and credit cards represented only 19% of total loans compared to 33% in 2012 (BRSA, 2019; 2022). The distribution of bank loans to the construction sector also increased dynamically after 2013 (BRSA, n.d.).

Private capitals blended with the state as construction-sector capital groups engaged in infrastructural "mega-projects" which relied on state support via public-private partnerships (PPPs) and politicized public procurement. TOKI promoted a threefold increase in PPP construction between 2003 and 2013 (Demiralp et. al., 2016; Sonmez, 2014 cited in Bozkurt, 2021: 14; Buğra and Savaşkan, 2012; Marschall et. al., 2016; Arslanalp, 2018). However, this trajectory was repeatedly destabilized by global liquidity shocks following policy shifts by reserve currency central banks: the Fed's 2013 taper tantrum spurred new waves of capital outflows and volatility in 2013–14 and 2015–16 (Akçay and Gungen, 2019; Bozkurt, 2021: 26). After a third phase of capital flight in 2018, CBRT responded with DFS interventions: These included an amendment to CBRT law authorizing the Bank to obtain any data required to monitor the foreign exchange transactions of real persons and legal entities, regulations to allow export rediscount credit borrowers to make payments in lira equivalent, facilitation of domestic currency based trading through a swap agreement with China, and the centralization of bank collateral management under CBRT (CBRT, 2017: xii, 26, 28; CBRT, 2018: 23). These interventions deepened CBRT's involvement in the management and supervision of corporate finances and currency risk. Interest rate hikes led to debt servicing problems and bankruptcies by domestic firms concentrated largely in the construction sector (Erol, 2019: 738). This dynamic turned the currency crisis into a more systemic debt crisis while also making CBRT more complicit and constrained (Akçay and Gungen, 2019). By the end of 2018, the official inflation rate almost doubled within a year and settled at 20.30% (CBRT, 2018: 20; Figure 11.9).

CBRT tackled these challenges after 2018 by enhancing OFS interventions to stabilize credit provisioning for NFCs and continuous policy rate cuts in the second

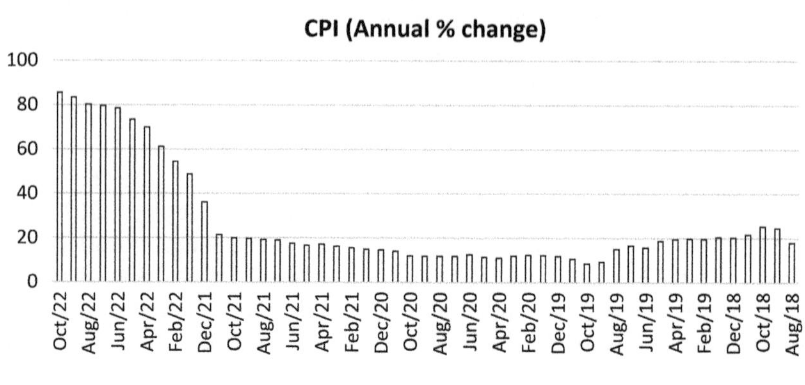

Figure 11.9 Inflation in Türkiye

Source: CBRT (n.d.),

half of 2019 (CBRT Annual Report, 2018: xii, 23–25). It also utilized reserve requirement ratios (RRRs) to keep monetary expansion in check: A crucial regulation introduced in December aimed to channel the loans to "production-oriented sectors rather than consumption-oriented ones" with the aim of encouraging "long-term commercial loans that had a strong relation with production and investment, and long-term housing loans that had a weak relation with imports" (CBRT, 2019: xii).

Part II: Deepening Authoritarian Financialization under COVID-19 (2020–21)

Hungary

Green lending and asset purchase programs (APP) launched before the pandemic to deepen financial markets via securitization were reframed under COVID-19 as countercyclical policies (MNB, 2019). MNB emulated the low interest rates, APPs, and green lending of Core economies: Instead of convergence with AE templates, however, the semi-peripheral features of authoritarian financialization were reinforced. An apparent deepening of financial markets masked a recapitalization of state-dependent crony capital groups tied to the finance-real estate nexus, the concentration of banking assets under state control and the shoring up of the rentier social contract via the financialization of housing.

MNB's monetary policy toolkit to tackle COVID-19 contained limited DFS interventions to contain the risk of ballooning public and private debt: a loan repayment moratorium was announced for the private sector, and an Asset Purchase Program (APP), under which MNB purchased government securities with long maturities to help finance public debt. By contrast, OFS interventions involved multiple instruments such as low rates, greenwashing the financialization of housing, new subsidized instruments, macroprudential regulations to boost lending and an APP to recapitalize domestic capital groups.

MNB kept base rates under 1% until May 2021 and expanded its mission creep by rebranding itself as a green central bank, mimicking the EIB's transformation into a climate bank (Mazzucato and Penna, 2016; Griffith-Jones and Carreras, 2021). The green mandate empowered MNB to use macroprudential interventions to incentivize "green" retail lending and create new asset classes such as green mortgage-backed bonds.

A Mortgage Funding Adequacy Ratio (MFAR) for green-certified mortgage-backed funds would be weighted at a preferential rate. A "Green Preferential Capital Requirement Program" for retail banks reclassified household loans for energy-efficient housing as less risky and conceded lower capital requirements to retail banks. MNB also launched a new Green Home Program in October 2021, offering 0% refinancing for banks to lend at a capped 2.5% to households for the purchase or refurbishing of energy-efficient flats. To support the uptake of green instruments, a Green Mortgage Bond Purchase scheme to buy forint-denominated, fixed-rate "green" mortgage-backed bonds to the tune of HUF 200 billion was announced in 2021 (MNB, 2021a). In continuity with preferential loans to SMEs since 2013, MNB launched the FGS

GO! Program under which it provided 0% refinancing loans for banks to lend at capped interest rates to SMEs: between April 2020 and September 2021, 40 655 firms benefited from this subsidized scheme (MNB, 2021b). To support the largest domestic firms, MNB launched in July 2019 an Asset Purchase Program called "Bond Funding for Growth Scheme" with a HUF 300 billion window to purchase bonds issued by NFCs, modelled after the ECB's Corporate Sector Purchase Programme (CSPP) and the 2016 BoE Corporate Bond Purchase Scheme (CBPS) (MNB, 2019). By 2022, over 30% of retail credit was subsidized, while MNB acknowledged the pacifying role of state-driven financialization noting that "*buying a new home without subsidies would currently represent an excessive financial burden for families in Budapest*" (MNB, 2022a). MNB acknowledged that it had created a housing bubble overvalued by at least 18% compared with fundamentals (MNB, 2022a).

The APP spurred one of the largest Central Bank balance sheet expansions in EMEs: between 2020 and 2021, MNB assets grew from 7% to 20% of GDP. While MNB purchased up to 5% of government debt, Hungarian QE also involved massive purchases of collateralized bonds issued by NFCs, making it an outlier among EMEs which primarily used APPs to stabilize sovereign bond markets instead of recapitalizing domestic firms (Arena et al., 2021). The APP strengthened the finance-real estate nexus: 35% of the large firms benefitting from the APP were involved in construction and real estate (Figure 11.10) just as most subsidized SME loans were channelled to the sector (Figure 11.11).

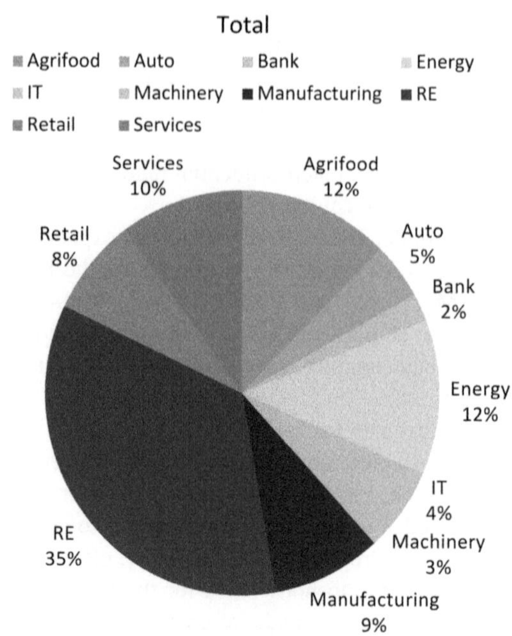

Figure 11.10 The APP and the finance-real estate nexus

Source: own calculations based on MNB and press (see Appendix).

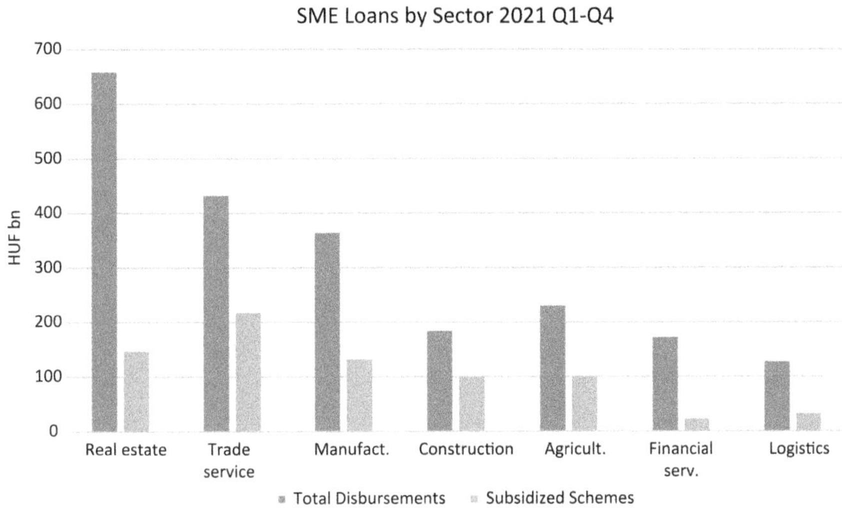

Figure 11.11 Sectoral composition of SME loans

Source: MNB (2022d).

The APP also circumvented EU state aid rules which had limited MNB's ability to capitalize crony firms: 50 out of 90 large firms benefitting from the APP were connected to the Prime Minister's inner circle. Multiple recapitalized crony capital groups expanded their foreign corporate and residential real estate portfolios during COVID-19 (HVG, 2020; Mester, 2020; Kassay, 2022; Kuzmanovic, 2022). Finally, the APP also created a hitherto inexistent private bond market: Between 2018 and 2022, the corporate bond market grew from 1.5% to 5% of GDP. However, these asset-backed bonds didn't trade on the secondary market and failed to kickstart a broader expansion of securitization (Szekeres, 2021): banks only purchased bonds issued by NFCs because of preferential yields on corresponding deposit accounts stored at the Central Bank. Overall, neither green lending nor the APP delivered the sought-after deep capital markets, but they were effective in shoring up the rentier social contract supported by the finance-real estate nexus.

Türkiye

The transition to the Presidential System of Government (PSG) in 2018 accelerated authoritarian financialization in Türkiye. The centralization and personification of power represented an authoritarian fix to address global liquidity shocks in 2015–16 and the deepening legitimacy crisis of the AKP regime after 2013 (Akçay, 2018; Akçay, 2020; Araj and Savran, 2021). However, the politicization of economic management dramatically heightened conflicts over monetary policy between the Presidency and CBRT. While this tension had been present since 2001, the shift to PSG after 2018 empowered the Erdogan regime with stronger coercive

Table 11.3 Macroeconomic fundamentals

Macroeconomic fundamentals	*Turkey*	*Hungary*
General government debt (2020)	Low (<50% of GDP)	High (>70% of GDP)
General government fiscal deficit (2019)	High (>5% of GDP)	Low (<5% of GDP)
Local currency government debt (2019)	Low (<20% of GDP)	High (>50% of GDP)
Size of domestic government securities markets	Small	Large
State ownership of the banking sector (2016)	High (>30%)	Low (<30) (increased after 2016)
Inflation rate and expectations	High	Low
Pre-pandemic current account balance (2017–19)	Deficit –(funding through portfolio flows)	Surplus
Foreign reserves (2020)	Below the IMF's reserve adequacy metric (<80%)	Above the IMF's reserve adequacy metric (>100%)
Post-Covid APPs		
Duration	Mar-Jul 2020	May 2020- Dec 2021
Asset type	Government securities	Government securities, mortgages, and corporate bonds
Amount	1.6% of GDP (2020)	7.2% of GDP (by end-June 2021)

Compiled from Arena et al. (2021: 29–33, 56, 59).

capabilities to directly dismiss central bank governors and policymakers (Akçay, 2020; Bedirhanoğlu, 2021a).

Throughout 2020, CBRT relied on loose monetary policy and macroprudential incentives for lending to weather the pandemic-related economic distress (CBRT, 2020: xii-xiii, 25, 35). The Bank also initiated an asset purchase programme (APP) accompanying its policy rate cuts from March 2020 to July 2020 (more modest than in Hungary) to offset capital outflows (Arena et al., 2021: 6, 12; Table 11.2). These policy choices preserved the OFS objective of pursuing financialization as a growth strategy while introducing graver inflationary and political risks for the post-GFC power bloc.

A consequence of incentivizing credit was the sharp rise in domestic demand-driven imports (CBRT, 2020: 20; CBRT, 2021: 1). This, in turn, increased the indebtedness ratio of the corporate sector from 56% in January 2020 to 69% in August while the previously declining household financial leverage ratio flattened at 36% during the pandemic (CBRT, 2020: 36). These dynamics, alongside excessive FX reserves loss (over USD 100 billion in the course of 20 months) brought the economy to the verge of crisis once again (CBRT, 2021: 2; Figure 11.12).

Consequently, CBRT moved to stem credit by increasing its policy rates between September 2020 and 2021 (Figure 11.13) and the Covid-era OFS instruments were

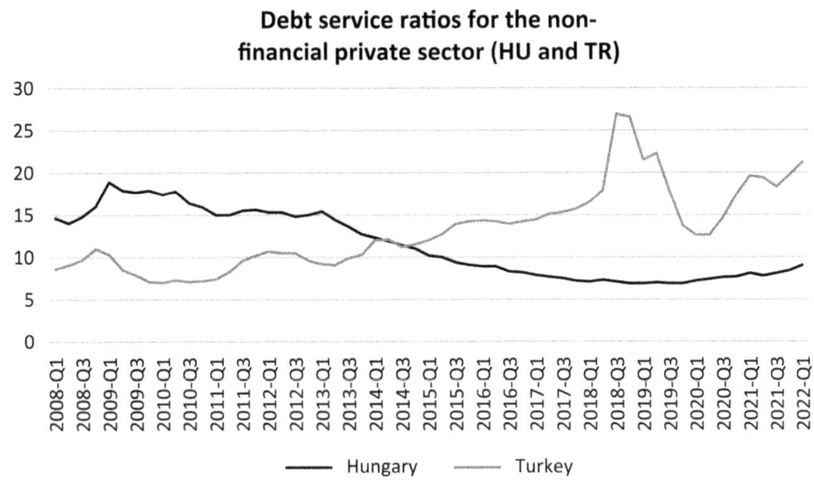

Figure 11.12 NFC Debt Service

Source: BIS (n.d.).

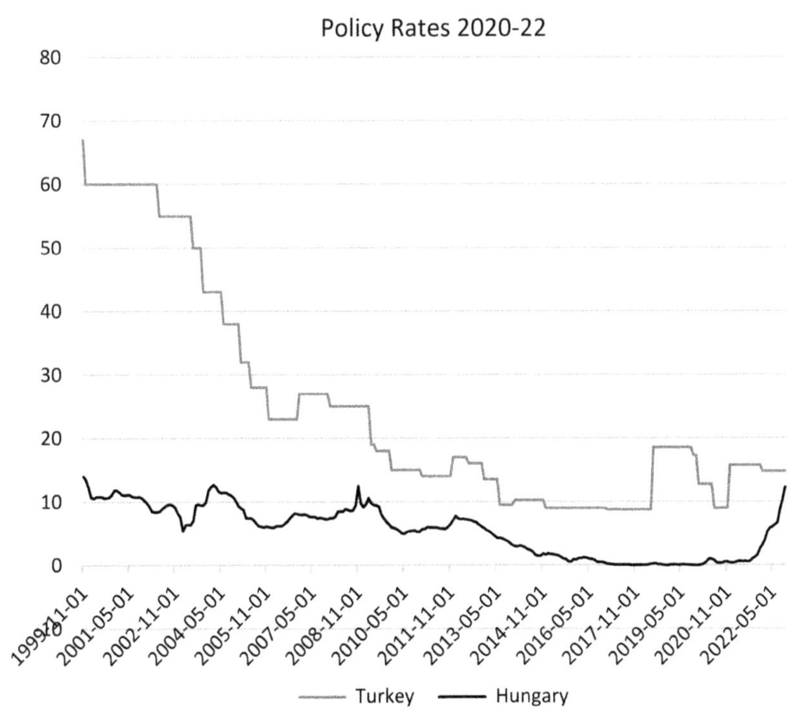

Figure 11.13 Monetary policy divergence *(Continued)*

Source: BIS (n.d.).

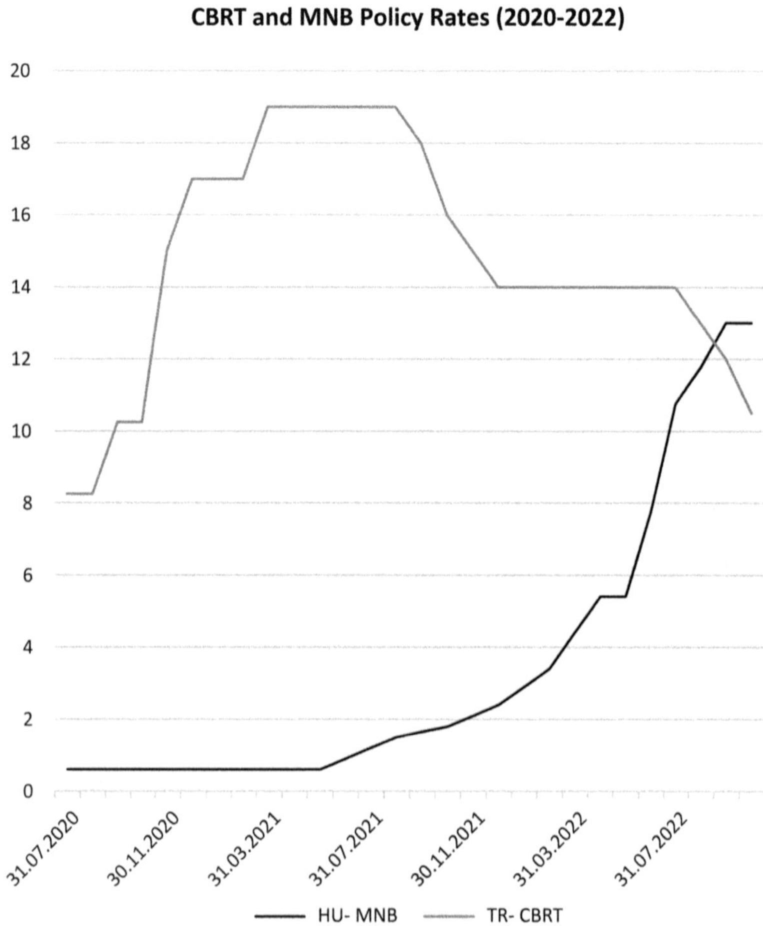

Figure 11.13 (Continued)

gradually rolled back after November 2020. The earlier onset of monetary contraction was an element of divergence between Türkiye and other emerging economies and worsened due to the pre-pandemic vulnerabilities of the economy (CBRT Annual Report, 2020: 20).

In response to CBRT's stubborn pursuit of price stability, the President resorted to frequent dismissals of several central bank governors and policymakers in 2020 and 2021 (Guardian, 2020; Al Jazeera, 2021; Michaelson, 2021). A similar battlefield formed between the Turkish Statistical Institute and the executive with respect to the announced official inflation rate which led to the dismissal of the head of the Institute by the President in early 2022 (Pitel, 2022).

The contractionary monetary response of CBRT was countered by the expansionary pressures on credit growth and deepening financialization led by several OFS practices of the executive: the inclusion of new debt instruments as eligible collateral for repo and reverse-repo transactions of banks and intermediary institutions in December 2020 and February 2021, an extension of credit support packages to SMEs, micro and small enterprises (MSEs) in the manufacturing and technology sectors as well as long-term loan support for targeted manufacturing investments in specific regions, financial support programmes for income loss and rent. Additionally, a presidential decree issued in December 2020 introduced significant interest discounts to loans that were extended by one of the main public banks (Halkbank) and the Ministry of Treasury and Finance was tasked with covering the income losses arising from the extension of these loans. In February 2021, the Ministry of Environment and Urbanization extended credit interest support for urban transformation and construction (CBRT, 2021: 6, 8).

CBRT also started reporting on green finance and bond developments, and their impact on financial stability more substantially from 2021 onwards (CBRT, 2021: 14). Sustainable and green bond issuance by the Turkish banking sector commenced in 2016, and while it is not as developed as in the advanced capitalist economies and in Hungary (World Bank, 2022: 21), the post-Covid era demonstrated a visible upsurge in this regard. CBRT reports that green/sustainable bond issuance has reached a total of USD 2.7 billion in Türkiye since 2016. However, USD 1.75 billion of this total amount has been issued since August 2020 (CBRT, 2021: 17). The degree of attention paid to green finance is discernible in the announcement of the Monetary Policy Committee's decision to "support sustainable finance initiatives as a long-term policy without prejudice to the main objectives of monetary policy" in October 2021 (CBRT 2021d; 2021c: 10; CBRT, 2021a: 6).

Part 3: Crises of Authoritarian Financialization (2021–22)

Hungary

After the GFC, Fidesz proposed two justifications for executive control over monetary policy and credit: the first was to deleverage and domesticate debt, which enhanced the state's relative financial autonomy vis a vis capital markets. The second was to engineer a controlled housing asset price bubble via subsidized loans provided by the re-politicized Central Bank and a renationalized retail banking sector, which benefitted SMEs, crony capital groups and households. The global liquidity squeeze of 2022 undermined both. By late 2021, previous DFS objectives became unsustainable: A political deadlock with the EU Commission over systemic corruption blocked EU transfers. These frozen funds, combined with widening current account deficits and a phase of fiscal populism before general elections in April 2022 destabilized a model which had relied on fiscal restraint and on MNB's stick-and-carrot approach which had forced bank reserves and savings into forint denominated bonds via the quantitative limit instrument (see part I) and subsidized bonds for households. Anticipating monetary tightening, the Treasury launched its largest-ever FX bond auction of $4.25 billion and EUR 1 billion in September 2021. After a decade spent on reducing it, the share of FX debt increased to 23,3% in July 2022 from an absolute low of 15,4% in February 2020. While price controls on energy and food introduced in 2022 failed to stem a 21% core inflation and a collapsing exchange rate (IMF, 2022b), MNB hiked interest rates from 0.6% in 2020 to 18% by October 2022 (Figure 11.13), ending the era of cheap credit.

Blocked EU transfers were highly salient in reversing DFS objectives: they depleted Central Bank FX reserves and explained a more severe depreciation of the forint compared with regional counterparts (Zsiborás, 2022). They also threatened the finance-real estate nexus: the largest sectoral impact of EU transfers had been in real estate transactions and construction where they accounted for 9% and 4.6% of growth (KPMG, 2017). EU transfers in Hungary thus played a comparable role in sustaining the finance-real estate nexus to foreign portfolio investments in Türkiye.

Fiscal tightening forced the government to phase out the APP and subsidized green lending schemes introduced under COVID-19 to prop up financialization. After aggressive rate hikes, year-on-year housing loans dropped by 31% by July 2022 (MNB, 2022b). With the return to orthodox monetarism, the executive sacrificed the real estate bubble it had created to contain inflation and depreciation.

The government and MNB had closely coordinated de-financialization in 2010–15 and re-financialization in 2015–20. In the new stagflationary, high interest rate environment, however, conflicts erupted over monetary policy. The governor of the Central Bank accused the government of locking in a credit-fuelled construction-driven growth model by "investing in concrete and steel instead of brains", and "a fiscal program composed for two thirds of construction" (Matolcsy, 2021). Conversely, the Orbán-aligned chairman of the Chamber of Commerce attacked MNB for being dovish on inflation (Hornyák, 2022). Far-right opposition party Jobbik blamed both the government and MNB for the forint's depreciation and proposed to constitutionalize a strong exchange rate (MTI, 2022).

Internal conflicts within the state translated into degraded policy coherence: MNB contracted money supply while pretending to leave the base rate untouched. In fact, it made an 18% overnight deposit rate into the new, implicit policy rate, decoupling it from the official 13% base rate which lost its relevance. This mirrored Türkiye where CBRT tightened money supply after 2018 while placating the President's refusal of high policy rates by introducing multiple rates which made monetary policy purposefully less transparent (Yağcı, 2018, Apaydin and Çoban, 2022b).

The priorities of MNB and the government also conflicted regarding the externalities of subsidized lending and shielding indebted households and NFCs: In 2020, the government introduced a temporary interest rate cap on housing loans and mortgages indexed on interbank and MNB base rates: to avoid a wave of defaults, these were extended until December 2022. Capped rates were indexed on the 2021 MNB base rate of 2% and an interbank rate of 2,4% - while they had in fact increased to 18% and 16% respectively by October 2022. In October 2022, the government further extended capped interest rates to SME loans. In March 2022 however, MNB had already warned that the scale of subsidized lending (above 30%) and protections actually hindered monetary policy transmission (MNB, 2022d) given how many interest rates were frozen by fiat.

The conflict-ridden consolidation of an anti-inflationary coalition should be appraised in light of Fidesz' social bloc. Unlike Turkish export-oriented SMEs which are vital for AKP, Hungarian domestic capital is concentrated in import-intensive and non-tradable sectors (Vakhal, 2020): 39% of SMEs rely on imported intermediary goods, while 80% of export value is realized by foreign-owned multinationals (KSH, 2018). Domestic capital is highly sensitive to cost-push inflation (Karas, 2021), and to exchange rate volatility: containing both appeared as a shared concern for domestic capital and for wage earners. In conjunction with structurally high public debt and a deep exposure of the renationalized banking system to the sovereign, austerity and monetary contraction attempted to contain inflation, depreciation, and the degradation of public balance sheets.

Türkiye

As noted earlier, several upheavals splintered the power bloc (Akçay, 2020) between a first-generation bourgeoisie (older, highly internationalized, large financial and holding groups) and a second-generation bourgeoisie (younger, gradually internationalizing, small and medium-scale capital groups in construction and light manufacturing) with opposing demands on interest rate policy (Bozkurt, 2021). The state temporarily addressed their conflicts by increasing the repression of societal dissent and resistance, centralizing political power in the executive branch, and deepening financial statecraft (e.g. Gezi uprisings in 2013, 2016 coup attempt, and the shift to the presidential system in 2017, 2018 crisis, post-pandemic and the 2021–22 inflation cycle) (Akçay and Jungmann, 2022: 22).

In late 2020 and 2021, the CBRT's tight monetary policy to address high inflation and exchange rate volatility once again conflicted with the government's stimulus policies (CBRT, 2021: 4–9, 21; CBRT, 2020a: 5). CBRT maintained a restrictive monetary policy by preserving its policy rate (which was raised in March 2021 once again) between April and August (CBRT, 2021b: 4), used macroprudential instruments (CBRT, 2021: 4–5), and signed three separate swap agreements with the central banks of Korea, China (increasing the limit of the previous agreement), and Qatar (extending the expired swap agreement for three more years) between May and September (CBRT, 2021b: 10).

Rapid policy rate cuts, continuously demanded by Erdogan (Deutsche Welle, 2021; Reuters, 2022), reversed these measures in the last four months of 2021 amidst the executive's announcements that Türkiye was adopting a "Chinese model" of export-oriented growth supported by competitive depreciation (Hurriyet, 2021). This policy rollback resulted in yet another episode of currency crisis and depreciation, dramatic inflation and capital outflows (CBRT, 2022; Figure 11.9). The latter was exacerbated by the global liquidity squeeze following the Fed's interest rate hikes throughout 2022.

As of October 2022, the official inflation rate reached 85.5% in Türkiye (CBRT Consumer Prices, n.d.; Figure 11.9) whereas the independent ENAG report set the same rate at 185.3% (ENAGrup, 2022). Facing a hyperinflationary crisis, the executive counter-intuitively pressured CBRT to reduce its policy rate in August 2022 (CBRT, 2022b). The post-2018 shift to PSG has enabled more direct executive interventions in monetary policymaking. The endorsement of loose monetary policy aligned with the short-term interests of export-driven capital groups by facilitating the depreciation of the lira.

The new monetary policy simultaneously alienated the highly internationalized, big capital groups which maintained a strong presence in finance/banking sectors as well as higher value-added industrial sectors which favoured a strong lira and high interest rate policy (Bozkurt, 2021; Akçay and Jungmann, 2022: 14–18). Wage earners paid the price of a weak lira in a hyperinflationary context, which enhanced dispossession and further proletarianization (Inanc, 2021).

A low value-added export-driven growth strategy, already mobilized in the previous crisis cycles of the 1980s and 1990s, has deepened the cracks of the social bloc (which includes the power bloc made up of the state and dominant capital groups as well as the subordinated classes), enhancing the accumulation/legitimation dilemma of the Erdogan regime (Akçay and Jungmann, 2022: 22–23). These cracks were visible in criticisms voiced by the representatives of the first-generation bourgeoisie against the new economic policies (TUSIAD, 2022). But representatives of the second-generation bourgeoisie also expressed concerns over high inflation and exchange rate volatility given their impact on the external debt payments and pricing practices (Dunya, 2021; MUSIAD, 2022).

The low interest rate policy accelerated the lira's collapse and produced new and more visibly authoritarian DFS interventions: the government attempted to reverse dollarization with the "permanent and strengthened liraization" (CBRT, 2022a) and indirect capital controls (Reuters, 2022; Ahval, 2022) by attempting to appropriate NFC dollar revenues and household dollar deposits to stem the current account deficit and replenish depleting FX reserves needed to support the lira's exchange rate.

Nevertheless, these DFS instruments neither managed to convert large volumes of FX deposits to lira (Kubilay, 2022) nor stopped depreciation and hyperinflation. They also eroded the consent and co-optation of subordinated classes exacerbating the legitimation dilemma of the Erdogan administration despite renewed attempts to pacify low-income households via a vast social housing programme announced in September 2022 (Pitel, 2022a)

The executive attempted to stem inflation and depreciation without a monetary tightening which would have undermined its social bloc: To do so, it forced the introduction of indirect capital controls, tried to appropriate the forex deposits of private actors, and boosted CBRT's FX reserves with international swap agreements. Controversially, it also recycled massive Russian capital inflows attempting to evade US sanctions (Pitel and Samson, 2022). Under these adverse circumstances, state-driven financialization only sustains a radically narrowed power bloc in the eve of the 2023 general elections while the cost-of-living crisis amid hyperinflation erodes the societal consent rapidly.

Conclusion

Our intervention contributes to the state of the art in three ways: Firstly, we link the research agendas on monetary policy, financialization and authoritarianism in EMEs without reifying a monocausal link: we don't explain authoritarianism with financialization – instead, we identify the features of a specific, authoritarian statist mode of financialization (AF) in EMEs. We show how exposure to global liquidity- and exchange rate volatility under subordinate financialization can spur EME states to develop new forms of financial statecraft, which aim to re-govern finance and to govern society through finance (Braun et al., 2018). AF shares with AE modalities of financialization the objectives of sustaining finance-based growth and pacifying society with cheap credit and asset price bubbles (Adkins et al., 2020) and solving the interrelated problems of financing sovereign debt, enhancing monetary policy transmission and fuelling credit-based growth (Braun and Gabor, 2020). Whereas this project is carried out by depoliticized, independent Central Banks in AEs, under AF, the very visible hand of the executive fuels credit-based growth by centralizing political control over the social allocation of money in ways that parallel state monopolies over resource rents.

Secondly, we emphasize that convergence to state-engineered asset price bubbles shouldn't deflect attention from significant variation in external financing conditions, the macroeconomic and political function of sovereign debt in a national economy, as well as the social and sectoral compositions of rentier social contracts enabled by financialization. As monetary policy plays a dual role in managing both sovereign and private debt, these underlying differences are important to explain different policy preferences when AF regimes face zero-sum trade-offs between the external and internal functions of monetary policy.

Thirdly, we point out the crisis-ridden nature of AF as a state capitalist strategy to mitigate the destabilizing impacts of financialization, while harnessing the opportunities of credit-based growth for stabilizing authoritarian regimes. Transposing the arguments of Poulantzas and Offe to financialization, we observe that authoritarian state control over money in EMEs merely internalized distributive conflicts within the state, eroded monetary policy coherence and locked in pathways of coercive escalation instead of delivering macro-financial stability or unlocking new growth models. In an era when financial sovereignty has become a politicized question in many EMEs (Ben Gadha et al., 2021), our study signals the limits of nationalist authoritarian statist strategies to expand the state's relative financial autonomy. The EU's crisis management under COVID-19 showed that Core economies and Central Banks have the capacity to stabilize peripheral bond markets (Eichacker, forthcoming): AF fills the void of comparable mechanisms of macro-financial stabilization at a global level.

Acknowledgments

The earlier versions of this chapter were presented in the British Political Studies Association (PSA) and the Society for the Advancement of Socio-Economics (SASE) annual conferences as well as the University of Birmingham POLSIS Political Economy Research Group 'work-in-progress' workshop 'Political Economy after the Covid

Crisis: Shifting research agendas' in 2022. We would like to especially thank Ilias Alami, Mehmet Kerem Coban, Agnes Gagyi, Dora Piroska, Sean Kenji Starrs, Mustafa Yagci, and 'Helyzet' Working Group for Public Sociology for their critical engagement with and feedback on the ideas presented in the paper. All errors and omissions are our own.

Note

1 Erol (2019: 738) argues that these measures have contributed to the rapid commodification of housing and a speculative construction boom in the country; however, household and housing consumption financialisation have not accompanied this process to the same degree due to the legal and institutional set up of the mortgage system in the cautious post-2001 policy environment, the high inflation and unemployment rates, and the low income levels. During this period, housing credit market has remained accessible mainly to upper- and middle-class households (ibid.: 732-3; see also Arslanalp, 2018: 26-7).

Bibliography

Adaman, F., Akbulut, B., Madra, Y., & Pamuk, Ş. 2014. Hitting the Wall: Erdoğan's Construction-Based, Finance-Led Growth Regime. *The Middle East in London*, 10, 7–8.

Adkins, L., Cooper, M., & Konings, M. 2020. The Asset Economy. Property Ownership and the New Logic of Inequality. Cambridge: Polity.

AHVAL 2022. Turkey limiting lira loans for firms holding foreign currency 'further step towards capital controls' – analysts. [Online]. Available: https://ahvalnews.com/turkey-economy/turkey-limiting-lira-loans-firms-holding-foreign-currency-further-step-towards [Accessed 7.7.2022].

Akçay, Ü. 2018. Neoliberal populism in Turkey and its crisis, Working Paper, No. 100/2018, Hochschule für Wirtschaft und Recht Berlin. Institute for International Political Economy (IPE). Berlin.

Akçay, Ü 2020. Authoritarian Consolidation Dynamics in Turkey. *Contemporary politics*. 27:1, 79–104, DOI: 10.1080/13569775.2020.1845920

Akçay, Ü, & Gungen, A. R. 2019. The making of Turkey's 2018–2019 economic crisis, Working Paper No. 120/2019, Institute for International Political Economy Berlin.

Akçay, Ü, & Jungmann, B. 2022. *Political Economy of Growth Regimes in Poland and Turkey*, Berlin, Institute for International Political Economy Berlin.

Alami, I. 2020. *Money Power and Financial Capital in Emerging Markets. Facing the Liquidity Tsunami*, London and New York, Routledge.

Alami, I., Alves, C., Bonizzi, B., Kaltenbrunner, A., Koddenbrock, K., Kvangraven, I., & Powell, J.. 2022. International Financial Subordination: a Critical Research Agenda. *Review of international political economy*. https://www.tandfonline.com/doi/full/10.1080/09692290.2022.2098359

Alami, I., & Dixon, A. D. 2021. Uneven and Combined State Capitalism. *Environment and planning a: Economy and space*, 0.

AL JAZEERA 2021. Turkey: Erdogan central bank firing clears way for more rate cuts. 14 October. https://www.aljazeera.com/economy/2021/10/14/turkey-erdogan-central-bank-firing-clears-way-for-more-rate-cuts accessed on 19/7/2022.

András, B., & Motyovszki, G. 2016. Ideje tisztázni, mit is csinálnak éppen az MNB-nél (It's time to clarify what they are doing at the MNB). *Portfolio.hu* [Online]. Available: https://www.portfolio.hu/gazdasag/20160727/ideje-tisztazni-mit-is-csinalnak-eppen-az-mnb-nel-235303 [Accessed 07.08.2022].

Apaydin, F., & Çoban, M. K. 2022a. Growth Models, Growth Regimes and Bureaucratic Autonomy: The Case of Turkey. *PSA 2022 Politics from the Margins*. York, UK.
Apaydin, F., & Çoban, M. K. 2022b. The Political Consequences of Dependent Financialization: Capital Flows, Crisis and the Authoritarian Turn in Turkey. *Review of international political economy*. https://www.tandfonline.com/doi/abs/10.1080/09692290.2022.2083658?journalCode=rrip20
Araj, V., & Savran, A. Y. 2021. Neoliberal De-Development in Turkey and the AKP's Socio-economic War on the Counterhegemony. In Aydin H, Langley W. (eds.) *Human Rights in Turkey, Philosophy and Politics - Critical Explorations*. 15, pp. 383–410.
Arena, M., Bems, R., Ilahi, N., Lee, J., Lindquist, W., & Lybek, T. 2021. *Asset Purchase Programs in European Emerging Markets*, Washington DC, IMF.
Armijo, L. E., & Katada, S. N. (eds.) 2014. *The Financial Statecraft of Emerging Powers. Shield and Sword in Asia and Latin America*: Palgrave Macmillan.
Arslanalp, M. 2018. Coalitional Politics of Housing Policy in AKP's Turkey. *Social policy in the middle East North Africa* POMEPS Studies. 31, pp. 25–33.
Ashworth, L. 2022. Who's stuffing Turkey? *Financial Times* [Online]. Available: https://www.ft.com/content/4addf2a1-7fdd-4cfd-9565-ac2ef0a7fca1 [Accessed 13.09.2022].
Aslan, A. S., & Dincer, I.. 2018. The Impact of Mortgage Loans on the Financialization Process in Turkey. *Planlama*. 28(2), pp. 143–153.
Bahçe, S., & Köse, A. H. 2016. Financialisation/Borrowing Circle as a Solution to an Unpleasant Conundrum: Observations from the Mature Neoliberalism in Turkey. *Research and policy on Turkey*. 1(1), pp. 63–74. DOI: 10.1080/23760818.2015.1099782
Ban, C., & Bohle, D. 2020. Definancialization, Financial Repression and Policy Continuity in East-Central Europe. *Review of international political economy*, 1–24.
Ban, C., & Helgadóttir, O. 2022. Financialization and Growth Regimes. *In:* Blyth, M., Pontusson, H. J. & Baccaro, L. (eds.) *Diminishing Returns: The New Politics of Growth and Stagnation*. New York: Oxford University Press.
Ban, C., Scheiring, G., & Vasile, M. 2021. The Political Economy of National-Neoliberalism. *European Politics and Society* 24(1): 96–114.
Banai, Á, Pankov, D., Fábián, G., & Nagy, T. 2018. *Hogyan alakította át a CSOK a hazai lakás- és hitelpiacot? (How did the CSOK program transform the real estate and credit market?)*, Budapest, MNB (Hungarian Central Bank.
BANKING REGULATION AND SUPERVISION AGENCY OF TURKEY (BRSA) (2019) Turkish Banking Sector Main Indicators Report. December.
Beckmann, E. 2017. *How does foreign currency debt relief affect households' loan demand? Evidence from the OeNB Euro Survey in CESEE*, Vienna, Österreichische Nationalbank (Austrian Central Bank).
Bedirhanoğlu, P. 2020. Social Constitution of the AKP's Strong State Through Financialization: State in Crisis, or Crisis in State? *In:* Bedirhanoğlu, P., Dölek, Ç., Hülagü, F. & Kaygusuz, Ö. (eds.) *Turkey's New State in the Making. Transformations in Legality, Economy and Coercion*. Zed.
Bedirhanoğlu, P. 2021. Global Class Constitution of the AKP's "authoritarian Turn" by Neoliberal Financialization. In Babacan E. et. al. (eds.) *Regime Change in Turkey*, Routledge, 68–84.
Bedirhanoğlu, P. 2021a. Economic Management Under the Presidential System of Government in Turkey: Beyond the Depoliticization Versus Repoliticisation Dichotomy. *Journal of balkan and near Eastern studies*, 24(1), pp. 97–113 DOI: 10.1080/19448953.2021.1992183
Ben Gadha, M., Kaboub, F., Koddenbrock, K., & Sylla, N. S. (eds.) 2021. *Economic and Monetary Sovereignty in 21st Century Africa*, London, Pluto Press.

Benczúr, P., & Kónya, I. 2015. Interest Premium, Sudden Stop, and Adjustment in a Small Open Economy. *Eastern European Economics* 54.

BLOOMBERG. 2022. Türkiye'de bankadaki her 100 liradan 71'i 'dolarize' (In Turkey, 71 out of every 100 liras in the bank are 'dollarized'). Available: https://www.bloomberght.com/turkiye-de-bankadaki-her-100-liradan-71-i-dolarize-2312299.

Bohle, D. 2013. Post-Socialist Housing Meets Transnational Finance: Foreign Banks, Mortgage Lending and the Privatization of Welfare in Hungary and Estonia. *Review of international political economy*, 21, 913–948.

Bohle, D. 2017. Mortgaging Europe's Periphery. *LEQS Working Papers* [Online]. Available: https://papers.ssrn.com/sol3/papers.cfm?abstract_id=3042205.

Bohle, D., & Greskovits, B. L. 2012. *Capitalist diversity on Europe's periphery*, Ithaca, Cornell University Press.

Boitan, I. A., & Marchewka-Bartkowiak, K. 2021. The Sovereign-Bank Nexus in the Face of the COVID-19 Pandemic Outbreak—Evidence from EU Member States. *Risks*, 9.

Bonefeld, W. 2014. *Critical theory and the critique of political economy: Subversion and negative reason*, New York and London, Bloomsbury.

Bonizzi, B., Kaltenbrunner, A., & Powell, J. 2020. Subordinate Financialization in Emerging Capitalist Economies. *In:* Mader, P., Mertens, D. & Van Der Zwan, N. (eds.) *The Routledge International Handbook of Financialization (Kindle edition)*. London and New York: Routledge.

Bonizzi, B., Kaltenbrunner, A., & Powell, J. 2022. Financialised Capitalism and the Subordination of Emerging Capitalist Economies. *Cambridge Journal of economics*, 46, 651–678.

Borchert, J., & Lessenich, S. 2016. *Claus Offe and the Critical Theory of the Capitalist State*, New York and London, Routledge.

Bozkurt, U. 2021. State-Bourgeoisie Relations Under Neoliberalism With Turkish Characteristics. *Historical materialism*. pp. 1–41.

Braun, B., & Gabor, D. 2020. Central Banking, Shadow Banking and Infrastructural Power. *In:* Mader, P., Mertens, D. & Van Der Zwan, N. (eds.) *The Routledge International Handbook of Financialization (Kindle edition)*. London and New York: Routledge.

Braun, B., Gabor, D., & Hübner, M.. 2018. Governing Through Financial Markets: Towards a Critical Political Economy of Capital Markets Union. *Competition & change*, 22, 101–116.

BRSA 2022. Turkish Banking Sector Main Indicators Report. March.

BRSA n.d. Monthly Banking Sector Data. Available: https://www.bddk.org.tr/BultenAylik/en/Home/Gelismis [Accessed 22.11.2022].

Bruff, I. 2016. Neoliberalism and Authoritarianism. In: Springer S, Birch K and MacLeavy J (eds) *The Handbook of Neoliberalism*. New York and London: Routledge, pp.107–117.

Bryan, D. Martin, R., & Rafferty, M. 2009. Financialization and Marx: Giving Labor and Capital a Financial Makeover, *Review of Radical Political Economics*, 41(4), 458–472.

Buchholtz, A. 2020. The Hungarian Guarantee Scheme. *Journal of financial crises*, 2, 739–756.

Büdenbender, M., & Lagna, A. 2020. Statecraft Strategies and Housing Financialization at the Periphery: Post-Socialist Trajectories in Russia and Poland. *Finance and society*, 5, 105–125.

Buğra, A., & Savaşkan, O. 2012. Politics and Class: The Turkish Business Environment in the Neoliberal Age. *New perspectives on Turkey*. 46, 27–63, DOI: 10.1017/S0896634600001503

Buğra, A., & Savaşkan, O. 2014. *New Capitalism in Turkey: The Relationship between Politics, Religion and Business*, Cheltenham, UK & Northampton, MA, USA, Edwar Elgar.

Buljan, A., Deskar-Škrbić, M., & Dumičić, M. 2020. What Drives banks' Appetite for Sovereign Debt in CEE Countries? *Public sector economics*, 42, 179–201.
Burnham, P. 1994. Open Marxism and Vulgar International Political Economy, *Review of International Political Economy*, 1(2), 221–231.
Callison, W., & Manfredi, Z. 2020. Theorizing mutant neoliberalism. In: Callison, W., & Manfredi, Z. (eds.) *Mutant Neoliberalism: Market Rule and Political Rupture*. New York: Fordham University Press, pp.1–38.
Carney, R. W. 2015. The Stabilizing State: State Capitalism as a Response to Financial Globalization in One-Party Regimes. *Review of international political economy*, 22, 838–873.
Cassetta, J. M. 2022. The Geopolitics of Swap Lines. *M-RCBG Associate Working Paper Series*. Harvard Kennedy School Mossavar-Rahmani Center for Business and Government.
Central Bank of the Republic of Turkey (CBRT) (n.d.) International Reserves And Foreign Currency Liquidity Data, 2000–2022 https://evds2.tcmb.gov.tr/index.php?/evds/serieMarket/collapse_18/5092/DataGroup/english/bie_ulusdovlkd/ accessed on 28/7/2022.
CBRT (n.d) Consumer Prices (Turkstat Data), https://www.tcmb.gov.tr/wps/wcm/connect/en/tcmb+en/main+menu/statistics/inflation+data accessed on 21/11/2022.
CBRT 2017. *Annual Report*, Ankara, CBRT.
CBRT 2018. *Annual Report*, Ankara, CBRT.
CBRT 2019. *Annual Report*, Ankara, CBRT.
CBRT 2020. *Annual Report*, Ankara, CBRT.
CBRT 2020a. *Monetary and Exchange Rate Stability Report for 2021*. December, Ankara, CBRT.
CBRT 2021. *Financial Stability Report*. Vol. 32, May, Ankara: CBRT.
CBRT 2021a. *Financial Stability Report*. Vol. 33, November, Ankara: CBRT.
CBRT 2021b. *Monetary and Exchange Rate Policy for 2022*. December, Ankara, CBRT.
CBRT 2021c. *Inflation Report, 2021–4, 28 October*, Ankara, CBRT.
CBRT 2021d. Press Release No: 2021-47. 28 October. Available: https://www.tcmb.gov.tr/wps/wcm/connect/EN/TCMB+EN/Main+Menu/Announcements/Press+Releases/2021/ANO2021-47 [Accessed 4.4.2022].
CBRT 2022. *Inflation Report, 2022–1, 27 January*, Ankara, CBRT.
CBRT 2022a. Press Release, No: 2022-30. 30 June. Available: https://www.tcmb.gov.tr/wps/wcm/connect/EN/TCMB+EN/Main+Menu/Announcements/Press+Releases/2022/ANO2022-30 [Accessed 7.7.2022].
CBRT 2022b. Press Release, No: 2022-35. 18 August. Available: https://www.tcmb.gov.tr/wps/wcm/connect/EN/TCMB+EN/Main+Menu/Announcements/Press+Releases/2022/ANO2022-35 [Accessed 11.5.2023].
Clarke, S. (ed.) 1991. *The State Debate*, London, Macmillan.
Cordeiro Santos, A. 2022. Conceptualising State Financialisation: from the core to the Periphery. *New Political Economy* 28(1), 142–154.
Deghi, A., Fengoglu, S., Iyer, T., Tabarraei, H. R., Xu, Y., & Yenice, M. 2022. *The Sovereign-Bank Nexus in Emerging Markets in the Wake of the COVID-19 Pandemic*, Washington D.C, International Monetary Fund.
Demiralp, S., Demiralp, S., & Gümüş, İ 2016. The State of Property Development in Turkey: Facts and Comparisons. *New Perspectives on Turkey*. 55, 85–106, DOI: 10.1017/npt.2016.3
Deutsche Welle. 2021. 'Turkey: Lira falls as Erdogan cites Islam on monetary policy'. Available: https://www.dw.com/en/turkish-lira-hits-turbulence-as-erdogan-cites-islam-as-reason-for-monetary-policy/a-60202309 [Accessed 20.11.2022].

Dönmez, P., & Zemandl, E. 2019. Crisis of Capitalism and (De-)Politicisation of Monetary Policymaking: Reflections from Hungary and Turkey. *New political economy*, 24, 125–143.

DUNYA 2021. 'MUSIAD Baskani Asmali: Kurdan etkilenmiyorum diyen sanayici dogru soylemiyordur' [MUSIAD Chair Asmali: The industrialist that claims he/she is not affected by the exchange rate is not telling the truth] Available: https://www.dunya.com/ekonomi/musiad-baskani-asmali-kurdan-etkilenmiyorum-diyen-sanayici-dogru-soylemiyordur-haberi-642150 [Accessed 9.10.2022].

EBF 2018. *Hungary's banking sector: Facts and Figures*, Brussels, European Banking Federation.

Eichacker, N. Forthcomming. Institutional Constraints, Liquidity Provision, and Endogenous Money in the Eurozone Core and Periphery Before and After Crises: A Preliminary Comparison of the Eurozone Crisis and the Coronavirus Pandemic. *PSL Quarterly Review*.

ENAGrup 2022. ENAGroup – Inflation Research Group. Available: https://enagrup.org/?hl=en [Accessed 21.11.2022].

Ergüven, E. 2020. The Political Economy of Housing Financialization in Turkey: Links With and Contradictions to the Accumulation Model. *Housing Policy Debate*, 30, 559–584.

Erol, I. 2019. New Geographies of Residential Capitalism: Financialization of the Turkish Housing Market Since the Early 2000s. *International Journal of Urban and Regional Research* 43(4), 724–740.

Erol, I., & Unal, U. 2015. Role of Construction Sector in Economic Growth: New Evidence from Turkey. MPRA Paper No. 68263. Available at: https://mpra.ub.uni-muenchen.de/68263/

Feng, Y., Wu, F., & Zhang, F. 2021. Changing Roles of the State in the Financialization of Urban Development Through Chengtou in China. *Regional studies*, 56, 1259–1270.

Fabry, A. 2019. *The Political Economy of Hungary. From State Capitalism to Authoritarian Neoliberalism*. London: Palgrave Macmillan.

Fernandez, R., & Aalbers, M. B.. 2020. Housing Financialization in the Global South: In Search of a Comparative Framework. *Housing policy debate*, 30, 680–701.

Gabor, D. 2010. (De)Financialization and Crisis in Eastern Europe. *Competition & change*, 41, 248–70.

Gagyi, Á, & Mikuš, M. 2022. Housing Finance in the Aftermath of the Foreign-Currency Mortgage Crisis in Eastern Europe: Editorial. *Critical housing analysis*, 9, 39–47.

Garcia, J. G., & Martinez Lopez, M. A.. 2021. State-led Actions Reigniting the Financialization of Housing in Spain. *Housing, Theory and Society*.

GOVERNMENT_OF_HUNGARY 2012. Risk indicators regarding Hungary have improved. Budapest.

GOVERNMENT_OF_HUNGARY 2021. Hungary's Recovery and Resilience Plan. Budapest.

Griffith-Jones, S., & Carreras, M. 2021. *The Role of the EIB in the Green Transformation*, Columbia University: The Foundation for European Progressive Studies (FEPS) and the Initiative for Policy Dialogue (IPD).

GUARDIAN 2020. Turkey's central bank chief ousted after lira plunges to record lows. [Online]. Available: https://www.theguardian.com/world/2020/nov/07/turkeys-central-bank-chief-ousted-after-lira-plunges-to-record-lows [Accessed 29.6.2022].

Güngen, A. R. forthcomming. The Shifting Politics of Debt. *Middle East Report*.

Holloway, J., & Picciotto, S. 1991. Capital, Crisis and the State. In: Clarke, S. (ed.) *The State Debate*. London: Macmillan.

Hornyák, J. 2022. Parragh László: a rendszerváltás óta nem látott sokkhatás érkezik (Laszlo Parragh: a shock on the scale of the regime change is coming). *Portfolio.hu* [Online]. Available: https://www.portfolio.hu/gazdasag/20220920/parragh-laszlo-a-rendszervaltas-ota-nem-latott-sokkhatas-erkezik-567707.

HVG. 2020. A Cordia lakásfejlesztő Nagy-Britanniában terjeszkedik (Housing developer Cordia is expanding in Great Britain). *HVG* [Online]. Available: https://hvg.hu/ingatlan/20200907_Magyarorszag_vezeto_lakasfejlesztoje_NagyBritanniaban_terjeszkedik [Accessed 14.03.2022].

IMF 2018. Hungary. 2018 Article IV Consultation. Press Release and Staff Report. Washington D.C.: International Monetary Fund.

IMF 2019. Hungary. Selected Issues. *Selected Issues Papers*. Washington D.C.: International Monetary Fund.

IMF 2022a. Global Financial Report April 2022. Shockwaves from the War in Ukraine Test the Financial System's Resilience. Washington D.C.: International Monetary Fund.

IMF 2022b. *Hungary: Staff Concluding Statement of the 2022 Article IV Mission*, IMF.

IMF 2022c. Sovereign Debt Investor Base for Emerging Markets. April 29, 2022 ed. Washington D.C: International Monetary Fund.

Inanc, Y. S. 2021. 'Turkey lira crisis leaves workers and middle class struggling to make ends meet'. *Middle East Eye [Online]*. Available: https://www.middleeasteye.net/news/turkey-lira-middle-working-class-struggle-crushing-inflation [Accessed 9.10.2022].

Johnson, J., & Barnes, A. 2015. Financial Nationalism and Its International Enablers: The Hungarian Experience. *Review of international political economy*, 22, 535–569.

Kaltenbrunner, A., & Painceira, J. 2018. Subordinated Financial Integration and Financialisation in Emerging Capitalist Economies: The Brazilian Experience. *New political economy*, 23, 290–313.

Karacimen, E. 2015. Interlinkages between Credit, Debt and the Labour Market: Evidence from Turkey. *Cambridge Journal of Economics* 39(3), 751–767.

Karacimen, E. 2016. Consumer Credit as an Aspect of Everyday Life of Workers in Developing Countries: Evidence from Turkey. *Review of Radical Political Economics* 48(2), 252–268.

Karas, D. 2021. Financialization and State Capitalism in Hungary after the Global Financial Crisis. *Competition & Change*, 26(1), 29–52.

Karwowski, E. 2020. Economic Development and Variegated Financialization in Emerging Economies. *Financial Geography Working Paper Series*. University of Hertfordshire.

Kassay, T. 2022. Indotek Group expands on the Greek Hotel Market. Hungarian Hotel Investors Step Onto the International Stage. Available: https://spabook.net/blog/hotelek/indotek-group-gorogorszag-terjeszkedes-oscar-hotel-athen/.

Khmelnitskaya, M. 2014. Russian Housing Finance Policy: State-Led Institutional Evolution. *Post-communist economies*, 26, 149–175.

Kolozsi, P. P., Banai, Á, & Vonnák, B.. 2015. Phasing Out Household Foreign Currency Loans: Schedule and Framework. *Financial and Economic Review*, 14, 60–87.

KPMG 2017. *A magyarországi európai uniós források felhasználásának és hatásainak elemzése (Analysis of EU transfers utilization and impacts in Hungary in the 2007–2013 MFF)*, Budapest, KPMG.

KSH 2018. *Külföldi irányítású vállalkozások Magyarországon, 2018 (Foreign-Owned Enterprises in Hungary 2018)*, Budapest, Hungarian Central Statistical Office (KSH.

KSH 2022. *Housing Prices Report*, Budapest, Hungarian Central Statistical Office (KSH).

Kubilay, M. 2022. 'As Turkey's economic woes worsen, a new currency crisis is approaching'. https://www.mei.edu/publications/turkeys-economic-woes-worsen-new-currency-crisis-approaching, accessed on 9/10/2022.

Kuzmanovic, J. 2022. Hungary's Indotek Buys Sberbank Stake in Biggest Balkan Retailer. *Bloomberg* [Online]. Available: https://www.bnnbloomberg.ca/hungary-s-indotek-buys-sberbank-stake-in-biggest-balkan-retailer-1.1749607.

Lapavitsas, C., & Soydan, A.. 2022. Financialisation in Developing Countries: Approaches, Concepts, and Metrics. *International review of Applied Economics* 36(3), 424–447.

Marschall, M., Aydogan, A., & Bulut, A. 2016. Does Housing Create Votes? Explaining the Electoral Success of the AKP in Turkey. *Electoral Studies* 42, 201–212.

Matolcsy, G. 2021. Áttérés az okostőke-intenzív pályára (Transition to a smart capital-intensive pathway). *Magyar Nemzet* [Online]. Available: https://magyarnemzet.hu/pc19/2021/07/atteres-az-okostoke-intenziv-palyara.

Matolcsy, G., & Palotai, D. 2018. The Hungarian Model: Hungarian Crisis Management in View of the Mediterranean Way *Financial and economic review*, 17, 5–43.

Mattioli, F. 2020. *Dark Finance. Illiquidity and Authoritarianism at the Margins of Europe*, Stanford, CA, Stanford University Press.

Mazzucato, M., & Penna, C. R. 2016. Beyond Market Failures: the Market Creating and Shaping Roles of State Investment Banks. *Journal of economic policy reform*, 19, 305–326.

Mester, N. 2020. Beindult a magyar úthenger - Tízmilliárdokat keres több hazai ingatlanos cég külföldön (Several domestic real estate companies are earning tens of billions abroad). *mfor.hu* [Online]. Available: https://mfor.hu/cikkek/vallalatok/beindult-a-magyar-uthenger--tiz-milliardokat-keres-tobb-hazai-ingatlanos-ceg-kulfoldon-.html [Accessed 14.03.2022].

Michaelson, R. 2021. 'There's jobs but no money': Turkey's economic crisis begins to bite. *Guardian [Online].* Available: https://www.theguardian.com/world/2021/dec/19/theres-jobs-but-no-money-turkeys-economic-crisis-begins-to-bite?fbclid=IwAR21pPAh3W6lH7Bb4XS7m1e99giZQNPmtvFP2yKzMJXbOpfj1ts9vY8xiBQ [Accessed 21.12.2021].

MINISTRY_OF_NATIONAL_ECONOMY 2013. *Change in the budget and general government debt on the basis of data reported for the Excessive Deficit Procedure*, Budapest, Government of Hungary.

Mishura, A., & Ageeva, S.. 2020. Financialization and Authoritarian State: The Case of Russia. *Financial Geography Working Paper Series*. Oxford: FinGeo Global Network on Financial Geography.

MNB 2018. *Considerations behind the launch of the Funding for Growth Scheme Fix (FGS FIX) and main features of the programme*, Budapest, MNB (Hungarian Central Bank).

MNB 2019. *Considerations Behind the Launch of the Bond Funding for Growth Scheme (BGS) and Main Features of the Programme*, Budapest, Hungarian Central Bank (MNB).

MNB 2021a. *Notice on the terms and conditions of primary market purchsases in the MNB's Green Motgage Bond Purchase Programme*, Budapest, MNB.

MNB 2021b. *Press Release on the Utlisation of the Funding for Growth Scheme Go!* Budapest, MNB.

MNB 2022a. *Housing Market Report May 2022*, Budapest, MNB (Hungarian Central Bank).

MNB 2022b. *Inflation Report September 2022*, Budapest, Hungarian Central Bank (MNB).

MNB 2022c. *Report on the Balance of Payments April 2022*, Budapest, MNB (Hungarian Central Bank).

MNB 2022d. *Trends in Lending March 2022*, Budapest, MNB.

MTI. 2022. Jobbik Proposes Amendments to Constitition, law on Central Bank. *The Budapest Times* [Online]. Available: https://www.budapesttimes.hu/hungary/jobbik-proposes-amendments-to-constitution-law-on-central-bank/ [Accessed 25.10.2022].

MUSIAD 2022. 'MUSIAD Genel Baskani Mahmut Asmali: KGF destek paketi, sanayicimizin imkanlarini genisletecek' [MUSIAD Chair Mahmut Asmali: CGF support package will expand our industrialists' opportunities] Available: https://www.musiad.org.tr/icerik/haber-detay-39/p-1168 [Accessed 9.10.2022.]

Nagy, M., & Kolozsi, P. P. 2017. The Reduction of External Vulnerability and Easing of Monetary Conditions With a Targeted Non-Conventional Programme: The Self-Financing Programme of the Magyar Nemzeti Bank. *Civic review*, 13, 99–118.

Nölke, A., & Vliegenhart, A. 2009. Enlarging the Varieties of Capitalism: The Emergence of Dependent Market Economies in East Central Europe. *World politics*, 61, 670–702.

Offe, C. 1974. Structural Problems of the Capitalist State: Class Rule and the Political System. On the Selectiveness of Political Institutions. *In:* Beyme, V. (ed.) *German Political Studies Vol. 1*. Sage.

Orhangazi, O., & Yeldan, A. E. 2021. The Re-Making of the Turkish Crisis. *Development and change*. 52 (3), 460–503.

Piroska, D., Gorelkina, Y., & Johnson, J. 2020. Macroprudential Policy on an Uneven Playing Field: Supranational Regulation and Domestic Politics in the EU's Dependent Market Economies. *Journal of Common Market Studies* 59(3), 497–517.

Piroska D. (2021) Financial nationalism and democracy: Evaluating financial nationalism in light of post-crisis theories of financial power in Hungary. Financial Geography Working Paper No. 33.

Pitel, L. 2022. Turkish president sacks statistics chief as inflation tension escalates. *Financial Times [Online]*. Available: https://www.ft.com/content/8ea4f3ea-cdbf-45ff-b4f1-d77451109453 [Accessed 18.7.2022].

Pitel, L. 2022a. Erdoğan gears up for huge pre-election spending spree in Turkey. *Financial Times [Online]*. Available: https://www.ft.com/content/b8ed297d-c054-4454-878b-e07656e764aa [Accessed 20.11.2022].

Pitel, L., & Samson, A. 2022. Turkish finance minister defends economic links with Russia. *Financial Times [Online]*. Available: https://www.ft.com/content/d1b33e56-2835-4d04-8387-ba1d8dc55646 [Accessed 19.11.2022].

Pósfai, Z., & Nagy, G. 2017. Crisis and the Reproduction of Core-Periphery Relations on the Hungarian Housing Market. *European Spatial research and policy*, 24, 17–38.

Poulantzas, N. 2014. *State, Power, Socialism*, London, Verso.

Pyrkalo, S. 28.09.2022 2022. Emerging markets and advanced economies differ on tackling energy prices. *www.ebrd.com* [Online]. Available from: https://www.ebrd.com/news/2022/emerging-markets-and-advanced-economies-differ-on-tackling-energy-prices-.html.

REUTERS 2022. Turkey's Erdogan advises central bank to cut rates at upcoming meetings. [Online]. Available: https://www.reuters.com/markets/europe/turkeys-erdogan-advises-central-bank-cut-rates-next-meeting-2022-09-29/ [Accessed 20.11.2022].

REUTERS 2022a. Rising risk of more capital controls in Turkey - S&P Global. [Online]. Available: https://www.reuters.com/markets/rates-bonds/rising-risk-more-capital-controls-turkey-sp-global-2022-06-08/ [Accessed 7.7.2022].

Rodrigues, J., Santos, A. C., & Teles, N. 2016. Semi-Peripheral Financialisation: the Case of Portugal. *Review of international political economy*, 23, 480–510.

Scheiring, G. 2021. Varieties of Dependency, Varieties of Populism: Neoliberalism and the Populist Countermovements in the Visegrád Four. *Europe-asia studies*, 73, 1569–1595.

Scheiring, G., & Szombati, K. 2020. From Neoliberal Disembedding to Authoritarian Re-Embedding: The Making of Illiberal Hegemony in Hungary. *International sociology*, 35, 721–738.

Sebők, M. 2018. Institutional Entrepreneurship and the Mission Creep of the National Bank of Hungary. *In:* Bakir, C. & Jarvis, D. S. L. (eds.) *Institutional Entrepreneurship and Policy Change. Theoretical and Empirical Explorations*. Cham, Switzerland: Palgrave Macmillan.

Sonmez, M. 2022. Money inflows of unknown origin headed for record in Turkey. *Al-Monitor* [Online]. Available: https://www.al-monitor.com/originals/2022/08/money-inflows-unknown-origin-headed-record-turkey [Accessed 16.08.2022].

Szekeres, K. 2021. Mit adott nekünk a Növekedési Kötvényprogram? (What did the Asset Purchase Program give us?). *Portfolio.hu* [Online]. Available: https://www.portfolio.hu/gazdasag/20211229/mit-adott-nekunk-a-novekedesi-kotvenyprogram-518274 [Accessed 02.06.2022].

Tansel, C.B. 2017. *States of Discipline. Authoritarian Neoliberalism and the Contested Reproduction of Capitalist Order*. London: Rowman and Littlefield.

Tansel, C. B. 2019. Reproducing Authoritarian Neoliberalism in Turkey: Urban Governance and State Restructuring in the Shadow of Executive Centralization. *Globalizations*. 16:3, 320–335, DOI: 10.1080/14747731.2018.1502494

Thomas, M. 2022. Inflation in Turkey surges to 83%. *BBC* [Online]. Available: https://www.bbc.com/news/world-europe-63120478 [Accessed 03.10.2022].

TUSIAD 2022. TUSIAD Baskani Orhan Turan'in Ekonomist Dergisi soylesisi: 'Onceligimiz enflasyon sorununu cozmek olmali' [TUSIAD Chair Orhan Turan's interview with the Economist magazine: 'Our priority must be the resolution of the inflation problem'] Available: https://tusiad.org/tr/basin-bultenleri/item/10980-tusi-ad-baskani-orhan-turan-in-ekonomist-dergisi-soylesisi-onceligimiz-enflasyon-sorununu-cozmek-olmali [Accessed 9.10.2022].

Vakhal, P. 2020. Magyar Kis- és Középvállalkozások a Globális értékláncokban (Hungarian SMEs in Global Value Chains). *Külgazdaság (foreign trade)*, 64, 30–59.

Vaughn, A. L. 2019. *Ties that Bind: The Geopolitics of Bilateral Currency Swap Agreements*, Princeton Niehaus Center for Globalization and Governance.

Voszka, É. 2018. Nationalisation in Hungary in the Post-Crisis Years: A Specific Twist on a European Trend? *Europe-asia studies*, 70, 1281–1302.

WORLD BANK 2022. *Selected Capital Markets Options To Promote Long-Term Finance For Türkiye*, Washington DC, The World Bank Group.

Yağci, M. 2018. The Political Economy of Central Banking in Turkey: The Macroprudential Policy Regime and Self-Undermining Feedback. *South European Society and politics*, 23, 525–545.

Yeldan, A. E., & Ünüvar, B. 2016. An Assessment of the Turkish Economy in the AKP Era. *Research and policy on Turkey*. 1:1, 11–28.

Yeşilbağ, M. 2020. The State-Orchestrated Financialization of Housing in Turkey. *Housing policy debates*, 30, 533–558.

Yesilbag, M. 2021. Statecraft on Cement: The Politics of Land-Based Accumulation in Erdogan's Turkey. *Urban studies*. pp. 1–16, doi:10.1177/00420980211044044

Zsiborás, G. 2022. Interju: Nem látom azt a durva szándékot, hogy a forint árfolyamát bármi áron megerősítsék (Interview: I don't see a strong commitment to strengthen the forint). *Forbes* [Online]. Available: https://www.forbes.hu/penz/hold-moricz-befektetes-forint-energia/ [Accessed 25.10.2022].

12 Diversity of Monetary Regimes and Reactions to the COVID-19 Pandemic Crisis in the Balkan Countries

Nikolay Nenovsky and Tsvetelina Marinova

Introduction

COVID-19 has had a disruptive economic impact in 2020 causing a severe global recession, significant increases in unemployment, income inequality, state budget deficits and public debt-to-GDP ratios in the developed and developing countries. How long its impact will persist remains unclear (Emmerling et al. 2021). Moreover, the Russia-Ukraine war, which has started in February 2022, has been among the major drivers of soaring energy and food prices and inflation and has further worsened economic performance and prospects in Europe and in the world (IMF 2022). During the coronavirus pandemic, the economic policy response (fiscal, monetary and regulatory) encompassed various compensatory mechanisms across countries.[1] Similar to the global financial crisis from 2008, the COVID-19 crisis has led to a remarkable state intervention in the economy through massive fiscal policy measures and further expansion of the lender of last resort of the major central banks. Big central banks have acted as classic lender of last resort (Bagehot concept), buyer of last resort (QE) and third and perhaps the most radical step was that some of the biggest central banks became a lender of last resort even to nonfinancial firms and companies (Bernanke et al. 2022).

During the pandemic, central banks' stimulative monetary policy of low and negative interest rates (in the eurozone) included direct purchases of government debt to finance fiscal stimulus, which in turn led to a strong increase in their balance sheets. Central banks provided unlimited liquidity to commercial banks, at a subsidised cost and at a significant reduction in the quality of the collateral. Supervisory and regulatory policies in the banking sector included temporary reductions in the risk weights of certain exposures, and a uniform framework for temporary moratoria (private or public) on bank loan payments was established in the European Union (EU) (English, Forbes & Ubide (eds) 2021). Central banks aimed to limit the economic consequences of lockdowns and stabilising the economy. Administrative restrictions and containment measures during the pandemic determined the central banks' monetary policy measures and interventions (Brzoza-Brzezina et al. 2021)

DOI: 10.4324/9781003323280-13

Theoretical Framework for Understanding Monetary Regimes in the Balkan Countries during COVID-19 Crisis

First, we focus on the theoretical and legal characteristics of the different types of monetary regimes implemented in Bulgaria, Romania and Serbia. Unlike the other Central and Eastern European countries, Bulgaria implemented floating exchange rate and independent monetary policy at the beginning of the transition (after 1989). After a period of banking crisis, hyperinflation and loss of foreign reserves, under the pressure of the International Monetary Fund (IMF), it introduced currency board in July 1997. The currency board is a monetary regime based on rules that bring discipline in macroeconomic policy through market discipline and capital movement. It relies on two main effects: discipline effect (legal constraints on monetary policy) and the credibility effect stemming from the fixed exchange rate (1 euro = 1.95583 levs) and the coverage of monetary base. It maintains 100% foreign exchange coverage for the total amount of the Bulgarian National Bank (BNB) monetary liabilities (banknotes, coins and deposits). These are government deposits and commercial banks' reserves. Hence, no monetary policy is carried out (Nenovsky & Rizopoulos 2003). The currency board constraints do not allow the government to rely on money issuance in order to finance budget deficits and it enforces prudent and conservative fiscal policy. Strict fiscal limitations apply to all the economic agents who have to bear the costs from their action alone (Marinova 2016). Under the currency board regime, the BNB can perform a strictly limited function of lender of last resort. It is allowed to refinance private banks only in case of a systemic risk and the amount of extended loans should not exceed the deposit (bank reserves) of the Banking Department placed with the Issue Department. Moreover, the BNB may provide loans only to solvent banks experiencing pressing need for liquidity only against collateral of liquid assets. The currency board is a conservative and dependent monetary regime (pursuing the monetary policy of the ECB) having limited opportunities for reactions to shocks and systemic crisis.[2]

Unlike Bulgaria, Romania and Serbia have been implementing monetary policies of inflation targeting. In fact, both countries pursue the monetary policy of the ECB despite preserving their monetary independence and the execution of discretionary monetary policy. Starting in 2013, Romania has applied inflation targets which are formulated in terms of the annual change in the consumer price index and are set as midpoints within a target band of ±1 percentage points. The inflation target is set at 2.50% with variation band of ± 1pp. The National Bank of Romania (NBR) has announced that this is an intermediate stage meant to ensure the transition towards the phase of long-term continuous inflation targeting in line with the ECB's definition of price stability.[3] The main monetary policy instruments available to the NBR are open market operations, standing facilities and reserve requirements.

The National Bank of Serbia (NBS) has been implementing a managed floating exchange rate regime since 1 January 2009. The inflation target is set for three years ahead until the process of nominal, real, and structural convergence to the EU is finished. Headline inflation target from January 2021 to December 2023 is set at the level of 3%, with a tolerance band of ±1.5 percentage points. The NBS strives to achieve the targeted rate of inflation by changing its key policy rate.[4]

Unlike inflation targeting rule in other contexts, central banks are allowed to apply all the tools of conventional and non-conventional monetary policy to react to economic shocks and crises. Moreover, there are no institutional restrictions to fiscal policy. Hence, governments have bigger fiscal space and can execute expansionary fiscal policy.

Figure 12.1 illustrates the dependence of the monetary regimes and the monetary policies in Bulgaria, Romania and Serbia on the ECB's common monetary policy executed in the eurozone as well as their direct relation, interaction and impact on the fiscal policies and the state of the public finances in the countries. We reveal the short-term implications of the monetary policy as well as the long-term implications of the fiscal policy for the Balkan economies. Bulgaria and Romania are not yet part of the eurozone and Serbia is a candidate country for EU membership. Bulgaria applies currency board and a fixed exchange rate of the lev against the euro as well as it participates in ERM2. Romania and Serbia, on the other hand, pursue a monetary policy of inflation targeting based on the ECB's definition of price stability.

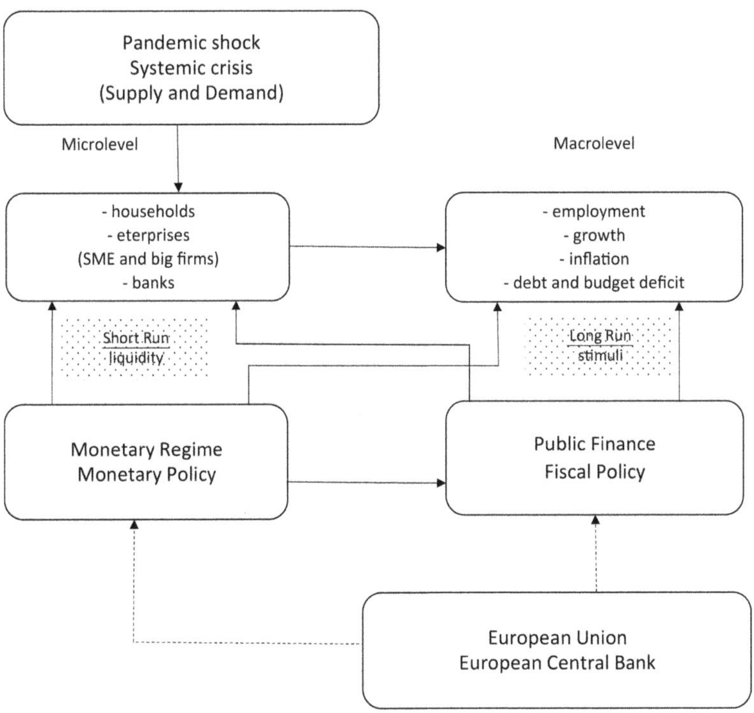

Figure 12.1 Theoretical framework for understanding monetary regimes in the Balkan countries during COVID-19 crisis

Source: Sahling et al. (2021, p. 279).

The pandemic has brought to the fore the need for timely and proper coordination and interaction between countries' fiscal and monetary policies. In the short term, monetary policy measures relate to the provision of liquidity to households, firms and banks, while in the long term, banking regulations and fiscal measures are of paramount importance to sustainable growth. At the same time, Bulgaria and Romania have to respect the rules for sound public finance set out in the EU institutional framework (Maastricht Treaty, Stability and Growth Pact) and they have to avoid excessively high budget deficits and public debt.[5] While for Bulgaria there are both internal and external constraints to monetary and fiscal policy, for Romania and Serbia these are mostly external, coming from the EU.

Fiscal and Monetary Policies during COVID-19

Before the pandemic, the three Balkan countries had stable growth, decreasing unemployment, moderate inflation, and stable fiscal positions (budget surpluses in Bulgaria and Serbia and lower public debt in the three countries compared to the other EU countries). The COVID-19 pandemic led to a sharp decline in economic activity and a rapid deterioration in the budgetary positions of the three countries. In 2020, Bulgaria experienced the biggest decline in the economic activity among the three countries. The Bulgarian economy contracted by 4.4% and the Romanian[6] and the Serbian economies by 3.9% and 0.9% respectively. Slight increases in the unemployment rate were recorded in Bulgaria and Romania. In Bulgaria, the unemployment rose from 5.9% in 2019 to 6.7% while in Romania it increased from 2.9% in 2019 to 3.4% in 2020. It is noteworthy, that in Serbia the unemployment rate declined from 11.2% in 2019 to 9.7% in 2020. The governments increased public expenditure mostly in Serbia where it reached 49.4% of GDP in 2020, while in Bulgaria and Romania, it was 41.8% and 42.0% of GDP respectively. The fiscal measures to address the effects of the pandemic have worsened the budgetary positions. The budget deficit in Bulgaria grew to 4.0% of GDP and the public debt rose to 24.7% of GDP. Nevertheless, the Bulgarian sovereign debt is still among the lowest in the EU27.[7] In Romania, the budget deficit doubled (9.3% of GDP) and the public debt reached 47.3% of GDP. In Serbia, the budget deficit was 8.3% of GDP and the government debt rose to 57% of GDP.

In the three Balkan countries, the financial stability has been sustained and further strengthened due to the monetary and regulatory policy measures. Moreover, the banking system has remained excessively liquid. Furthermore, the delayed consumption and investment by economic agents have led to a significant accumulation of savings and credit decline for households and non-financial companies in 2020.

Fiscal Policy Measures during COVID-19

According to the analysis of the IMF (2021) governments have implemented two types of fiscal measures worldwide: demand-support measures and emergency lifelines. Demand support measures have been applied to boost demand and households/firms' disposable income which included: wage subsidies and targeted transfers to households, enhancement of unemployment benefits, paid sick leave and support to parents for school closures; tax relief measures for firms and households, and deferrals of tax and social security payments for firms and households, etc. This group of fiscal measures have exacerbated fiscal imbalances, the government debt and the borrowing needs have risen in the short run. They are considered as above-the-line measures. Meanwhile, emergency lifelines refer to liquidity measures that provided sustained cash flow support to firms and households, especially during the lockdown phase of the pandemic, when firms needed to shut down production in order to maintain social distancing. Such measures include loans to firms and households, state guarantees, government provisions of loans, and equity injections. These measures have no upfront impact on the fiscal deficit but they increase debt or liabilities in the long-term and are considered to below-the-line measures.

Similarly to the other European countries, the governments of the three Balkan states have pursued countercyclical fiscal policies by increasing transfers to economic agents, programmes to preserve employment and boost government consumption and investment. The demand support measures and health spending became a major part of the fiscal packages and fiscal stimuli. In Bulgaria, total government spending was Bulgarian lev (BGN) 10.9 bn or USD 6.4 bn. According to the IMF estimations (2021) the demand support measures and health spending amounted to 5.3% of GDP (BGN 6.3 bn or USD 3.7 bn). The fiscal measures included subsidised employment programmes (60/40 programme), payment of pension supplements, health spending, including for frontline medical staff, credit guarantees from the state-owned Bulgarian Development Bank, and tax relief (reduction of the VAT rate on certain goods and services, extension of corporate tax payment deadlines and increase in the amount of personal tax allowances).

In Romania, the demand support measures and health spending constituted 3.4% of GDP Romanian leu (RON) 36 bn or USD 8.5 bn) They also included: partially covering the wages of parents staying home during school closure as well as partially covering the wages of self-employed and workers in danger of being laid off, partially subsidising the wages of those returning to work, deferral of utility payments for SMEs (small and medium enterprises), bonus for corporate income tax payments, grants for the businesses which totaled 2.5% of GDP (RON 26 bn or USD 6.1bn). In addition, the government has rescheduled the payment of certain taxes for companies in difficulty. Other measures included: faster reimbursement of VAT, suspending foreclosures on overdue debtors, suspending tax authorities' control, discounts for paying corporate income taxes, postponement of property tax by three months, exempting the hospitality industry from the specific tax for 90 days, changes in the insolvency legislation. The possibility to reschedule tax payments was extended in 2021 (IMF 2021).

In Serbia, the demand support measures and health spending introduced by the government amounted to 12.2% of GDP Serbian dinar (RSD) 664 bn or USD 6.4 bn). The fiscal measures announced in 2020 included: wage subsidies (RSD 93 bn):

(i) Payment of three minimum wages for all employees in SMEs and entrepreneurs; (ii) Payment of 50% of minimum wages to big companies for employees who were not working; one-off payment to all pensioners (RSD 7 bn); new loans to SMEs from the Development Fund (RSD 24 bn); universal cash transfer of EUR 100 to each citizen over 18 years old (about RSD 71bn); support to 14,000 most vulnerable women in 50 municipalities across Serbia in hygiene packages and essential foods (RSD 12 bn); one-off fiscal support to help city hotels through a fixed subsidy per room and per bed, with an estimated cost of RSD 1.3 bn. Most of these measures were prolonged in 2021: three additional months of wage subsidies (RSD 73bn); payments for employees in travel and hospitality; universal cash transfers to all adult citizens paid in May and November (RSD 43bn); pension bonus (RSD 8.5bn); support for the transport sector and for city hotels (RSD 3bn); one-off financial assistance to all the registered unemployed people, of EUR 60; a one-off payment to vaccinated citizens (RSD 9 bn).

In Bulgaria the limited capacity of the government to use fiscal policy to tackle the crisis was partly offset by EU funds. The financial support measures utilising national and EU resources amounted to 3.9% of GDP (BGN 4.6 bn or USD 2.7 bn). They consisted of capital increase in the Bulgarian Development Bank (BGN 700 mn) as well as liquidity provided through state-owned entities and other EU institutions. The Bulgarian Development Bank, the Fund of Funds, the JEREMIE initiative ("Joint European Resources for Micro to Medium Enterprises") and Urban Development Funds executed quasi-fiscal operations on behalf of the government which amounted to 2.5% of GDP (BGN 3 bn or USD 1.8 bn).

Unlike Bulgaria, the Romanian government provided loan guarantees and state guarantees for SMEs and big companies which amounted to 4% of GDP (RON 42 bn or USD 10 bn). The IMF (2021) estimated that below-the-line measures corresponded to 4.2% of GDP (RON 44 bn or USD 10.4 bn).

In Serbia state guarantees amounted to 3.2% of GDP (RSD 175 bn or USD 1.7 bn). In 2020 a state guarantee scheme for bank loans to SMEs was approved (RSD 56.5bn). In 2021 the existing scheme for state-guaranteed bank loans to SMEs was expanded by EUR 500 mn (1% of GDP) and a new EUR 500 mn scheme for vulnerable companies was implemented. Quasi-fiscal operations totaled EUR 200 mn (0.4% of GDP), including subsidised loans (1% interest rate) to SMEs from the Development Fund (IMF 2021).

Monetary and Macro-Financial Policy Measures

The monetary and macro-prudential policy tools during the COVID-19 pandemic can be divided into four categories: interest rate cuts, asset purchases, liquidity provision and credit support as well as regulatory easing. The specific tools used by each central bank depended on local macroeconomic conditions, the state of the banking system and the financial sector as well as of the institutional constraints of the applied monetary regime.

In March 2020, the **Bulgarian National Bank** adopted an anti-crisis package for the banking sector which totaled BGN 9.3 bn. Its main objectives were to further strengthen the resilience of the banking sector and to temporarily ease payments to businesses and households on bank loans. The regulatory measures included:

- Prohibition on distribution of retained earnings from previous years to strengthen the capital base;
- Restrictions on the level of concentration and quality of assets in which banks can invest their liquid assets;
- Repeal of the planned increases in the countercyclical capital buffer;
- Private moratorium on bank loan payments.

In March 2020, the BNB adopted a decision to cancel the increases in the countercyclical capital buffer applicable to domestic credit risk exposures scheduled for the second quarter of 2020 and the first quarter of 2021 and maintaining its 0.5% level during 2020–2021. In September 2021, the BNB decided to increase the countercyclical capital buffer applicable to credit risk exposures to 1.0%, effective from 1 October 2022. The main reason for this measure was the accelerated growth rates of housing loans and the risks of increasing indebtedness and non-performing loans, with a negative change in economic conditions. The countercyclical capital buffer will be raised to 1.5% with effect from 1 January 2023. In December 2021 the BNB confirmed a 3% systemic risk buffer of 3% (BNB 2021). The measures taken do not inject liquidity into the banks. They preserve and reallocate available resources within the banking system, as the currency board rules prohibit the BNB from creating money and financing the government through securities purchase programmes. Nevertheless, the ECB can provide liquidity through swaps and repo transactions. In April 2020, for the first time, the ECB and the BNB set up a swap line of EUR 2 bn which was in place until end-2020.[8]

Unlike the BNB, the Romanian and Serbian central banks implemented almost all monetary policy instruments during the pandemic. Foreign exchange interventions were undertaken to smooth excessive volatility and stabilise the exchange rate in order to further strengthen financial stability The Romanian and Serbian central banks acted as lender of last resort and applied quantitative easing. **The National Bank of Romania (NBR)** reduced the monetary policy rate by 1.2 percentage point to 1.25% and narrowed the corridor defined by interest rates on standing facilities around the monetary policy rate to ±0.5 percentage points from ±1.0 percentage points. The NBR purchased government securities on the secondary market and implemented measures to ensure the smooth functioning of payment and settlement systems. The NBR performed open market operations and provided liquidity to credit institutions via repo transactions (repurchase transactions in government securities). The repo transactions stood at around RON 42 bn in 2020 and more than RON 2 bn in 2021. The total volume of leu-denominated government securities purchased on the secondary market in the period April 2020–March 2022 amounted to RON 5.895 bn.[9] The banks deferred loan repayments for households and businesses affected by COVID-19 for up to nine months (applicable until March 2021). The ECB set up a euro repo line with NBR worth a maximum of €4.5 bn. Extended until March 2022 (IMF 2021).

On 11 March 2020 the **National Bank of Serbia** cut main interest rates. The key policy rate was lowered to 1.75%, the deposit facility rate to 0.75% and the lending facility rate to 2.75%. The main interest rates were further lowered and the terms of financing became even more favourable than before the beginning of the pandemic. In April, June and December, the NBS Executive Board further trimmed the key policy rate by a total 0.75 pp, to its historical low of 1.00%, while the deposit facility rate was decreased to 0.10% and the lending facility rate set at 1.90%.[10]

During COVID-19 the NBS continued to promote the use of the dinar in the national financial system (*dinarization*). The domestic financial sector was supplied with additional dinar and FX liquidity to sustain unhindered flow of credit to local businesses and households. From March to May 2020, the NBS provided to banks with additional dinar liquidity worth RSD 41.1 bn and FX liquidity amounted to EUR 96.0 mn via additional FX swap auction, regular swap auctions and three repo securities purchase auctions. The commercial banks were given the opportunity to tap two dinar liquidity lines – additional FX swap purchase auctions and repo securities purchase auctions. The NBS supplied additional liquidity to banks which totaled RSD 145.1 bn (repo purchase amounted to RSD 101.4 bn and FX swaps worth RSD 43.7 bn) (IMF 2021). In July 2020, dinar loans were approved under the guarantee scheme at lower interest rates. Moratorium on debt payments was introduced during 2020–2021. Housing loan requirements were facilitated.[11]

In May 2020, for the first time, local-currency denominated corporate bonds became eligible for open market operations and as collateral for banks to receive daily liquidity loans and short-term liquidity from the NBS. Thus, the NBS acted as lender of last resort also for the non-financial companies. On 17 July 2020, the ECB and the NBS set up repo line to provide euro liquidity extended until end-March 2022.

The NBS has intervened heavily in the foreign exchange market to maintain a relatively stable exchange rate during the crisis.[12]

Table 12.1 Central Banks' policy measures during COVID-19 (2020–2021)

Tool type	*Measures*	*Bulgaria*	*Romania*	*Serbia*
Interest rate	Policy rate cut		X	X
Lending operations/ liquidity provision and credit support	Liquidity provision		X	X
	Use of swap line/repo line (with ECB)	X	X	X
	FX operations		X	X
Asset purchases	Government bonds/sovereign debt		X	X
	Corporate bonds			
Reserve policy/ regulatory easing	Capital requirements			
	Countercyclical capital buffer	X		X
	Systemic risk capital buffers			
	Easing collateral eligibility rules			

Source: Bulgarian National Bank, National Bank of Romania, National Bank of Serbia, IMF, Authors

The Effects of Fiscal and Monetary Measures on the Balkan Economies

In this part we refer to Figure 12.1 on the theoretical framework of monetary policy regimes to analyze the effects of the monetary and fiscal measures implemented by the national institutions. In 2021, the three Balkan economies have started to recover from the crisis. In Bulgaria, the GDP growth reached 4.2% and private consumption was the main driver of growth. The unemployment rate declined to 4.8%. The major causes of inflation were the price hikes of primary energy commodities (oil, natural gas and electricity) and food in international markets, as well as the rising consumption expenditure of households and the higher consumer goods prices in Bulgaria's major trading partners. To curb inflation the government imposed a moratorium on regulated prices of electricity, water and sewerage services and heating in December 2021 which expired on 31 March 2022. For the first quarter of 2022 the CPI rose to 10.5% while the CPI compared to the previous period reached 4.3%. In March 2022, the CPI was 12.4% year-on-year. The harmonised index of consumer prices (HICP) reached 8.9% on an annual basis. The continuation of fiscal stimulus in 2021 resulted in a further increase in the budget deficit and government debt while the fiscal reserve which provides some scope for stimulative fiscal policy, remained at high levels during the pandemic.

The banking system continued to be liquid and stable in 2021. The commercial banks' reserves on the BNB's balance sheet more than doubled. The Banking Department's deposit with the Issuance Department also continued to grow, which has further strengthened the confidence and stability of the financial system because it enables the BNB to serve, albeit in a limited capacity, as a lender of last resort in the event of a systemic crisis.

In 2021, the deposit growth slowed in comparison to 2020 due to the retention of very low deposit interest rates coupled with accelerating inflation which stimulated economic agents to redirect part of their savings to consumption as well as to seek investment opportunities as alternatives to deposits. At the same time, lending to households and businesses almost doubled in 2021.

According to the BNB analysis (2022) risks to lower GDP growth are mainly associated with the military conflict in Ukraine and the emergence of additional disruptions in the supply of prime and raw materials from the countries involved in the war. There are risks to the inflation forecast of a stronger increase in prices. These risks are associated mainly with international commodity price dynamics. Other risks stem from possible changes in the regulated prices of electricity, water and sewerage services, and heating for household consumers in line with substantial rise in energy prices.

The European Commission Spring forecast (2022) reveals that annual inflation will rise to 11.2% in 2022 and start to decline in 2023. The unemployment rate is expected to remain at 5.4% in 2022. The budget deficit will exceed 3% of GDP in 2022 while the government debt will remain at 25% of GDP.

In Romania, economic growth reached 5.9% in 2021. The unemployment fell to 2.7%, a level lower than before the pandemic. The HICP accelerated to 4.1%

Table 12.2 Macroeconomic and financial indicators for Bulgaria

Indicators	*2018*	*2019*	*2020*	*2021*	*2022*	*2023*
GDP growth, %	2.7	4.0	–4.4	4.2	2.1	3.2
Private consumption growth, %	3.1	3.9	1.2	8.0	2.7	3.0
Total deposits, lei million, annual change %	7.3	9.7	9.7	9.1	7.2	7.0
Household deposit growth, %	7.7	8.0	9.7	9.0		
Non-financial corporations deposit growth, %	5.2	14.3	10.5	8.5		
Financial corporations deposit growth, %	16.9	2.4	2.0	16.9		
Foreign direct investment, % of GDP	2.7	3.2	5.2	2.6		
Gross capital formation, % of GDP	18.8	18.6	19.2	16.6		
HICP, %	2.3	3.1	0.0	6.6	9.6	3.9
Unemployment rate, %	6.1	5.9	6.7	4.8	5.2	4.9
Public sector expenditure, % of GDP	36.9	35.5	41.8	43.1		
Gross external debt, % of GDP	66.1	61.3	64.9	61.8		
Government debt, % of GDP	22.1	20.0	24.7	25.1		
Budget deficit/surplus, % of GDP	1.7	2.1	–4.0	–4.1		
Average monthly wage in euro	573	633.5	695.5	775.5		
Money supply, % of GDP	84.8	85.1	94.7	94.8		
Monetary base, million BGN	32,590.2	32,477.6	43,810.5	47,779.7		
Central bank balance sheet, BGN thousand	51,264,563	50,881,190	62,539,687	69,964,089		
Key interest rate	0.00	0.00	0.00	0.00		
Deposit of the Banking Department, BGN thousand	5,721,320	6,150,286	6,909,195	8,963,406		
Commercial banks reserves, BGN thousand	15,267,214	14,462,625	23,518,532	24,313,910		
Fiscal reserve at BNB, thousand BGN, as at 31 December	10,719,427	8,853,715	8,646,875	9,531,918		
Gross international foreign reserves, million BGN	49,036.9	48,574.2	60,333.9	67,666.3		
Loans to non-government sector, annual growth, %	8.4	9.3	4.4	8.7		
Household loans, annual growth, %	11.2	9.5	6.6	13.4		
Loans to non-financial corporations, annual growth, %	5.4	5.9	3.0	4.6		
Loans to financial corporations, annual growth, %	23.7	26.9	3.6	15.0		
House Price Index, total	6.6	6.0	4.6			
Current account balance, % GDP	0.9	1.9	–0.1	–0.4	–5.4	–2.8

Source: BNB, Eurostat

on an annual basis, with the main contributors again being the increase in private consumption and rising food and energy prices in the international market. In 2021, the budget deficit declined to 7.1% of GDP. As a result of expansionary monetary policy, the NBR balance sheet has substantially grown. While in 2019 total assets amounted to RON 194,556.1 mn, in 2020 it grew to 231,794. 0 mn and continued to rise in 2021. In February 2020 net foreign assets amounted to RON 203,671.7 mn that augmented to RON 231,314.8 mn in 2021 (NBR 2021, 2022).

Since the beginning of 2022, the NBR has continued to tighten monetary policy, raising the monetary policy rate by 0.50 percentage points, to 2.50%. Moreover, it decided to raise by 0.50 percentage points both the lending facility rate and the deposit facility rate, to 3.50% and 1.50% respectively, as well as to maintain firm control over money market liquidity. Furthermore, the NBR decided to keep the existing levels of minimum reserve requirement ratios on both leu- and foreign currency-denominated liabilities of credit institutions at 8% and 5% respectively.[13] In March 2022 the annual inflation reached 10.15%. This was mainly due to the increase in production costs, as a combined result of the energy crisis triggered in mid-2021 and the shock wave generated by the Russia-Ukraine war on the commodities markets. On 5 April 2022 the NBR decided to increase the monetary policy rate from 2.5% to 3% per year to counter the rising inflation (NBR 2022).

According to the European Commission (2022) Romania's economy is set to slow down to 2.6% in 2022 as high inflation erodes disposable income and Russia's war of aggression against Ukraine affects economic sentiment, supply chains and ultimately investment. Unemployment is projected to stay at 5.5% while price level growth will peak in 2022. The general government deficit is forecast to reach 7.5% of GDP before decreasing to 6.3% in 2023, bringing the debt-to-GDP ratio up to 52.6% by 2023.

The Serbian economy recorded a strong rebound in 2021. Real GDP growth reached 7.4%, mostly driven by private consumption, gross fixed capital formation and public consumption. The unemployment rate slightly increased in 2021. It is expected to decline in 2022 and 2023. The general government deficit and the debt-to-GDP ratio, after decreasing to 4.1% of GDP and 57.1% respectively in 2021, are expected to decrease in 2022 and 2023.

Banking sector stability has been preserved and further reinforced in 2021. At the same time, the central bank's balance sheet has grown due to the expansionary monetary policy. It expanded from RSD 1,789,983 mn in 2019 to RSD 1,935,018 mn in 2020 and to RSD 2,211,996 mn in 2021. The foreign assets rose from RSD 1,584,736 mn in 2019 to RSD 1,598,360 mn in 2020 and to RSD 1,947,103 mn in 2021. The net foreign assets were RSD 1,287,399 mn in 2019, and then increased to RSD 1,347,165 mn and RSD 1,744,488 mn in 2021.

Similar to Bulgaria and Romania, the European Commission's forecast (2022) reveals that the Serbian economy will grow more moderately by 3.4% in 2022 and by 3.8% in 2023. The inflation has accelerated since the second half of 2021. In March 2022 it rose to 9.1% and it is projected to peak in the middle of 2022. In May 2022, the NBS decided to increase the key policy rate by 0.5 pp to 2.0% due to the inflationary pressures in the global and domestic markets.

Table 12.3 Macroeconomic and financial indicators for Romania

Indicators	*2018*	*2019*	*2020*	*2021*	*2022*	*2023*
GDP growth %	4.5	4.1	−3.9	5.9	2.6	3.6
Private consumption growth, %	7.7	3.9	−5.1	7.9	2.9	3.5
Total deposits, annual change %	5.9	5.4	10.5			
Household deposit growth, annual change %	6.0	7.5	11.3			
Non-financial corporations deposit growth, annual change %	5.1	3.3	11.6			
FDI, % of GDP	3.0	2.9	1.4	3.7		
Gross fixed capital formation, % of GDP	−1.1	12.9	4.1	2.3	4.8	8.1
HICP, %	4.1	3.9	2.3	4.1	8.9	5.1
Unemployment rate, %	3.3	2.9	3.4	5.6	5.5	5.3
General government expenditure, total % GDP	34.9	36.3	42.0	39.9		
External debt, total, % of GDP	48.8	49.2	57.7			
Government debt, % of GDP	34.7	35.3	47.3	48.8	50.9	52.6
General government balance % GDP	−2.8	−4.3	−9.3	−7.1	−7.5	−6.3
Money supply (M3), % GDP	40.0	39.9	46.2			
Reserve money, lei million, December	100,349.8	108,249.3	132,624.8	143,265.2	Feb. 134,648.0	
Central bank balance sheet, lei million, December	190,252.5	194,556.1	231,794. 0	258,265.5	Feb. 262,029.5	
Monetary policy rate, % p.a	2.50	2.50	1.50	18/01/2021 −1.25%; 06/10/2021 −1.50%; 10/11/2021 −1.75%	11/01/2022 −2.00%; 10/02/2022 −2.50%; 06/04/2022 −3%; 07/07/2022 −4.75%; 08/08/2022 −5.50%	

(*Continued*)

Table 12.3 (Continued)

Indicators	*2018*	*2019*	*2020*	*2021*	*2022*	*2023*
Lending facility rate, % p.a	3.50	3.50	2.00	18/01/2021 –1.75%; 06/10/2021 –2.00%; 10/11/2021 –2.50%	11/01/2022 –3.00%; 10/02/2022 –3.50%; 06/04/2022 –4.00%; 07/07/2022 –5.75%; 08/08/2022 –6.50%	
Deposit facility rate, % p.a	1.50	1.50	1.00	18/01/2021 –0.75%; 06/10/2021 –1.00%; 10/11/2021 –1.00%	11/01/2022 –1.00%; 10/02/2022 –1.50%; 06/04/2022 –2.00%; 07/07/2022 –3.75%; 08/08/2022 –4.50%	
Due to domestic credit institutions and other financial institutions lei thousand	3,867,447	4,357,228	4,893,048			
Current account of the State Treasury lei thousand	37,424,485	2,301,090	40, 318,645			
International reserves, total million euro	36,800.2	37,450.4	42,517.6	45,830.7		
Loans to the private sector – total, annual change %	1.9	3.6	2.4			
Loans to households, total, annual change %	4.5	3.8	3.4			
Loans to non-financial corporations, total, annual change %	−1.3	3.1	0.9			
Current account, balance, % of GDP	−4.6	−4.9	−5.8	−7.0	−7.5	−6.3

Sources: National Bank of Romania, NBR Annual reports 2019, 2020, Eurostat, NBR Monthly bulletin December 2019, 2020, February 2022, European Commission Spring 2022 Economic Forecast

Table 12.4 Macroeconomic and financial indicators for Serbia

Indicators	*2018*	*2019*	*2020*	*2021*	*2022*	*2023*
GDP growth, %	4.5	4.3	−0.9	7.4	3.4	3.8
Private consumption growth, %	3.1	3.7	−1.9	7.6	3.6	3.8
Deposits, total, annual change %	8.77	8.80	8.54	8.76		
Household deposits, total, annual change %	9.2	8.9	8.9	8.8		
Deposits from non-financial corporations, total, annual change %	8.1	8.6	8.0	8.7		
Foreign direct investment, % of GDP	8.0	8.3	6.5			
Gross fixed capital formation, % of GDP	17.5	17.2	−1.9	12.5	4.4	4.8
CPI, %	2.0	1.7	1.6	4.0	8.5	4.6
Unemployment rate, %	13.7	11.2	9.7	11.0	10.0	9.3
General government expenditure total % GDP	40.9	42.3	49.4			
Government debt % of GDP	53.6	51.9	57.0	57.1	54.5	52.5
General government balance % GDP	0.6	0.2	−8.3	−4.1	−3.1	−1.8
Monthly average wage in euro	419.8	466.0	510.9	560.2		
M3, annual change %	14.5	8.4	18.1	11.8		
Total reserve money, in million RSD	776,599	810,724	1,009,731	1,074,875		
Central bank balance sheet, in million RSD	1,558,164	1,789,983	1,935,018	2,211,996		
Key policy rate, %	3.0	2.25	1.00	1.00	1.50 (April) 2.00 (May) 2.50 (June) 2.75 (July) 3.00 (August) 3.50 (September)	

(Continued)

Table 12.4 (Continued)

Indicators	*2018*	*2019*	*2020*	*2021*	*2022*	*2023*
Discount rate, %	3.00	2.25	1.00	1.00	1.50 (April) 2.00 (May) 2.50 (June) 2.75 (July) 3.00 (August) 3.50 (September)	
Deposit facilities interest rate	1.25	0.75	0.10	0.10	0.50 (April) 1.00 (May) 1.50 (June) 1.75 (July) 2.00 (August) 2.50 (September)	
Lending facilities interest rate	4.25	3.50	1.90	1.90	2.50 (April) 3.00 (May) 3.50 (June) 3.75 (July) 4.00 (August) 4.50 (September)	
Banks' reserves with the NBS, million RSD	549,295	566,902	705,596	731,690		
Government deposits, million RSD	237,890	361,455	365,857	471,652		
Foreign exchange reserves, in million RSD	1,331,088	1,573,213	1,586,352	1,934,756		
Loans to the private sector - total, annual change %	9.15	9.21	9.10	9.20		
Loans to households, total, annual change %	8.9	9.2	8.9	9.0		
Loans to non-financial corporations, total, annual change %	9.4	9.3	9.2	9.3		
Loans to financial organisations, total, annual change %	−11.4	8.5	9.3	−10.5		
Current account, balance, % of GDP	−4.8	−6.9	−4.1	−4.4	−6.5	−6.4

Source: National Bank of Serbia, NBS Statistical bulletin January 2022, Eurostat, Macroeconomic developments in Serbia May 2022, European Commission Spring 2022 Economic Forecast

Conclusion

Based on the reactions and measures of the monetary and fiscal authorities during the pandemic, we can draw the following conclusions:

First, the nature of the measures and the scale of the interventions by the governments and the central banks in the three Balkan countries depend mostly on the monetary regime in place and the constraints it imposes on monetary and fiscal policy. Our analysis confirms the limited capacity of Bulgaria's conservative currency board regime to respond to external shocks. Unlike Bulgaria, the two inflation-targeting countries have used both conventional and unconventional monetary policy tools to mitigate the negative effects and recover from the crisis.

Second, under currency board regime, the central bank cannot influence interest rates, cannot create liquidity through the purchase of securities, through quantitative easing, and cannot carry out open market operations. Therefore, the creation of a monetary base and the growth of the central bank's balance sheet is tied to the balance of payments. Unlike the currency board arrangement in inflation-targeting regimes, central banks acted as a lender of last resort for banks and the government and increased their balance sheets significantly during the pandemic. Furthermore, the NBS was also a lender of last resort to non-financial corporates, as local-currency denominated corporate bonds became eligible for open market operations and they could be used as collateral for banks to receive daily liquidity loans and short-term liquidity from the central bank.

Third, the constraints on fiscal policy under currency board have led to limited government intervention and have resulted in the smaller fiscal package in Bulgaria compared to those in Romania and Serbia. The limited fiscal space in Bulgaria is partly compensated by payments from EU funds and programmes. Despite the maintenance of a high fiscal reserve, which provides some opportunities for a government response, the fiscal policy has been restrictive and conservative in order to maintain the fixed exchange rate and the stability of the financial system.

Fourth, unlike in Romania and Serbia, where central banks used almost all conventional and unconventional monetary policy tools, in Bulgaria only supervisory and regulatory measures to the banking sector were implemented. In Bulgaria, these measures included a ban on the distribution of retained earnings from previous years to strengthen the capital base, restrictions on the level of concentration and quality of assets in which banks can invest their liquid assets, maintaining the level of the countercyclical capital buffer, and a private moratorium on bank loan payments. The regulatory measures applied in the three countries broadly follow those taken by the ECB and the European Banking Authority.

Fifth, although in all three Balkan countries the banking system was highly liquid and stable before the pandemic, national central banks entered into precautionary swap (Bulgaria) and repo lines (Romania and Serbia) with the ECB to further strengthen financial stability in the crisis. The main reason is that the BNB cannot act as a lender of last resort. In Romania and Serbia, central banks have further increased their capacity to act as lenders of last resort.

Sixth, banks in the three countries are predominantly foreign, which is a major reason for their high liquidity before and during the pandemic, as they have access to funding from their parent banks and therefore have access to the ECB instruments. As a result, there was no sharp contraction in credit to both households and firms during the pandemic.

Seventh, as regards to the effects of monetary and fiscal measures on growth, employment and inflation, it is noteworthy that the two countries with inflation targeting achieved a lower decline in GDP than Bulgaria in 2020. In 2021, the Romanian and Serbian economies have achieved a faster recovery, recording higher growth and lower inflation. However, Romania and Serbia have increased their budget deficits and public debt significantly during the COVID-19 crisis, while Bulgaria continues to be among the EU member states with the lowest deficit and government debt.

In the light of these findings, we can deduce that now inflation control has become a major challenge for central banks in the post-pandemic time in the context of increased consumption and rising global energy and food prices, supply problems as well as the Russia – Ukraine war. Since the beginning of 2022, the inflation has rapidly surged in the three Balkan countries mainly due to geopolitical tensions and the negative developments in the world economy, imported inflation.

Since the beginning of the year, inflation has been growing rapidly in the three countries under consideration, with the strongest growth in Bulgaria. In Bulgaria, for August the general inflation on an annual basis reached 17.7%, or a monthly rate of 1.2% (for July, 17.3% and a monthly rate of 1.1%), and for food it was even higher, or 24.1% for August and 23.8% for July. Housing and utilities also grew significantly, or 26.8% for August and 18.5% for July. In Romania the numbers were lower, the general inflation on an annual basis for August was 15.32% (monthly 0.56%) and 14.96% for July (monthly 0.89%), and for food it was 18.22% for August and 16.05% for July. In Serbia, the figures for general inflation on an annual basis were even lower, namely, 13.2% for August and 12.8% for July. For food, it was higher, or 20.4% for August and 19.7% for July.

While the BNB does not have the tools to react to soaring prices, the NBR and NBS have started tightening monetary conditions by raising key monetary policy rates as well as lending and deposit facilities interest rates. From the beginning of 2022, the central banks of Romania and Serbia raised 6 times the key interest rates, which reached 5.5% in Romania and 3.5% in Serbia, respectively. The corridors of the marginal lending and deposit facilities rates have a margin of 1% around the key rate.

The monetary authorities in Bulgaria have little choice, and interest rates in Bulgaria follow those of the ECB. For now, the exchange rates in Romania and Serbia are relatively stable, and in Bulgaria the exchange rate is fixed within the framework of the currency board. The inflationary challenge to monetary policies is very strong, both in Romania and Serbia it will require a significantly higher rise in interest rates than in the euro area, as well as efforts to maintain the level of the exchange rate, which could become a major factor in pass-through inflation. In Bulgaria, things are more unpleasant, and only regulatory measures remain at the disposal of the monetary authorities, and above all an increase in capital buffers – anti-cyclical, systemic and, under certain conditions, sectoral (greater provisioning for real estate loans). In any case, apart from inflation, it is clear that bank balance sheets will deteriorate, and this requires pre-emptive action by regulators.

It remains to be seen to what extent central banks will be able to fight inflation and ensure sustainable economic growth.

Notes

1 See Bighelli, Lalinsky & Vanhala 2022 and also Deb et al. 2021
2 Dependent monetary regimes in the Balkans are studied by Nenovsky & Magnin, 2022
3 https://www.bnr.ro/Inflation-Targets-3241-Mobile.aspx
4 National Bank of Serbia's Memorandum on Inflation Targets until 2023
5 See Nenovsky, Turcu & Tochkov 2013
6 For the impact of the pandemic on the export-import activities of the companies see Belu 2021
7 For economic trends and risks during the pandemic see Yotsov et al. 2022
8 https://www.ecb.europa.eu/press/pr/date/2020/html/ecb.pr200422~962a743486.en.html.
9 Leu-denominated government securities purchased by the NBR on the secondary market in 2020: RON 1,882.9 mn in April; RON 1,611.5 mn in May; RON 533.1 mn in June; RON 748.5 mn in July; RON 504.3 mn in August.
Leu-denominated government securities purchased by the NBR on the secondary market in 2021 and in the first quarter of 2022: RON 112.7 mn in March; RON 134.7 mn in April; RON 367.3 mn in March 2022 (NBR 2020, NBR 2022)
10 See Martin 2020
11 https://nbs.rs/en/drugi-nivo-navigacije/pres/covid19/
12 https://www.nbs.rs/en/drugi-nivo-navigacije/pres/covid19/
13 https://www.bnr.ro/Reserve-requirements-3658-Mobile.aspx

Bibliography

Belu, M 2021, COVID-19 pandemic impact on the exports and imports, *The Romanian Economic Journal*, Year XXIV no. 82

Brzoza-Brzezina, M, Kolasa, M & Makarski, K 2021, Monetary policy and COVID-19, IMF, WP/21/274

Bernanke, B, Carstens, A, Geithner, T, Shanmugaratnam, T & Shirakawa, M 2022, Economic policy lessons from Covid-19: The big picture, Occasional Paper No. 97, Group of Thirty Washington, D.C.

Bighelli, T, Lalinsky, T & Vanhala, J 2022, Covid-19 pandemic, state aid and firm productivity, Bank of Finland Research Discussion Papers 1/2022

Bulgarian National Bank, Annual report 2018, 2019, 2020, 2021

Bulgarian National bank, Macroeconomic forecast March 2022

Bulgarian National Bank, Economic review, April 2021

Bulgarian National Bank, Monetary, deposit and credit indicators, February 2022

Deb, P, Furceri, D, Ostry, J, Tawk, N & Yang, N 2021, The effects of fiscal measures during Covid-19, IMF, WP/21/262

Emmerling, J, Furceri, D, Monteiro, F, Loungani, P, Ostry, J, Pizzuto, P & Tavoni, M 2021, Will the economic impact of COVID-19 persist? Prognosis from 21st century pandemics, IMF, WP/21/119

English, B, Forbes, K & Ubide, Á 2021, Monetary policy and central banking in the Covid era, Centre for Economic Policy Research

European Commission, Spring economic forecast 2022

IMF World economic outlook, War sets back the global recovery, April 2022

IMF, Fiscal Monitor: Database of country fiscal measures in response to the COVID-19 pandemic, 2021

Marinova, T 2016, 'Comparative study on monetary and fiscal policy in the eurozone and Bulgaria', *Economic Alternatives Journal*, vol. 2016/3, pp. 367–78. (in Bulgarian)

Martin, V 2020, The response of the monetary and fiscal policies on COVID 19 in Serbia, *Bankartsvo, 2020*, vol. 49, Issue 2

National Bank of Serbia, Monthly bulletin, February 2021, 2022

National Bank of Serbia, Statistical bulletin January 2022

National Bank of Serbia, Macroeconomic developments in Serbia May 2022

National Bank of Serbia, Annual report 2019, 2020

National Bank of Serbia, Inflation Report May 2022 Year XVIII, No. 68

National Bank of Serbia's Memorandum on inflation targets until 2023

National Bank of Romania (NBR) 2022, Monthly bulletin, February 2022 Year XXX, No. 340

National Bank of Romania (NBR) 2021, Monthly bulletin December 2020 Year XXVIII, No. 326

Nenovsky, N, Turcu, K & Tochkov, K 2013, 'Monetary regimes, economic stability, and EU accession: Comparing Bulgaria and Romania', *Communist and Post-Communist Studies*, vol. *46*, no. 1, pp. 13–23.

Nenovsky, N & Magnin, E 2022, *Diversity of capitalism in Central and Eastern europe. Dependent economies and monetary regimes*, Palgrave Macmillan.

Nenovsky, N & Rizopoulos, Y 2003, 'Extreme monetary regime change: Evidence from currency board introduction in Bulgaria,', *Journal of Economic Issues*, vol. 37, no. 4, 2003, pp. 909–41.

Sahling, C, Nenovsky, N & Chobanov, P 2021, 'Diversity of monetary regimes And reactions to the pandemic crisis: Bulgaria, Romania, And Serbia Compared', in Pantelis K. (ed.), *Bridging microeconomics and macroeconomics and the effects on economic development and growth*, IGI Global, pp. 276–96.

Yotsov, V, Minasyan, G, Lukanova, P, Zlatinov, D & Sariyski, G 2022, 'Bulgaria's economy during the pandemic', *Economic Thought Journal*, vol. 67, no. 2, pp. 121–149(in Bulgarian).

13 The PBOC in the Post-Covid World: Multitasking, Perseverance and Self-Discipline

Orhan Yazar

Introduction

China has been going through a political transformation since the 18th Party Congress in late 2012. This transformation has generated significant consequences for China's governance and international relations. COVID-19 outbreak in 2020 and China's effective measures to contain the virus before any other country around the world strengthened the actors behind this political transformation despite visibly less impressive economic outcomes and increasing diplomatic frictions. This environment has affected Chinese bureaucracy and how it operates as well. This paper intends to offer an analysis of the workings of the Chinese bureaucracy in the post-Covid world by focusing on one of the stronger bureaucratic agents in China, the PBOC (People's Bank of China), and its behavior in various policy areas.

The paper first introduces the changing policy-making environment and the role of the bureaucracy after the 18th Party Congress. Secondly, the shape of the Chinese economy is discussed in the aftermath of the initial COVID-19 outbreak. Third, policy actions of the PBOC in the post-COVID world are investigated in a range of issues from green finance to economic inequality. Lastly, the constraints that the PBOC is working within presented followed by the conclusion.

The Role of the Chinese Bureaucracy after the 18th Party Congress

China had suffered quite dearly during the Mao years as a result of disastrous policy decisions that were made predominantly by a small group of individuals and in some cases by a single individual. The leaders of the post-Mao China adopted 'collective leadership' and 'decision-making through deliberation' principles in order to avoid similar policy mistakes. However, in the early 2010s party leaders believed the pendulum swung too much and fragmentation of the bureaucratic authority and constant negotiations between various levels of government and agencies generated a less effective state apparatus. Hence, starting with the 18th Party Congress, we have witnessed a reversal of deliberative policy-making and re-centralization of decision-making power (Düben, 2018). The expansion of 'leading small groups'

DOI: 10.4324/9781003323280-14

in recent years (see Johnson and Kennedy, 2017) is a sign of such rebalancing act by the Party and the desire of the leadership to assert a more hands-on approach in matters ranging from finance to environment.

The restitution of authority by the party leadership was not limited to adding more guiding layers of governance for bureaucracy but also included greater ideological training, demands to follow the party line without questioning and mechanisms to punish those who failed to comply. One of the most potent tools of such disciplining efforts was China's Central Discipline and Inspection Commission which has been overly active since the 18th Party Congress. The organizational, ideological, and disciplinary constraints on the bureaucracy diminished independent policy-making capacity and space for adjustments when policy guidelines contradicted with the conditions on the ground.

This situation has been exacerbated by the party leadership's ideological hardening and departure from pragmatism in economic policy-making. On one hand increased economic inequalities during China's rapid growth years and growing might of the private entrepreneurs at times challenging the officialdom generated a desire to pushback against the laissez-faire market capitalism internally. On the other hand, Western governments' policy flip-flops on issues ranging from the 2008 Global Financial Crisis to COVID-19 pandemic gave credence to the 'demise of the West and the rise of the East' narrative which made policy recipes with foreign origins less likely to be adopted. In this environment, policy-makers adopted a set of policies that were less market-friendly and advocated greater regulatory oversight in areas where they have seen excesses. Even when the adopted policy measures resulted in negative economic outcomes, the policy reversals were rare. The resurgence of the centralism in the country's governance was generating escalation commitment and pragmatism that has helped the country navigate its economic development for so long has become a less sought-after principle.

Moreover, geopolitical and geo-economic tensions intensified competition between China and the West and accelerated China's efforts to establish alternative institutions to assert itself in the international economic and political order in line with its 'great rejuvenation' objective. China's desire to be assertive and to relentlessly defend its national interest manifested itself in the form of a hardened discourse towards other international actors which have been popularly characterized as 'Wolf Warrior' diplomacy. The bureaucracies had to consider the national security implications of their decisions more carefully and seek ways to support government's initiatives that will give an edge to the country in the new competitive environment.

Overall, after the 18th Party Congress, China's bureaucrats were operating under the greater direct supervision of the Party's top leadership with less flexible policy directions in a tense international political environment with a greater risk of being purged in the case of non-compliance with Party leadership's directives or failure to reach goals set by the Party. It is important to keep in mind this context as we try to understand the role of the PBOC in the post-COVID world.

The Chinese Economy in the Post-Covid World

After the 18th Party Congress, the new Chinese leadership adopted a more balanced economic growth approach that aimed for slower but higher quality growth. This 'new normal' was aimed at mending some of the negative externalities generated by the earlier fast-growth model in the form of high levels of debt, environmental pollution, and social inequality. This broad framework guided economic policies deployed by the state at various levels. Sectors and local governments with high leverage were encouraged to deleverage while the regulators and central bank were called to limit the credit channeled to these risky actors. One of these sectors was the real estate sector which accounts for almost one third of the country's economy. Real estate is the main store of wealth for many ordinary citizens through home ownership and generates much-needed revenue for local governments through land sales.

Before the pandemic, the Chinese leadership also viewed the real estate market as an imbalanced marketplace rife with social injustice and a cause for political dissent among citizens due to unequal access. The speculative price movements causing housing prices in major cities to soar and making it almost impossible for the young working classes to own a house which is a requirement to start their own families according to unwritten social rules of the country, was an issue that Chinese government could no longer ignore. However, the timing to reign in the real estate market came at a very precarious moment in the summer of 2020 as the market was recovering from the slump generated by country-wide COVID-19 restrictions. The 'three red lines' of the government restricted further debt acquisition of real estate companies if they were unable to meet financial thresholds regarding their asset to liability, net gearing, and cash to short-term debt ratios (UBS, 2021). Illustrating the restrictiveness of the measures adopted, only 6.3% of the real estate developers rated by the rating agency S&P, was expected to meet the criteria set by the government and continue to acquire debt (S&P Global, 2020). Moreover, the talk of pilot property tax legislation in some provinces dulled property sales further and made the situation worse, precipitating a slowdown in sales and new projects.

Another headwind for the Chinese economy in the post-covid era is the country's adherence to its zero-Covid policy which was successful at preventing large-scale transmission of the virus across the country in early 2020. However, while the rest of the world seems to have moved towards living with the virus towards the end of 2021, Chinese leadership reiterated its commitment to the preventative measures that it deems necessary to prevent fatalities due to human and equipment deficits in its healthcare system and vulnerability of the country's vast elderly population. Hence, despite adopting various iterations of the policy after the initial wave of the pandemic had passed, the Chinese leadership's zero-Covid approach with strict lockdowns remained in place. As the transmissibility and stealth of the virus increased with the new variants, China has experienced more sporadic and frequent flares of cases and local authorities had to implement longer lockdown periods to bring the case numbers down to zero. The results of these Covid related restrictions were crippling impediments to the mobility of people and goods, struggling small and medium enterprises, depressed economic activity, poorer households and weakened local government budgets. Overall, the zero-Covid policy is expected to cause the country to fall behind its 5.5% growth target in 2022 when such undershooting will be politically very costly due to the very much anticipated 20th Party Congress in October 2022.

In the external environment, China faced greater challenges as international economic circumstances turned from favorable to unfavorable rapidly. China's quick recovery from the first wave of the pandemic as many parts of the world continued to struggle with production and supply chain disruptions helped the country achieve high levels of positive trade balance initially. However, with the adverse impact of domestic lockdowns and recovery of production capacities in other economies, the export growth slowed down. Moreover, Russian invasion of Ukraine in early 2022 hit global economic growth prospects and caused increases in already high energy and commodity prices hurting Chinese exports and competitiveness further. The soaring inflation in the US and ensuing rate hike in May 2022 diminished the attractiveness of Chinese capital markets and weakened China's currency. The international investors, who were already spooked by possible secondary sanctions on China by the West due to China's strategically ambivalent stance in the Russia–Ukraine conflict, have become much more bullish and some capital left the country.

The PBOC is quite adept when it comes to dealing with internal and external economic challenges, however the level of complexity it faces today, due to the domestic political picture depicted earlier and the unchartered global risk environment, is greater than ever.

The PBOC in the Post-Covid World

The PBOC has responded to the first wave of pandemic in early 2020 with relatively measured response by offering liquidity and monetary easing, when necessary, in order to avoid 2008 style credit expansion binge. The swift control of the pandemic in the country with ample monetary support allowed the Chinese economy to experience a strong 'V'-shaped recovery. This allowed Chinese central bank to focus on other policy tasks that were set by the new leadership in China. Unlike many other central banks around the world which have very limited mandates, the effectiveness and influence of the PBOC in guiding the financial system made it a target for top policy makers who wanted every institution to be behind their economic policy agenda. This agenda included stricter regulation of the internet economy, financial support for small and medium enterprises (SMEs), deleveraging of private sector, greater income equality, price stability in the real estate market and support for development of green economy.

Regulation of the 'Internet Economy'

The economic vision of the new leadership sought better regulation of the 'internet economy' and the expansion of the digital finance in the country. The scandals and public protests around failed digital financing platforms prompted swift action from the PBOC from 2015 onwards. The target for PBOC was two-fold in these efforts; first to prevent expansion of shadow banking loans through these platforms, second to prevent possible social unrest caused by masses who lost their life savings with vanishing internet finance platforms. In late 2020, the nature of the PBOC's regulatory efforts took a different turn, when one of the richest entrepreneurs behind China's biggest financial platform Ant Financial Group, made remarks about how the regulators were stifling innovation in finance (McMorrow and Yu, 2021). The Party leadership was not happy about the brazen criticism of the state regulators by a businessman and demanded swift action.

The digital divide between the public sector and the private tech companies in China which have been early investors in the digital payments systems and online financial products, tilted the balance of power in fin-tech towards private companies. The first mover advantage in this field allowed the private companies to amass users and user data ensuring their supremacy and attracted the envy of public agencies. PBOC used this opportunity to force these companies to share their data with public agencies and support the efforts of the PBOC in issuing its own digital currency, e-CNY. After launching the e-CNY or the digital renminbi (*shuzi renminbi)* in several Chinese cities as a part of a pilot program in April 2021, the PBOC showcased the digital currency at the 2022 Beijing Olympics signaling the global ambitions for the digital yuan. However, the e-CNY is still not used countrywide or nor available overseas and nowhere close to the popularity of major online payment systems like Alipay and WeChat Pay (Laskai, 2022). It is quite a challenge for the PBOC to convince the users and business owners to switch to e-CNY as current payment systems serve the market quite well. Hence, the PBOC has to resort to arm-twisting of major Chinese internet companies like Alibaba, Tencent, Meituan and JD for the adoption of e-CNY through their platforms.

The e-CNY serves the PBOC and the state as a tool for tracking transactions and financial control as well. While the e-CNY offers an option to users to hide their identities from vendors which will restrict the access of internet platform giants hosting these vendors like Alibaba to user data, ultimately users can be traced by the authorities (Deutsche Bank, 2021). In the long run, the PBOC can weaken the data supremacy of the internet giants and their fintech arms and strengthen its capacity to oversee financial transactions. This is in line with the PBOC's earlier efforts to control capital movements by limiting alternative ways to store, manage and move wealth for individuals. An illustration of such behaviour was the PBOC's ban of all cryptocurrency transactions in September 2021 which had global implications (BBC News, 2021). The PBOC was worried that the virtual currencies were becoming tools for evading China's capital controls and offering an option to store wealth beyond the PBOC's supervision. Along with the ban of cyrptocurrencies, the regulatory crackdown on internet finance companies and offering state-sanctioned alternatives like e-CNY meant that the state authority remained supreme in finance along with the vision of the new Party leadership.

Financing SMEs

PBOC has to walk a fine line when regulating fintech as it is seen as a solution to chronic funding problems of SMEs in China. 140 million Chinese SMEs generate 85% of employment in the country making them extremely important for the central government, which sees unemployment rate as a key factor for political stability (Liu, 2022). SMEs are also seen as the future growth engines of China's high-tech development by the central government. Replicating the success of the German SME model, the Chinese government wants to generate 'little giants' among its SMEs to reinvigorate its industry. Despite the rapid development of internet economy and related services in the country, the leadership in China keenly emphasizes the centrality of the 'real' economy. Hence, supporting SMEs to make them more innovative and competitive in high-end manufacturing is an important goal which has also been ingrained into the 14th Five Year (2021–2025) Plan of the country (Shijia, 2021).

However, banks in China tend to ignore SME credit demands as they are riskier borrowers and less politically connected than state-owned enterprises or large corporations. During the COVID lockdowns, these businesses feel the brunt of city-wide closures and ensuing lackluster of consumer demand. Being aware of the vitality of the SMEs, PBOC provided 1.8 trillion RMB (257 billion USD) worth of preferential loans to the financial system after the initial COVID wave in China to ease their pain in early 2020. However, illustrative of the banking system's hesitancy on lending to SMEs, only 19% of the available funds were used by SMEs at the end of the first quarter of 2020. It seems that bank managers who are accountable for non-performing-loan ratios, were reluctant to lend funds to struggling SMEs.

As China continues to implement its zero-COVID strategy facing highly transmissible, harder to contain variants of the virus; strict lockdowns or highly restrictive COVID protocols became China's new normal in many cities across the country in 2022. On one hand, the Chinese leadership wants to keep the zero-COVID approach for political and healthcare reasons, on the other hand it wants SMEs to flourish and be the driver of China's economic growth. These contradicting policy objectives of the country's leadership once again pushes the PBOC to go beyond its traditional mandate of price stability and step in to help struggling SMEs. Recently, the PBOC announced an additional 1 trillion RMB (157 billion USD) worth of funding to support businesses (Bloomberg.com, 2022). How much of these funds will be used by the SMEs remains to be seen given the current shape of the overall economy and the low-risk appetite of banks. However, this time, an important political meeting in late 2022 is approaching and stability is at the top of Chinese leadership's agenda. The upcoming 20th Party Congress of the CCP is expected to extend the tenure of the current leadership for at least another five years diverging from the post-Mao era political norms limiting the terms of each party leadership to two consecutive five-year terms. This critical moment in Chinese politics necessitates every organ of the state to present a stellar performance in their respective fields in the run up to the meeting to dispel any doubts about the competence of the current leadership. Hence, the PBOC and other regulators will need to prioritize economic recovery. The Chinese banking regulator already issued a statement 'encouraging' large banks 'to reduce the provision coverage ratio' signaling willingness to accept higher NPLs in the banking sector which will be a reversal of a long stated central government policy objective of deleveraging.

Preventing Excessive Lending and Debt

Since the 2008 GFC, Chinese leaders are wary of excessive lending and debt crises. They are not only worried about the adverse social impacts of a collapsing financial system, but also the lingering effects of high debt levels on the country's sustained economic growth. Hence, when the new leadership in China took power in late 2012, they intended to make deleveraging a priority economic policy. However, reducing debt is not an easy task when economic growth is a crucial political legitimacy objective and heavily relies on accumulation of new debt. Consequently, the PBOC had to follow an 'orderly' deleveraging path which had limited impact on the expansion of corporate and household debt. The PBOC should be credited with better regulation of debt formation though along with other regulatory agencies especially with their efforts to curb 'shadow banking' and 'shadow lending'.

Limited success in managing debt was washed away with initial wave of the pandemic and recovery efforts, generating a surge in corporate debt levels. In the summer of 2020, when China thought it was out of the woods regarding the COVID pandemic, a new push for deleveraging started targeting one of the most notorious debt accumulators in the economy, the real estate sector. Heating up in the real estate sector was targeted as possible burst of asset bubbles were considered 'gray rhinos' for the economy and the new leadership deemed 'houses are for living not speculation', targeting multiple house purchases by households in urban areas. In reaction to these demands, the PBOC sat with 12 major real estate developers and handed them the 'three red lines' policy which would determine the amount of new debt they can acquire according to their financial health measured by how they fare against these 'three red lines'. According to the stipulations, the real estate developers would not exceed a liability-to-asset ratio of 70%, have a net gearing ratio of less than 100%, and a cash to short-term borrowing ratio of at least 1 (Jing, 2022).

Later that year in December 2020, the PBOC targeted bank loans to property companies and home buyers by capping their ratio to the bank's total loans. This had no impact on the growth of new home sales or property investment, both of which increased significantly in the first months of 2021. However, the real estate market plummeted in the rest of the year along with the confidence in the sector and ability of its major players to service their existing debts. When one of the biggest names in China's property sector, Evergrande, missed payments on its offshore bond payments, market sentiment in the real estate market has turned sour and a 'systemic' impact on the economy was unleashed. The real estate sector in China roughly generates one third of the country's GDP growth, employs millions of people through connected industries and is the main investment vehicle for ordinary citizens. Failing property companies and depressed housing prices were in no ones' interest, hence PBOC tried to reassure the market that liquidity issues were limited to a few property developers and this was not China's 'Lehman' moment as some suggested in the media.

PBOC had to walk on a tight rope on this matter, as it did not want a total collapse in the real estate sector nor generate moral hazard by bailing out the troubled companies. However indirect support was offered through various government agencies and arrangements, as the PBOC cut the reserve-requirement-ratio allowing 1.2 trillion RMB (188 billion USD) to flow to the financial system in December 2021. Despite these attempts, the property sector weakness and problems of property developers continue to haunt the Chinese economy as zero-COVID strategy continues to depress the demand in the country. As a major reversal of deleveraging efforts in the real estate sector, the PBOC dropped the five-year loan prime rate, which is the benchmark for mortgage rates, by fifteen basis points in May 2022. Many local governments announced policies to support the real estate sector in their cities in the same month.

Overall, the demand for deleveraging from the Chinese leadership pushed the property sector to the brink of collapse. The 'three red lines' were too restrictive and sudden stop in the flow of funds to the sector precipitated a crisis with economy-wide implications. PBOC once again had to rebalance the economy in the debt-growth dichotomy of the country. This episode of policy-making by orders and mantras of the new leadership illustrates how the PBOC's institutional capacity is eroding as it tries to respond to policy demands from the 'center', instead of relying on more pragmatic and flexible way of collective decision-making.

Global Challenges

Despite the cut in the five-year loan rate, the PBOC's policy steps to stabilize the faltering Chinese economy through further monetary easing are also constrained by the global environment. The US central bank started reversing its loose monetary stance to tame its decades-high inflation at the beginning of May 2022, generating headaches for many emerging market economy central bankers including the PBOC. China's ability to get out of the first wave of pandemic earlier while other major economies endured long COVID battles gave the Chinese financial markets an edge and the attractive rates in China allowed capital flows to the country. While the economic slowdown in China due to lockdowns and mismanagement of corporate debt in the real estate sector necessitates the PBOC to take stronger monetary easing action, the PBOC is reluctant to decrease shorter term rates as such action will generate capital outflows and weaken the already sliding renminbi further.

Capital outflows coupled with disgruntled foreign direct investors considering alternative locations in Asia due to China's strict lockdowns may hurt the Chinese economy. The weakening of renminbi will decrease the real value of the incomes of Chinese households who have already reduced their consumption due to lockdowns. This might be in contradiction with the objectives of the 'dual circulation strategy' set by the current leadership to establish an economic development pattern that will be sustainable even global environment becomes less predictable for or hostile to Chinese economic interests. This strategy puts greater emphasis on domestic consumption, development of innovative capacities for technological self-sufficiency and securing key supply chains while maintaining country's strong international economic presence (CSIS, 2021). If China wants to transform its economy that relies not only on exports but also on domestic consumption as the 'dual circulation' strategy proposes, the PBOC cannot allow the renminbi to depreciate too much too fast. The pressure to keep the renminbi stable is exacerbated by the high commodity prices around the world due to the impact of war in Ukraine which makes monetary policy execution more challenging for the PBOC.

Supporting Green Economy

Another area where the influence of the new leadership can be observed over the PBOC policy-making is the 'green economy'. For long, Chinese economic development disregarded the environmental impact of rapid industrialization. Pollution of air, water and land were acceptable externalities as the country was lifting millions out of poverty. However, as the middle classes in China has grown, they demanded smog-free clean air in major cities and a more sensitive government to environmental issues. When the new leadership came to power in late 2012, the desire to protect the environment was cited as one of the objectives of lower, more sustainable economic growth targets. Effectively, the new leadership was responding to the demands of the middle classes to preserve its political legitimacy. The government also saw green technologies and clean energy generation as an alternative source of economic growth that will generate jobs for the masses. Moreover, as the US formally withdrew from the Paris Climate Accord in late 2020, the Chinese government stepped in for the leadership of global climate change politics by making a pledge to become carbon neutral by 2060 in September 2020. Hence, there is a lot at stake for the Chinese leadership and it wants to divert more resources to environmentally friendly industries and decrease the country's carbon footprint with both political and economic motivations. The policy guidance within the Chinese bureaucracy regarding environmental objectives is so stringent and strict that some cities had to ration electricity use (Hoskins, 2021) to comply with energy intensity rules in late 2021.

The PBOC has been at the forefront of green finance initiatives and its actions are commended internationally. According to UK-based advocacy group PositiveMoney's 2021 green central banking scorecard evaluating the support of G20 central banks for environmental protection, the PBOC outperforms its peers in green finance (Barmes and Livingstone, 2021). This result is understandable as the PBOC has been giving growing attention to 'green' economy and development of 'green' finance with its 'Guidelines for Establishing Green Financial System' since 2016. With various schemes subsidized 'green' loans and bonds have been offered increasingly by the PBOC to support investment in renewable energy and conservation projects as Figure 13.1 illustrates. The Achille's heel for China's green energy efforts however has been the heavy use of coal which accounts for 56% of country's energy consumption. This heavy reliance on coal in China's energy mix also made the PBOC more conservative regarding elimination of financing for coal and PBOC supported clean coal initiatives with its green bonds. Recently, this discrepancy between Chinese green bonds and international standards regarding financing of coal projects was addressed by the 2021 Green Bond Catalogue which took coal projects outside the scope of green bonds (Lin and Hong, 2022).

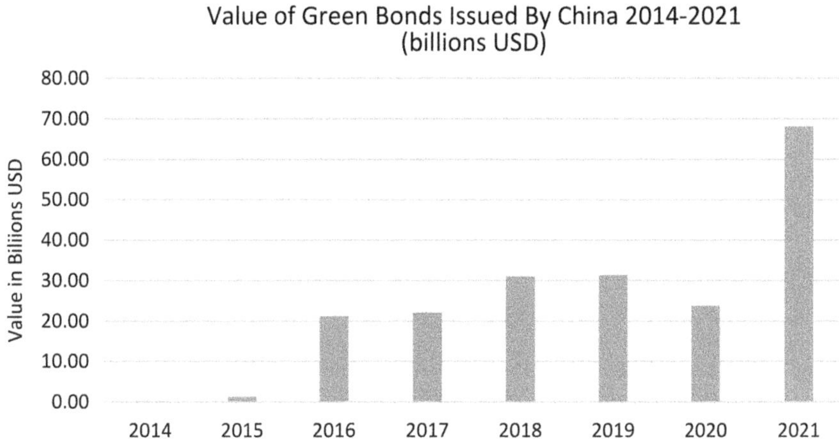

Figure 13.1 Value of green bonds issued in China from 2014 to 2021

Source: Climate Bonds Initiative (via Statista)

PBOC's approach to coal is an extension of government's position regarding the use of coal. Until late 2021, the government was quite adamant on stomping on coal use. Episodes of energy crunches at the end of 2021 and trade tensions between Australia and China hurting coal imports to the country prompted a renewed interest in coal and the government directed banks to support the domestic coal industry. The new leadership understood that pushing clean energy initiatives too much could hurt the economic growth and pulled back. Moreover, the war in Ukraine, pushed the energy prices to record highs at the end of the first quarter of 2022. Seeking energy security and a hedge against inflationary pressures, the PBOC offered 100 billion RMB (15 billion USD) credit line for the domestic coal industry in early May 2022 (Global Times, 2022). The approach of the central bank and the new leadership towards environmental protection and especially the use of coal illustrates that they are very much coordinated and the PBOC takes cues from the new leadership regarding their policies.

Addressing Economic Inequalities through 'Common Prosperity'

As the Chinese leadership aims to build political legitimacy with delivery of blue skies, they are also under pressure to address economic inequalities in society for the same purpose. The rapid development of the country allowed some of its citizens especially in urban areas to prosper while vast numbers of people are still struggling economically and fell behind in their access to quality social services in education, health, and housing. The new leadership reintroduced the term 'common prosperity' from the Party's ideological discussions spanning over several decades to emphasize its resolve to diminish the huge wealth gap between its citizens and improve the quality of life for the masses. This emphasis is important for the Party's consistent messaging regarding the nature of the country's economic system which claims to unite socialist principles of an egalitarian society and market principles of a vibrant competitive private economy. After officially reaching its centennial goal of making China a moderately prosperous society in the summer of 2021, the next step for the Party leadership was sharing wealth through 'common prosperity'. The regulation in tech, education and calls for greater contributions from the wealthy businesses to society illustrated the new approach of the government. The new leadership reiterated its commitment to the market economy by denying 'return to the old path of the planned economy', while the new set of policies showed its distrust against how markets operate and desire to 'address blindness of the markets'.

The PBOC also took action to comply with the Party's 'common prosperity' by using its 'inclusive finance' initiatives. These initiatives aimed at allowing a greater flow of financial resources to micro and small businesses, revitalization projects in rural areas and support for social risk groups. As an extension of its inclusive finance initiative the PBOC wants to educate public about finance and achieve higher financial literacy (Liu, 2021). The PBOC's approach to common prosperity also emphasizes macroeconomic policy elements like balanced growth, prudent monetary policy, and stability of the exchange rate. With an analogy from farming, this approach advocates 'drip' irrigation emphasizing targeted financial support rather than 'flood' irrigation which depicts earlier credit expansion initiatives. Beyond extending existing policies to address inequality, the PBOC also set more concrete inequality elimination targets. At the end of 2021, the PBOC announced its desire to decrease the country's Gini coefficient from 0.47 (see Figure 13.2 below) to 0.4 by 2025 and to 0.35 by 2035 (Hancock, 2021).

Figure 13.2 China's Gini index: 2004 to 2020

Source: National Bureau of Statistics of China (via Statista)

Despite these pledges and policy announcements PBOC's role in the common prosperity drive is mostly shaped by the central government's priorities. As the war in Ukraine and COVID lockdowns decreased prospects of China reaching its annual growth targets, the central government softened its messaging regarding monopolies in the tech sector. In early May 2022, the PBOC announced 'normalized' regulation of financial arms of platform economies (Caixin Global, 2022) like Alibaba, signaling that regulatory crackdown in the name of common prosperity was put on hold for the time being.

RMB Internationalization in the Post-Covid Era

China has systematically worked towards making its currency, *renminbi*, an international reserve currency since the 2008 Global Financial Crisis. The efforts of the PBOC in this arena have been supported by other key government agencies, ministries and commissions guided by current leadership's desire to eliminate China's vulnerabilities in a US dollar-denominated international trade and finance order. The global economic and political environment in the post-Covid era served well for China's ambitions to internationalize RMB (see Figure 13.3). On one hand, China's strong trade presence during and after COVID increased the use of RMB in trade settlements, especially with China's trading partners in the developing world and ASEAN (Association of Southeast Asian Nations). On the other hand, the much deeper involvement of China in global affairs, growing tensions between the US and China on multiple fronts, and the war between Ukraine and Russia generated a moment of historical inflection that encouraged many governments around the world especially in the developing world to hedge against further erosion of the US-centric world order by establishing closer ties with China through commercial agreements that increasingly involved currency swap deals.

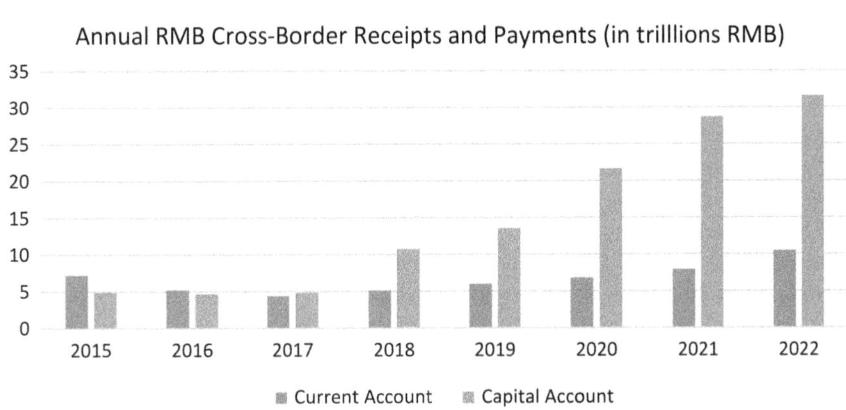

Figure 13.3 Annual RMB cross-border receipts and payments 2015–2022

Source: PBOC (2022).

The war between Russia and Ukraine and ensuing sanctions brought by Western governments preventing Russian banks from using established financial transaction ecosystems like SWIFT (Society for Worldwide Interbank Financial Transactions) accelerated China's efforts to establish a parallel financial transaction system that will allow capital flows without impediments in case similar sanctions are imposed on China in the future. However, China's alternative payments system Cross-Border Interbank Payments System (CIPS) established in late 2015 is well behind SWIFT both in the number of financial institutions participating in the system and the volume of transactions, despite recent strong growth (Eichengreen, 2022). PBOC continues to give great importance to and invest in the CIPS by improving its infrastructure and diminishing its current reliance on SWIFT messaging system as the launch of the second generation RMB Cross-border Payment Management Information System (RCPMIS) indicates (PBOC, 2022). For China, the success of CIPS is a matter of national security and an extension of its dual-circulation strategy.

China understands that the road ahead to internationalize RMB as a rival to US dollar is a long and steep one. Regardless, efforts are being made at different levels of China's financial bureaucracy, including PBOC, to reach this objective. Wins, here or there, like the IMF's decision to increase the weight of Chinese RMB from 10.92% to 12.28% (Anon, 2022) strengthens the resolve of the Chinese state in this area. However, incomplete capital account liberalization and currency convertibility remain to be the Achille's heel for RMB internationalization. As these two policy areas are closely linked to the role of the state in the economy and to the preferred economic development model that emphasizes guidance of state, change is incremental and attritional. Although policy-makers and central bankers in various countries are willing to diversify their foreign reserves with the use of RMB despite shortcomings of China's financial openness, for market actors driven by profit and with access to hassle-free lucrative alternatives investing in RMB is still risky, exotic and half-rewarding (Yeung, 2021).

From Financial Discipline to Disciplining the PBOC

The PBOC rose to become a competent economic bureaucratic agent in the Chinese political system. Despite the wild swings of inflation in the early years of economic reform, the PBOC's emphasis on prudent financial policies has allowed China to experience relatively stable prices starting from the second half of the 1990s. The power of the PBOC has increased under steady and strong leadership of Zhou Xiaochuan who was the central banker of China between 2002 and 2018. After the GFC, the PBOC became the systemic risk monitor for the whole financial system, regaining some of its regulatory and supervisory powers lost to various financial oversight agencies established in the early 2000s. In the Chinese bureaucratic organization, PBOC is one of the handful government agencies that have a seat in China's State-Council. The PBOC also has a representative in the Office of the Central Leading Group Financial and Economic Affairs, which guides country's economic and financial policies under the leadership of trusted top economic adviser Liu He.

Despite their competency and rank, the PBOC members are bound by following the new leadership. Unlike their counterparts in other countries, central bankers in China cannot execute policy independent of political considerations. This lack of independence has become more pronounced as like many other bureaucratic agencies, the new leadership demanded absolute adherence to policy choices of the Party's 'core'. This has generated an atmosphere where the PBOC had to watch very closely the guidance by the central government and make adjustments as demanded. The policy issues we have seen so far illustrated this approach of guided central banking.

One of the most potent tools of making sure vast cadres across the country follow the party core is fear of purge. A leadership change in China has always precipitated anti-corruption campaigns to get rid of opposition strongholds or uncooperative factions. However, since the 18th Party Congress, anti-corruption campaigns have become sustained, periodical, extensive and systemic. Millions have been investigated while close to 1% of CCP member were expelled from the Party as a result of the new leadership's anti-corruption drive to date (Anstey, 2022). This new feature of Chinese political system ensures party cadres and bureaucrats administer self-control not only in matters requiring them to uphold public interest but also in their ideological acts and deliberations. This panopticon of constant surveillance administered by the Central Discipline and Inspection Commission (CDIC) allows the new leadership to discipline all participants in the state apparatus regardless of their heft. The PBOC, which is believed to be a competent and devout bureaucratic agency, has also been the target of CDIC recently among other major financial regulatory agencies. As a result of CDIC's investigations, the PBOC was accused of paying lip service to the new leadership's goals and one of the key figures in the Bank, the head of the monetary-policy department was removed from his position at the beginning of May 2022 (Reuters, 2022). The repercussions of these investigations can be long-lasting on the policy-making capacity of the central bank as central bank bureaucrats now need to pay even more attention to the demands of the central government.

Conclusion

Since the 18th Party Congress, Chinese governance is moving away from collective leadership and pragmatism is less of a concern in economic management. The recentralization efforts are affecting the way economic policy is made and bureaucrats are losing room for maneuvering. The PBOC, one of top economic bureaucracies in the country, is not immune to this new economic governance model. Especially, after the pass of the baton to a new central banker in 2018, the PBOC is feeling greater pressure to follow the party line in economic thinking.

The new leadership also 'summoned' economic development on their own terms. While addressing issues like environmental pollution, income inequality and overreliance on debt for growth has been a critical policy objective for the new leadership, the way and speed these can be achieved have been debated little. Hence the objectives are set but the strategy is not clear. In this policy environment, the PBOC as a competent bureaucratic actor, is expected to assist the central government with multiple objectives ranging from supporting green economy to decreasing inequality in addition to its traditional price stability mandate. Beyond expansion of duties, the real consequence for the PBOC will be the erosion of credibility with policy failures and reversals in these policy areas. As continuity of current leadership is anticipated for at least another five years, the PBOC will be expected to fulfill multiple objectives both domestic and international to transform China's existing economic development model and eliminate its global vulnerabilities. The acceleration of rising tensions with the West and increasing fragility of domestic economic conditions may complicate PBOC's agenda and its prudent approach.

From a global perspective, the experience of the PBOC mirrors the debates about the more involvement of elected governments in economic governance around the world when delegation and independent authorities are viewed as causes of failure rather than mechanisms enabling smooth operation of economic institutions. The reflection of this hands-on approach in the central banking space is the erosion of central bank authority and independence which is more pronounced in the emerging market economies where economic institutions were set up to comply, in most cases with the IMF and World Bank conditionalities, rather than being a result of domestic policy deliberation. The performance of the PBOC as a guided central bank may embolden or generate hesitation for future emerging market governments regarding their level of involvement in central banking.

References

Anon, 2022. IMF Executive Board Concludes Quinquennial SDR Valuation Review and Determines New Currency Weights for SDR Valuation Basket. *IMF.* [online] 14 May. Available at: https://www.imf.org/en/News/Articles/2022/05/14/pr22153-imf-board-concludes-sdr-valuation-review [Accessed 20 October 2022].

Anstey, C., 2022. China's Government Disciplinarians Target 'Disorderly' Capitalism. *Bloomberg News.* [online] Available at: https://www.bloomberg.com/news/newsletters/2022-01-29/china-s-disciplinarians-target-disorderly-capitalism-new-economy-saturday#xj4y7vzkg [Accessed 14 June 2022].

Barmes, D. and Livingstone, Z., 2021. The Green Central Banking Scorecard: How Green Are G20 Central Banks and Financial Supervisors? *Positive Money.* [online] Available at: http://positivemoney.org/wp-content/uploads/2021/03/Positive-Money-Green-Central-Banking-Scorecard-Report-31-Mar-2021-Single-Pages.pdf [Accessed 14 June 2022].

BBC News. 2021. *China Declares All Crypto-currency Transactions Illegal.* [online] Available at: https://www.bbc.com/news/technology-58678907 [Accessed 14 June 2022].

Bloomberg.com. 2022. *China's Central Bank Pledges Support for Businesses Hit by Covid.* [online] Available at: https://www.bloomberg.com/news/articles/2022-04-18/china-s-central-bank-pledges-support-for-businesses-amid-covid#xj4y7vzkg [Accessed 14 June 2022].

Caixin Global. 2022. *China's Central Bank Vows Normalized Supervision of Tech Sector.* [online] Available at: https://www.caixinglobal.com/2022-05-05/chinas-central-bank-vows-normalized-supervision-of-tech-sector-101880293.html [Accessed 14 June 2022].

Climate Bonds Initiative. (2022). *Value of Green Bonds Issued in China from 2014 to 2021 (in Billion U.S. Dollars). Statista*. Statista Inc. [online] Available at: https://www-statista-com.surrey.idm.oclc.org/statistics/1289032/value-of-green-bonds-issued-china/ [Accessed 16 October 2022].

CSIS (2021) *Will the Dual Circulation Strategy Enable China to Compete in a Post-Pandemic World?, ChinaPower Project.* Available at: *https://chinapower.csis.org/china-covid-dual-circulation-economic-strategy/* [Accessed 10 May 2023].

Deutsche Bank. 2021. *Digital Yuan: What Is It and How Does It Work?* [online] Available at: https://www.db.com/news/detail/20210714-digital-yuan-what-is-it-and-how-does-it-work [Accessed 14 June 2022].

Düben, B. 2018. Xi Jinping and the End of Chinese Exceptionalism, *Problems of Post-Communism*, 67(2), 111–128.

Eichengreen, B., 2022. Sanctions, SWIFT, and China's Cross-Border Interbank Payments System. *CSIS Briefs.* [online] Available at: https://www.csis.org/analysis/sanctions-swift-and-chinas-cross-border-interbank-payments-system [Accessed 20 October 2022].

Global Times. 2022. *Central Bank Issues More Credit Lines to Inspire Coal Production, energy storage*. [online] Available at: https://www.globaltimes.cn/page/202205/1264817.shtml [Accessed 20 October 2022].

Hancock, T., 2021. China Needs Cut to Inequality for Common Prosperity: PBOC's Cai. *Bloomberg News*. [online] Available at: https://www.bloomberg.com/news/articles/2021-11-29/china-needs-cut-to-inequality-for-common-prosperity-pboc-s-cai#xj4y7vzkg [Accessed 14 June 2022].

Hoskins, P., 2021. China Power Cuts: What Is Causing the Country's Blackouts? *BBC News.* [online] Available at: https://www.bbc.com/news/business-58733193 [Accessed 14 June 2022].

Jing, L. 2022. *China's Real Estate Problem 1. The 'Three red lines', CKGSB.* Available at: *https://english.ckgsb.edu.cn/blog/the-three-red-lines/* [Accessed 10 May 2023].

Johnson, C. and Kennedy, S., 2017. *Xi's Signature Governance Innovation: The Rise of Leading Small Groups*. Csis.org. [online] Available at: https://www.csis.org/analysis/xis-signature-governance-innovation-rise-leading-small-groups [Accessed 14 June 2022].

Laskai, L., 2022. *Let's Start With What China's Digital Currency is Not – DigiChina.* DigiChina. [online] Available at: https://digichina.stanford.edu/work/lets-start-with-what-chinas-digital-currency-is-not/ [Accessed 14 June 2022].

Lin, L. and Hong, Y. 2022. Developing a Green Bonds Market: Lessons from China, *European Business Organization Law Review*, 23(1), 143–185.

Liu, G., 2021. High-quality Development of Inclusive Finance for Common Prosperity, *International Forum for China Financial Inclusion (IFCFI) 2021,* Taizhou, 16 December 2021. Available at: http://www.bis.org/review/r211229f.htm [Accessed 14 June 2022].

Liu, Y., 2022. Job Market Key to Maintaining GDP Growth, Stability This Year. *China Daily*. [online] Available at: https://www.chinadaily.com.cn/a/202204/11/WS6253836ea310fd2b29e56241.html [Accessed 14 June 2022].

McMorrow, R. and Yu, S., 2021. The Vanishing Billionaire: How Jack Ma Fell Foul of Xi Jinping. *Financial Times*. [online] Available at: https://www.ft.com/content/1fe0559f-de6d-490e-b312-abba0181da1f [Accessed 14 June 2022].

National Bureau of Statistics of China. 2021. Gini Index: Inequality of Income Distribution in China from 2004 to 2020. *Statista*. Statista Inc. Available at: https://www-statista-com.surrey.idm.oclc.org/statistics/250400/inequality-of-income-distribution-in-china-based-on-the-gini-index/ [Accessed 16 October 2022].

PBOC. 2022. Zhongguo Huobi Zhengce Zhixing Baogao 2015 to 2022.PBOC. Available at: http://www.pbc.gov.cn/zhengcehuobisi/125207/125227/index.html [Accessed 02 March 2023].

Reuters. 2022. *China's Anti-graft Watchdog Investigating Former Central Bank Official Sun*. [online] Available at: https://www.reuters.com/article/china-economy-pboc-probe-idUSL2N2XA0MZ [Accessed 14 June 2022].

S&P Global, 2020. *China Property Watch: Issuers Go on a Debt Diet*. [online] Available at: https://www.spglobal.com/ratings/en/research/articles/201112-china-property-watch-issuers-go-on-a-debt-diet-11728306 [Accessed 14 June 2022].

Shijia, O., 2021. New 5-Year Plan to Turbocharge SMEs. *China Daily*. [online] Available at: https://global.chinadaily.com.cn/a/202112/18/WS61bd4ea0a310cdd39bc7c269.html [Accessed 14 June 2022].

UBS, 2021. *China's Three Red Lines: Opportunities in China Real Estate*. [online] Available at: https://www.ubs.com/global/en/assetmanagement/insights/thematic-viewpoints/apac-and-emerging/articles/china-three-red-lines.html [Accessed 14 June 2022].

Yeung, K., 2021. China's Yuan Internationalisation Faces Coronavirus, geopolitical Threats Despite Record Cross-border Use. *South China Morning Post*. [online] 25 Aug. Available at: https://www.scmp.com/economy/china-economy/article/3146130/chinas-yuan-internationalisation-faces-coronavirus [Accessed 20 October 2022].

14 Central Banking and the Impact of the COVID-19 Pandemic: Some Insights from Ghana

Patrick K. Tutu, Franklin Nakpodia and Geofry Areneke

Introduction

In recent years, the world has witnessed increasing awareness of the impact of climate change and biodiversity on humans and the ecosystem (Sintayehu 2018). Climate change is a global phenomenon evident in the past three decades. Its potential long-term hazards have become a fundamental policy concern among international organisations, governments and the general public (Hansen 2022). Various parts of the globe have experienced the devastating impact of climate change and its ensuing harm (Verma 2021). As highlighted in the Fifth Assessment Report of the Intergovernmental Panel on Climate Change (IPCC), the globe has been experiencing rising land and ocean temperature by 0.85°C from 1880 to 2012 (IPCC 2013).

In response, the United Nations (UN), in September 2015, endorsed the Sustainable Development Goals (SDGs) with the focal aim of stimulating global action towards sustainable development (Pizzi et al. 2020). This move coincided with growing public awareness of the risks posed by climate change and the international community's commitment to addressing these challenges (Savaresi 2016; Schnell et al. 2016). The growing concern for environmental sustainability has instigated the desire among stakeholders to demand that policymakers, business managers, and the public make informed decisions to stabilise the climate, conserve biodiversity, and prevent harm to humanity and ecosystems (Kørnøv, Lyhne & Davila 2020; Pizzi et al. 2020).

While considerable strides have been achieved in promoting and implementing the sustainability agenda among developed economies, the same cannot be said of developing countries (Omisore 2018). The impact of climate change and sustainable development challenges have become dominant concerns in developing economies, owing mainly to the dearth of resources needed to drive the agenda. Thus, Omisore (2018) observes various poor sustainable development practices and weak implementation across many of these countries. Specifically, on the African continent, where the UN SGDs were intended to foster rapid socio-economic growth and minimise environmental risks, the implementation of SDGs remains in its infancy. Many African countries need an enabling environment to cultivate sustainable development principles. This expectation benefits from political stability, good governance, equal rights, and responsive institutions that are in short

DOI: 10.4324/9781003323280-15

supply (Jaiyesimi 2016). While it is worth noting that some African countries have made marginal progress in this direction, Mo Ibrahim Foundation (2017) Report observes that the overall improvement rate has slowed in the last decade.

The COVID-19 pandemic has exacerbated the many challenges confronting sustainable development on the African continent. The pandemic precipitated a global humanitarian and economic crisis that deepened the region's sustainability concerns (Ekwebelem et al. 2021) and undermined the minimal gains from a decade of action on the continent (Nchanji & Lutomia 2021). Arguably, the pandemic has unearthed a new world that challenges the status quo. In essence, governments and other stakeholders are now expected to innovate to meet their sustainability targets while overcoming the effects of the pandemic. Consequently, many African countries must rebuild to get back on the sustainability track. Rebuilding requires countries to adopt a sustainability framework, and African governments are well-positioned to do so. Many governments have strongly endorsed sustainable development and incorporated it into their national strategies and development plans (Omisore 2018).

Nonetheless, these countries face several challenges, from communication and information-sharing, insufficient stakeholder engagement and, most importantly, a lack of financial resources to support the implementation and monitoring of sustainability initiatives (Mthembu & Nhamo 2021). So, to realise the SDGs, such countries have engaged various institutions and agencies to champion the cause. In certain instances, the central banks in these countries have been saddled with the responsibility of promoting, supporting, and steering sustainability plans (Asogwa 2015). Ghana is not different in this respect. Before and during the COVID-19 pandemic, the Ghanaian government consistently engaged the Central Bank, i.e., the Bank of Ghana (BoG), in its sustainability drive (Anaman & Pobbi 2019). To catalyse change, central banks are expected to implement fiscal and monetary policies to regulate economic activities and help finance sustainable development projects. This mandate of central banks is particularly critical during and after a pandemic (Mosser 2020; Wagner 2010). The preceding is the motivation for this book chapter. Relying on insights from Ghana, a developing economy, this chapter discusses how central banks are addressing their sustainability responsibilities in a post-pandemic world.

The rest of the chapter is presented as follows; First, we present the BoG, followed by the discussion of the sustainability agenda and the sustainability focus of the BoG. Next, we examine the challenges in implementing sustainability initiatives in the country. We then present SDGs and COVID-19, emphasising the implications of COVID-19 on SDGs. This enables us to discuss the BoG's response to the pandemic. The chapter concludes by reflecting on the pandemic's lessons and offering suggestions for future research.

The Bank of Ghana (BoG)

The BoG is the central bank of Ghana, established in 1957, just ahead of the declaration of the country's independence. Similar to central banks across the globe, the initial objective of the bank, as enshrined in the 1957 ordinance that birthed it, was to issue and redeem banknotes and coins, manage the country's reserves, maintain monetary stability and the external value of the Ghanaian currency, and acting as the banker and financial adviser to the government. Over time, these functions have been refined in response to contemporary developments in the global financial system. For instance, Nashiru and Singh (2015) reflect on how the BoG seeks to promote knowledge creation, implementation, and practice across the banking sector. Primarily, the functions of the BoG can be classed into two broad categories, i.e., regulating the financial system and implementing government policies.

The primary mandate of the BoG is to maintain stability in the general price level and support government economic policies to promote growth and development through efficient and effective banking and credit system (BoG Act 2002, Act 612). To ensure price stability, the BoG, like Nigeria and South Africa, officially adopted an Inflation Targeting (IT) framework underpinned by a flexible exchange rate regime in 2007 (Kabundi & Mlachila 2019). The BoG is independent of instructions from the Government and other authorities as enshrined in the 1992 constitution of Ghana.

Regarding the regulation of the financial system, the BoG's remit is formulating and implementing monetary policies and stabilising its currency within and outside Ghana. They also handle the banking and credit system, supervise payment and settlement systems, control currency notes and coins, and ensure effective management of the country's external financial wealth. Their role includes licencing, promoting, regulating and supervising non-banking financial institutions and maintaining relations with international banking and economic systems. It also implements government policies to ensure effective fiscal management (Abdallah 2015). In this regard, the BoG establishes measures that ensure a favourable balance of payment, control government expenditure and stimulate overall economic development.

As noted, the evolving nature and contemporariness of the business environment have meant that the role of central banks continues to evolve. A good example is the role of central banks in supporting the sustainability agenda (Anaman & Pobbi 2019). In many countries, the central bank was co-opted to drive the realisation of the SDGs. While Ghana has equally adopted this approach, the next section addresses the primary focus of sustainability by the Ghana government.

Sustainability in Ghana

Over the years, Ghana has demonstrated significant effort towards achieving the UN sustainable development goals despite facing several challenges. According to the 2022 UN Sustainable development report, Ghana is ranked 110/163 with an index score of 63.44%, ranking among the top 10 countries in Africa. Among sub-Saharan African countries, Ghana ranks 3rd, next to Mauritius and South Africa. A review of the SDG report reveals that Ghana has reasonably achieved SDG 12 and is on track to achieving SDG 13. In addition, the country has also demonstrated improved performance towards achieving SDG goals 1, 4, 5, 6, 7, 8 and 9, although significant challenges still impede progress. Ghana's progress toward goals 2, 3, 11, 14, 16 and 17 has remained stagnant.

In Ghana's context, sustainable development integrates the three pillars of sustainability, namely the socio-cultural, economic, and natural resources, into the country's policies, plans, and programmes. In addition, Ghana has identified institutional development as the fourth pillar for sustainability, recognising the vital role that robust and efficient institutions play in delivering sustainable development outcomes. These four pillars emphasise development planning, implementation, monitoring, and evaluation across the various facets of government. The country customised the Strategic Environmental Assessment Tools for mainstreaming sustainability to provide valuable insights and lessons for policy coherence and synergies.

Ghana National Climate Change Policy (NCCP) and Ghana National Climate Change Master Plan Action Programmes for Implementation: 2015–2020 (Cobbinah et al. 2019; Lawson 2016) are the leading national policies in place to accelerate climate change and environmental sustainability awareness. Other sectoral policies address unsustainable mining practices, deforestation, water, and land management. Emphasis has also been placed on aiding local governments in mainstreaming the green economy into regional development strategies and establishing the capacity to compute indicator values based on the SDGs' metadata requirements.

In the medium-term national development policy framework – Agenda for Jobs (2018–2021) – the Social Development focus area encompasses measures to ensure fair and balanced allocation of national resources across ecological zones, gender, income, and socio-economic groups and to empower vulnerable people to access necessities of life. Its specific strategies include investment in human capital, health, social protection, and the promotion of viable and sustainable economic livelihood schemes for vulnerable people and persons with disabilities. The government's flagship programmes, such as 'Planting for Food and Jobs' (Tanko, Ismaila & Sadiq 2019) and 'One District One Factory' (Mensah et al. 2021), aim to promote agriculture and industrial development while creating job opportunities at the local level. These are critical given the recent slowdown in poverty reduction and the rise in spatial disparities. The Agenda for Jobs (2018–2021) also focuses on strengthening the capacity of oversight institutions regarding poverty reduction.

As a principal player in Ghana's economy with the mandate of assisting the government in implementing economic policies, the BoG has proposed various sustainability initiatives in the country's banking sector. The BoG has been working hand in hand with the Government to ensure economic stability and promote sustainable development in the country. They do this through the use of central banking tools such as monetary and fiscal policies as well as regulatory and monitoring activities. To this extent, the BoG plays a pivotal role in the overall government sustainability policies by ensuring that the economic parameters required for attaining the SDGs are regulated through sustainable banking practices. In effect, the sustainable banking initiatives issued by the central BoG in 2019 are not distinct from the Government's frameworks towards achieving sustainable development goals but rather enhance them through the financial sectors of the economy. It is mandatory for all commercial banks in Ghana to comply with the provision of sustainable banking principles and report on the same to BoG annually.

Sustainability Strategies by the BoG

As Durrani, Volz and Rosmin (2020) indicate, the need for central banks and financial regulators to address risks posed by climate change and sustainability is gaining traction. This is evidenced by the establishment of the Central Banks Financial Supervisors and Network for Greening the Financial System (NGFS) (Battiston, Dafermos & Monasterolo 2021), as well as the Sustainable Banking Network (SBN) (Bukhari, Hashim & Amran 2020). The overarching purpose of these networks is to strengthen global responses to the SDGs by enhancing financial systems' role in managing risk, mobilising for green and low-carbon investment and defining, promoting, and implementing best practices. The BoG has embraced these responsibilities. It promotes sustainability in the country, using various policies and guidelines to ensure financial institutions carry out their operations with an SDG focus. The primary focus of sustainability policies of the BoG is to reinforce sustainability practices by upholding policies geared toward improving the environmental, social and governance issues within the financial sector (Anaman & Pobbi 2019).

Against this backdrop, the BoG has presented creative ideas about supervising banks for excessive climate risk-taking. As a means of ensuring the safety of commercial banks, the BoG, since 2019, routinely examines and assesses these institutions along several dimensions. The banking supervisory role has been expanded to incorporate climate change parameters by evaluating the commercial bank's risk management procedure in relation to climate exposure and the efficacy of their ESG policies. In addition, the BoG also employs regulatory measures to provide incentives for banks to make their investments greener. Through sustainable banking principles, commercial banks, effective January 2020, are encouraged to help finance green businesses and report the same in their annual reports.

Socially Responsible Stewardship

The banking sector can positively influence the society in which it operates. The environment relies on the financial sector for credit to facilitate its operation. Banks, in this instance, can support the environment by providing financial products and services to businesses that promote sustainable development (Avrampou et al. 2019). Achieving this objective requires engagement with stakeholders to encourage them to follow good environmental and social practices. This process provides a two-way benefit to the business and the banks. Companies will integrate good environmental and social practices into their operations, reducing exposure to environmental and safety (E&S) risks. When banks' clients consider E&S dangers in their line of operation, the bank can be exposed due to the economic consequences that clients may have to deal with because of E&S cases. Thus, banks must understand their clientele's E&S risk exposures and how they affect the bank's overall risk profile. Therefore, banks should be aware of the commercial opportunities of dealing with clients that implement robust E&S policies.

To curtail such occurrences, the BoG, since January 2020, has instructed licenced commercial banks to develop and implement E&S risk management policies endorsed by the bank's top management. The banks must also demonstrate their intention to apply E&S risks policy provisions in their business activities and report the same to the central bank annually. As an implementation process, the requirements of this policy should be communicated to all relevant employees, and such communication must include incentives to encourage compliance. Employees must be reminded that the policy will be viewed using the same lens as other internal risk management policies. The industries and clients the bank works with, their client's location, and the product type all influence the bank's E&S risk exposure. Therefore, banks must identify client activities' risk areas before mitigation and control. The bank's ability to identify and mitigate their clients' E&S risks allows them to identify companies that uphold socially responsible actions and support them, especially in granting credits. Although the effectiveness of the policies cannot be assessed since it is still in its infancy, the commercial banks have demonstrated willingness and sensitization plans to comply with the guidelines while the central banks intensify supervision and monitoring (Bank of Ghana 2020).

Gender Equality

Gender equality is another vital component of the SDGs (Susan Solomon, Singh & Islam 2021), and it has been a central component of sustainability policies in Ghana. SDG No. 5 emphasises pursuing and attaining gender equality and empowering all women and girls (Agarwal 2018). Ghana's effort to build a more robust economy requires inclusive participation across all sectors. The proportionate representation of gender across various sectors of the economy increases diversity and workplace harmony, which is instrumental to productivity. Despite the government's relentless efforts to ensure a more balanced gender representation, women still face gender inequalities and discrimination that limit their ability to access or participate in the financial services sector and the economy (Mannah-Blankson 2018; Sossou 2011). Studies in Ghana suggest that men are two to three times more likely to be appointed to senior management positions or have credit access than women (Kuada 2009).

Banks can play a crucial part in redressing gender inequality in the financial sector while ensuring that their practices are fair to all employees and clients (Seguino 2019). The benefit of women's economic empowerment goes beyond their families to encompass a country's overall financial performance by boosting innovation and productivity that support the emergence of a more prosperous society (Adeabah, Gyeke-Dako & Andoh 2018). Diverse teams in an organisation are associated with greater innovative capacity, increased institutional trust, improved decision-making, better performance, better ability to retain talented employees, higher market share gains and better financial performance (Ogbo, Anthony & Ukpere 2014; Saxena 2014).

Drawing on the preceding, the BoG requires licensed financial institutions to ensure gender equality in their workforce and business activities starting January 2020. Through a blend of guidelines, the BoG mandates banks to demonstrate support for gender equality by establishing a corporate leadership framework that encourages women to strive for top management positions. It also motivates banks to set gender-sensitive recruitment and retention agenda within their respective establishments. Banks are also required to ensure health and safety for male and female workers, promote training and professional development for women, foster equality through community initiatives, and provide grievance mechanisms to address work-related grievances equitably across gender.

Corporate Integrity

Sustainability in the business literature focuses on a firm's capacity to undertake its entrepreneurial activities, maximise its shareholder's wealth over the long term, balance the expectations for short-term performance and implement strategies that assure value creation in the long term (Maletič, Maletič & Gomišček 2018). Wan, Chen and Ke (2020) contend that businesses are legally expected to maintain an integrity compass that emphasises ethical values and regulatory compliance to meet these prospects.

Businesses and enterprises are the primary economic units that play a critical role in economic growth and social development. Therefore, companies must be more socially responsible by seeking avenues to give back to society through, for example, charitable donations, safe production, employment promotion, employee rights protection, product quality, environmental protection, and resource conservation (Wan, Chen & Ke 2020). Achieving social responsibility among businesses requires embedding corporate integrity and ethical culture in the organisation's core values (Wan et al. 2020). According to Erhard and Jensen (2017), corporate integrity is fundamental to a firm's continued survival. It also assists in attracting socially responsible investments (Denison & Mishra 1995), reducing transaction costs (Gosling & Huang 2009), enhancing operating efficiency (Hsu 2007), and improving corporate profitability and performance (Erhard & Jensen 2017; Reichheld & Teal 1996; Simons 2002).

Corporate integrity also catalyses firms' contributions to the SDGs. Due to its relevance in promoting sustainable development, the BoG's sustainability policies are designed to improve corporate integrity among Ghanaian firms. The BoG expects licensed financial institutions to conduct operations ethically by developing policies that identify client behaviours that the bank finds unacceptable. These behaviours include the non-appointment of qualified staff to manage the critical functions of the client, poor management of bribery and other operational risks, engaging in illegal activities, employing aggressive tax avoidance tactics, and failing to follow appropriate local and international regulations, among others.

BoG also requires licensed banks to establish procedures detailing the processes needed to identify and avoid working with clients that demonstrate poor corporate governance or unethical behaviour. These procedures should describe how to screen new clients and monitor existing clients. When implementing these procedures, the BoG expects the respective institutions to examine the scope of their existing processes and consider enhancements. In particular, the guidelines should emphasise the processes and penalties when a new or existing client demonstrates poor governance and unethical behaviour.

Challenges in Implementing Sustainability Initiatives

While the BoG has achieved some positive outcomes in its sustainability interventions, some challenges have minimised the payoffs from the bank's sustainability policies. In this section, we focus on three main challenges the bank faces.

The first problem concerns the country's financial institutions' response to BoG's sustainability policies. The BoG sustainability policies require banks to tackle environmental and social risks in their business activities, promote ESG practices, and enhance corporate governance, ethical standards, gender equality, and financial inclusion. These principles demand that financial institutions build the capacity to cope with these requirements. Though the banks have pledged their commitment to the environmental regulations and standards that guide their activities, most still grapple with the problem of securing the necessary resource to operationalise these expectations. In pursuit of resource efficiency, banks need to be active players to drive this objective. The banks must be mindful of how they consume energy, water, and other input materials. This challenge impedes the full implementation of BoG's sustainability policies.

The second main challenge the BoG faces in implementing the sustainability policies is the bank's (BoG) limited capacity and resources to push its sustainability initiatives (Gyasi, Phillips & Adam 2021). The BoG needs to build sufficient monitoring and evaluation tools and the requisite expertise to access compliance with requirements as specified in the sustainable banking framework. They must educate stakeholders on internalising their operations to conform to the policies. Though various stakeholder forums have since been established, there are traces of inconsistency in compliance levels (Bank of Ghana 2020). Educating key stakeholders and establishing a consensus on sustainability principles must feature prominently in BoG's plans. Building regulators' and financial institutions' capacity, enhancing cooperation among financial institutions, and providing incentives for sustainable initiatives must be consistently explored by the BoG in its sustainability drive.

The third major issue hampering the implementation of sustainability policies by the BoG is the low public awareness of sustainability principles (Duah, Ahenkan & Larbi 2020). Sustainable practices imply carrying out banking operations and business activities with conscious consideration of these activities' environmental and social impacts. Banks must implement sustainable banking in their internal processes and activities relating to external interactions with clients and the types of projects they fund. The public understanding of sustainable practices in Ghana is still in its infancy. The public has exhibited a scant reaction to the sustainability agenda because there is no consensus regarding the significance of sustainability to their well-being. This situation draws from poor awareness and inadequate public education. The onus rests on the BoG to raise public awareness of its sustainability objectives. Such increased awareness could generate public support for the regulations while positioning them to demand accountability from the banks.

SDGs and COVID-19 Pandemic

As anticipated, the COVID-19 pandemic created fresh economic challenges and frustrated key global economic policies. In addition to the global economy (Priya, Cuce & Sudhakar 2021), employment (Blustein & Guarino 2020), education

(Tarkar 2020), mental health (Pfefferbaum & North 2020), and the United Nations (UN) Sustainable Development Goals (SDGs), were impacted significantly. As Heggen, Sandset and Engebretsen (2020) note, COVID-19 has been a foremost impediment in attaining the UN SDGs as it halted or reversed decades of development progress. The pandemic pushed over 124 million people back into poverty and chronic hunger and accounted for global deaths of over 4 million as of July 2021. Concerning the SDGs, the pandemic provoked increased inequality toward women and children. A UNDP Report notes that women are the most affected by the COVID-19 crisis, as they are increasingly likelier to lose their source of income and less likely to be covered by the government's social welfare packages. In fact, the poverty rate among women exceeded 9%, which is equivalent to about 47 million women. Similarly, the crisis caused a spike in child poverty levels to around 15%. The education of millions of children worldwide was interrupted, with about 24 million children at risk of dropping out of school.

Understandably, these problems attracted the attention of governments and their agencies worldwide (Heggen, Sandset & Engebretsen 2020). While some governments sought collaborative opportunities to tackle the effects of the pandemic, many governments sought internal strategies to manage the crisis. In this instance, many governments engaged critical stakeholders in their domain. In Ghana, for example, the BoG was actively involved in implementing the country's government's policies to fight COVID-19 impacts (Aduhene & Osei-Assibey 2021). A selection of the primary interventions by the BoG is presented next.

BoG's Response to the COVID-19 Pandemic

The impact of the COVID-19 pandemic on economic, social and environmental sustainability was felt globally, and policymakers and regulators responded accordingly (Ranjbari et al. 2021). The crisis imposed immense pressure on the global economy and business activities with significant adverse financial consequences, increased GDP losses, and raised poverty and hunger levels (Iwuoha & Ukamaka 2020). It became clear that ignoring the impact will impede countries' recovery policies and sustainability strategies since mainstreaming sustainability is critical to rebuilding stronger and deeply rooted sustainable systems (Assaf & Scuderi 2020). As the OECD (2021) highlights, returning to the traditional business model would mean missing a vital opportunity to confront underlying and interconnected environmental, social, and economic challenges pre-dating the COVID-19 pandemic. It is relevant to note that addressing the sustainability mayhem prompted by the pandemic requires social and economic changes across society (Ranjbari et al. 2021). Hence, policies and practices cannot remain the same. Undeniably, COVID-19 triggered forceful actions to temporarily alleviate the pandemic's impact on the economy, environment, and society.

Like most countries, the BoG and the Ghanaian government implemented a raft of policies to cushion the detrimental effects of COVID-19 on the country's economy. Given its role as a central bank, the BoG introduced some monetary policies intended to raise the money supply in the economy. Some monetary policies include cutting the interest rate by 1.5%, from 16% to 14.5% (Aduhene & Osei-Assibey 2021).

This reduction, which left the interest rate at an 8-year low, was intended to stimulate economic growth, as lowering the interest rates can encourage borrowing and investment even during crises. Also, the BoG reduced the reserve requirements for lenders from 10% to 8%. Central banks deploy the reserve requirement tool to increase or decrease the money supply in an economy. Reserve requirements denote the amount of funds banks could hold in reserve to cope with sudden withdrawals. Traditionally, credit reserve asset is used primarily for precautionary purposes, based on reserve adequacy metrics (International Monetary Fund 2016). The aim is to assure markets that banks can meet their financial obligations, thereby fostering public confidence in the domestic economy (Fender et al. 2020). By reducing this limit, Ghanaian banks were able to pump more money into the economy to cope with the increasing demand occasioned by the pandemic. It is also necessary to note that this move ensured that the critical sectors of the Ghanaian economy could access the necessary liquidity needed to support their continued operation.

Further monetary policies launched by the BoG include decreasing banks' conservation buffers (Asante & Mills 2020). This reduced from 3% to 1.5%, translating to a decrease in the capital-adequacy ratio to 11.5% from 13%. Like the cuts in interest rates and reserve requirements, lowering the capital adequacy ratio means that there is greater scope for banks to make a portion of their capital available to the economy as risk assets. This further reinforces the country's capacity to deal with the impact of the crisis. A report by Deloitte (2020) hinted at another monetary intervention. The report notes that the BoG updated the loan provisioning model in Ghanaian banks to offer capital relief to financial institutions. Targeting the 'Other Loans Especially Mentioned' (OLEM) category, the BoG slashed the provisioning of loans for OLEM by 50%, from 10% to 5% for all banks and Specialised Deposit-Taking Institutions (SDIs). This move became necessary as loan repayments might be challenging for many clients due to the slowdown in economic endeavours. Therefore, the reduction in funds set aside to cover non-performing loans raises monies available to financial institutions to lend to the public to incentivise economic activities.

Another monetary intervention that the BoG utilised to boost the money supply in the Ghanaian economy to combat the debilitating consequences of COVID-19 was a directive disallowing the country's financial institutions from paying dividends or making any other payments to their shareholders for the years 2019 and 2020. The decision to implement this policy ensured that banks did not take advantage of the many incentives the BoG, following the COVID-19 pandemic, offered. However, the BoG stipulated conditions wherein this directive can be overruled. Where Ghanaian banks and SDIs have met all standard prudential obligations, and evidence suggests that the banks have relied on the additional liquidity released by the BoG to compensate for COVID-19, banks may pay dividends and make other statutory distributions to their shareholders.

Still on the financial system, the BoG, to enhance financial inclusion (Valencia et al. 2021), leveraged opportunities offered by its mobile payment system, specifically the popular mobile money payment platform. The idea is to encourage the public to use mobile money services to promote the country's effort to move to a cashless economy. To avoid a transaction slowdown, the BoG reduced the cost of fund transfers through mobile money. It further mandated banks and service suppliers to desist from charging on transactions below GH100 (USD18) for three months, subject to review at the end of the timeframe. In addition, the BoG increased the daily limits for mobile money transactions to boost transactions. These interventions explain the 22% growth in the volume of transactions on mobile money platforms during the COVID-19 crisis.

While the above interventions can be considered internal, the BoG also sought to access monetary opportunities outside Ghana. As the pandemic had global ramifications, global institutions such as the IMF and the World Bank were increasingly open to supporting countries with financial assistance and debt relief to counter the economic shocks triggered by the pandemic. The organisation's Catastrophe Containment and Relief Trust (CCRT) financed the IMF lending facilities and debt service relief. As of March 2020, IMF lent its member countries about $250 billion. Ghana also benefitted from this opportunity. The BoG and the country's government applied to the IMF to disburse a credit facility to enable the country to face the adverse economic effects of COVID-19. According to the IMF, USD1 billion and Special Drawing Rights (SDR) of US$738 million were approved for Ghana in April 2020 via its Rapid Credit Facility (RCF) programme. Deloitte (2020) notes that the facility will assist in managing the urgent fiscal and balance of payments needs that Ghana is encountering. The disbursement is also anticipated to improve overall confidence, boost economic activity and performance, and catalyse support from other development partners.

COVID-19 Lessons and the Future Roles of Central Banks

Despite the various global strategies implemented by central banks (including the BoG) to minimise COVID-19 effects, it is apparent that there are lessons for financial sector regulators to reflect on to ensure that similar future crises do not produce a comparable damaging impact on the economy.

As the pandemic dawned, the first apparent issue was the lack of crisis preparedness. While there have been significant crises in the past, e.g., the global economic recession of 2008-09, the COVID-19 pandemic presented challenges that the financial system was hitherto unaccustomed to. Unfortunately, many Ghanaian banks and the BoG do not possess the requisite experience to deal with the subsequent developments. Conventional practices were dismantled and replaced by agility to cope with unforeseen marketplace disruption. COVID-19 exposed the lack of effective cross-border cooperation, coordination and risk-sharing among financial institutions. Therefore, the BoG must emphasise the need for banks to establish a crisis management framework that provides for similar future crises. This framework must articulate best practices in crisis management and recognise areas such as risk-sharing opportunities, decision-making, and relevant policies during emergencies.

Related to the lack of crisis preparedness is the resilience of the markets and institutions (Beyens, Failler & Asiedu 2018). This concern was prevalent in many less-developed countries as they struggled to manage the outcomes of the crisis.

The adjustment of monetary policies at short notice by the BoG created its own problems. For instance, the increased inflation rate in the first quarter of 2021 draws from the reduction in bank interest rates. These problems reveal the extent of the economy's fragility. Besides, while the banks could quickly deploy resources to cope with the government's monetary directives, this was not the case with the non-bank financial institutions. Thus, the BoG must explore the necessary parameters that help strengthen the resilience of non-bank financial institutions to deal better with crises in the future. This is particularly critical given that non-bank financial organisations enjoy a significant presence in the Ghana financial system.

The COVID-19 pandemic also exposed operational resilience issues among Ghanaian organisations. Notably, many of these organisations had not established robust risk management frameworks to deal with exogenous shocks. However, as the industry regulator, the BoG should be held accountable for this anomaly as it indicates a poor monitoring mechanism. This is critical, considering that the various banking regulations in the country need a robust risk management mechanism. Therefore, the BoG must reevaluate its monitoring mechanism and identify best practices for the types of information architecture banks and non-banks financial firms should establish to maximise their resilience in managing operational elements such as exogenous shocks.

The pandemic also brought to the fore the issue of work-life balance (Putri & Amran 2021). Pre COVID-19, it was almost unthinkable to render banking services from home. While this traditional practice heightened work-life balance concerns, the COVID-19 crisis compelled businesses to rethink their modus operandi. Some Ghanaian banks have established systems that now allow their staff to work from home, thus promoting increased flexibility and potentially helping to ease work-life issues (Irawanto, Novianti & Roz 2021). However, there have not been definitive guidelines from the BoG regarding this arrangement. As the industry regulator, the BoG must take advantage of this opportunity to design industry-wide policies that support this new arrangement. Promoting working from home could mean significant cost savings for banks (e.g., office running costs and transportation costs for employees) while helping to lighten work-life balance concerns.

Lastly, the crisis fostered greater internal and external teamwork and collaboration across the industry. For instance, organisations collaborated on technologies to facilitate connectivity within virtual environments. Such collaborations are expected to continue post-COVID-19, further enhancing quality service offerings to clients. Internally, employees in similar job bundles were deployed to support priority business areas. While this reinforces teamwork, it also helped organisations reassess their value chain by focusing on business areas that significantly impact their clients and contribute considerably to their bottom line.

Summary and Conclusion

This chapter focuses on the role of the BoG in relation to the sustainability programmes of the country's governance and how the COVID-19 pandemic necessitated a rejig of policies to deal with the effects of the pandemic. Following an introduction that detailed the motivation and objective of this chapter, the chapter proceeds by presenting the BoG, highlighting its core and emergent responsibilities in light of the COVID-19 pandemic. We focus on sustainability-related initiatives in Ghana, presenting the government's sustainability agenda, how the BoG has advanced specific areas of the government's sustainability plan and the critical challenges faced by the BoG in supporting the agenda. Moving on, the chapter considers how the COVID-19 pandemic impacts the SDGs and concludes by presenting the various BoG responses to the COVID-19 pandemic and the lessons learnt from the crisis.

In conclusion, the primary limitation of the chapter is the lack of empirics to generate richer insights into the SDGs, COVID-19 and the central banking nexus in Ghana. Notwithstanding, it is essential to highlight that the country is one of the fastest growing economies in Africa and has, over the period, embarked on significant initiatives towards achieving the UN sustainable development goals. This is evidenced in the UN sustainable development report 2022, where Ghana ranks among the top 10 African countries in terms of contribution towards achieving the SDGs, and the role of BoG in this effort cannot be over-emphasized. The BoG has implemented several initiatives through both monetary and regulatory tools to boost the government's policies to achieve the SDGs. By acknowledging the institutional variations across varieties of capitalism, the chapter presents an insight into the initiatives central banks in Africa are employing to enhance the achievement of the UN Sustainable development goals. This knowledge is needed to enable stakeholders and regulators to refocus their scarce resources on SDG areas that suffered the most losses following the crisis.

References

Abdallah, MI. 2015. Financial sector regulatory and supervisory framework in Ghana. *International Journal of Economics, Commerce and Management*. 3(5):1043–1055.

Adeabah, D., Gyeke-Dako, A. and Andoh, C., 2019. Board gender diversity, corporate governance and bank efficiency in Ghana: a two stage data envelope analysis (DEA) approach. Corporate Governance: *The International Journal of Business in Society*, 19(2):299–320.

Aduhene, D.T. and Osei-Assibey, E. 2021. Socio-economic impact of COVID-19 on Ghana's economy: challenges and prospects. *International Journal of Social Economics*. 48(4):543–556

Agarwal, B. 2018. Gender equality, food security and the sustainable development goals. *Current Opinion in Environmental Sustainability*. 34:26–32.

Anaman, EA & Pobbi, M. 2019. Analysis of financial performance and sustainability of microfinance institutions in Ghana. *International Journal of Accounting, Finance and Risk Management*. 4(1):34–43.

Asante, LA & Mills, RO. 2020. Exploring the socio-economic impact of COVID-19 pandemic in marketplaces in urban Ghana. *Africa Spectrum*. 55(2):170–181.

Asogwa, RC. 2015. Governments' options for financing the sustainable development goals (SDGs) in a period of economic downturn. *Economic and Financial Review*. 53(4):11.

Assaf, A & Scuderi, R. 2020. COVID-19 and the recovery of the tourism industry. *Tourism Economics*. 26(5):731–733. https://doi.org/10.1177/1354816620933712.

Avrampou, A, Skouloudis, A, Iliopoulos, G & Khan, N. 2019. Advancing the sustainable development goals: Evidence from leading European banks. *Sustainable Development*. 27(4):743–757.

Battiston, S, Dafermos, Y & Monasterolo, I. 2021. Climate risks and financial stability. *Journal of Financial Stability*. 54:100867.

Beyens, Y, Failler, P & Asiedu, B. 2018. Institutional challenges and constraints for Ghana in exporting fishery products to the European union. *Food Reviews International*. 34(3):265–289.

Blustein, DL & Guarino, PA. 2020. Work and unemployment in the time of COVID-19: The existential experience of loss and fear. *Journal of Humanistic Psychology*. 60(5):702–709.

Bukhari, SAA, Hashim, F & Amran, A. 2020. Green banking: A road map for adoption. *International Journal of Ethics and Systems*. 36(3):371–385.

Bank of Ghana. (2020). *Sustainable Banking Principles and Sector Guidance Notes – Bank of Ghana*. Bank of Ghana. Available from: https://www.bog.gov.gh/news/sustainable-banking-principles-and-sector-guidance-notes.

Chukwunyere Iwuoha, J & Adaeze Ukamaka, J-I. 2020. Challenge to SDG and globalization. *Electronic Research Journal of Social Sciences and Humanities*. 2(Iii). Available from: www.eresearchjournal.com.

Cobbinah, PB, Asibey, MO, Opoku-Gyamfi, M & Peprah, C. 2019. Urban planning and climate change in Ghana. *Journal of Urban Management*. 8(2):261–271.

Deloitte. 2020. Economic impact of the covid-19 pandemic on the economy of Ghana economic impact of covid-19 at a glance. *Summary of Fiscal Measures and Deloitte Views*. (April 2020):1–5.

Denison, DR & Mishra, AK. 1995. Toward a theory of organizational culture and effectiveness. *Organization Science*. 6(2):204–223.

Duah, EF, Ahenkan, A & Larbi, D. 2020. Mainstreaming sustainable development goals (SDGs) into local development planning: Lessons from adentan municipal assembly in Ghana. *Journal of Sustainable Development*. 13(5):1–13.

Durrani, A., Rosmin, M. and Volz, U., 2020. The role of central banks in scaling up sustainable finance–what do monetary authorities in the Asia-Pacific region think?. *Journal of sustainable finance & investment*. 10(2):92–112.

Ekwebelem, OC, Ofielu, ES, Nnorom-Dike, OV, Iweha, C, Ekwebelem, NC, Obi, BC & Ugbede-Ojo, SE. 2021. Threats of COVID-19 to achieving United nations sustainable development goals in Africa. *The American Journal of Tropical Medicine and Hygiene*. 104(2):457.

Erhard, W & Jensen, MC. 2017. Response to Deirdre Nansen Mccloskey's comment On 'Putting integrity into finance: A purely positive Approach'. *Capitalism & Society, Response*. 12.

Fender, I, Mcmorrow, M, Sahakyan, V & Zulaica, O. 2020. Reserve management and sustainability: The case for green bonds? *BIS Working Papers*. (849). Available from: www.bis.org.

Foundation, MI. 2017. Africa at a tipping point. *Forum Report*. (March). https://mo.ibrahim.foundation/sites/default/files/2021-06/2017-forum-report-africa-at-a-tipping-point.pdf.

Gosling, M & Huang, HJ. 2009. The fit between integrity and integrative social contracts theory. *Journal of Business Ethics*. 90(3):407–417.

Gyasi, RM, Phillips, DR & Adam, AM. 2021. How far is inclusivity of financial services associated with food insecurity in later life? Implications for health policy and sustainable development goals. *Journal of Applied Gerontology*. 40(2):189–200.

Hansen, LP. 2022. Central banking challenges posed by uncertain climate change and natural disasters. *Journal of Monetary Economics*. 125:1–15. https://doi.org/10.1016/j.jmoneco.2021.09.010.

Heggen, K, Sandset, TJ & Engebretsen, E. 2020. COVID-19 and sustainable development goals. *Bulletin of the World Health Organization*. 98(10):646.

Hsu, S-H. 2007. A new business excellence model with business integrity from ancient Confucian thinking. *Total Quality Management and Business Excellence*. 18(4):413–423.
International Monetary Fund. 2016. IMF annual report 2016 finding solutions together. *IMF Annual Reports*. 1:131. Available from: https://www.imf.org/external/pubs/ft/ar/2016/eng/pdf/ar16_eng.pdf.
IPCC. 2013. *Climate Change 2013: The Physical Science Basis*. Available from: https://www.ipcc.ch/report/ar5/wg1/ [Accessed 2 June 2022].
Irawanto, DW, Novianti, KR & Roz, K. 2021. Work from home: Measuring satisfaction between work–life balance and work stress during the COVID-19 pandemic in Indonesia. *Economies*. 9(3):96.
Jaiyesimi, R. 2016. The challenge of implementing the sustainable development goals in Africa: The way forward. *African Journal of Reproductive Health*. 20(3):13–18.
Kabundi, A & Mlachila, M. 2019. The role of monetary policy credibility in explaining the decline in exchange rate pass-through in South Africa. *Economic Modelling*. 79:173–185.
Kørnøv, L, Lyhne, I & Davila, JG. 2020. Linking the UN SDGs and environmental assessment: Towards a conceptual framework. *Environmental Impact Assessment Review*. 85:106463.
Kuada, J. 2009. Gender, social networks, and entrepreneurship in Ghana. *Journal of African Business*. 10(1):85–103.
Lawson, E.T. 2016. Negotiating stakeholder participation in the Ghana national climate change policy", *International Journal of Climate Change Strategies and Management*. 8(3):399–417.
Maletič, M, Maletič, D & Gomišček, B. 2018. The role of contingency factors on the relationship between sustainability practices and organizational performance. *Journal of Cleaner Production*. 171:423–433.
Mannah-Blankson, T. 2018. Gender inequality and access to microfinance: Evidence from Ghana. *Journal of African Development*. 20(2):21–34.
Mensah, CN, Dauda, L, Boamah, KB & Salman, M. 2021. One district one factory policy of Ghana, a transition to a low-carbon habitable economy? *Environment, Development and Sustainability*. 23(1):703–721.
Mosser, PC. 2020. Central bank responses to COVID-19. *Business Economics*. 55(4):191–201.
Mthembu, DE & Nhamo, G. 2021. Domestication of the UN sustainable development goals in South Africa. *South African Journal of International Affairs*. 28(1):1–28.
Nashiru, ZM & Singh, RK. 2015. Exploring knowledge creation, implementation and practice by banking leaders at the Central Bank of Ghana. *Leadership & Organizational Management Journal*. 2015(3):42–53.
Nchanji, EB & Lutomia, CK. 2021. Regional impact of COVID-19 on the production and food security of common bean smallholder farmers in sub-Saharan Africa: Implication for SDG's. *Global Food Security*. 29:100524.
OECD. 2021. *COVID-19 Emergency Government Support and Ensuring a Level Playing Field on the Road to Recovery*. Available from: https://www.oecd.org/coronavirus/policy-responses/covid-19-emergency-government-support-and-ensuring-a-level-playing-field-on-the-road-to-recovery-1e5a04de/ [Accessed 2 June 2022].
Ogbo, AI, Anthony, KA & Ukpere, WI. 2014. The effect of workforce diversity on organizational performance of selected firms in Nigeria. *Mediterranean Journal of Social Sciences*. 5(10):231.
Omisore, AG. 2018. Attaining sustainable development goals in sub-Saharan Africa: The need to address environmental challenges. *Environmental Development*. 25:138–145.
Pfefferbaum, B & North, CS. 2020. Mental health and the covid-19 pandemic. *New England Journal of Medicine*. 383(6):510–512.

Pizzi, S, Caputo, A, Corvino, A & Venturelli, A. 2020. Management research and the UN sustainable development goals (SDGs): A bibliometric investigation and systematic review. *Journal of Cleaner Production*. 276:124033.

Priya, SS, Cuce, E & Sudhakar, K. 2021. A perspective of COVID 19 impact on global economy, energy and environment. *International Journal of Sustainable Engineering*. 14(6):1290–1305.

Putri, A & Amran, A. 2021. Employees work-life balance reviewed from work from home aspect during COVID-19 pandemic. *International Journal of Management Science and Information Technology*. 1(1):30–34.

Ranjbari, M, Shams Esfandabadi, Z, Zanetti, MC, Scagnelli, SD, Siebers, PO, Aghbashlo, M, Peng, W & Quatraro, F, et al. 2021. Three pillars of sustainability in the wake of COVID-19: A systematic review and future research agenda for sustainable development. *Journal of Cleaner Production*. 297:126660. https://doi.org/10.1016/j.jclepro.2021.126660.

Reichheld, FF & Teal, T. 1996. *The Loyalty Effect: The Hidden Force Behind Growth, Profits, and Lasting Value*. Harvard Business School Press. Boston, Massachusetts.

Savaresi, A. 2016. The Paris agreement: A new beginning? *Journal of Energy & Natural Resources Law*. 34(1):16–26.

Saxena, A. 2014. Workforce diversity: A key to improve productivity. *Procedia Economics and Finance*. 11:76–85.

Schnell, JL, Prather, MJ, Josse, B, Naik, V, Horowitz, LW, Zeng, G, Shindell, DT & Faluvegi, G. 2016. Effect of climate change on surface ozone over North America, Europe, and East Asia. *Geophysical Research Letters*. 43(7):3509–3518.

Seguino, S. 2019. Macroeconomic policy tools to finance gender equality. *Development Policy Review*. 37(4):504–525.

Simons, T. 2002. Behavioral integrity: The perceived alignment between managers' words and deeds as a research focus. *Organization Science*. 13(1):18–35.

Sintayehu, DW. 2018. Impact of climate change on biodiversity and associated key ecosystem services in Africa: A systematic review. *Ecosystem Health and Sustainability*. 4(9):225–239. https://doi.org/10.1080/20964129.2018.1530054.

Sossou, M-A. 2011. We do not enjoy equal political rights: Ghanaian women's perceptions on political participation in Ghana. *Sage Open*. 1(1):2158244011410715.

Susan Solomon, D, Singh, C & Islam, F. 2021. Examining the outcomes of urban adaptation interventions on gender equality using SDG 5. *Climate and Development*. 13(9):830–841.

Tanko, M, Ismaila, S & Sadiq, SA. 2019. Planting for food and jobs (PFJ): A panacea for productivity and welfare of rice farmers in Northern Ghana. *Cogent Economics & Finance*. 7(1):1693121.

Tarkar, P. 2020. Impact of COVID-19 pandemic on education system. *International Journal of Advanced Science and Technology*. 29(9):3812–3814.

Valencia, DC, Calabuig, C, Villa, E & Betancur, F. 2021. Financial inclusion as a complementary strategy to address the SDGs for society. In: *Sustainable Development Goals for Society Vol. 1: Selected Topics of Global Relevance*. Springer, Cham, pp. 79–89.

Verma, AK. 2021. Influence of climate change on balanced ecosystem, biodiversity and sustainable development: An overview. *International Journal of Biological Innovations*. 3(2). https://doi.org/10.46505/IJBI.2021.3213.

Wagner, H. 2010. The causes of the recent financial crisis and the role of central banks in avoiding the next one. *International Economics and Economic Policy*. 7(1):63–82.

Wan, P, Chen, X & Ke, Y. 2020. Does corporate integrity culture matter to corporate social responsibility? Evidence from China. *Journal of Cleaner Production*. 259:120877.

Index

Note: *Italicized* numbers refer figures, **bold** tables and "n" notes in the text.

ABBC *see* Brazilian Association of Banks
ABCD *see* Brazilian Association of Digital Credit
Accenture 37
accountability 81, 85, 245, 264, 268
Account Information Service Providers (AISP) 130
Action Plan on Sustainable Finance 178
ACTU *see* Australian Council of Trade Unions
Aden 21
Adkins, L. 93, 97
Afghani Central Bank 25
Afghanistan 26, 27; United States financial sanctions 25
Africa 21, 30
Africa's last colonial currency: the CFA franc story (Pigeaud and Sylla) 20
Agenda for Jobs (2018–2021) 260
AI *see* artificial intelligence
AIDS 23
AISP *see* Account Information Service Providers
Aizenman, J. 63
AKP 190–194, 203, 209
Albania 168, 171
Alberta 12
Algeria 29
Alibaba 35, 45, 46
Alipay 35, 46
Alonso, N. 79
The American Conservative (Hendrickson) 26
Anglo-America 23
ANPD *see* National Data Protection Agency
Ant Financial Group 244
apartheid 65; Fed and 61–64; virtual 63
APP *see* asset purchase programme (APP)
Arauz, A. 46
artificial intelligence (AI) 127
ASEAN *see* Association of Southeast Asian Nations
Asia 180
Asset-Backed Reserve Requirements 23
asset capitalism, financialized 92–96
asset inflation 31, 92, 96, 98–100, 102–104
asset purchase programme (APP) 6–7, 53, 115, 120, 170, 176, 201–202, 204
Association of Southeast Asian Nations (ASEAN) 251
Attlee, C. 21
Auer, R. 44
Australia 19, 20, 22, 23, 24, 25, 27–28, 31, 59, 249
Australian Council of Trade Unions (ACTU) 24
Austria 21
authoritarian financialization (AF) 186–212; COVID-19 and 201–207; crisis tendencies of 189; in Hungary 193–197, 201–203, 207–209; literature review 187–193; in Türkiye 198–201, 203–207, 209–210
autonomy 46, 63, 121, 134, 145–152, 158–162, 186, 188, 194–195, 207, 211
Avant smart card 35

Balkan Countries, COVID-19 crisis and 222–224, *223*
Bank Act (1871) 22
Banka Slovenije 179
Bank for International Settlements (BIS) 36, 37, 40; Committee on Payments and Market Infrastructures 41

Bank of Canada (BoC) 19–21, 36, 59
Bank of England (BoE) 6, 20–22, 28, 31, 37, 43–45, 59, 115–117, 119, 178, 202
Bank of Finland 35
Bank of Ghana (BoG) 258–259, 265–267
Bank of Japan (BoJ) 21, 36–37, 38, 59
Bank of Korea 43
Bank of Montreal 36
Bank of Slovenia 181n5
Bank of Slovenije (2022a) 173
Banque de France 20, 21
BCB *see* Brazilian Central Bank
Beijing Winter Olympics (2022) 35
Belarus 157–158, 161; macroeconomic **153**; monetary regime transformations in 146–152
Belgium 21
Bernanke, B. S. 22
Biden, J. 25–28
bilateral swap lines 55, 57–58, 64, 65
BIS *see* Bank for International Settlements
Blinder, A. S. 4
Blockchain 39, 40
BoC *see* Bank of Canada
BoE *see* Bank of England
Boehme, R. 44
Bofinger, P. 43
BoG *see* Bank of Ghana
BoJ *see* Bank of Japan
Bosnia 168, 169
Brady bonds 46, 47n4
Braun, B. 74, 188
Brazil 59, 62; open banking in 131–132, **135**
Brazilian Association of Banks (ABBC) 141n12
Brazilian Association of Credit Card Companies and Services (Abecs) 141n12
Brazilian Association of Digital Credit (ABCD) 141n12
Brazilian Association of Fintechs (ABFintechs) 141n12
Brazilian Association of Payment Institutions (Abipag) 141n12
Brazilian Central Bank (BCB) 127, 129, 131–134, 136, 138–140
Brazilian Chamber of Electronic Commerce (Câmara-e.net) 141n12
Brazilian Federation of Banks (FEBRABAN) 141n12
Brazilian Internet Association (Abranet) 141n12
Brazilian Regulatory Model **135**
Brazilian System for the Defense of Competition 136
Bretton Woods 34, 55, 58, 65
Brexit 31
BRICS 161
brokerage operations 82
Bulgaria 168, 169, 222; macroeconomic and financial indicators for **230**
Bulgarian Development Bank 225, 226
Bulgarian National Bank 226

Caixa Econômica Federal 137
Canada 20, 22, 30–31, 36
capitalist bank market 19
capitalist military firms 25
capitalist money 20–21
capital markets union (CMU) 73–74
carbon taxation 11, 14
Cartelier, J. 20
Carter, J. 28–29
Cassetta, J. M. 63
Catastrophe Containment and Relief Trust (CCRT) 57, 267
CBDCs *see* Central Bank Digital Currencies
CBE *see Corporación Bancaria de España*
CBPS *see* Corporate Bond Purchase Scheme
CBR *see* Central Bank of Russia
CBRT *see* Central Bank of the Republic of Turkey
CDIC *see* Central Discipline and Inspection Commission
Cecchetti, Stephen G. 103
Central Bank Digital Currencies (CBDCs) 34–47; account-based 38; definition of 34; design of **39**; global projects 35–37; reason for implementation 41–46; technology 39–41; types of 38–39
Central Bank FX 208
Central bank of Bahamas 47n1
Central Bank of China 43, 45
Central Bank of Croatia 173, 179; Climate Declaration, of 172
Central Bank of Greece 30
Central Bank of Hungary 175; Green Programme 172
Central Bank of Montenegro 172
Central Bank of Nigeria 47n1
Central Bank of Russia (CBR) 27, 145
Central Bank of the Republic of Turkey (CBRT) 200, 203, 204, 206–210
central banks (CBs) 18–31; autonomy 146–152; climate change recognition 168–169; Covid

and 22–25; declarations 171–172; disclosure and reporting on climate-related risks 172–173; exchange rate policies 96; finance 25–30; forward guidance over private banks 19; governors **147**; independence of 4, 163n15; mandates, risk impact on 168–169; objectives of 4; pledges 171–172; policy measures during COVID-19 **228**; potential losses 6; reputation of 4; response to pandemic 110–117; strategic frameworks 171–172; variations in 19–22
Central Banks Financial Supervisors 261
Central Discipline and Inspection Commission (CDIC) 241, 253
Central Europe (CE) 167, 168, 170, 171, 180
challenges: in implementing sustainability initiatives 264; monetary policy 14–15; PBOC (People's Bank of China) 247–248
Chamber of Commerce 208
Champ, B. 43
Charles II (King) 20
Chen, X. 263
Chen, Y.-S. 81
China 23–26, 28–29, 31, 34, 35, 58; forward guidance 19; Gini index *250*; green bonds *249*; NetsUnion Clearing Corporation 45; State-Council 252; United States nuclear missiles around 28
Chinese Digital Currency Institute 35
classical liberalism 20
"Climate Action Incentive Payment" 12
climate change 167–181; climate finance initiatives 171–177; economic inequalities and 10–12, *11*; emerging strategies and policy 169–171; green credit allocation 178–179; green prudential tools 177–178; inequalities and 5; information-based policy tools 171–177; monetary policy adjustments 178–179; recognition by central banks 168–169; risk impact on central bank mandates 168–169; risk in regulatory and supervisory framework 169–171; soft powers 171–177
Climate Declaration of the Central Bank of Croatia 172
climate finance initiatives 171–177
Climate Pledge of the National Bank of Slovakia 172
climate-related risks 167, 171–172; assessment of 170; climate-related challenges to mitigate 169; disclosure and reporting on 172–173; disclosure of 175; impact on central bank mandates 168–169
climate-risk exposures 175–177
climate risk management 175–177
CMA9 140n4
"CO2levy" 12
Commercial Credit Data Sharing (CCDS) 129
Commercial Paper Funding Facility 113
common prosperity 249–251
Commonwealth Development Corporation 79
Competition and Markets Authority (CMA) 130, 133
consumer inflation 97–98, 100–102, *101*, 103–104
Corporación Bancaria de España (CBE) 81, 82, 85
Corporate Bond Purchase Scheme (CBPS) 202
corporate integrity 263
Corporate Sector Purchase Programme (CSPP) 202
corrective tax 11
COVID-19 13, 23, 34, 37, 53; authoritarian financialization and 201–207; central bank response to 110–117; central banks (CBs) and 22–25; Chinese economy and 242–243; crisis in Spain 75–78; effects on global economies 3; fiscal and monetary policies during 224–226; global distribution of dollar liquidity 54; impact on production 75–76; impact on the labour market 76; inequality, poverty, and social exclusion 76–77; lessons and future roles of central banks in Ghana 267–268; monetary measures in **155**; monetary regimes of Balkan Countries during 222–224, *223*; open banking during 137–139; RMB internationalization in 251–252; SDGs and 264–265
credibility theory 4
credit bureau 129
credit entity 82
Credit Reference Agencies 129
credit reserve asset 266

credit risk 61, 83, 156, 159, 175, 227
Croatia 168, 169, 171
Croatian Financial Stability Report 173
Croatian National Bank 174, 181n4
Cross-Border Interbank Payments System (CIPS) 252
Cull, R. 72
Czech Republic 168, 171

dala 21
dalar 21
Debt Management Office 117
debt profiles **192**, 192–193
decarbonization 11
decentralization 134, 137, 139
declarations, central bank 171–172
defensive financial statecraft (DFS) 189, **189**, 191, 194, 200–201, 207–208, 210
de-financialization 188, 208
deflation 4, 7, 25, 97, 117–118, 119, 121
Delaware 30
Deloitte 266–267
Denmark 24, 59–60
developing countries 11, 93; affect of climate change in 5
DFS *see* defensive financial statecraft
Dietrich, A. 7
Digital Currency Electronic Payment (DCEP) 42
Digital Currency Initiative 36–37
Digital Currency JPY (DCJPY) 37
Digital Dollar Project 37
digitalization 38, 127, 137
dilemmas, monetary policy 14–15
di Mauro, W. 7
dinarization 228
Dinero Electrónico (DE) 35
direct operations 82
disintermediation, risk of 42
distributed ledger technology (DLT) 36, 39–40; types of 40–41
DLT *see* distributed ledger technology
domestic capital 191, 193, 201, 209
Dominican Republic 5
Donetsk 157
Durkheim, E. 20
Durrani, A. 261

East Asian 18, 23
Eastern Bloc 178
Eastern Caribbean Union 47n1
Eastern Europe 145–146
East India Company (EIC) 21
ECB *see* European Central Bank
Eccles, M. 21
economic growth 3
economic inequalities 7–12, *8–9*, 10–12, *11*, 249–251; climate change and 10–12, *11*
economic recovery 4, 81, 85, 138, 157, 160
Economides, G. 7
Ecuador 35, 46
efficiency gains 42
Eichengreen, B. 58
18th Party Congress 240–241
Eisenhower, D. D. 21
e-krona 36–37
electronic Chinese Yuan (e-CNY) 35, 38, 47n2, 244
EMDE *see* emerging market and developing economies
emerging market and developing economies (EMDE) 54, 55, 57, 63
emerging market economies (EMEs) 186
emerging strategies and policy, climate change 169–171
EMEs *see* emerging market economies
e-Naira 47n1
energy social dividend 13
Engebretsen, E. 265
England 20
environmental, social and governance (ESG) 169, 173–175, 177, 178, 180, 264
environmental and safety (E&S) 261–262
environmental sustainability *5*, 5–7, 14, 85, 169, 173, 257, 260, 265
Epstein, G. 20
Erhard, W. 263
Erol 212n1
ESG *see* environmental, social and governance
Ethiopia 30
EU Commission 193, 207
EU Member States 168, 172
Eurasian Fund for Stabilization and Development (EFSD) 154, 156
Europe 14, 20, 21, 23, 25, 178
European Central Bank (ECB) 36, 38, 43, 59, 74, 75, 91–92, *94*, 114–115, 175; 2021 pledge on climate change action (ECB 2021a) 172; Guide on Climate-Related and Environmental risks (ECB 2020) 175; Quantitative Easing programme 114; secondary objectives 6; unconditional distribution 13

European Commission 5, 79, 84–85, 231; Sustainable Finance Action Plan 177
European Commission Spring 229
European Data Protection Board (EDPB) 140n1
European Financial Reporting Advisory Group 177
European Fund for Strategic Investments (EFSI) 73–74
European Green Deal 5–6
European Investment Bank (EIB) 73–74, 79, 84
European Parliament and the Council of the European Union 130
European Union (EU) 31, 168, 207–208, 221, 226, 236; in Brexit 31; financial instrument of economic policy 82; government support and legislated mandates 118; sanctions 163n17; sustainability reporting standards 177
European Union Directives 130
Eurozone 8, 109, 115; income inequality *9*; interest rate *9*
executive order No. 79 164n20
'*expedientes de regulación temporal de empleo*' (ERTE) 76
Experian 138
Extended Credit Facility 56
external financial conditions 193

Faccia, D. 7
Facebook 34, 45
Family Housing Allowance (CSOK) program 196
family-owned businesses 93
Federal Reserve 3, 21, 37
Fed's Open Market Committee (FOMC) 58, 61
FGS GO! Program 201–202
Fidesz 190, 192, 194, 196, 207, 209
FIMA *see* Foreign and International Monetary Authorities
finance: central banks (CBs) 25–30; economics 23; sustainable 169
finance-real estate 187, *198*, 201, *202*, 208
financial crisis of 2007–2008 3, 110
financial industry 127
financial instrument of economic policy 82
financialization 92–95
Financialization of Housing (FoH) 187
financial repression 188
financial risk 40, 72, 74, 85, 170, 172, 174–178, 187
Financial Stability Report for 2021 173
The Financial Times 60
FinTech 34, 36, 41–42, 45–46
fiscal policy 4; Balkan economies 229–231; during COVID-19 224–226; institutional independence 117–120
Foreign and International Monetary Authorities (FIMA) 54–55, 59, 61, 64; repo facility, 113 58–64
401(k) plans 95
France 20, 21, 29; "yellow vest" 11
full employment (FE) 22–23, 30–31
Funding for Lending Scheme 178
funding operations 82
Fund of Funds 226
FX: deposits 191, 210; household 194; interventions 154, 157, 160; liabilities 154, 156; loans 156; regulation 159; swap auction 228

Gabor, D. 188
Gad, A. G. 40
Gaddafi, M. 30
Gallup 95
Garratt, R. 46
GDP *see* gross domestic product
GDPR *see* General Data Protection Regulation
gender equality 262–263
General Board of the National Committee for Macroprudential Oversight (NCMO) 171
General Data Protection Regulation (GDPR) 128
Georgia State University 37
Germanwatch 11
Germany 92–93, 103; stock ownership 95
GFC *see* 2008 Global Financial Crisis
Ghana 257–269; Bank of Ghana (BoG) 258–259, 265–267; challenges in implementing sustainability initiatives 264; COVID-19 lessons and future roles of central banks 267–268; SDGs and COVID-19 pandemic 264–265; sustainability in 259–260; sustainability strategies by 261–263
Ghana National Climate Change Master Plan Action Programmes for Implementation: 2015–2020 260
Giuliani, D. 7
global climate risk index 11, *11*
global financial safety net 54, 55–58
Gosplan 146

governance, open banking 132–137
government debt 91, 92; FX liabilities 156; legitimate and justifiable 118; monetizing 120
government-led reregulation 199
Great Britain 22, 24, 28, 109; war debt 21
Great Depression 111
Great Recession 3–4, 10, 22, 82; stimulus measure to cope with 13
green credit allocation 178–179
green economy in PBOC 248–249
Green Finance Report 173
Green Home Program 201
green lending 201
Green Mortgage Bond Purchase Programme 179
greenness 175
Green Preferential Capital Requirement Program 201
green prudential tools 177–178
Greenspan, A. 22, 103
Griffith-Jones, S. 74
gross domestic product (GDP) 3, 75–79, 114, 116, 133, 194, 202, 224–226, 231, 246

Haas, T. 43
Haiti 5
Halkbank 207
Hardie, I. 62
harmonised index of consumer prices (HICP) 229
Heggen, K. 265
Helsinki University of Technology 35
Hendrickson, D.: *The American Conservative* 26
Herzegovina 168
High-Level Task Force 36
Hilmi, N. 7
Household Finance and Consumption Survey (HFCS) 99
HSBC 36
Huang, Z. 40
Hungary 168, 180–181; authoritarian financialization in 191, 193–197, 201–203, 207–209; export competitiveness crisis *196*
hypostatisation of money 20

Idrissa, R. 21
IMF *see* International Monetary Fund
imperial preference 21
income inequality: Eurozone *9*; United States *8*
independence 147, 149–151; of central banks 4; described 4
India 20, 62
inequalities: climate change and 5; COVID-19 76–77; economic 10–12, *11*; socioeconomic 11
inflation 3, 23, 30; by businesses and central bankers 102–103; dynamics 6; evolution of 6; political economy 96–97; in Türkiye *200*; war 26
information-based policy tools 171–177
'*ingreso mínimo vital*' (basic minimum income) 77
instability, risk of 42–43
institutional independence 109–122; central bank response to the pandemic 110–117; fiscal policy 117–120; monetary policy 117–120
Instituto de Crédito Oficial (ICO) 75, 76, 82–83, *83*
Inter-American Development Bank 79
interdependent challenges 10–14
interest rates 3, 227, 268; Eurozone *9*; negative 117, 191; securitizing mortgages 93; spread 140n6; United States *8*
Intergovernmental Panel on Climate Change (IPCC) 257
International Central Bank Digital Currency 44
international lender of last resort (ILOLR) 58
International Monetary Fund (IMF) 53, 55, 145, 150–151, 156, 222; (in) effectiveness as the lender of last resort 55–57
International Monetary Governance 58–64
international motives 43–44
internet economy 243–244
Iraq: United States financial sanctions 25; US invasion of 27
Ireland 20
Italy 21

James I 20
Japan 23, 24, 28, 31, 58; forward guidance 19
Jensen, M. C. 263
Jobbik 208
jobless 198
Johnstone, C. 27
Joint European Resources for Micro to Medium Enterprises 226
Jourdan, S. 13
Juncker Plan 73

Ke, Y. 263
Keynesian heterogeneous agent models (HANK) 10
Kim, Y. S. 43
Klenert, D. L. 11
Konradt, M. 7
KPMG 130
Krugman, P. 24
Kumhof, M. 43
Kwon, O. 43

labour market, COVID-19 impact on 76
Lagarde, Christine 114
"lean against the wind" strategy 21
Lei Geral de Proteção de Dados (LGPD) 128
lender of last resort 21, 42, 53–54, 55–58, 62, 221, 222, 227–229, 236–237
lending and debt 246–247
lending and exports *197*
Libra/DIEM project 45
"Libra" project 34
Lima, G. 74
liquidity shortages 57–58
liquidity traps 3
literature review 187–193
Liu He 252
loanable funds 22
Lombardi, D. 58
London: Crown in Parliament 20; defaulting merchant-lenders 20
long-term interest rates *190*
Luhansk 157
Lyutova, M. 164n21

machine learning (ML) 127
macroeconomic fundamentals **204**
macro-financial policy 226–228
Magyar Nemzeti Bank (MNB) 169, 171, 173, 175, 181n1, 182n12, 195–196; Funding for Growth Scheme (FGS) 178, 196; green mandate 201; Green Toolkit Strategy 178; interest rates 208; mission creep 195; stick-and-carrot approach 207; subsidized lending instruments 197
Main Street Lending Program 112–113
Malaysia 34
Mali 30
Malkin, A. 58
Manitoba 12
marginal propensity to consume (MPC) 10
market-based banking 73
Market-based Lending Scheme (MLS) 196
Martin, M. 21
Massachusetts Institute of Technology (MIT) 36–37
Matolcsy, G. 195
McCauley, R. N. 65n1
McDowell, D. 61
Médecins sans Frontiers 27
Media Lab 36
Medicare 24
mega-projects 200
Merchant Savvy 45
Mertens, D. 74
Mexico 21, 59
micro and small enterprises (MSEs) 207
Middle East 26
Ministry of Treasury and Finance 207
MKB 196
MNB *see* Magyar Nemzeti Bank
Modenesi, A. 74
Modern Monetary Theory (MMT) 122
Mo Ibrahim Foundation 258
monetary base **154**
monetary financial policy 226–228
"monetary helicopter" 12
monetary policy 3–15; Balkan economies 229–231; challenges 14–15; during COVID-19 224; dilemmas 14–15; economic inequalities and 7–12, *8–9*, *11*; environmental sustainability and *5*, 5–7; innovation 3; institutional changes in 3; institutional independence 117–120; interdependent challenges 12–14; objectives of 3, 4; opportunities 14–15; political aspects 18, 30; unconventional 12; wealth inequality linked to 9
monetary policy adjustments 178–179
Monetary Policy Committee 207
monetary policy divergence *205–206*
monetary regimes, Balkan Countries 222–224, *223*
monetary sovereignty 149
Money Market Mutual Fund Liquidity Facility 113
Montenegro 168, 171
mortgage funding adequacy ratio (MFAR) 201
Muellbauer, J. 13
Municipal Liquidity Facility 113
Murau, S. 54, 63
Myanmar 5

Nabiullina, E. 28
Namibia 30

Naqvi, N. 74
Nashiru, Z. M. 259
National Assembly 169
National Bank of Romania (NBR) 171, 172, 222, 227
National Bank of Serbia (NBS) 173, 222–223, 228
National Bank of Slovakia 172; Climate Pledge, of 172
National Bank of the Republic of Belarus (NBRB) 145–147, 154, 159, 161; policy framework for 2005–2021 **150**
National Bank of the Republic of North Macedonia: Strategic Plan 2022–2024 172
National Bank of Ukraine (NBU) 145, 147, 157
National Climate Change Policy (NCCP) 260
National Committee for Macroprudential Oversight 172
National Data Protection Agency (ANPD) 136
national development banks (NDBs) 73–74
National Monetary Council 133
NATO 26, 30
natural disasters, frequency of *5*
NBR *see* National Bank of Romania
NBU *see* National Bank of Ukraine
NCCP *see* National Climate Change Policy
neoclassical economics 19
NetsUnion Clearing Corporation 45
Network for Greening the Financial System (NGFS) 172, 261
New York District Fed 21
New Zealand 20, 24, 59–60, 62
Next Generation EU funds 80
NFC Debt Service *205*
NGFS Glasgow Declaration (NGFS 2021) 172
NHS 31
Nigeria 30, 259; *dala* 21
Nölke, A. 23; *Post-Corona capitalism* 19
non-financial corporations (NFCs) 187
non-performing loans (NPL) 196
Noone, C. 43
Norman, M. 20
North Africa 30
Northern Rock 22
North Macedonia 168, 171
Norway 59–60
NPL *see* non-performing loans
NYT 24, 25

Obama, B. 18, 27, 29, 30
OECD 24, 75, 265
offensive financial statecraft (OFS) 189, **189**, 191, 194, 198–201, 204, 207
OFS *see* offensive financial statecraft
Omisore, A. G. 257
One District One Factory 260
Ontario 12
open banking (OB) 127–140; in Brazil 131–132, **135**; defined 127; during the pandemic 137–139; regulation and governance 132–137; in United Kingdom 129–131, **135**
Open Banking Implementation project 129
Open Banking Workshop Opening 131
opportunities, monetary policy 14–15
Organization of Brazilian Cooperatives (OCB) 141n12
Orléan, A. 23
orthodoxy 22; capitalist money and 20
Other Loans Especially Mentioned (OLEM) 266
Ottawa Parliament 22
Oxford 24
Oxford Severity Index (OSI) 78

Pacific Island 27
Pakistan 5
Pandemic Emergency Purchase Program 115
Panetta, Fabio 36
Pape, F. 54
Paris Climate Accord 248
Passos, N. 74
Paycheck Protection Program Liquidity Facility 113
payment: e-krona project 36; guidelines 130; nature and properties **38**; pre-crisis period 43; transactions 137–138
Payment Initiation Service Providers (PISP) 130
Payments Canada 36
Payment Service Directive 2 (PSD2) 130
Payment Services Regulations 130
Payment Systems and Services and Electronic Money 130
PayPal 34
People's Bank of China (PBOC) 35, 38, 47n1, 240–254; addressing economic inequalities through common prosperity 249–251; Chinese bureaucracy after the 18th Party Congress 240–241; Chinese economy in the post-Covid world 242–243; financial discipline to disciplining the 252–253; financing

SMEs 244–245; global challenges 247–248; green economy 248–249; internet economy 243–244; in the post-Covid 243–251; preventing excessive lending and debt 246–247; RMB internationalization in the post-Covid 251–252
Pérez-Moreno, S. 7
Pew Research Center 102
Pforr, T. 54
Philippines 5
Pigeaud, F.: *Africa's last colonial currency: the CFA franc story* 20
Pigouvian carbon tax 11
Pigouvian tax 12
PIX 138
Plaitakis, A. 138
Planting for Food and Jobs 260
pledges: central bank 171–172; declarations and 167
Plosser, C. 120
Poland 168, 169, 171
polarization 11
political economy 91–104; asset capitalism 92–96; asset inflation 98–100, 102; consumer inflation 97–98, 100–102, *101*, 103–104; inflation 96–97, 102–103
PositiveMoney 248
Post-Corona capitalism (Nölke) 19
post-GFC deleveraging *194*
post-pandemic public banking in Spain 78–81
poverty: COVID-19 76–77; inequality and 11; reduction 260
prenatal baby support loan scheme 196
pre-pandemic crisis 3
Presidential System of Government (PSG) 203
price stability 6–7, 12–14, 115, 117, 120, 160, 167–169, 186, 206, 222–223, 243, 245, 254, 259
Primary Dealer Credit Facility 113
Primary Market Corporate Credit Facility 113
privatisations 19
Project Jasper 36
Proof of Concept (PoC) Phase 1 37
public banking definition of 78
public banking in Spain 72–86; COVID-19 crisis 75–78; evolution of 81–82; *Instituto de Crédito Oficial* (ICO) 82–83, *83*; need for post-pandemic 78–81; reorientation of 83–85
public-private partnerships (PPPs) 200
Puerto Rico 5
Putin, V. 26

quantitative easing (QE) 19, 22, 91, 111, 114, 117, 160, 179, 227; Australia 25
quarantine 23–24

Rapid Credit Facility (RCF) 56, 267
Rapid Financing Instrument 56
RBA *see* Reserve Bank of Australia
RBC 36
RCF *see* Rapid Credit Facility
Reagan, R. 23
real estate bubbles *190*
recapitalization 156, 201
re-financialization 208
refinancing operations 76, 115, 178–179
regional financial arrangements (RFAs) 55
regulation, open banking 132–137
regulatory capture problems 4
regulatory framework 169–171; climate change 169–171
Reiter, S. 164n21
rentiers 19, 25; social contracts 193
Republic of Korea 59
reputation of central banks 4
Reserve Bank of Australia (RBA) 19–23, 25, 27, 30
Reserve Bank of India 63
reserve requirement ratios (RRRs) 201
return on equity (ROE) 131
Riester pension 95
RMB Cross-border Payment Management Information System (RCPMIS) 252
Romania 168, 169, 171, 222; economic growth 229–231; economy of 231; macroeconomic and financial indicators for **232–233**
Roosevelt, F. D. 18, 21
Rosmin, M. 261
Royal Decree-Law 12/1995 81
Russia 14, 25, 28–29; Biden's threats against 25; invasion of Ukraine 3, 27, 30, 91, 101, 145–146, 186; macroeconomic **153**; monetary regime transformations in 146–152; United States financial sanctions 25–26
Russia-Ukraine conflict of 2022 119

safe-haven 53
Sahasrabuddhe, A. 63

Sandset, T. J. 265
SARS 24
Saskatchewan 12
Sberbank 79
Schenk, C. R. 65n1
Schnabel, I. 6
Schoenmaker, D. 7
Schumpeter, J. A. 22
Scotiabank 36
SDG 12 259
SDG 13 259
SDGs *see* Sustainable Development Goals
Secondary Market Corporate Credit Facility 113
security gains 42–43
self-financing *195*
Serbia 168, 171, 173, 222; macroeconomic and financial indicators for **234–235**
Setterfield, M. 74
SFN 131
Shanghai 23
Shanghai and Hong Kong Stock Exchange 46
Short-term Liquidity Line 57
Simmel, G. 20
Singapore 34, 59
Singh, R. K. 259
Single Supervisory Mechanisms (SSM) 170, 180
Slovakia 168, 169
Slovenia 168, 169, 171
small- and medium-sized enterprises (SMEs) 74, 129, 130; domestic credit provision 199; financial support to 84; financing 79, 244–245; loans *203*; Turkish export-oriented 193
Small Business Enterprise & Employment Act (SBEEA) 129
SMEs *see* small- and medium-sized enterprises
Smith, A. 22
Smoliy, Y. 156
social contexts 20
social exclusion, COVID-19 76–77
socially responsible stewardship 261–262
"social tax or dividend" 12
societal attitudes 100–102
socioeconomic inequalities 11
soft powers 171–177
South Africa 259
South America 180
Southeast Europe (SEE) 167, 168, 169, 170, 171, 180
South Korea 24, 25, 28, 31, 34; forward guidance 19
sovereign bonds 113
sovereign debt *192*
Soviet Gosbank 145, 146, 161
Spanish influenza 24
Specialised Deposit-Taking Institutions (SDIs) 266
stable coins 44–45
Stand-By Arrangement (SBA) 56, 156
Staschen, S. 138
state financial agency 82
"Stella" project 36
Stracca, P. M. L. 7
strategic frameworks, central bank 171–172
supervisory engagement activities 173–174
supervisory expectations 173–174
supervisory framework, climate change 169–171
Survey on Income and Living Conditions 76
sustainability: challenges in implementing 264; finance 169; in Ghana 259–260; strategies in Ghana 261–263
Sustainable Banking Network (SBN) 261
Sustainable Development Goals (SDGs) 257, 265; COVID-19 and 264–265
Sustainable Finance Action Plan 177
Sveriges Riksbank 36–37
swaps 57, 59–61, 64, 156, 227–228
Sweden 19, 30, 59
Swedish Rehn-Meidner model 20
SWIFT (Society for Worldwide Interbank Financial Transactions) 252
Swiss National Bank 59
Switzerland 12, 62
Sylla, N. S.: *Africa's last colonial currency: the CFA franc story* 20

taxation 5, 7, 11–12, 99
tax cuts 23, 53, 91
Technical Expert Group 175
technology, CBDCs 39–41
Tencent 35, 45
Term Asset-Backed Securities Loan Facility 113
Thailand 24, 25, 34
thaler 21
Thatcher, M. 23, 28
Thiemann, M. 74
Thompson, H. 62
trade-offs 13
transformation: digital 34; economic and social 79; financial industry 127; monetary regime transformations 146–152; urban 207

Treaty on European Union (TEU) 169
Treaty on the Functioning of the European Union 6
Trillo, D. 79
Trump, D. 23, 28
Trunin, P. V. 147
Turkish Statistical Institute 206
Türkiye: authoritarian financialization in 191, 198–201, 203–207, 209–210; inflation in *200*
20th Party Congress 245
2010 European debt crisis 114
2022 Beijing Olympics 244
2008 Global Financial Crisis (GFC) 18, 22, 91, 117, 187, 199 56, 241

Uchida, S. 37
UK Market Access Fund 129
UK Open Banking 136
Ukraine 19, 26; financial assistance 162n6; indirect monetary financing in *151*; macroeconomic **153**; military invasion in 157, 159; monetary regime transformations in 146–152; oligarchs 30; Russia invasion of 3, 27, 30, 91, 101; war in 13
UK Treasury 119
unconventional 3; monetary policy 7, 12–13, 115
Union of Soviet Socialist Republics (USSR) 147
United Kingdom 133; open banking in 129–131, **135**
United Nations (UN) 27, 257, 265
United States 8, 22, 24, 92–93, 103; dollar hegemony 19; finance promotion 20; financial and real warfare 23; financial sanctions on Iraq, Afghanistan, Venezuela, and Russia 25–26; income inequality *8*; inflation 101; interest rate *8*; nuclear missiles around China 28; rising housing prices 99; sovereign currency 21; "war on coal" 11
Urban Development Funds 226
USA post-1945 26
US Democrats 23
US Fed Board Chairs 21
US Federal Reserve (Fed) 18, 21, 22, 24, 31, 53–54, 58–64, 112–114; global dominance 19; motivations and emergent apartheid 61–64
US Treasury 22, 60, 119
US Treasury Securities 113

Venezuela 25
virtual apartheid 63
VISA 34
Vodaphone 46
volatility 13, 44, 45, 167, 187, 189, 200, 209–211, 227
Volz, U. 261

Waller, Christopher 47
Wall Street 19, 21–22, 28, 93
Wan, P. 263
war debt 21
"war on coal" 11
Weber, M. 20
WeChat Pay 35, 46
Weidmann, J. 118
West Germany 100
White, Alison 136
White House 25, 30
William, K. 20
William III 20
William of Orange 20
Wirtschaftswunder 100
World Bank 53
World Bank Study 137
World War I 21, 28
World War II 18, 19, 26, 30, 53

Xepapadeas, A. 7

"yellow vest" 11

Zerbib, O. 7
Zhang, T. 40
Zhou Xiaochuan 252

For Product Safety Concerns and Information please contact our EU representative GPSR@taylorandfrancis.com
Taylor & Francis Verlag GmbH, Kaufingerstraße 24, 80331 München, Germany

www.ingramcontent.com/pod-product-compliance
Ingram Content Group UK Ltd.
Pitfield, Milton Keynes, MK11 3LW, UK
UKHW020151200926
475702UK00016B/2654
* 9 7 8 1 0 3 2 3 4 6 7 1 7 *